Piercing the Cosmic Veil

Piercing the Cosmic Veil

You shall not be afraid

of the terror by night

Joseph G. Jordan and Jason Dezember

2020

First Printing: 2020

Published by Seekye1 Publishing in the United States of America.

ISBN-13: 978-1-893788-31-2
ISBN-10: 1893788-31-8

Artwork by Robert Marsee.

www.CE4Research.com

In loving memory of our Sister in Jesus Christ, Joyce Ahrens. Hers was a most powerful testimony, supporting the truth and Hope for so many others to come. We miss her. May God bless her family.

Contents

Part 3 – The Testimonies   173

Introduction
By Jason Dezember

"Put on the whole armor of God that you may be able to stand against the wiles of the devil - For we do not wrestle against flesh and blood, but against principalities, against powers, against the rulers of the darkness of this age, against spiritual hosts of wickedness in the heavenly places." Ephesians 6:11-12

I wish I could have understood those words a few years back.

After a life of drug addiction, rock 'n' roll music, two failed marriages, anger, resentment, and unforgiveness, I was at a point of utter despair.

On October 6, 2013, my life changed forever.

That's the night the ships came.

They came quietly, silently over my head. There were many types of ships in numerous shapes and sizes. Some were as large as your local mall, others the shape and size of a train, and some appeared disc-like. The armada lasted an hour and a half. The next three to four years manifested itself into a horror which I never imagined I could have endured. I experienced multiple sightings and UFO encounters, various beings present in videos on my phone, and finally what you would call an alien abduction. My mind was at the point of madness - suicide seemed the only way out. I understood that this would be the end of me.

It was at that time I started searching anywhere and everywhere I could. I looked to UFO/alien abduction experts, who wanted to charge me money to help me, the famous Mutual UFO Network (MUFON) organization, the hospital, strangers – nobody could help, or even seemed willing for that matter. I was in a void, feeling invisible, like no one could see me and definitely could not understand me. By the grace of God, I randomly came across a testimony by Joe Jordan, a Mutual UFO Network (MUFON) researcher, and the head of CE4 Research, an alien abduction research group, from the mid-90s. He was speaking about alien abductions, and Hope for a way out of the experiences.

This is what I had been waiting for.

The solution had finally come. And it was free.

Thanks to the Lord my God, by the name of Jesus Christ, and with the help of an angel that he put in my life to suffer the things that I was experiencing for that horrific four year period, I was able to overcome. I overcame the torment, the fear, the pain, the lies, the manipulation, the deception, and the unimaginable horror that plagued me.

I was free. Free indeed.

The information in this book that you are about to read is probably the best kept secret in the entire UFO/Alien Abduction Research realm.

Why is this important to me, you say? Because the many polls taken over the years show that either you, or somebody close to you, has had a UFO/Alien Abduction experience. Most likely they are afraid to talk about it. And it most definitely has changed the way they perceive reality, but usually not in a good way. This book is their Hope.

The UFO/Alien Abduction research community has an agenda, and we at CE4 Research are not part of that agenda. We stand alone with a small group of truth seekers that have found truth, and only want it to be heard. Over the many years, our research findings have been referred to as "The Unwanted Piece of the Puzzle".

As honest researchers, we only ask that every piece of the UFO/Alien Abduction Puzzle be allowed to be brought to the table. Without every piece of the puzzle, you do not have an honest, clear picture of what we are dealing with.

The information shared here may challenge many who read this book. But we ask that you keep an open mind to the end, and leave your preconceived notions behind. You should always view the other side of the coin, too. Only then can you make an honest decision about what is truth and what is delusion.

We ask that you do not trust us personally. Why would you? You don't know us. But trust the research findings and the evidence. They stand on their own. The evidence has been tried and tested for over two decades now, and it is even repeatable, as is required for scientific research.

We dedicate this book to those who have overcome this powerful delusion, to those who have the courage to testify of this powerful delusion, and to those who are still held captive by this powerful delusion. God bless you all.

WARNING

The following information

may change your pre-conceived notions

of the UFO and Alien Abduction phenomenon.

You have been warned.

The Lonely Road

Spring of 1964

Orleans, France

Sergeant J. was up early that morning. The alarm had gone off at 5:00 am. He had made an appointment to have his car looked at by the auto garage at the Base Exchange on the Army base near Fontainebleau.

Sergeant J. had ordered the car special from the United States. This car was kind of unique for its model and year: a family station wagon, a 1964 Rambler Ambassador, 990, Cross-Country. Sergeant J. had ordered the car with a stick shift with overdrive. The car had a 327 cubic inch V-8 and, for a station wagon, it would really get up and go. But there was a problem that plagued the car since it first arrived in France. It had been burning a lot of oil. For some reason too much oil was getting past the rings and into the cylinders, so Sergeant J. decided to let the mechanics at the Base Exchange garage have a look at it.

After getting himself ready he woke up his young son, who would ride with him. By 6:00 am, the two of them climbed into the car to head out down the road. His son got into the backseat, still sleepy from having to get up so early. He could stretch out on the big back seat and sleep some more until they got to the Base Exchange. The morning sky was black and clear, sprinkled with stars, and the air cool and crisp; it was going to be a nice morning ride.

The road to Fontainebleau was a two-lane blacktop highway, nothing like the highways you see today. The road passed through scenic French farmland and forests. But, because of the early time of the morning, and it still being dark, there wasn't much to see of the French countryside.

There were very few cars traveling at that time that morning. Occasionally, a car coming from the opposite direction would pass, its yellow headlights approaching, then passing by. In France the law required all vehicle headlights to be yellow, unlike the white or blue-white we are more familiar with in the United States. Every once in a while, you would see a vehicle from another country, traveling in through France from another country, that had the white lights. It was uncomfortable to see the white headlights after getting used to seeing only the mild yellow ones.

Sergeant J. was cruising along at about 80 to 90 kilometers an hour, his young son fast asleep in the back seat. The traffic was very sparse. He noticed a white light fast approaching from behind in his rear view mirror. "Guy must have his high beams on. Come on man, dim your lights", he thought to himself. The bright white light kept coming, faster and faster. He couldn't make out if it was a truck or a car. It was just a big bright white light. He reached for the adjustment on his rear view mirror to cut down the glare. He was starting to get nervous; maybe the guy wouldn't slowdown as he got closer. Maybe he was asleep at the wheel. He was thinking about the safety of his young son in the back seat. His eyes were glued to the road ahead, hoping the vehicle would hurry and pass by safely. The white light kept getting closer and brighter. Then the whole inside cab of the car was engulfed in the bright light. It was hard to see anything. The light got so bright he couldn't even see the road ahead. The light was not two headlights, but one huge bright light source.

The light, filling the inside of the cab of the car, seemed as if it was actually inside of the car, bouncing off of the dashboard, the door panels, the seats, the ceiling; it was everywhere at once, instead of coming from a single source.

In the instant that the vehicle should have passed him, the light blinked out completely. He saw only total darkness, his eyes not yet adjusted to the sudden change in light, and feeling panic; he slams on the brakes, coming to a stop on the shoulder of the road. The engine quit. That fast moving vehicle should have blown by him.

Very angry and shaken, he jumped out of the car to yell at the person in the vehicle that should have passed him by. But: no vehicle. No lights. He expected to be seeing tail lights leading away from him, but the road was empty.

Maybe it had stopped before getting to him. He looked back the other way, but saw just empty road. A dark empty lonesome road and a starry sky.

Then he noticed something really strange: there was no sound, just absolute, total silence. Like time was standing still around him. Why is there no sound? Not even that of the wind rustling the trees, or of the birds in the early morning. Not even the ticking sound that a hot car would make of the engine cooling down after it stops running. Very strange, very strange indeed.

Something was very wrong here. Sergeant J. started to shake, lips quivering, his body reacting to something very terrifying. He looks into the backseat window to check on his son in the car. He was still sound asleep in the back seat. He paused to regain his composure for a couple of minutes before continuing on to the Base Exchange. He got back into the car and it fired right up, everything okay. Still disheveled, he continued on with the day's plans.

Sergeant J. was a career Army man. He, his wife, and three children had been stationed in France since 1960. This was the family's second tour of duty overseas. They had already spent two years stationed in Germany

The events of that spring day in France, in 1964, would forever haunt the memory of Sergeant J. This shouldn't have been something that would leave that type of impression on him. He had entered the Army during the Korean War at 17 years old. He was a member of the regiment called the Polar Bears. He was a combat infantryman. He had looked death in the face many times in Korea. He received his Combat Infantry Badge there.

After his tour of duty in Korea, he had spent time stationed in Ft Meade, Maryland, outside of Washington, DC. He was part of a radar gun unit in the nation's capital, located in the Four Corners, Maryland area. It was the time of the Cold War. It was 1952. He was actually part of the events of that year that involved reported and recorded unidentified flying objects over Washington, DC. These objects were being tracked by the Air Force Base nearby, and by the very same radar gun units he was attached to.

Sergeant J's next tour of duty for the Army was in the South Pacific. He spent time on a small atoll —Eniwetok Atoll— where he was an observer of the early atomic blasts in the Marshall Islands. It was quite an incredible experience for a boy who grew up hunting and fishing in the forests and creeks around Norfolk, Virginia. After all he had lived through in his young life, the events of that early morning in France should not have been that disturbing to him.

What was that bright light that quickly approached from behind, only to blink out completely? What made everything so absolutely silent, no wind, no birds, and no crickets? Why that feeling of time standing still? What had caused the deep body shaking fear after the event? Was there something he wasn't remembering? What the heck happened? That event has haunted his conscious memory for 45 years.

It wasn't until the 1980's, 25 years after that strange event, that he saw that this was an experience that was being talked about by many others. He saw television shows on UFOs and alien abductions and he saw people sharing testimonies of encounters like the one he had experienced that early morning in France. That type of experience was referred to as the "lonely road experience". The people that talked about this type of experience reported seeing a bright lighted object or light either following or approaching them. They also reported being engulfed in the light. Their experience of feeling like time was standing still, and no sound at all, was also talked about. The frozen time and reports of no sound had been termed the "Oz factor" by some UFO researchers. Seeing these shows only brought back feelings of anxiety and dread. What HAD really happened that morning in 1964 to Sergeant J. and his son? Would he ever find an answer? Or would it only lead to more questions?

Like many people who have had experiences like this, if affects your worldview. You start to question reality itself. It's difficult to share experiences like this with others who have not had something similar happen to them. You unwillingly become a member of a very special club, (albeit, an unorganized one) of people who have experienced something very life changing.

Like others, Sargent J. had memories of what he could only call persistent "dreams". God forbid that they actually were real.

In his "dreams", he says there is more to that event that happened to him in France in 1964.

In the dreams, after he stopped the car and got out to see what the light was, he looked to his right, down by woods. He saw a wall. He couldn't describe the wall. It had no color, no texture, but it was a wall of some sort.

He went down by the wall and saw an opening. The opening resembled a large porthole on a ship. But it wasn't round, it was oblong, narrower on the top and the bottom.

He wasn't scared at all while it was happening; he was more just curious. He said he was pretty cocky at that age. No fear.

He stuck his head in through the hole. Then he climbed inside. It was big enough to step in through. He said it was another world of some sort. No trees, no nothing. No sound at all. And when he tried to see himself, he couldn't. He knew he was there inside, but he was invisible, even to himself.

All of a sudden he saw these little wispy clouds float by. Then a voice spoke in his mind, it startled him for a moment. It wasn't an audible voice.

The voice started telling him things about himself, and things he would do in the future. He felt that there were more present than just the voice speaking to him.

The "dream" ends there. But the memory lives on for decades, always leaving a question unanswered. Leaving that seed of doubt, and that hunger for truth.

The story that you have just read is not unlike the many stories reported, heard about, and researched over the past decades, but to no avail, till now.

"Today they call them angels, demons, tomorrow they will call them something else." - Aleister Crowley

Close Encounters of the Fourth Kind

Alien Abductions

"Alien abduction, sometimes also called abduction phenomenon, alien abduction syndrome, or UFO abduction, is a personally held belief in which the alleged "abductee" describes "subjectively real experiences" of being secretly kidnapped by nonhuman entities (aliens) and subjected to physical and psychological experimentation. Most scientists and mental health professionals explain these experiences by factors such as suggestibility (e.g. false memory syndrome), sleep paralysis, deception, and psychopathology."

https://en.wikipedia.org/wiki/Alien_abduction

CE4 Research Group
Testimony of a UFO Researcher
By J. G. Jordan

Chapter 1

It was June of 1992 in Cocoa, Florida. I was finally getting to take that much anticipated vacation trip to Alaska. I was headed up to visit with my brother and his family in Anchorage, and to see the many sights of the northern frontier. My brother was in the Air Force and stationed at Elmendorf Air Force Base.

I was flying out that morning from Orlando International Airport in Central Florida. My mother and my six year old son were accompanying me on the trip. I was going to visit for a week's vacation that had been a long time coming. My mother and son were going to stay a full month.

It was going to be a long flight, a ten and a half hour trip, including the stopover in Salt Lake City.

I thought I had best get something to read for the duration of the flight, so, when we got to the airport, I headed to the airport book and news stand to see what I could find.

I didn't see anything of interest to purchase as I browsed through the magazine section, so I headed to the paperbacks. I looked specifically through the fiction section, looking for maybe something I might be familiar with.

I had been a fan of science fiction when I was much younger. I saw it as a form of escapism from life's worries and troubles. You can lose yourself in a future time, or on a different world, far, far away from life as we know it here and now. I grew up without much television at all until high school. My father had been a career Army soldier and we had lived overseas for many years. So, not knowing the languages, we resorted to the American radio station on the bases near where we lived, or we read books and comic books to pass the time.

Walking through the paperback section, a particular book caught my eye. The cover looked like it would be a science fiction story, but the synopsis on the back cover stated that it was a scientific investigation. An investigation of an alleged alien spacecraft that had crashed near the small New Mexico town of Roswell in July of 1947.

Seriously? An alien spacecraft, an unidentified flying object, a flying saucer? That is science fiction. No life has been found anywhere in the Universe yet; there are no aliens visiting earth, right? Who would take this as real? You would have to be crazy.

The whole idea that this book was alluding to was fuzzing the fine line that separates fantasy from reality. It was either real, or it wasn't. I had to find out what the researchers were using as their evidence and basis for it to be real. I had to buy this book.

I purchased the book. Its title: <u>UFO Crash at Roswell</u>, by Kevin D. Randle and Donald R. Schmitt, July 1, 1991.

I read as much of the book as I could on the plane flight to Alaska. I also had a few bits of down time while I was in Alaska where I would get in a few more pages.

Within a week of arriving back to my home in Florida I had completed the book. Now, I had a thousand questions to ask, but no one to ask them to. I didn't know anybody that followed this idea of UFOs and aliens. I know I didn't have any interest in this subject matter before I read the book.

About three weeks after arriving back home from my Alaska trip, I was sitting in my living room watching the local news on my TV, when a news story of a new business opening up on International Drive in Orlando caught my attention. It was an interview with a gentleman named Jim that had just opened a UFO museum there. He took the reporter on a walk-through of his collection of UFO memorabilia and news articles that he had assembled into a museum for people to experience. Now, this guy might be able to answer my questions. I had to go see him.

A couple of weeks went by and I decided to make the trip to Orlando to see the UFO museum. I drove over on a Saturday morning, early, arriving as they were opening.

As I entered the lobby of the museum, I was greeted by Jim, the owner, who then introduced me to his wife, Mary, who was there with him. It wasn't busy when I arrived, so it gave me a chance to talk one on one with Jim. I told him about the book I had read and how it had only raised many more questions for me. And I would really like some answers.

Jim and Mary were really good people and very knowledgeable concerning the UFO phenomenon and its history. The museum was a walk-through exhibit of the historical time-line of the UFO phenomenon. It also had a section as you left that included sales of many types of UFO and alien memorabilia and books on the UFO phenomenon. I loved going to visit with them, which I did many times over the next few months. On one of my later trips I took the time to look over the books Jim and Mary had for sale to see if there was one or two that might help my understanding this mystery. There were many from the world's leading researchers and investigators of the UFO subject. There were also many books that seemed to contain a more spiritual type of content, but somehow strangely connected to this phenomenon. I really didn't understand how the two subjects could possibility be connected. I held off from exploring that avenue of research until another time.

At this time in my life I was pretty much an agnostic humanist, a worldly person, just surviving and trying to enjoy what I could get out of life. This is the world view I had, and the perspective from which I would be viewing and investigating this strange phenomenon. I just wanted to investigate the nuts and bolts aspect of this UFO realm. It's okay to be an agnostic humanist and a researcher in Ufology, right?

I didn't think much of there being a spiritual realm, or gods, or angels. I had followed Christian teachings when I was younger, but pretty much fell away from all of that in my senior year of high school. That was twenty years before. I do have to admit, though, I felt something was missing in my life, and I was determined to find it. I just didn't know what it was. Maybe I would find it here.

After a while, Jim, recognizing how much my interest had grown in the subject, asked me if I would like to get more involved in the investigative and research side of the UFO phenomenon. I said, "Of course I would, what else can I do?" That's when Jim introduced me to the Mutual UFO Network (MUFON).

MUFON is an all-volunteer, non-profit, 501(c) 3 charitable corporation, and the world's oldest, and largest, civilian UFO investigative & research organization. MUFON was founded in 1969.

Jim explained how the organization worked and how it was structured. There was an International Director over the organization. Under him were National Directors and US State Directors. Each State Director had State Section Directors that were working at the county level. The State Section Directors would set up chapters for MUFON in their county or counties of responsibility. They would hold monthly meetings, open and free to the public, for the sharing of information and education on the UFO phenomenon. The monthly meetings would also encourage membership into the MUFON organization. The State Section Directors were also responsible for recruiting and training Field Investigators to follow up on sighting reports that may come in from MUFON

Headquarters, or local police and sheriff's departments, local news reporting outlets, or even public call-ins.

After Jim shared with me the advantages of working with an organization like MUFON, and the support it gives its Field Investigators, I knew it was for me. Jim helped me sign up as a Journal Subscriber/Member.

Alright: now I was on my way to finding some answers to this crazy phenomenon.

I wanted to get my Field Investigator status right away. I purchased the MUFON Field Investigators Manual, studied it thoroughly, and took the test. I sent it to MUFON HQ for scoring and received the status of Field Investigator a couple of weeks later.

A few months went by and Jim asked me if I would like to do even more for MUFON and its search for UFO truth. He told me how he was the State Section Director for Orange County, Florida, which includes metropolitan Orlando. He stated that MUFON did not have an organized group established in Brevard County, where I lived. Brevard County is east of Orange County and nicknamed the Space Coast, due to the Kennedy Space Center and Canaveral Air Station being located in the county. He asked if I would like to take the position of State Section Director for Brevard County and set up its own group. I said "Heck yea, I would!" I thought to myself, what an awesome opportunity, to have a chapter which included one of the most highly protected and watched airspaces in the world.

Jim set up a phone interview for me with the Florida State Director. With my responses to his questioning, and Jim's personal referral in late 1993, I was appointed the Sate Section Director of Brevard County, Florida, for the Mutual UFO Network. The State Director did give me one word of caution as I was on to setting up my own county MUFON chapter. He wanted me to be aware of people who might come to the meetings sharing metaphysical or New Age ideas. He stated that this type of thinking could not be scientifically investigated, so stick to the nuts and bolts of UFOs. I said OK, not really sure what he was referring too, though.

On to putting together a team for Brevard County. Over the next few months I found five interested candidates for an investigation team. I trained them up, had them take their tests, and got them qualified. As we received sighting reports from within our county, we would follow up with witness statements and performing investigations the best we could. We would then send in the reports to MUFON HQ to add to their database of reports which reached back to 1969, when MUFON was founded. Back then a report consisted of many printed pages of questions, answered by hand, and sent in, unlike today, where a UFO witness files the initial report themself online through the MUFON website.

I found a free room I could book once monthly at the local public library where I could host my meetings. They even offered all of the video tools I might need for free use, like TV's, recorder/players, overhead projector, etc. All at no charge, as long as we did not charge for the meetings. Free to the public they would be.

The Brevard County MUFON group was now off and running. I hung up a sign on the door of the room where we were to have our first meeting. It said, "UFO Group Meeting, Free to the Public".

Now, let me ask you this question: if you were to hang a sign like that on the door to a meeting room, what kind of people do you think would show up? Weird people, crazy people, delusional people, or regular everyday people like yourself? You're right: all of the above. The meetings were quite a mishmash of interesting attendees.

Many of those coming to the meetings had a story to share of something they had seen, or experienced, in relation to the UFO phenomenon. Some just came to listen, to see what it was all about. And others came looking for answers to what they had experienced. Then there were those that came looking for help. What they had experienced had turned their lives upside down, and they wanted their normal lives back. Those looking for answers or help thought we would be the ones to answer their questions, or offer them help, because we were MUFON, and we were supposed to be in the know. But we didn't have answers, we only had the same questions that they did. We were looking for those same answers, we were looking for that same help for them. The best we could offer them was that we would do it together, with them. With their UFO and/or their alien abduction experience testimonials, and our investigative abilities and research support from MUFON, maybe, just maybe, we could find answers and help.

As the months of monthly meetings went by, I started seeing something relating to the experiencers that caught my attention. A majority of them talked amongst themselves about topics that seemed to have a spiritual nature to them. Not in a spiritual manner that I had heard when I was a church goer in my much younger years, but something much different. Many of them talked as if they thought that the ETs (extraterrestrials) were of a higher spiritual nature. Some thought they might be more interdimensional than physical beings. And some believed that they were probably our real gods of old. I heard terms like metaphysical, Enlightenment, and New Age, but I had no idea what they meant. Some of this seemed familiar to me. Maybe it had to do with some of the literature I had seen for sale in Jim's UFO museum.

As I explored this "spiritual" area of study, I realized that this was what the MUFON State Director had warned me about. That people with these views might come to the meetings and share these views.

But, you know something, the more I listened to what they had to say, the more I realized that this thinking, or these ideas, were actually part of the UFO phenomenon. Somehow there was a connection. No, you probably can't scientifically investigate most of it, but it was still a piece of the UFO puzzle. And if you were honestly going to do research and find answers, you had to include all the pieces of the puzzle, no matter how strange it might be.

Strange as the ideas of the New Age and metaphysical realm were, I had to check it out. I started looking at their information and listening to their teachings on the spiritual aspects of the UFO phenomenon. Something about all of it felt good. It was truly seductive, this quest for information, hidden information; I felt important. It gave me purpose. I wanted to reach this "enlightenment".

It seemed to fill that hole in me that I had been feeling for many years, feeling that something was missing in my life. Here, these people were offering a form of spirituality, albeit, without accountability. None of those rules and burdens of organized Christianity were there that I had been part of long before. It reminded me of the "forbidden fruit" from an old Bible story I had been told. Come on, give it to me, I'll eat that whole thing.

With no real grounded foundation to work from, I bought into this "spirituality without accountability". I consumed every piece of literature I could get my hands on concerning the subject of New Age and metaphysical thinking. I visited New Age and metaphysical book stores and hangouts. I even followed a self-proclaimed "Pleiadian channeler", someone who said they were being channeled through by a higher spiritual alien entity from the star system called the Pleiades, who was sharing special information to those who were ready to receive it. I studied and practiced the power of "crystals" and "healing" tools. Every time I found out something new it just made me want more. Looking back now, I can see my ego was getting quite puffed up from all the "special knowledge" I was acquiring.

I spent three years involved with the New Age and metaphysical world, thinking, studying, and researching. I even tried to convert my friends and family to this new "special knowledge". Especially amongst Christians, most of the ones I knew were weak in their faith and understanding of God's Word. It didn't take much of me spreading a little doubt about their beliefs to sway them over. I could show them, that they, too, could be like God.

All during this time I was still investigating and researching UFOs and alien abductions. But the perspective from which I viewed the strange phenomenon had changed. I was now seeing it from a second viewpoint, and it had opened me up to many new and different questions about the UFO subject matter.

Now I was more open to the things we can't explain, wanting to see things more from a metaphysical or esoteric viewpoint. It's okay to be a New Ager and a researcher in the field of Ufology, right? I mean, if you were okay with me being an agnostic humanist when I started out, I would hope it'd still be alright, now that I was "woke".

I continued to hold our monthly meetings at the library and the group was getting larger and larger. Other groups opened up in other towns that I would also visit and share information with. The town of Edgewater north of me had a fair sized group. I started working pretty close with them, sharing findings and information. Another opened up in Orlando that I visited too.

Then, one day, I had this thought. The people claiming to have alien abduction experiences were saying that the aliens abducting them were in the UFOs we were chasing as Field Investigators. Wouldn't it make more sense to focus on their experiences, rather than chasing sighting reports to get to the truth? They seem to be the front line of this phenomenon.

I ran the idea by my Field Investigators to see what they thought. They agreed that I might be on to something, so we decided to focus the majority of our work on abductions. But we would still continue to do UFO investigations as needed when they came in, so we put together a plan.

First, we would set up as a separate entity, or group, outside of MUFON to do the investigations, research, and the findings compilation, because MUFON was not structured at that time to do that. The name that was agreed upon for the group was the CE4 Research Group. The CE4 stood for close encounters of the fourth kind, the UFO encounter classification representing Alien Abductions. The research group would be a totally voluntary group with a rotating door membership. Members would be able to come and go as they wanted or needed. There have been many people over the past twenty-plus years that have come and gone from the group, but all made great contributions to the research.

We all agreed that the research findings would be available to MUFON or the public to review at all times. We had nothing to hide.

We expressed that, as much as possible, that group members be trained MUFON Field Investigators, following the scientific method for research that we were trained on through MUFON. We wanted to be as credible as we could be in this strange field of Ufology. We wanted our peers to know that we had done the research the right way.

One of the things we had already recognized from the group meetings was that the people we were encountering with stories of alien abductions were not happy people. They were quite miserable, in fact. These people had their world views turned upside down by these unexplainable experiences that they were having. They questioned what reality was, and what it was not. These experiences were happening against their will, totally unexpected. Sometimes it was recalled from a dream memory. Sometimes, fragments of the memory of an abduction experience would be triggered by a photo, a TV show, or a Hollywood movie. They felt alone and segregated from everyone. They couldn't share their experiences with friends, or family members, or co-workers, for the fear of being labeled crazy or delusional. Many resembled victims of Post-Traumatic Stress Disorder (PTSD), suffering from traumatic events.

For this reason, we agreed to study as much of the Alien Abduction phenomenon as we could. We did this through books, articles, and interviews of other researchers in the field. This was so we would not cause any more harm to these people.

We studied the works of John Mack, David Jacobs, Jacques Vallée, Budd Hopkins, Whitley Strieber, J. Allen Hyneck, and John Keel, just to name a few. Our focus was to find out why it was happening to them, and was there a way to actually help them, as well as understanding who was behind it, and why.

So were the humble beginnings of the CE4 Research Group, in Cocoa, Florida, U.S.A., in 1996.

Chapter 2

As we were looking at where we would be heading in our research, we realized that this was going to be a definite challenge to our way of thinking. This was going to prove to be a very bizarre field of research and study.

What was this Alien Abduction experience? This is what Wikipedia, the free encyclopedia on the Internet, says about alien abductions:

"The terms alien abduction or abduction phenomenon describes "subjectively real experiences" of being secretly kidnapped by nonhuman figures (aliens) and subjected to physical and psychological experimentation.

Typical claims involve forced medical examinations that emphasize the subject's reproductive systems. Abductees sometimes claim to have been warned against environmental abuse and the dangers of nuclear weapons. The contents of the abduction narrative often seem to vary with the home culture of the alleged abductee.

Reports of the abduction phenomenon have been made around the world, but are most common in English speaking countries, especially the United States.

The precise number of alleged abductees is uncertain. One of the earliest studies of abductions found 1,700 claimants, while contested surveys argued that 5–6 percent of the general population might have been abducted.

In a study investigating the motivations of the alleged abductors, Jenny Randles found that in each of the 4 cases out of 50 total where the experiencer was over 40 years of age, they were rejected by the aliens for "what they (the experiencers) usually inferred to be a medical reason." Randles concludes "The abduction is essentially a young person's experience." Given the reproductive focus of the alleged abductions it is not surprising that one man reported being rejected because he had undergone a vasectomy. It could also be partially because people over the age of 40 are less likely to have "hormonic" or reproductive activity going on.

Although abduction and other UFO-related reports are usually made by adults, sometimes young children report similar experiences. These child-reports often feature very specific details in common with reports of abduction made by adults, including the circumstances, narrative, entities and aftermaths of the alleged occurrences. Often these young abductees have family members who have reported having abduction experiences.

As a category, some studies show that abductees have psychological characteristics that render their testimony suspect, while others show that "as a group, abduction experiencers are not different from the general population in term of psychopathology prevalence". Dr. Elizabeth Slater conducted a blind study of nine abduction claimants and found them to be prone to "mildly paranoid thinking," nightmares and having a weak sexual identity, while Dr. Richard McNally of Harvard Medical School concluded in a similar study of 10 abductees that "none of them was suffering from any sort of psychiatric illness."

There have been a variety of explanations offered for abduction phenomena, ranging from sharply skeptical appraisals, to uncritical acceptance of all abductee claims, to the demonological, to everything in between

Some have elected not to try explaining things, instead noting similarities to other phenomena, or simply documenting the development of the alien abduction phenomenon.

Others are intrigued by the entire phenomenon, but hesitate in making any definitive conclusions. The late Harvard psychiatrist John E. Mack concluded, "The furthest you can go at this point is to say there's an authentic mystery here. And that is, I think, as far as anyone ought to go." (emphasis as in original) Mack was unconvinced by piecemeal counterclaims, however, and countered that skeptical explanations naturally need to "take into account the entire range of phenomena associated with abduction experiences," up to and including "missing time," directly contemporaneous UFO sightings, and the occurrence in small children.

Putting aside the question of whether abduction reports are literally and objectively "real", literature professor Terry Matheson argues that their popularity and their intriguing appeal are easily understood. Tales of abduction "are intrinsically absorbing; it is hard to imagine a more vivid description of human powerlessness." After experiencing the frisson of delightful terror one may feel from reading ghost stories or watching horror movies, Matheson notes that people "can return to the safe world of their homes, secure in the knowledge that the phenomenon in question cannot follow. But as the abduction myth has stated almost from the outset, there is no avoiding alien abductors."

Matheson writes that when compared to the earlier contactee reports, abduction accounts are distinguished by their "relative sophistication and subtlety, which enabled them to enjoy an immediately more favorable reception from the public."

Some writers have said abduction experiences bear similarities to pre-20th century accounts of demonic manifestations, noting as many as a dozen similarities. One notable example is the Orthodox monk Fr. Seraphim Rose, who devotes a whole chapter in his book Orthodoxy and the Religion of the Future to the phenomena of UFOs and abductions, which, he concludes, are manifestations of the demonic."

https://en.wikipedia.org/wiki/Alien_abduction

As the monthly meetings came and went, we were definitely getting plenty of practice interviewing Abduction Experiencers. We were not finding anything unusual or different from what we had read about from the leading researchers in the field. Many of them were using hypnotic regression on their subjects, but we refrained from using that technique for memory recall. I had done a lot of reading on the history, methodology, and criticisms of hypnosis and hypnotic regression, and decided it was not reliable enough to base our research findings on, especially if they were to be peer reviewed. We would opt for relying only on conscious memories that had been recalled by the experiencer. As we interviewed an experiencer, we would let the narrative of their testimony guide us into asking the right questions, digging deeper into their stories, if it was possible. Sometimes we would just come to a dead end, and what we had was all we were going to get from them.

During the spring and summer of 1996, I became really busy on other projects, taking some of my time away from the research.

I had been contacted by a gentleman that worked at the Jet Propulsion Laboratory (JPL) in Pasadena, California, asking if I would be interested in being part of a simultaneous public rally concerning the upcoming return to Mars launch of the Mars Global Surveyor, which was going to remap the planet Mars for future missions.

He had contacted me because I was the MUFON State Section Director, for the area of the Kennedy Space Center (KSC), where the Surveyor Satellite would be launched from. His idea was to hold two simultaneous public rallies the day of the launch to Mars, one at JPL, the other at KSC. They would be held at the main entrances to both locations for the best publicity coverage.

The reason for the rally was because the Surveyor Satellite was not going to include photography of the infamous "Plain of Cydonia" on Mars, where the so-called "Face on Mars" was located, which was previously photographed during the 1976 Viking Mission to Mars and made famous by researchers like Richard Hoagland with his well-known book, The Monuments of Mars: A City on the Edge of Forever, published in 1987.

Supposedly, the ruins of a whole ancient city could be seen there in the Viking photos. This whole "ancient aliens" idea was very well known amongst the more fringe UFO crowd. I know what you must be thinking: the whole UFO subject is fringe as it is. I don't disagree with you. I really had no interest or knowledge in this area of study (ancient cities on Mars), but I was open to giving a fellow UFO nut with a good cause a helping hand.

Just to let you know how "fringe" this field of study can get, there are areas of investigation and research such as: time travel, interdimensional travel, intergalactic travel, worm holes, crop circles, cattle mutilations, shadow people, reptilians, alien hybrids, Nordics, hollow earth, flat earth, transhumanism, cloning, Ancient Aliens, Secret Space Fleets, orbs, past life regressions, Bigfoot, reincarnation, ghosts, missing time, sleep paralysis, hypnotic regressions, and on, and on, and on. I kind of considered this to be only mildly fringe. Right.

This group of interested parties in JPL wanted to publicly pressure NASA to change the photography and surveying docket of the Surveyor Satellite, to add the "Plain of Cydonia" to its mission, helping answer the twenty year old questions that came from the Viking photos. They felt that, with my support, with two simultaneous rallies, they might be able to pull it off. This was their goal.

After talking with the guys at JPL and getting the gist of what they expected to do, I felt that I could pull this off on the KSC side with them. But, to get my group and any other local UFO group to participate, I needed to be able to make sure they understood the idea behind it. They had made the comment that they knew and were in touch with Richard Hoagland. I asked if they could get permission from him for us to publicly show one of his recorded video talks to help everyone understand why this event was important. They replied that they would talk to him for us.

A week went buy, and the gentleman I was working with from JPL said he had talked with Richard Hoagland, and he had stated that he would do one better for us and this rally. He offered to come and speak publicly for free and be present for the rally at KSC on launch day.

Richard was excited to be able to come to the Kennedy Space Center again. He had once been a Science Advisor to CBS News during the Apollo program, from 1968–1971.

This whole thing just got real big. Our group was going to have a lot to do in preparation for this event. But we were all excited.

We spent two months planning and organizing the talk venue for Richard Hoagland. We planned the rally point for the west entrance to the Kennedy Space Center on NASA Causeway. We prepared promotional items, posters, signs, newspaper advertisements, and personnel support for the rally events. Everyone was working hard. Even though we had regular jobs and families as well as this event to prepare for, we still supported the UFO group and investigations.

When the time for the rally came, everyone was ready. Richard Hoagland flew in on Saturday and spoke at a local junior college auditorium we booked for him that seated over five hundred people. The place was totally packed, even standing room areas were filled to capacity. He spoke for fours, non-stop, about his research on Mars and new information about the Moon.

The Mars Global Surveyor launch was scheduled for Tuesday. We were all at the rally point early that morning. We set up our big banners and signs, and greeted the thousands of KSC workers headed to work on the Space Program.

We were set up in front of the KSC Badging and Security Station at the west entrance of the Space Center. Many of us took the day off from work to be at the rally. Richard Hoagland came by and visited for a while with us, then he got an opportunity to be present at the press viewing area on the Space Center for the launch. So he headed out there.

Many interested people came by and asked what the Rally was about. The local newspaper sent reporters and a photographer by. We had a radio show interview stand set up on site covering the Rally. Even NASA Security personnel would come by off and on and hang out and talk with us. It was a really good event, all in all.

The launch time for the Mars Global Surveyor came and went. We heard on the radio that it had been scrubbed due to high upper atmosphere winds, which could be detrimental to the launch of the rocket. They rescheduled for the next day. We all stayed till the end of the work day and workers had finished leaving the Space Center headed for home.

Before we left the rally that day, we had a NASA spokesperson that had come out to the rally near the end and shared with us that NASA had changed their minds and had added the "Cydonia" region of Mars to the photographic and surveying docket of the satellite's mission. The rally worked; we had achieved what we came for. It really felt good. We had taken a stand for a cause (however weird it was) and had actually made a difference.

A sidebar note: The rocket blasted off successfully the day after the rally and the Mars Global Surveyor took the pictures we wanted of the "Cydonia" region and the "Face on Mars". Months and months later when they were released, the area, and the Face, looked nothing like they had been seen in the Viking pictures from twenty years ago. To me, this was the end of the subject. The evidence spoke for itself. It had only been a play of light and shadows. But at least we got the evidence to prove it. For others, it wasn't that easy. They had a belief, a belief that no hard evidence against it could change. To this day, they still have conspiracy theories as to why the area didn't look the same.

I wanted to share all of this with you because it was an important event, one of many, leading up to another dramatic change in my life, a change which would give me another unique perspective to viewing the UFO and Alien Abduction phenomenon.

Chapter 3

It was now the second week in November of 1996. I was exhausted from the time spent putting the rally together. I had still been working my full-time job and helping raise my son, who was 11 years old. I wasn't married and had him staying with me on my weekends. I had been juggling all these responsibilities together for too long. I needed a break. Adding to all of this were these two bizarre abduction/contactee cases we were working on. These two cases were weighing on us. There was something dark and not right about them.

There was a really nice gal I had been dating for some time that was also working with us in our abduction investigations. I was happy to have her support because most of the experiencers of the alien abduction phenomenon were female, and many of their testimonies had a very sexual nature to them. It was better if she did the interviews with them, or, with us together. We were kind of a mixed couple you could say, she being a professing Christian, and me a crystal-rolling New Ager. But, we agreed to not pressure each other too much about our different beliefs.

Along about the second weekend in November, we were sitting at her place talking, when she stated that she was concerned for us. I asked what she meant by that. She said she could tell that we were tired and bothered by something in our work. There were a couple cases that we were working on that had a very, very dark effect on us. We couldn't put our finger on it, but something wasn't right. But I tried to convince her that we were alright, just in need of a little break. And with the holidays coming up, we would do just that.

But she pulled me aside one day, and she said, "You know, something is wrong here." She said, "These cases you're working on right now, there's something very dark about them. There's something that seems like there's almost an evil presence involved." And of course, me and my new age thinking, said, "You know, evil's just a perception you have of this, there's really no evil, it's all relative." She said, "No, no, no, there's really something wrong here. I know you feel it."

She said, "You know, when you're working in this area, I think you really need to have some type of protection on you as you go into this. I think there are some dark forces here that you need to be protected from." Of course, I reached in my pocket and pulled out my trusty crystals. And I said, "I got all the power I need right here." My New Age studies had taught me about the power of crystals and how they can protect us in many different ways. And she said, "No, no, no, that's not the kind of protection I'm talking about, that's not going to help you, it isn't helping you right now." And I said, "Well what kind of protection are you talking about?" And she said, "From evil that can be associated with this phenomenon. I know of a help that can help you and can protect you." And I said, "Yeah? What do you got?"

And she broke out a Bible, and set it on the table, and said, "It's in here." And I said, "Oh no, that's got nothing to do with what I do." She said, "I think it does. I think you need to take a look at it. And I was like, "No, no, we don't need to go there." I said, "That has nothing to do with what I am researching here." She asked if we could just take a look at it. I told her no, I didn't think it played any role in these investigations.

And she said, "Wait a minute… you said you're the most objective and open-minded objective investigator there is; you tell people that." I said, "I am." She said, "Then you'll take a look at this, right?" I had just been had. I agreed to look at it. So, we sat down, and I said, "Show me what you've got." And I gave her, her time.

In those next few moments, as I sat there listening, something amazing happened. She was sharing with me the Gospel message of Jesus Christ, and the power and authority in that name available to those that believed in Him. In those moments it was like a great weight was lifted off of my shoulders. I could see His truth as never before, I could hear His truth as never before. Even though I had followed Christianity in my younger years, it never came across to me as it had right then. I knew in my heart that this was truth, and that this was real protection, and I wanted it. That day, I accepted Jesus Christ into my life.

My life was to change once again.

In the following weeks, I made a public profession of faith in Jesus Christ in my parent's church for all to see that I meant business. I was baptized the following Sunday.

I'm now a Christian.

But what is a Christian? What is it all about? As a person with an inquisitive mind I needed to know more, and I was hungry to know now.

My Lead Field Investigator and co-founder of CE4 Research Group was also a Christian. He told me that a friend of his had a powerful two week VHS video study course on Christianity. He felt it would well educate us on Christianity in a short period of time. I told him that sounded like a good idea. I said that I had two weeks off from work in December that I could use to go through the course. We could watch a video presentation a night and be finished before I had to go back to work. He talked with his friend and we set it up.

We continued with our research with CE4 Research. We decided to put out a hypothesis or a question that we would make as the focus of the research: "Are Christians being abducted by aliens?" From what we had read from the research done by other peers in the field, this experience reached across all races and belief systems. But we were going to look at one specific group.

When my two week break came at the end of December we met at the house of the gentleman who owned the Bible study course. My partner introduced us and gave him a little background on me and the research we were doing. He set everything up in his living room for us. He popped in the first tape as we got relaxed on his couch.

The study course was very enlightening, packed with scripture study and biblical information that I had never been exposed to before. I was very thankful to have had the opportunity to study like this as a new believer in Jesus Christ. We would view a two hour tape a night, staying a little longer as we discussed each lesson.

As the nights of study went by, the studies got deeper and deeper into scripture. There was one specific night that I will never forget. As the tape started playing, the narrator of the study lessons on the tape said that we were going to look at Spiritual Warfare. I didn't know what that was, but it did sound pretty cool and interesting. After a few minutes the narrator turned to reading scripture from the book of Ephesians in the New Testament—Ephesians chapter six, verse twelve, to be exact: "For our struggle is not against flesh and blood, but against the rulers, against the authorities, against the powers of this dark world and against the spiritual forces of evil in the heavenly realms."

As he read that verse, I starting seeing a picture in my mind unfold. It was like I was seeing it right in front of me. I saw a picture of the atypical Hollywood style grey alien, then it starting morphing into the most horrific thing I could have ever imagined. I said to my friends, "Stop that tape". They were kind of startled by what I said. I shared with them what I had seen. They asked me what I thought it meant. I said that I think I was just shown what this UFO and Alien Abduction is about, and who was behind it. I told them I believed that scripture—Ephesians 6:12—is God's Word on who they really are: demonic evil entities, perpetrating a lie, a deception, a delusion if you will, on humanity.

I told my partner that I think it's probably wrong to be involved in the UFO phenomenon. I told him that I think I would do better not to be involved. He agreed with me. We went on to finish the Bible study, and planned to close out our work into the UFO realm.

You know, I've had people tell me that the Lord told them this or the Lord told them that. I really didn't know what to make of it when I heard that. I do believe the Lord speaks to us through His written Word.

Then one day, about two weeks after saying I wanted nothing else to do with the UFO realm, I kept getting this thought in my head, "Take what you now know back to where you came from."

I had made a commitment to stop dabbling in this area.

Again, "Take what you know back to where you came from." I thought to myself, could this be from the Lord? Nah, I must be going crazy. So I said out loud, "Lord, if this is you speaking to me, I can't take the truth back to where I came from. Those New Age folks don't accept your Word and the Word of the God of this Universe. You have to give me something better to reach them with." Hey, I was a new believer, nobody ever told me you don't talk back to God.

I kind of figured that was the end of all that. I wasn't hearing any messages anymore. Moving on. Until a couple of weeks later. Then, I hear in my mind, "You already have what you need." Lord, what do you mean I already have what I need, already have what? I was puzzled.

I talked with my research partner and told him what I had been experiencing and what I had heard in my mind. I asked him if he knew what was meant by, "already having what you need". He was as clueless as I was. I asked him if he thought it might have to do with something we found in the research. We agreed to go back through the video recordings of our case interviews and see if we were missing something. We reviewed one testimony after another, looking for something that maybe we had just not picked up on.

Then, one evening, we plugged in a tape of an interview of Bill D. that we had done at least six months before I gave my life to Jesus Christ. Bill D. had had many encounters, some even at work. He worked at the Kennedy Space Center on the evening shift. He was also a recent Christian, attending a small church near where he lived in Christmas, Florida. We had met Bill D. when he started coming to our monthly MUFON meetings at the Cocoa Library.

After a few minutes into his taped interview, things got interesting.

Bill D. "I couldn't move...gray fog. I couldn't see anything, but it was like someone was there." I felt myself lifted off the bed. "I was terrified, so helpless... screaming inside, but I couldn't get it out."

"I thought I was having a satanic experience; that the devil had gotten hold of me and had shoved a pole up my rectum and was holding me up in the air... so helpless. I couldn't do anything."

"I said, 'Jesus, Jesus, help me', or 'Jesus, Jesus, Jesus!' And when I did, there was a feeling or a sound or something. That either my words that I had thought, or the words that I had tried to say or whatever, hurt whatever was holding me up in the air on this pole.

"And I felt like it was withdrawn, and I fell. I hit the bed, because it was like I was thrown back in the bed. I really can't tell what it was. But when I did, my wife woke up and asked why I was jumping on the bed."

My partner and I looked at each other and asked why we hadn't caught that earlier. This man had just testified that he had stopped his Abduction experience while it was happening. We were told that that was not possible by the leading Abduction researchers in the UFO realm. What did this testimony of Bill D. mean? Was it real? Because, if it was, it was huge. If it was real, it was showing that this was more than what anyone else knew. This would unmask these entities for what they really were. It would validate the vision I had during the reading of Ephesians 6:12 during the Bible study. It would also validate what I what I had asked for, "something better" to take back to where I came from. This showed the power and authority in the name of Jesus Christ, validating God's Word is real. Wow, just wow.

I had to validate this testimony of Bill D. the best I could. I decided to take to peer review. I contacted some of the leading researchers in the UFO and Alien Abduction realm for opinions of this experiencer testimony. Each one that I called and shared the testimony with asked me if we could talk off the record. Off the record means I can tell you what was said, but I cannot tell you who said it. This is asking for anonymity, something we take really important in this field. As a MUFON researcher and Investigator, I have to respect it when asked for.

I said, sure, that's fine, I'm just trying to find out if this testimony is valid or not, in their opinion. Each one I talked with stated that in their research, they too, had come across experiencers that had stopped an abduction experience by quoting Bible scripture, humming or singing a Christian hymn, praying, or even calling on the name Jesus Christ for His aid. I asked them why we had not heard about this before. We usually hear that the experience cannot be stopped. All, most all of them, had the same reply: "We didn't know what to make of it." You know, I would have been fine with that answer and moved on. But they just had to add another reason, as if the first wasn't enough. And that reason was, "We were afraid to go there because it might affect our credibility in the UFO realm."

So, let me get this straight in my head. You were afraid to share all of your research findings, which we rely on for truth, because you might have your credibility damaged in the UFO realm? Excuse me, isn't that what a cover-up is all about? All over the UFO realm you hear the Government covers this up, the Government covers that up. But the true cover-up, I found, is coming from the same researchers you rely on for UFO truth. The same ones you buy books and DVDs from. The same ones you pay to see at conferences with your hard earned money.

Sure, our Government keeps secrets for national security reasons, but that's not the same as what these UFO researchers are doing, withholding information to support their own agendas in the UFO realm. After twenty plus years working alongside of them, I really don't think they want the answers. It would put an end to the traveling UFO circus. Don't get me wrong, there are some researchers trying to the right thing and dig for truth, no matter which direction it goes in. But, the show boaters of Ufology, that's a whole different thing.

My response to all of these researchers I went to for help was, thank you for validating this testimony for me as something that they too had come across before. It meant that there were probably more testimonies out there like this to be found. I told them I would take on this piece of the UFO puzzle, and find those testimonies, and document them, and share them. Bringing this unwanted piece of the UFO puzzle to the table so that we will get an honest picture of what this phenomenon is about.

They all told me, "Please do, because we can't."

In the twenty plus years that I have been collecting these testimonies and sharing them, these researchers that I confided with have never come against me or our research findings. But those that I had not talked to have come at me with an anger and hatred that I've never seen before. All because of what I had found and shared. Now I knew what the other researchers feared.

Now, without a doubt, I knew I had something I could take back to where I came from: The Word of God and the testimonies of the ability of the name and authority of Jesus Christ to stop these horrific experiences. That was something powerful. Finally, a Hope for these broken people that they could stop this experience. A Hope offered nowhere else in this UFO realm. And evidence leading to the true nature of the entities behind this strange deceptive phenomenon.

I was starting to see this phenomenon from a new, third perspective-the Christian perspective. A spiritual perspective. And, as I would soon find, the only perspective that answers all of the questions that all the secular researchers are still asking.

Before we move on, I have to ask: it's okay to be a Christian and a researcher in the field of Ufology, right? If you had no problem so far accepting me, as an agnostic humanist researcher or a New Ager researcher, I would hope you can also accept me as a Christian researcher. We are still going to be tolerant of other people's beliefs, right? Good, let's move on.

It was around this time that I got a "spiritual" smack in the face that I never saw coming. I was still trying to grasp the whole understanding of what this all meant.

While all of this new "revelation" was going on, I was still working full time at the boat company and helping raise my son. In other words, I was still trying to lead a normal life. After all the years at the boat company, my co-worker friends had seen me go through these changes in my beliefs. Many thought I was absolutely crazy, I'm sure. I know Hippie Bob did.

I got to know Hippie Bob through my good friend Rick W. Rick and Bob worked in the lamination building at the boat company manufacturing facility on day shift. I was working second shift in the welding and mold and master reinforcement department next door at the Product Development and Engineering facility at the time.

Hippie Bob was definitely quite the character. I really liked him. He was a guy that was really hard not to love. He had more jokes about aliens than anybody I knew. He ribbed me every chance he had about my research into UFOs. At this time, I had not shared with anyone outside of the CE4 Research group anything about what we had found about an abduction being stopped in the name and authority of Jesus Christ. We just were not ready to release that yet.

It happened one Tuesday evening. I had just gotten home from work on second shift at 11:30pm. The phone rang. I thought who's calling me this late at night? I picked up the phone and it was Hippie Bob. Hippie Bob had never called me at home before. He was kind of agitated from the sound of his voice. I asked him "What's up?" He said he wanted to talk with me about some things that had been happening to him lately. Well, I was pretty tired myself, and just wanted to relax, so I asked him if we could get together maybe Friday, as we both had Friday off from work (we worked four ten hour days at the boat company.) He agreed that would be best, and I said I would see him then.

Friday wasn't soon enough. I got home from work on Thursday night around midnight and the phone rings as soon as I get into the house. It's Hippie Bob again, and he is freaking out. He's going on about being taken somewhere, it's not nice like it was before, shooting billiards at the bar…I told him to calm down a minute and tell me what was happening.

He apologized first for having joked about my research on aliens. He said he now knows it's real. He said he had been taken twice that evening while traveling between the bars where he and his girlfriend were playing billiards on a team. He said he had been having good pleasant experiences up till then. But after talking to me on Tuesday evening, things got real strange and real scary for him.

I asked him why he thought that was. I was just trying to calm him down. Right about that time Bob said he felt they were coming again. I asked him if his girlfriend was there, he said she was. I told him to put her on now.

His girlfriend picked up the phone and asked who the heck I was to Bob. I explained how I knew him and what I did in my research. I asked her what was going on right now with him and she said he is out again. I told her that he will be OK, just to bear with me a few minutes. I asked her to tell me about the evening and what had happened to him. She said they were on a billiards team and were playing at two bars this evening. On the way to the first one he was in the passenger seat and she was driving. He started getting agitated and cursing when he just blacked out. It was only for a couple of minutes. When he came to, he was really upset and scared. He wouldn't tell her what happened. They played at the first bar but I could tell his heart wasn't into it. After they finished at the first bar and were headed to the second one it happened again. He said they're coming again. And he slumped over. She thought he might be having a heart attack or something. But as quick as he went out, he came to, agitated and angry again. That's when he said he needed to talk to me, so she brought him home and he called.

By the time all this conversation went between me and Bob's girlfriend, he came to again. Now angrier than ever.

He grabs the phone and yells, "They are pissed at you." I asked, "Why are they pissed at me?" He said, "Because you know what the heck is going on."

That brought me to my knees. These beings sent a message back, through him, to me. That is *wayyyyy* too personal. Now I'm shaking. I asked Bob if he knew what they were referring to and he said he had no idea. This just got scary and more real than I ever imagined.

I told Bob he was going to be okay, they would not harm him, and to try and get some sleep. I told him that I needed to sleep and I would come see him in the morning.

I don't think I slept a wink that whole night. I doubt Bob did either. I do know I did a lot of praying.

The next morning I contacted my girlfriend Melinda, who had been working with us in abduction research, and me and Bob's friend Rick and shared with them what had happened the evening before. I asked both of them to accompany me when I went to visit Bob. The reason I wanted them there was they too were both Christians, and this was spiritual warfare. I could surely use the backup.

We all met at Hippie Bob's place at around 10:00 that Friday morning. I could see Bob was still quite shaken from the ordeal from the night before.

I had Bob start out with what he had been doing and what had been happening prior to the events of Thursday evening. He told us how, for a while now, he had been looking into the supernatural, things like meditation and out-of-body-experiences. He said he had been having experiences where in a relaxed state, laying on the couch, he would levitate out of his body and go to a different place, a place that had beings of colored light. He stated it was an extremely pleasant experience. He said it felt like he seemed to be gone for a long period of time, but actually it was for only a few minutes.

He knew he could not share this with anyone but probably me. He hoped I would not think he was crazy. This is why he had called me on Tuesday night.

Then Thursday night everything changed for the worst. It went from him wanting to induce the experience to "them" forcing the experience upon him. He said their appearance had changed too. There was communication. He said again that he felt like he had gone for a long period of time, but his girlfriend said it was only a couple of minutes that he was out, limp, and lifeless. And she testified that he had not physically gone anywhere; he stayed in the front passenger seat of the car the whole time.

Bob relayed to me what they told him that last time after he called me on Thursday evening. They told him they were angry that he was talking to me. He said, "They are pissed at you." Because I knew the truth about them. I asked Bob again if he knew what they were referring to, and he said he did not.

Right then Bob reached for his chest and said, "They are back, they are here to take me again, and I'm scared."

Immediately, my girlfriend stood up and walked over behind Bob, he was sitting in a small kitchen table chair across from us, and put her hands on his shoulders. She started praying out loud for Jesus Christ to come and protect Bob, to stop the work of these entities. Over and over she prayed.

Then, all of a sudden, Bob relaxed, a small smile started to appear on his face, and he said, "How did you do that?"

I told him she did nothing that he could not do himself. I took the next half hour and shared with Bob what we had come across in our research. He made the connection of why "they" were "pissed at me."

We witnessed to Bob that day the Hope he could have through Jesus Christ. Bob said he had been raised Catholic and had been an altar boy. He knew of Jesus Christ but had never made that personal relationship with him.

I never heard Bob state that he had any more experiences. I believe he had shut that door for good.

Hippie Bob's case, by far, was one of the most important ones I came across in our research. It showed this to be a non-physical experience. He was taken physically nowhere, verified by a witness, yet to him he believed he was taken somewhere. There was the "time distortion" as we see in cases termed "the Oz factor". And the communication from these entities to Bob, they knew what I was doing and he didn't.

I regrouped with my partner and some of the group members working with us at CE4 Research. I shared with them the conversations that I had with the other leading researchers, and what they said. I showed them that we had a brand new discovered piece of the UFO puzzle to explore, document, and present to the world. This was the beginning of the twenty plus years of research for CE4 Research Group.

I recommended putting forward a question to go after for the group. We chose, "Are Christians being abducted by aliens?"

We knew the usual statistics of those who have had abduction experiences, but this specific one was not addressed. We as a group would try and answer this one.

At this same time, we knew that there were more testimonies like Bill D.'s to find. We still needed to build the database, to reinforce this specific piece of the UFO puzzle. But we had no idea at the time how to go about doing that. We would have to think about that.

Chapter 4

I decided to give my newspaper reporter friend a call and see what he thought about what we had found. Maybe he would think it was a newsworthy piece to write. My friend was Billy Cox, a reporter for the <u>Florida Today</u> newspaper, in Brevard County, Florida. Billy was also very knowledgeable about the UFO realm. He had many articles submitted and printed in the newspaper over the years. Many times he would have an article on the UFO subject he was working on, and he'd contact me for a comment, to add as the local MUFON representative. He even covered us at the Mars Global Surveyor Rally that we did at the Space Center. I thought for sure he would bite on this one.

I called Billy and gave him a rundown on what we were working on and had come across. He said he thought it would be better if another reporter wrote the article other than him. He felt since it had a "religious" content that it would best be covered in the Spiritual section of the newspaper, so he put me in contact with Rita Elkins of the <u>Florida Today</u> newspaper. I called Rita and told her that Billy had recommended that I talk to her about what we had found. She was very interested and we set up an interview.

My co-founder of CE4 and I met with Rita at his home and laid it all out for her, some pictures were taken, and she said it looked to be a good story to be printed.

The article did get published, printed, and released on Sunday, August 17, 1997. We were plastered on the front and second page of the <u>Florida Today</u> "People" section of the Sunday paper. Now that's coverage. There might be someone out there who will read this that might have another testimony like Bill D's to add to the database we were compiling.

"SPIRITUAL WARFARE?"
SOME LOOK TO BIBLE FOR ANSWERS TO ALIEN ABDUCTIONS
By Rita Elkins
Originally Published August 17th 1997 in Florida Today

Big Stretch: Imagine that alien abduction experiences and demons are equally real.

Hey, we said it'd be tough. But you were halfway there watching the recent movie, "Fire in the Sky," right? One more step and you're in the strange and trendy world of UFOlogy theology, where extraterrestrials could be even scarier than you think.

Odd as it sounds, the spiritual life of aliens is being taken seriously in wide-ranging discussions among religious leaders. Magazine articles, books and even evangelists are engaging in Bible-based speculations about the nature and intention of entities that allegedly kidnap, paralyze, physically abuse and sometimes sexually molest victims - many of whom, more strangely still, come to believe the experience was worthwhile.

Religious leaders are alarmed about a growing train of thought that "wants us to reject traditional Judeo-Christian ideas about God" in favor of benign "Space Brothers" who will save humanity from itself, writes journalist William M. Alnor in his book, "UFOs in the New Age" (Baker, Grand Rapids, Mich.) Alnor concludes this new belief is a set-up for apocalyptic deceptions predicted in the Bible's Book of Revelation.

He's not alone.

"The similarity between the abduction experience and demonic possession is very, very close," says Joe Jordan of Cocoa, Brevard/Volusia state director for the Mutual UFO Network (MUFON), a widely respected clearinghouse for UFO-related research.

"These (alien contact) experiences these people are having are real. It does exist. But you just need to understand what's doing it."

Jordan and his partner, Wes Clark, have begun a research group called CE-4 (close encounters of the fourth kind, i.e. abductions), dedicated to studying alleged alien abductions. Its 15 members also belong to MUFON, but "nothing we do is necessarily sanctioned by them," says Clark, a quality control engineer at Kennedy Space Center.

MUFON principals did not respond to inquiries about CE-4's unusual hypothesis, summarized by Jordan:

"This whole thing is spiritual warfare. And the method the enemy's using is deception. Strong deception."

In other words, entities really are abducting people against their will. Only, they're not aliens from other planets. They're demons from the pit of hell.

Joe Jordan is addressing a "New Millennium Symposium" in Titusville. With his intense brown eyes and shoulder-length hair, he mingles easily with New Age folks who paid $44 to study pyramids, Mayan dream spells, Lakota prophesies, and to hear Jordan talk about "UFO Abductions."

Jordan, who works in product development and engineering for Sea Ray Boats, speaks calmly, his voice firm, with good grammar and diction. Kooks don't get to be state directors with science-orientated MUFON, for whom he has chased lights for seven years.

Last year he focused on CE-4 research, and encountered a Central Florida abductee whose otherwise-typical experience had one unique aspect. "They had stopped the experience while it was happening. In all the time I've been researching, I'd never heard that before."

Jordan punches buttons on a tape recorder. A nameless, 30-something man with an intelligent-sounding voice, slightly southern, tells his story. Calmly, at first.

There were strange lights in a nearby woods at bedtime, barking dogs. He is up and down a few times, yelling at the dogs while his wife sleeps soundly. Then, lying down again...

"I couldn't move... gray fog. I couldn't see anything, but it was like someone was there." He felt himself lifted off the bed. I was terrified, so helpless... screaming inside, but I couldn't get it out."

The voice is less calm now, but still certain, not hesitant.

"I thought I was having a satanic experience that the devil had gotten hold of me and had shoved a pole up my rectum and was holding me up in the air... so helpless. I couldn't do anything."

A non-religious person, he'd been to church with his wife a few times.

"I said, 'Jesus, Jesus, help me' or Jesus, Jesus, Jesus!' And when I did, there was a feeling or a sound or something. That either my words that I had thought, or the words that I had tried to say or whatever, hurt whatever was holding me up in the air on this pole.

"And I felt like it was withdrawn, and I fell. I hit the bed, because it was like I was thrown back in the bed. I really can't tell what it was. But when I did, my wife woke up and asked why I was jumping on the bed."

Yeah, but...

Relentless anonymity is a given in abduction research. Nobody in their right mind wants family, friends and co-workers to know they've had their personal space violated against their will by strange-looking creatures whose existence isn't even proven.

So they can't give names. But Jordan and Clark swear they have three verifiable cases in which apparent abduction experiences were halted by believers who called on the name of Jesus. And Jordan says as many as 400 cases may be documentable nationwide.

"It makes you wonder: if these beings are extra-terrestrial at all, why would they respond to that name?" Jordan asks. "We think we found the answer in the Bible, in Mark 16:17 where Jesus said, 'In my name they shall cast out demons.' That seems to be exactly what we came across."

Three major researchers told Jordan, off the record, that they had similar cases. But "They were afraid for their credibility," he says. "They felt they already had put their credentials out far enough dealing with extra-terrestrials." Other "so-called researchers (are) sitting on this information," Jordan says. "There's something wrong there. They're just as bad as the people they say have conspiracies in other ways."

Why would anyone suppress such research findings? Jordan, who became a Christian last year, says most UFOlogists share his former New Age beliefs, which dismiss Christianity and Judaism. "These people go from one thing to another looking for development of a higher consciousness," he says. Anyplace but in traditional religion.

Stranger still...

An estimated 40 percent of Americans say they believe aliens have visited Earth. More than a million people worldwide claim CE-4 experiences. Still, mainstream Christianity mostly side-stepped the issue - until March's mass suicide at Heaven's Gate showed just how misleading some alien link-thinking could be.

Suddenly, the religious press is full of articles about UFOs.

The May cover story in Central Florida's discovery Christian newspaper focused on UFOlogy theology, interviewing Berkley-trained scientist and Christian author, John Weldon. That was reprinted from Rutherford Institute's nationally-distributed October newsletter.

Even Jewish believers are connecting UFO experiences with the Torah, or Jewish Bible. "Many serious people who have been studying UFOs around the world have reached the consensus that the Bible is a convincing UFO story," said journalist Barry Chamish, quoted in a chapter titled, "UFOs in the Holy Land" from sightings: UFOs, by television writer Susan Michaels (Simon and Schuster, New York, due out in September).

July's Charisma magazine, a 200,000-plus circulation monthly, featured Christian evangelist and author Paul McGuire's article, "Alien Invaders." McGuire cites the evolution of popular New Age author Whitley Strieber's interests - from his first alien contacts in Communion, Transformation and Breakthrough to his latest titles, The Secret School: Preparations for Contact and Evenings with Demons - as an example of a progressive deception.

Indeed, Strieber fans often comment - albeit positively - on their favorite author's change. From experiencing his first alien encounters as terrifying and torturous, he began to seek them out and welcome them, finally advocating them as a religious experience.

That, say religious leaders, indicates a deceptive entity is at work.

"Both the seemingly benign and hostile entities... will play an increasing role in preparing a segment of humanity for the reception of the Antichrist," writes best-selling author David Allen Lewis and Robert Shreckhise in UFO: End-Time Delusion.

And the cover of The Agenda, The Real Reason They're Here, gives this premise: "In the near future, God will evacuate millions of people from the horrors to follow. Aliens will take the credit" for the Rapture (when Christians will be supernaturally airlifted to heaven), writes B. Fox, a MUFON researcher who resides in - of all places- Roswell, New Mexico.

Back in Titusville at the CE-4 office in Wes Clark's home, Joe Jordan and Clark continue to study, research and solicit abductees through the internet and with classified ads in MUFON's UFO Journal.

"The one thing we can offer people in this field, that nobody else elsewhere is offering, is hope. Hope that they can stop this experience," Jordan says.

"We're still researchers. It's not conclusive. But this is what we have so far."

http://www.alienresistance.org/ce4FLToday97.htm

Rita did a great job on the article for us. Even the pictures were awesome. Now, hopefully, someone who has had experiences would see this newspaper article and contact us with a testimony.

Over the next couple of weeks, I started receiving phone calls from people that had read the article and wanted to share their experiences and testimonies of stopping the experience through Jesus Christ. What puzzled me was, was when I looked at the ID Caller next to my phone, it was from outside of Brevard County. I asked them where they saw this article. They said they saw it in their local papers. I told them it only ran in the Brevard County local paper. How were they seeing it?

I called the paper and they told me that the <u>Florida Today</u> paper was an affiliate of Gannett News, as were many other newspapers throughout the US. The article had been printed in many of the other newspapers under Gannett around America. We were getting testimonies from all over. Now, that was coverage. More than we could have put together on our own.

The next thing we saw was that an Internet news service, CNI News, had picked it up, posted it, and people were seeing the article all over the US internet, and probably elsewhere.

Within about seven months of the release of the newspaper article, a friend in the UFO realm told me I should get the recent copy of <u>Flying Saucer Review</u>, the most prominent and oldest UFO magazine in print out of the United Kingdom. They had picked up the article and printed it verbatim in their magazine. We just went worldwide with our research.

We could not have planned the marketing of the research any better ourselves. It was a true Godsend. By the end of 1999 I had a good fifty testimonies showing that the name and authority of Jesus Christ could stop these experiences.

Right after we had our first few cases in 1997, I questioned if any Christian researchers had already written anything to support what we had come across.

There was a Christian bookstore near my home. I went to it looking for anything in print on the UFO subject. I wandered through the store for a while but didn't see anything on the subject matter, so I finally went to the counter and asked the gal working the register if she had a way to look up a book for me. She replied, "Sure, by title, by author, or by subject." I told her I had to go by subject. I told her the subject was UFOs. She gave me a strange look, wondering why that subject would be in a Christian bookstore. But, she did look it up, and actually found two books listed. The first one, <u>UFOs: What On Earth Is Happening?</u> Paperback – 1975 by John Weldon and Zola Levitt, and <u>UFO: End-Time Delusion</u> Paperback – July 1, 1991 by David Allen Lewis and Robert Shreckhise. I asked her if they were in stock at this time and she replied that they were not. But she said she could order them for me. I ordered them both before I left the store. But I did buy the July edition of <u>Charisma</u>, a Christian magazine that had just come out. It featured Christian evangelist and author Paul McGuire's article "Alien Invaders." It was the first of any information on the UFO subject I had read from the Christian perspective. And it confirmed my new Christian perspective on this phenomenon that this appeared to be a deception or delusion perpetrated by demonic entities. The main difference being, the testimonies I had come across were the actual evidence that proved the true nature of the entities behind the UFO and Alien Abduction phenomenon.

Of the two books that I had ordered, I felt that <u>UFO, End Time Delusion</u> was right on with my perception of the UFO phenomenon from my new Christian perspective. I had to contact Dr. David Allen Lewis and let him know what I had come across, the testimonies of experiencers stopping the abduction experience in the name and authority of Jesus Christ. I wanted him to know there was evidence to support his work, and we had it.

I found Dr. Lewis's phone number and gave him a call. He was excited by what I had to share with him. I told him how I had come across his book and felt it was right on in explaining this strange phenomenon. We talked a few times, sharing our findings into the UFO research realm.

A few months later, Dr. Lewis invited my partner and me to his home in Springfield, Missouri to meet and talk more in depth with him. He also had another visitor there at the time who wanted to talk with us also. He was the head of the Assemblies of God Christian Schools in Nigeria. He himself was in the process of putting a book together of how the New Age thinking was infiltrating the thinking in Nigeria. He was interested in our work with the Alien Abduction phenomenon, as it closely mirrored an experience that people of the Nigerian African culture were having and reporting. The main difference being, the experiencers were not abducted to an alien spaceship, but to a lake or body of water, where they were taken underwater, to a beautiful crystal city.

We all found the similarities amazing between the stories, but at the same time fitting the culture experiencing it. We had read about this in some of the abduction research we had explored earlier, but this just confirmed it.

In the fall of 1999, Dr. Lewis would be holding a Prophecy, Prayer, and Spiritual Warfare Conference in the Cornerstone Church of Springfield, Missouri. He invited us to come out and speak, our first time speaking at a Christian conference.

The conference was a four day event, three days of a spectacular lineup of Christian ministers, theologians, and researchers, followed by a panel question and answer time on Saturday. Many of the speakers had been doing the Lord's work for thirty, forty, or even fifty years. And yet, here we were, brand new to this. I truly felt unworthy, especially not being a practiced public speaker.

On the first two days as we sat through the fabulous talks, we twice heard our names mentioned as ones to especially listen to on Friday, when we were scheduled to talk. Those two times we were recognized, was by the head of the Worldwide Assemblies of God Church, and the second to the head of the Worldwide Assemblies of God Church. Both times when I heard us mentioned, I asked my partner, "Did he just mention us?" to which he replied, "He sure did." What was happening here?

I had tried to prepare something for Friday's talk, but I just couldn't make it come together in any organized manner. I knew what I needed to say, I prayed that it would make sense as I spoke it. The talk went without any problems. People were just flabbergasted by what they had just heard me say concerning the UFO realm. I had taken what they had suspected it to be and gave them the evidence to make it real. But oh, did it bring up a barrage of questions from them. I answered all of them the best I could, based on our research findings. I was really starting to see how important this all was, especially to the Church.

When we had first arrived in Springfield, I told my partner that I wanted to see what kind of demonic spiritual activity was present here. He asked me how we were to determine that. I said, let's see how many New Age bookstores or gathering places they have here in Springfield. That would give us an idea of the size of the New Age population they're supporting. And they most likely would advertise in the phone book, like any other businesses would. I asked my partner if he had ever been to one of these places. He said he had not, so I said, let's go visit one. I found one in the phone book that looked to be the biggest around, and off we went.

If you have never visited a New Age bookstore, you will be very surprised, by the diverse collection of ideologies, beliefs, and worldviews, all under one roof.

I had no idea what to expect when we got there. This place was huge. The store looked to be as big as most big name grocery stores in America. As we entered the store and started down the aisles, we found a section on Hinduism, Confucianism, Taoism, Metaphysical studies, Channeling, Tarot Cards, Big Foot, UFO's, Alien Abductions, Hypnotism, Starseed people, Satanic Worship, ESP, Poltergeists, Ghosts, American Indian beliefs, and on and on. Anything and or everything that is non-Christian, or even what the Bible would deem occult, all under one roof. Most of it contradicting each other, but as a whole in agreement of being non-Christian.

When it came time for the question and answer panel with the conference speakers on Saturday, I was given a question that led me into the story of visiting the New Age store with my partner. When I finished telling the congregation about the visit to the store, I told them about the ride back to the church. I told them I had counted more than twelve different independent churches between the New Age bookstore and the Cornerstone Church where the conference was being held. And as in most cities in America, these churches have nothing to do with each other. Not working together in any way. But all professing the same true God.

I asked them, "How can we defeat an enemy that is united in every non-Christian belief under one roof, and we, believing in the same one true God, can't come together. This new Space Age religion will soon be a force to reckon with if we don't come together, to expose the evil source behind it."

There was a moment of silence, then everyone clapped and gave us a loud amen. They got it. A seed had been planted. I felt good, and it felt right. I could keep doing this. I hoped I would be able to keep doing this.

Chapter 5

Over the next year I made acquaintances with Guy Malone, from Nashville, Tennessee, of Seek Ye One Ministry, and Dr. Chris Ward, from Leesburg, Florida, of Logos Christian Fellowship.

Guy Malone was a former Alien Abduction experiencer that had terminated his experiences through a personal relationship with Jesus Christ. He published his personal testimony in his book <u>Come Sail Away</u>, July 1999.

Dr. Chris Ward was a pastor of a Church in Leesburg, Florida, who had written his doctoral thesis on the "Origin of Demons." His church ministered to the "Rainbow People" during their Gatherings annually in the Ocala National Forest, and to the secular UFO community at UFO conferences.

The three of us, seeing we each had a lot to give to exposing the truth, decided to unite our mission under the heading of www.AlienResistance.org.

Guy Malone soon relocated to Roswell, New Mexico and set up the Alien Resistance HQ, an Internet coffee house and book store, sharing the Christian perspective of Ufology in the Mecca of the UFO community.

Chris Ward and I met Guy in Roswell, along with a close friend of mine and a former experiencer, Matt Kiss, for a weekend to commemorate the grand opening in 2000. We picked Saturday for a mini conference in Roswell at the coffee house, each of us taking a turn to speak. We had a pretty good turnout.

At the end of my talk, I opened up the floor to questions. A gentleman raised his hand and asked to share an experience. He relayed a story that actually had been published in a UFO magazine. He had a copy of it with him.

He had gotten caught up in running drugs in the high desert of New Mexico. He was of Mexican decent and had a Catholic background growing up. During a drug transaction on a high mesa one evening, his life changed. They had arrived a little early, it was night out, dark but bright stars overhead. While they were waiting, they saw something coming up towards them from the other end of the Mesa. Two large metallic craft moving silently towards them. He thought this was nothing of this earth. Remembering something that his mother had told him when he was younger, that if he was ever in need of help, to call on Jesus Christ to protect you, he did just that. When he did, the craft not only stopped, but they backed up and away to the other end of the mesa and then disappeared. He had come to share this with us as he had heard we had testimonies of the name and authority of Jesus Christ stopping experiences. This was the first I had heard of it being done to a UFO sighting experience. And his story had been published publicly in a UFO magazine.

This would be just the beginning of many, many years of UFO conferences we either held ourselves or spoke at, or attended as vendors, at least getting the information from the Christian perspective out through books, DVDs, and flyers.

Whenever I had the opportunity to speak, I would try to make sure I had a live testimony or two that would come up at the end of my talk as living testimony that they could question. I did not want people to only rely on what I was telling them, I wanted them to see (meet) the evidence for themselves. There were times at some of my talks I would have as many as a dozen of these live testimonies on stage. I would ask the audience, how many testimonies do you need to talk to, to make you believe what this research is saying? Because new ones are still coming in to this day.

I want to give a special thank you to those that were very instrumental in being there as that very live testimonials over the years; Bill Deffendall, Guy Malone, Kathy Land, Paradox Brown, Josh Jauz, Patrice Sheridan, Jackie Slack, Danny Ahrens, and the late Joyce Ahrens (I really miss her). I commend them, and the many, many others that were not afraid to stand with me, for their courage to testify that the name and authority of Jesus Christ terminates this so-called Alien Abduction experience.

Taking a minute to look back at the original posted hypothesis of CE4 Research—"Are Christians being abducted by aliens?"—we were finally able to give an answer, or sort of. Why sort of? Well, as far as were Christians having this "so-called" alien abduction experience, the answers were yes, and no. Why yes and no? Because we found that Bible-believing, God-worshiping, walk-the-walk Christians with a good personal relationship with Jesus Christ were not having these experiences. But, talk-the-talk Christians, still dabbling in things they should not be, were having these experiences.

It was around 2000-2002 that we got caught up in the thinking that was coming from other Christian Researchers in the field, that this Alien Abduction and alien/human hybridization idea was related Biblically to the verse in Genesis, Genesis 6:4, "The Nephilim were on the earth in those days-and also afterward-when the sons of God went to the daughters of humans and had children by them. They were the heroes of old, men of renown." This was supported by the idea taken from the Book of Matthew in the New Testament of, "As in the Days of Noah". It was thought that the Alien Abduction and alien/human hybridization reports, coming from the hypnotic regression sessions of the secular alien abduction researchers, were the prophesied events mirroring Genesis 6:4.

This actually sounded pretty feasible at first. This would answer a lot of questions about the Old Testament and how God worked with Israel, His chosen people, if it was correct in their interpretation of it. That would be assuming that the reports of alien/human hybridization were real; which, at this point, we had no real proof of alien/human hybrids. People were claiming to be hybrids, but there was no actual evidence to prove it to be true. The whole idea of alien/human hybrids came from the leading secular UFO and Alien Abduction researchers. They had tales of a hybridization program going on, coming from experiencers that they had regressed under hypnosis. So for the time being, I kind of went along with this thinking, leaving the idea open till something came along to confirm or disprove it. But many of my fellow Christian researchers bought into it hook, line, and sinker. They built their ministries on it being proven fact, which it wasn't.

I have to admit, when I first came to the truth of this phenomenon, it was easy to see the battle lines. There were the lost and deceived, and there was the Body of Christ (the Church). We were sharing the truth and giving Hope to those lost in the demonic delusion. We were freeing them and bringing them to a relationship with Jesus Christ. Then the attacks came. The first was from the publishing of a book that showed many different ways to stop the alien abduction.

In 1988, Ann Druffel, who has researched UFOs for 40 years, discovered a little-known fact that had been drowned in abduction hysteria-documented evidence that people have successfully fended off attack by the "greys," the short, big-eyed aliens now familiar through so much popular media. Using her database of 250 case studies, including 70 "resisters," Druffel has ascertained 9 techniques that witnesses use to ward off alien entities and even break off abductions in progress. And perhaps even more astonishing, this evidence pointed to the possible true identity of the greys and their link to the abducting entities of myth and folklore.

"Alien Abduction Resistance Techniques

1. Mental Struggle: Block their mind control
2. Physical Struggle: Fight back
3. Righteous Anger: Summon your inviolate rights
4. Protective Rage: Guard your loved ones
5. Support from Family Members: Seek strength in numbers
6. Intuition: Sense them coming
7. Metaphysical Methods: Create a personal shield
8. Appeal to Spiritual Personages: Get help from on high
9. Repellents: Use time-tested fend-off substances"

https://www.amazon.com/Defend-Yourself-Against-Alien-Abduction/dp/0609802631/

Ann supported the idea that calling on a "higher power" could stop an experience, but so could other means. That was a problem for our message. I talked with my partner in Alien Resistance, Pastor Chris Ward, about it. He believed we just had a problem with terminology. What we really had was the only way that the experience could be not only stopped, but also terminated from their lives, never to come back, and that was through the name and authority of Jesus Christ and a personal relationship with Him.

The second wave of attacks would be the introduction of "fringe" topics into the Church. Many of the same "fringe" topics were seen in the New Age belief system, but repackaged in a pseudo-Christian wrapping and sold for profit and gain to gullible new Christians, just coming out of the Enemy's lies. Because of this we would spend most of our energy trying to right wrong teachings by the "fringe" Christian teachers and researchers. Instead of these new believers getting grounded in God's Word, and brought into a Christian fold for covering, they are reintroduced to the Enemy's lies in pseudo-Christian wrappings. They are continuing in the bondage of deception, never really being free. It is a true battle for souls, and the Enemy is now working in the Church's camp.

Over the next few years we focused on getting the research findings out in many different avenues. Guy Malone was holding "The Ancient of Days" Christian perspective conferences in Roswell during the weekend of the Roswell UFO Festival, around Fourth of July each year, even mixing the lineup in 2004 with secular speakers and Christian speakers voicing their perspectives of the phenomenon together. Each of these conferences were videotaped/recorded so we could reach even more people afterwards. We also had multiple websites running that were getting hits of visitors in the millions. As Internet podcasts opened up, we started getting interviewed and archived the shows on our websites for even more to hear the truth.

In 2004 I was contacted by Gary Bates of the Answers in Genesis office in Brisbane, Australia. He was working on a book of his own on the UFO phenomenon from the perspective of Biblical Creationism. He had come across our work in CE4 Research and wanted to include it in his book, <u>Alien Intrusion, UFOs and the Evolution Connection</u>, Gary Bates, (Updated & Expanded, May 31, 2010) original print January 1, 2006. Gary committed a whole chapter to our research findings and my testimony. He and his family went on a US and world tour promoting his book, reaching many churches. He also was interviewed on the world famous paranormal radio show Coast to Coast AM with George Noory, reaching over 4 million people (mostly non-Christian) in one show. This was a major leap forward for reaching the church and the secular UFO realm with the truth about this phenomenon. Gary's book rose through the charts on Amazon, becoming one of the bestselling books on the UFO subject, and from a Christian perspective to boot.

Gary Bates soon after moved to the United States and became CEO of Creation Ministries International based out of Atlanta, Georgia. He was promoting more recorded talks on his book, and speaking at churches and conferences all over America. This included speaking as the keynote speaker at Guy Malone and Paradox Brown's *First Christian Symposium on Aliens*, a Christian conference on UFOs and Alien Abductions held during the 2009 Roswell UFO Festival. (http://www.ChristianSymposium.com)

Gary and I have continued to share our research with each other over the years, culminating with the release of *Alien Intrusion, Unmasking a Deception*, in 2018. This was a full-length movie treatment of the Amazon top-50 selling book Alien Intrusion: UFOs and the Evolution Connection. The movie aired in over 700 movie theaters in America, moving on to Australia, New Zealand, Canada, and then to DVD release. (https://alienintrusion.com)

Working with Gary Bates, and the research that Creation Ministries International was doing, finally helped me close the door on the idea of there being an alien/human (demon/human) hybridization program going on. Looking at the science aspect of this, which Creation Ministries has plenty of access to, through the many Christian scientists working with them, the Lord showed me that this is just more of the delusion of the UFO/Abduction phenomenon.

I came to see these so-called alien abductions as a spiritual experience only. Spiritual entities could not mix with human beings. Harass, influence, deceive, absolutely, but not mate and create hybrids. I believe the following article, "The Watchers and Genetic Diversity" from Dr. Robert Carter of Creation Ministries International explains what I mean best.

"Dr. Robert Carter obtained a BS in Applied Biology from the Georgia Institute of Technology in 1992. He then spent four years teaching high school biology, chemistry, physics and electronics before going to the University of Miami to obtain his PhD in Marine Biology. He successfully completed this program in 2003 with a dissertation on "Cnidarian Fluorescent Proteins." While in Miami, he studied the genetics of pigmentation in corals and other invertebrates, designed and built an aquaculture facility for Caribbean corals, performed well over 500 SCUBA dives, many of them at night, and licensed a spin-off product of his research (a patented fluorescent protein) to a biotech company. He is currently a senior scientist and speaker for CMI-USA in Atlanta, Georgia, and is currently researching human genetics and other issues related to biblical creation."

https://creation.com/dr-robert-carter

The Watchers and Genetic Diversity
Published: 22 February 2014

Bob M., U.S.:

I am looking for the genetic footprint of the Watchers, passed to the children known as the Nephilim. I am not interested in fan clubs and realize what I am after you may not be able to supply. We are talking about footprints right? Is your knowledge in order chronologically to be able to at least get close to my question? I like the declaration below. You may have my question but just how far along in understanding are you? I don't want to sound cynical I simply want to enjoy solid answers.

If the angels which left their first estate truly copulated with the daughters of man would there not be a genetic signature? Is this signature traceable as mine is? I am hoping to draw from your knowledge. With you or without you. What you do with this communication is yours. I am looking for answers that will produce understanding and knowledge. May God supply the wisdom.

Dr. Robert Carter, CMI-US, responds:

Dear Bob,

Thanks for writing in and for looking for answers to this difficult subject. There has been considerable debate over these topics for centuries, and it has only increased over the past few years.

Some have suggested that part of the reason for God sending the Flood was to stop the Nephilim problem.

Please take some time to consider the following even if it is not what you were expecting to hear.

First, a question: are you a Christian? If so, and this is important, I am going to implore you to apply a consistent biblical metric to the questions and to be willing to accept a straightforward biblical answer. [Editor's note: he replied in the affirmative in a follow-up e-mail]

If you are not a Christian, please accept this as an answer from a Christian. You can choose to disagree, but then you might be disagreeing with the very source of the original information (i.e., the Bible).

Second, where did you hear about this and are you allowing non-biblical, extra-biblical, or even anti-biblical, arguments to inform your opinion? It may be difficult to tease apart information sources, to critically examine assumptions and biases, and to see beyond what we want to be true, but it is certainly possible.

We have written many articles that explain our position clearly, including "The return of the Nephilim?" and "Who were the sons of God in Genesis 6?"

That last article is the single best analysis of the biblical statements on this subject of which I am aware. Some have suggested that part of the reason for God sending the Flood was to stop the Nephilim problem. If it were to continue after the Flood through more angelic-human interbreeding, God's purposes would have been to no avail and the statements of 2 Peter and Jude make no sense. If Nephilim genes carried through the Flood (on Noah's Ark), there would be no way to separate people from Nephilim, for the necessary inbreeding among the three original families would have distributed even a rare genetic variant among all family lines prior to the Babel dispersion, and continuing intermingling of people groups would have caused these traits to continue to circulate everywhere (we are all very closely related).

Also, keep in mind that the Bible does not say there were female Nephilim, not does it say that the Nephilim could, in turn, interbreed with people. To believe there are Nephilim genes in the modern human population is an assumption, a huge assumption, and it does not comport to the biblical details given in the previous paragraph.

You ask, "If the angels which left their first estate truly copulated with the daughters of man would there not be a genetic signature?" The answer is simple: no. There are strong reasons to say it should not be so, and only vague assumptions would make someone want it to be true.

You say, "I am hoping to draw from your knowledge." Since I am a geneticist, I can, without any reservation, tell you that there is nothing in the original human genome project data, in the over two thousand humans genomes sequenced since then, in the tens of thousands of human genomes in which only certain letters have been sequenced (and that often includes over 1 million letters scattered across the genome), in the six Neanderthal genomes or the one "Denisovan" genome sequenced to date, that in any way says there is anyone alive today, or who lived in the past, who carries Nephilim genes.

There are many today who are told they are a descendant of the "Watchers", but they, or those telling them such, are not appealing to the Bible for the answer. I also suspect there is no genetic data backing up the claim, or that if there is a claim to data it is easily explained by appealing to normal genetics.

You say, "I am looking for answers that will produce understanding and knowledge."

Many people reject an alternative answer because they are looking for confirmation, not critique. I have given you answers. Will you accept them?

"May God supply the wisdom."

The Bible is the very word of God, so where else would we turn for answers to these questions? Wisdom first comes in the form of biblical literacy. Additional wisdom can be gleaned from the pursuit of science. Applying both of these sources of wisdom leads one to reject the idea that there are descendants of the Nephilim on earth today. You are a child of Adam, a descendant of Noah, and a normal human being, created in the image of God and with the capacity to respond to His loving offer of salvation. Let nobody tell you otherwise.

Sincerely, Dr. Robert Carter

https://creation.com/watchers-genetic-diversity

This fringe idea of alien/human, or Nephilim hybrids, was taking hold among most of the leading Christian UFO researchers, and even many secular researchers. Nephilim became the buzz-word of the Christian Fringe community. But I had come to see it was a lie, just more of the deepening deception. These deceiving entities are very smart in perpetrating this delusion on humanity. They come at us from many different angles.

Coming to know the truth is not hard; admitting you had been deceived is what is difficult for most of us. It hurts, I know-I have had to admit I was wrong many times in my life. But it's the first step to moving towards and living in the truth.

I was at that point again, in my life and my research. I had supported the many researchers in the Christian and secular realms that were pushing the hybrid theory as fact. But I had now come to the point of having to admit that I had been deceived. I wrote a public statement and posted it, stating that I no longer supported the theory or ideas of any alien/human hybrids, or Nephilim/human hybrids, or any idea of a demonic human bloodline of any sort. I wrote that the so-called alien abduction experience was more a "spiritual experience" than a real life physical experience. That no-one is actually taken anywhere at all, especially up to an alien craft. And that the most important Biblical scripture supporting this was Ephesians 6:12, which states: "For our struggle is not against flesh and blood, but against the rulers, against the authorities, against the powers of this dark world and against the spiritual forces of evil in the heavenly realms." Did you get that? NOT against flesh and blood. It shows us this is not done by an extraterrestrial biological entity or even a biological being, but by spiritual beings. There was absolutely no evidence at all to support the hybrid idea or theory. And science itself points to the impossibility of it happening. It's only possible in the realm of pseudoscience or science fiction.

I have to tell you, this upset a whole lot of my former friends and peers in the Christian UFO research community. Some of them took this personal, as if I was out to destroy their work or research. But that was not my intention at all. I only wanted to make it known that I no longer followed the hybrid line of thought.

I really could not believe how some of these Christians behaved because of the new stance that I took. Some even threatened to shut down my work because of it. Imagine that, coming from devout Christians. I didn't even get that type of response from non-Christians in the research field. I stand by the rule that all the pieces of the puzzle are to be brought to the table for scrutiny, and peer review, to see if the puzzle fits the picture. Leave any piece of the puzzle out, you never complete the picture. They are absolutely welcome to bring their piece, as am I. Even if we don't agree with each other's viewpoints.

The whole thing ended up separating the Christian UFO research field into two camps. That division is still there today.

Chapter 6

The best support for what I now saw as being truth (this experience being more of a spiritual experience) came from the leading secular researchers in 2008.

In 2007, my partner in Alien Resistance, Guy Malone of Roswell, New Mexico, had been given the opportunity to direct the largest Roswell UFO Festival conference in the history of the event. The Sixtieth Anniversary of the (supposed) Roswell UFO crash of 1947 UFO Conference. It was huge; believe me, I was there, along with thousands of others.

As the conference was winding down, a question came up: "What about 2008?" Everyone was so exhausted from hosting and presenting this great 60th anniversary conference, nobody could even imagine what to do next. I talked about the idea with a couple of friends I had made in Roswell, and decided I would step out with their managerial assistance and volunteer our services to direct the 2008 Roswell UFO Festival conference.

The conference was fifteen talks over three days. I had invited some of the best researchers in the field at that time to come and speak, and I would of course leave time to present the findings of CE4 Research.

The most amazing thing about this conference was how much information came from the secular speakers showing this "visitor" to be more other dimensional than biological. I had no idea what the speakers were going to present; I gave them cart-blanche to cover what they wanted. But they ended up supporting my hypothesis of the "visitors" not being biological entities at all, but inter-dimensional, or spiritual, if you are a Christian.

Of course, the speakers said they felt "set up" because of the talk given on the findings of CE4 Research. But otherwise, it was well received by those that attended.

Getting back to talking with Gary Bates, our discussions led to the subject of hypnosis. Not about hypnotic regressions on the experiencers as many researchers were doing, but the similarities that Gary was seeing of stage hypnosis and the experience itself. The similarities were uncanny. The recall of an experience was very similar to the recall of someone who had been stage hypnotized and given powerful suggestions, like participating in a play on stage. There are props used that help set the atmosphere for the people watching a stage play. But only certain suggested props, to get the point across. Not everything needs to be there, as in reality, to know what idea is being put across.

I started to explore this a little on my own with some of the testimonies I had worked with over the years. I had only taken their recollection of their experiences and documented them for the record. With this new idea, I wanted to go back to them and ask more in-depth questions of the experience itself. As I did this, I started finding similarities that were unusual. Things were missing.

Let me give you an example. If I ask you to sit and recall everything you can remember about your last birthday, you would easily be able to do that. On your first round of sharing your memory, the most prominent things or important things to you will come out. If I question you about less remembered details I would be able to help you recall other suppressed memories that were still recorded in the memory banks of your brain. All of the senses would have been at work recording the experiences of the day. You just might need help bringing them forward. And keep in mind I am not using hypnosis for memory recall with experiencers. Just ask the right questions.

Even if you wake up from a very vivid dream and can remember it clearly, your own mind fills in every detail so a complete picture is created. It may be a puzzling dream, a nightmare, or a recollection of a lived event, but everything is filled in. It's complete, and actually quite amazing if you take the time to think about it.

But, when I did the same thing with the testimonies I re-interviewed, there were gaps of memory. Not all of the senses had recorded information of the experience. It was like the stage play setting, having only what was needed to make the play "seem" real. They were sensational, yes, but the sensational points were all that there was to the memory.

An example if you will. One of the best descriptions of the so-called alien abduction experience I have ever seen demonstrated comes from a Hollywood movie. The movie was not about abductions, but definitely explains what I am trying to share with you. The movie was *The Matrix* and the scene in question is the one in which Neo (Keanu Reeves) is first getting plugged in. He lays down on the bed and they hook him up from the back of his head, and he is instantly in this area that is all white, nothing else. Then Morpheus is there. They walk to a living room scene, only furniture is there, but you realize it's a living room setting. Now, here is the most important part of that scene in relation to abductions, Neo is still on the bed-he never went anywhere.

These visitors definitely have the ability to "pierce the veil" that separates us from them. It appears to be done in two separate but distinct ways. They can temporarily manifest as objects that people call UFOs or UAPs, and they can temporarily affect our thoughts in our dream state or when we are in an altered state of mind, as with the use of mind altering drugs, whether prescribed or not.

The question we have to ask ourselves is, if this experience is an implanted memory, put together like a stage play (sensational, but not complete), who is the playwright? Who or what is this intelligent force behind this?

Even the famous French researcher Jacques Vallee questioned this observation. His quotes below:

> "I will stress once again that we do not know the source from which the UFOs or the alien beings come. Whether or not, for example, they originate in the physical universe as modern astrophysics has described it. But they manifest in the physical world and bring about definable consequences in that domain.
>
> We are dealing with a yet unrecognized level of consciousness, independent of man but closely linked to the earth.... I do not believe anymore that UFOs are simply the spacecraft of some race of extraterrestrial visitors. This notion is too simplistic to explain their appearance, the frequency of their manifestations through recorded

history, and the structure of the information exchanged with them during contact.

Human beings are under the control of a strange force that bends them in absurd ways, forcing them to play a role in a bizarre game of deception.

The symbolic display seen by the abductees is identical to the type of initiation ritual or astral voyage that is embedded in the occult traditions of every culture...

We are dealing with a yet unrecognized level of consciousness, independent of man but closely linked to the earth...

If they are not an advanced race from the future, are we dealing instead with a parallel universe, another dimension where there are other human races living, and where we may go at our expense, never to return to the present? From that mysterious universe, are higher beings projecting objects that can materialize and dematerialize at will? Are UFOs "windows" rather than "objects"?

The 'medical examination' to which abductees are said to be subjected, often accompanied by sadistic sexual manipulation, is reminiscent of the medieval tales of encounters with demons. It makes no sense in a sophisticated or technical framework; any intelligent being equipped with the scientific marvels that UFOs possess would be in a position to achieve any of these alleged scientific objectives in a shorter time and with fewer risks."

https://www.azquotes.com/author/33226-Jacques_Vallee

As researchers, we also have to look at this from the aspect of the "false memory syndrome." But determining whether it is false memory or no memory in relation to the missing information that should be there, is difficult to determine.

Another issue when looking at the power of suggestion and how it plays into all of this, as in stage hypnosis, is the information gleaned from researchers that use hypnotic regression to recover memories that seem lost.

Most of the hundreds of experiencer testimonies that I've encountered over the past twenty plus years approached the subject by saying: "I've been having these dreams…" The reason they talk to me in the first place is because I am a UFO/Alien Abduction researcher. What I see is this: people have a memory of what seems like it could have been a dream. They relate it to what they have seen in the popular UFO culture and what others have reported. They put the two together and think, what if I have had an experience like they report of alien abduction? So, what do they do next? They go see their family doctor, right? Not hardly-he would think they are crazy. So they seek out a UFO researcher or investigator (someone who already believes this to be real) and asks for help. That researcher puts them under hypnotic regression to help them remember.

Stop. Did you catch that? The person has already set themselves up to give answers of an abduction experience to the hypnotist. The SUGGESTION has come from themselves. They are presupposing they already are experiencers. And subconsciously, they do not want to be failures. This is very similar to what happens to people who volunteer as participants in stage hypnosis.

Even Jacques Vallee had something to say about the use of hypnosis with the study of alien abductions:

> "Can help be provided to the traumatized witness who has experienced a close encounter and possibly an abduction? Absolutely. He or she should be directed to a qualified, professional hypnotherapist who is open-minded on the question of the UFO reality and who has reached no personal conclusion regarding the nature and origin of the phenomenon. And the ufologist should only be in the room at the request of, and under the control of, the therapist. Any other procedure, in my opinion, is unethical and unprofessional. Besides, it runs the risk of polluting the delicate, complex abduction database with fantastic and spurious material. It can drive UFO research over a very dangerous cliff." (p. 159)
> https://redstarfilms.blogspot.com/2007/04/jacques-vallee-on-abductionology.html

The worst part of this is that researchers take what is told by these individuals as absolute fact. The hypnosis can't be wrong, right? Listen to them, they swear by the results of the regressions they perform. But of course, they have to. They have nothing else to stand on. Because, after over 70 years of UFO research, there is still no proof of extraterrestrials visiting Earth.

Here is a real good piece from my friend and peer in this Christian UFO realm, Gary Bates. It's from his book <u>Alien Intrusion: UFOs and the Evolution Connection</u>, (Updated & Expanded) Paperback – May 31, 2010.

> "Gary has been speaking on the creation/evolution issue since 1990. With a background in management and marketing, in 2002, he was invited to join the ministry full-time in Brisbane and eventually became its Head of Ministry. Much in demand for his popular lay talks on creation, Gary and his family relocated to America to serve as CEO of CMI-US. He was also elected to the position of CEO of CMI-Worldwide, CMI's international Federation of ministries. He held this position from its inception in 2008 until mid-2016 when he decided to step down and concentrate on the task of managing the rapidly growing USA office and expanding the ministry's reach in other areas. This included co-writing and producing CMI's award-winning documentary Evolution's Achilles' Heels.

> Once a convinced evolutionist, the Creation message had a dramatic impact on Gary's life. He is now a biblical creationist with a heart to communicate this life-changing information to the average 'person in the street'.

> Concerned about the tremendous interest in UFOs and associated extraterrestrial beliefs, Gary undertook specialist research in an attempt to solve this seemingly baffling phenomenon. This led to his Amazon.com top 50 bestseller Alien Intrusion: UFOs and the Evolution Connection — (the only Creationist book ever to achieve this feat). This landmark book provides biblical answers to the many puzzling questions regarding UFOs, and whether there is intelligent, sentient alien life on other planets (our

theological position on this is no. Please read the first article below for why). As a leading Christian authority in this area, Gary has travelled extensively around the world, speaking and conducting literally hundreds of interviews on radio, television and various media. Gary has also undertaken the task of writing, producing and directing a movie-style documentary based upon his book called Alien Intrusion: Unmasking a Deception. It will be premiering in cinemas around the world early in 2018." https://creation.com/gary-bates

---

An excerpt from
Alien Intrusion: UFOs and the Evolution Connection
by Gary Bates

Hypnosis is actually just a label that has been applied to a very broad, imperfectly understood set of mind phenomena. However, the phenomenon of hypnosis is not new. When it comes to deceiving mankind, fallen angels do not need to "reinvent the wheel", and the Bible also indicates that man is only ever tempted by what is common to him (1 Corinthians 10:13).

When it comes to trying to unravel abduction episodes, there are many hypotheses percolating among the UFO community, with most resorting to unknown forces to explain what we cannot be sure is actually occurring anyway. None of these elegant hypotheses have any experimental or empirical basis to them. There is a distinct lack of physical evidence in these episodes, and there are no non-abductee eyewitnesses to abduction events, for example. While my own hypnosis theory is hypothetical, it appeals to mechanisms we know exist, to things that we know can actually be done via hypnosis. In mentioning some of these experiences earlier (and there are more below), I am pointing out that hypnosis is a known quantity that can be used to explain what is occurring during alleged alien abductions. Using the Ockham's razor approach (see chapter 4) I am suggesting that abduction episodes are an illusory spiritual deception that is being planted into the minds of experiencers to create the "reality"—a false memory in effect. This not only fits the

instances where individuals are concerned. In the case of the Allagash Four, too, the hypnosis theory fits the circumstances perfectly. Mass hypnosis episodes can also occur, and subliminal messages can be imposed on entire groups as shown earlier in the description of the shopping mall experiments.

So how can the appearance of a UFO in the sky lead to missing time and a recollection of being abducted by an alien?

Firstly, as we have shown, UFOs have changed their shapes over the years. They seem able to morph into a form that is culturally acceptable to the victim. This can help to create an openness to further suggestion. In the past UFOs appeared as flying canoes, and today they appear as spaceships, which automatically evokes the idea that they are piloted by extraterrestrial spacemen (and thus creates the opening for the alien abduction scenario). Jaques Vallée showed that the abductors have morphed over the years too. Anything from fairies and elves to ETs— whatever seems culturally acceptable to the population. Hypnotherapy is almost always done with relaxation and relatively gradual induction with a soft, soothing voice. But these are not even necessary with about 20% of the population (or well prepared subjects). Modern hypnotists also use lights and sounds to stimulate people to make them susceptible to suggestion. This is a characteristic also often used in sightings prior to abductions. Hypnotists can paralyze people—even when the patient is fully conscious. A clinical hypnotherapist confirmed to me:

Sleeping people do not usually transition into hypnosis, and are not subliminally suggestible, but waking up from an REM stage with shock and surprise would provide the perfect brainwave transition ... to induce an immediate deep state in "suggestible" subjects.

This was a common device in brainwashing techniques ... though usually with brutal shock and confusion. The gently repeated, soothing whispers "you're alright" or something similar would have less trauma, but should be very effective in leaving a "trigger" imprint in the subject's spirit that could be harnessed at a later time.

This method of waking people occurs commonly in alien abduction scenarios. Similarly, when entities appear in a room, many claim that they feel compelled to look into the entity's eyes—another method used by hypnotists. Once they are in this controlled state they are very prone to further suggestion. The idea that the entities communicate telepathically is also a common belief—something that fits no known scientific observations. But this could easily be believed if messages to that effect were being placed while under hypnosis.

There is also another pattern amongst abductees that I have discovered alongside of any pre-belief or openness to the idea of ETs, and it is that there seems to be an additional "entry point", so to speak. People who have unresolved trauma or issues in their past seem to be particularly vulnerable to alien abductions and False Memory Syndrome in general. This is something recognized by many medical experts operating outside of the UFOlogical area. In addition, those suffering from current problems such as alcoholism, drug addiction also seem to be susceptible. I have seen on occasions where people suffering with mental disabilities have had similar experiences as identified using the CAS categorization. Unfortunately, when these folks talk about their experiences they are largely ignored and the claims are passed off as the fruit of their illnesses. Of course, no amount of personal frailty can, by itself, explain such things as the seemingly shared experiences of the Allagash Four, for example. It seems that the master deceiver and enemy of God (the devil/Lucifer/Satan) and his cohorts (other fallen angels) are no respecter of persons, and seem to be largely opportunists.

Missing time

The missing time aspect is a fundamental key to understanding the methods used by these angelic beings. Earlier in the book we detailed the characteristics of angels. They are inter-dimensional, immensely powerful and intelligent sentient beings. If human beings can easily perform such deeds on their fellows, it cannot be any more difficult for angels to perform the same. Being able to appear instantly in a room would ensure anybody's attention, and once entities become the focus of the victim, most methods of hypnosis would become readily available. Experiencers usually only consciously remember the initial sighting of a UFO or an entity they believe to be alien. They then wake up several hours later with no conscious recollection of anything occurring during the missing time. However, when regressed, the victims are able to recount seeming events with incredible detail. Let's remember that all these entities have to do is to paint a picture to the unconscious victim—stories about cold metallic inspection tables, crude instruments, video screens—the works!

Gary Bates, <u>Alien Intrusion: UFOs and the Evolution Connection</u>, (Updated & Expanded) Paperback, May 31, 2010 <u>https://alienintrusion.com/</u>

The whole concept of hybrids arose because the regression stories collected by the secular UFO researchers by means of hypnotic regression were taken as absolute fact, were believed by the researcher, and were then published.

And then this was followed by people who wanted it to be real in order to substantiate their ideas, like Nephilim on the earth today.

But understand, there is no evidence today, nor has there ever been, that there are hybrids from an alien/human mix, or a demonic angel/human mix. None, *nada*, zip. It's falls into the realm of fantasy and make believe.

Sadly, its promotion as a valid theory or reality sucks hard earned money from gullible people who don't know any better. Some of them are the same people we have been trying to help all these years. Following this hybrid lie just keeps them in the same bondage of deception that they were in before becoming Christians. All of this is just New Age garbage, repackaged in a pseudo-Christian wrapping and sold to Christians for profit, preying on their weaknesses, by using an attractive sensational idea, with interjected Biblical scripture, to make it seem real.

Now you can see why my former Christian friends and peers are angry with me. They are promoting flawed secular research to support their beliefs of Nephilim or hybrids on the earth. They cannot accept the fact that the experience is not an actual physical experience in which people are actually taken somewhere, where things are done to them, nor can they accept that real hybridization is not taking place. It's actually a "spiritual" experience.

You might say physical things seem to happen to them. Well, it appears that way. But what I think is actually happening is that the physical marks, bruising, etc., are normal things happening to them, but are used by the entities to support the delusion of the experience being real.

We have human researchers playing on these same ideas. They ask people in the audience of their talks if they have noticed any marks on their bodies that they have no memory of how they got them. If they do, they are told that they might be experiencers. This is the use of the power of suggestion. Of course people can have marks or scars and not remember where they came from, but jumping straight to the idea of it being from alien abductions is absolutely ridiculous and should be criminal, due to where it leads some people.

Bottom line, many different conditions, situations, medical issues, drugs, mental disorders, or social environment and influences can be a reason for a person to believe they have had the so-called alien abduction experience. I have seen more damage caused to a person's life due to the "belief" that they have been abducted than by the abduction itself. Once the acceptance of the experience happening is made, the person takes that first step towards a new worldview. It changes them completely from who they were. For many it totally destroys their family relationships and work relationships. They are forever on a quest for answers, sadly, for something that may have never happened.

Don't get me wrong: I do believe that some, but very few, abduction experiences are due to this strange force that bends them in absurd ways; an evil, demonic, deceptive force.

I do believe experiencers are actually seeing these entities momentarily appear, "Piercing the Veil," meeting us in that state between awake and sleep. Or, in the matter of UFOs, the "wake" state, to initiate and/or perpetrate the experience, making the experiencer believe the entire experience was a real life physical event, very much along the concept of ghost appearances, or visions, or apparitions.

I would like to borrow from my friend and peer in this Christian UFO realm, Michael Heiser, as he does a great job putting it together in a clear precise answer:

> "Michael S. Heiser is an American biblical Old Testament scholar and Christian author who has criticized ancient alien astronaut theorists. His area of expertise is the nature of the spiritual realm in the Bible, namely the Divine council and hierarchy of the spiritual order. He is Executive Director of the School of Ministry at Celebration Church in Jacksonville, Florida. He was a Distance learning professor at Liberty University and Midwestern Baptist Theological Seminary. Until 2019, he was scholar-in-residence at Faithlife Corporation.
>
> He runs his own podcast, The Naked Bible and runs a ministry called Miqlat, dedicated to the production and dissemination of his content. Heiser appeared in the 2018 documentary film Fragments of Truth."
> https://en.wikipedia.org/wiki/Michael_S._Heiser

So what does Mike really think about alien abductions?
How does he approach the issue as an academic?

The short answer is that I think they're evil and I only really care to read credentialed academics who have worked in the field. And yes, there are scholars and health professionals who focus on such things. Now for the longer answer. Whoever is perpetrating such abductions—human or non-human—they are violent violations of human rights. This answer of course tells you that I don't think all the people who have claimed to be the victim of alien abduction are lying. Actually, I think many, perhaps even a majority, are telling the truth. That doesn't mean, though, that I think the perpetrators are really aliens like we have come to think of that term (as in, a physical being from a different planet who has a determinate lifespan, must eat and drink, must reproduce to further its species, etc.). I think "real" abductions (whatever isn't a hoax) are actually several things, but I can't put percentages on the options: (1) abductions by military personnel who implant an alien screen memory into the victim's mind, using technology that has been known (and further developed) since the 70s; (2) abductions where the victim's mind replaces their actual traumatizer with the alien - traumatization where the victim responds by what is known in psychology as dissociation - what used to be called multiple personality disorder); (3) ritual traumatization by cults or other groups for the purpose of deliberately producing "alters" (deliberately inducing psychological dissociation); (4) harassment and physical abuse on the part of a demonic entity; (5) harassment of physical abuse by some entity manufactured by a demonic entity. I haven't seen any evidence that undeniably points to a truly alien perpetrator (as in the above definition) or some sort of breeding program. I am well aware of the work of Professor David Jacobs (Temple University) on the subject, but what I'd need to believe we were really dealing with aliens would be some sort of hybrid offspring —tested and verified by a credible laboratory. All we really have are memories (mostly derived via hypnosis but not always) of sincere, mentally healthy people (the major studies on abductions have found no mental deficiencies in most abductees - see Mack and Jacobs in the bibliography at Question 15). I need more than memories. Yes, I believe these people are being truthful - something DID happen to them, and something physical in many cases. I don't believe its aliens.

Dr. Michael S. Heiser, http://www.michaelsheiser.com/FAQ.htm#q2

Chapter 7

A recent article from a fellow Christian researcher and longtime friend, Derek Gilbert, also supports our viewpoint that with certain cases, this is inter-dimensional, not extraterrestrial, in nature.

> "Derek Gilbert hosts SkyWatchTV, a weekly Christian television program, and co-hosts SciFriday, a weekly television program that looks at science news with his wife, author and analyst Sharon K. Gilbert. His broadcast career spans nearly four decades, with stops in Little Rock, Saint Louis, and Philadelphia, and he's been interviewing guests for his podcast, A View from the Bunker, since 2009. Derek is author of the groundbreaking books The Great Inception and Last Clash of the Titans. He's also the co-author with Josh Peck of The Day the Earth Stands Still, which exposes the occult origins of the modern UFO phenomenon. Bad Moon Rising: Islam, Armageddon, and the Most Diabolical Double-Cross in History was released in the summer of 2019. Derek and Sharon just released their newest book, Veneration: Unveiling the Ancient Realms of Demonic Kings and Satan's Battle Plan for Armageddon, about ancient death cults and the Bible" Find out more at www.derekpgilbert.com, www.gilberthouse.org, www.vftb.net, and www.SkyWatchTV.com."
> https://prophecyinvestigators.org/its-not-extraterrestrial-its-interdimensional/

It's Not Extraterrestrial, It's Interdimensional!
By Derek Gilbert
05/16/2020

With the recent admission by the U.S. Department of Defense that remarkable videos captured by Navy F-18s purporting to show UAVs—Unidentified Aerial Vehicles, the modern term for UFOs—are genuine, we're going to devote several columns to putting this subject in context. You may be surprised to learn that the modern UFO is just a sci-fi veneer on an incredibly old phenomenon.

It's not extraterrestrial, it's interdimensional.

Humans have wondered about the stars since forever. That is understandable; they are beautiful and mysterious, as out of reach as mountain peaks. And perhaps for the same reasons, the earliest speculation about the stars revolved around gods, not extraterrestrials.

As with mountains, humans have associated stars with deities since the beginning of human history. Three of the most important gods in the ancient Near East, from Sumer to Israel and its neighbors, were the sun, moon, and the planet Venus. To the Sumerians they were the deities Utu, Nanna, and the goddess Inanna; later, in Babylon, they were Shamash, Sîn, and Ishtar. The Amorites worshiped Sapash, Yarikh, and Astarte.

Yahweh not only recognized that the nations worshiped these small-G gods, He allotted the nations to them as their inheritance—punishment for the Tower of Babel incident.

When the Most High gave to the nations their inheritance, when he divided mankind, he fixed the borders of the peoples according to the number of the sons of God. (Deuteronomy 32:8)

> "And beware lest you raise your eyes to heaven, and when you see the sun and the moon and the stars, all the host of heaven, you be drawn away and bow down to them and serve them, things that the LORD your God has allotted to all the peoples under the whole heaven."
> Deuteronomy 4:19

In other words, God placed the nations of the world under small-G "gods" represented by the sun, moon, and stars, but He reserved Israel for Himself. The descendants of Abraham, Isaac, and Jacob were to remain faithful to Yahweh alone, and through Israel He would bring forth a Savior.

But the gods Yahweh allotted to the nations went rogue. That earned them a death sentence.

God has taken his place in the divine council; in the midst of the gods he holds judgment:

> "How long will you judge unjustly and show partiality to the wicked? Selah […]
>
> I said, "You are gods, sons of the Most High, all of you; nevertheless, like men you shall die, and fall like any prince." (Psalm 82:1-2, 6-7)

Ancient Aliens or Gods?

To be absolutely clear, those small-G gods are not to be confused with capital-G God, Yahweh, Creator of all things including those "sons of the Most High." We know the consensus view among Christians is to treat the gods of Psalm 82 as humans, usually described as corrupt Israelite kings or judges. With all due respect to the scholars who have held that view over the centuries, it is wrong. First, the Hebrew word elohim ("gods") always refers to spirit beings, and verse 7— "nevertheless, like men you shall die"—makes no sense if God was addressing a human audience.

Humanity has looked to the stars as gods for at least the last 5,000 years. End times prophecy, from the perspective of pagans, is about the return of the old gods, spirits defined as rebel angels and demons by the Hebrew prophets and apostles.

The Infernal Council has been playing an exceptionally long game. Once upon a time, Christians generally held a biblical worldview. The influence of the spirit realm on our lives was not perfectly understood, but at least it was acknowledged. And while the church of Rome can be fairly criticized for keeping the Bible out of the hands of lay people for nearly a thousand years, at least the learned scholars and theologians of the church made a fair effort to interpret their world through a biblical filter.

In our modern, enlightened age, however, the principalities and powers have nudged and prodded humanity through the Enlightenment and Modernism into Postmodernism, shifting us from a supernatural worldview to one that only accepts an external creator in the form of "ancient aliens," which allows us to account for the supernatural while simultaneously denying the existence of God.

In 1973, science fiction author Arthur C. Clarke wrote, "Any sufficiently advanced technology is indistinguishable from magic." By substituting advanced science for the supernatural, ancient aliens' evangelists have created a godless religion perfect for the 21st century. It offers mystery, transcendence, and answers to the big questions: Where do we come from, why are we here, and where do we go when we die?

Best of all, believers in E.T. do not need to change the way they think or act, except maybe to promise to our benevolent space brothers that we will live peacefully with our galactic neighbors. And, as surprising as it may seem, the followers of Eric von Däniken and Zecaria Sitchin are not the first to concoct a religion that includes a belief in extraterrestrial life.

Consider, for example, Emanuel Swedenborg, an 18th century Swedish scientist, philosopher, and mystic. He was undoubtedly brilliant, but sometimes the brilliant is blinded by their own light. His theology encompassed the following concepts:

- The Bible is the Word of God; however, its true meaning differs greatly from its obvious meaning. Furthermore, he and only he, through the help of angels, could discern the true meaning and message of the Scriptures.
- Swedenborg believed that the world of matter is a laboratory for the soul, where the material is used to "force-refine" the spiritual.
- In many ways, Swedenborg was quite universal in his concepts, for he believed that all religious systems have their divine duty and purpose and that this is not the sole virtue of Christianity.
- Swedenborg believed that the mission of the Church is absolutely necessary inasmuch as, left to its own devices, humanity cannot work out its relationship to God.

- He saw the real power of Christ's life in the example it gave to others and rejected the concept of atonement and original sin.

Swedenborg believed he heard directly from angels who lived elsewhere in the solar system. To this day, the Swedenborg Foundation offers a modern translation of the mystic's 1758 work <u>Life on Other Planets</u>, a book that "details Swedenborg's conversations with spirits from Jupiter, Mars, Mercury, Saturn, Venus, and the moon, who discuss their lives on other planets and how their cultures differed from those of earthly life.⊠

Swedenborg's teachings on spiritism and angelic ETIs and those who believe them are still around, although they have rebranded the faith as The New Church. (Maybe "Swedenborgianism" did not test well in focus groups.) It's a small sect, about 10,000 adherents worldwide, but the point is this: The messages Swedenborg received are very much like the telepathic contact some claim to receive from ETIs today—and similar to messages whispered into the minds of the demonically oppressed and possessed."

Of course, Swedenborg, who died in 1772, was not the last word in the rise of mystic scientism. Joseph Smith, who founded Mormonism about fifty years after Swedenborg's death, incorporated belief in the existence of many worlds in the doctrines of the Church of Latter-Day Saints. Smith taught that God was flesh and blood, formerly a mortal man who had earned godhood and, apparently, the right to create multiple earths. In <u>The Pearl of Great Price</u>, we read:

> "And [Moses] beheld many lands; and each land was called earth, and there were inhabitants on the face thereof.
>
> And it came to pass that Moses called upon God, saying: Tell me, I pray thee, why these things are so, and by what thou madest them?
>
> And behold, the glory of the Lord was upon Moses, so that Moses stood in the presence of God, and talked with him face to face. And the Lord God said unto Moses: For mine own purpose have I made these things. Here is wisdom and it remaineth in me.

And by the word of my power, have I created them, which is mine Only Begotten Son, who is full of grace and truth.

And worlds without number have I created; and I also created them for mine own purpose; and by the Son I created them, which is mine Only Begotten.

And the first man of all men have I called Adam, which is many."

Mormonism was just one among the waves of new spiritual movements that washed across the United States in the 19th century. Beginning with the Second Great Awakening in the 1790s, a reaction to the rationalism and deism of the Enlightenment, a series of revivals, cults, and camp meetings followed European settlers westward as the country grew and prospered. The raw, unspoiled nature of the frontier contributed to a desire to restore Christianity to a purer form, free from the formality and hierarchy of the churches of Europe.

The Second Great Awakening, which swelled the numbers of Baptists and Methodists especially, peaked by the middle of the 19th century, but other spiritual movements followed close behind. And here is where the Venn diagram begins to overlap ancient cults of the dead and a modern "scientific" worldview.

The Spiritualist Movement

The spiritualist movement, which emerged from the same region of western New York state that produced Joseph Smith, the so-called Burned-over District, first appeared in the late 1840s. Sisters Kate and Margaret Fox, ages 12 and 15, claimed to communicate with spirits of the dead through coded knocks or "rappings." They either convinced their 17-year-old sister, Leah, or brought her in on the gag, and she took charge of the younger two, managing their careers for years.

The Fox sisters not only enjoyed long careers as mediums, they left a legacy that continues to this day in the work of television mediums like John Edward, Theresa Caputo, and Tyler Henry—despite the fact that Margaret and Kate admitted in 1888 that they'd invented the whole thing. In Reuben Briggs Davenport's The Deathblow to Spiritualism, quoting Margaret Fox Kane, we read:

"That I have been chiefly instrumental in perpetrating the fraud of Spiritualism upon a too-confiding public, most of you doubtless know. The greatest sorrow in my life has been that this is true, and though it has come late in my day, I am now prepared to tell the truth, the whole truth, and nothing but the truth, so help me God! . . I am here tonight as one of the founders of Spiritualism to denounce it as an absolute falsehood from beginning to end, as the flimsiest of superstitions, the most wicked blasphemy known to the world."

The Fox sisters used a variety of techniques, one of which was simply cracking their toe joints, to produce the sounds that fooled gullible audiences into believing that spirits answered their questions. But even after their confession was published by a New York City newspaper, the spiritualist movement never skipped a beat. To this day, "many accounts of the Fox sisters leave out their confession of fraud and present the rappings as genuine manifestations of the spirit world."

Isn't that remarkable? Humans are so desperate for contact with the dead that the spiritualist movement lives on into our enlightened age even though its founders admitted their act was as real as professional wrestling. Well-known believers have included such powerful intellects as Sir Arthur Conan Doyle, the creator of Sherlock Holmes. In fact, Conan Doyle wrote <u>The History of Spiritualism</u> in 1926, and he pegged March 31, 1848—the very first time Kate and Margaret Fox claimed to hear from spirits—as the date the movement began.

https://prophecyinvestigators.org/its-not-extraterrestrial-its-interdimensional/

Chapter 8

The next couple of years would unexpectedly change my path through life. In 2008 the economy was showing signs of weakening in America. Financial collapse was on everyone's minds.

After 23 years with the world's leading pleasure boat manufacturer, and the last four years as their Safety Coordinator, I really didn't feel too worried about employment. But once the layoffs started coming, my thoughts changed. I felt it was probably time for a change of my own. I had heard of overseas contract employment supporting the war efforts in Iraq and Afghanistan, and the pay was said to be pretty high, too. Maybe a few years at that would be good for me, at least until the economy picked up again. So I started applying for jobs. I had lots of nibbles, but nothing solid. After a few months of looking, I started to get real nervous. I didn't want to be without employment, and I had a family to support.

Then, one day, I got a hit from a job recruiter about a local Safety Specialist position. I opened up the email and read it. It was for the Kennedy Space Center, right near the boat company I was working at. I couldn't believe it; for forty years I had tried to get employed out there. But it always seemed as if you had to know someone or have a relative working there to vouch for you, and I had none of those. But this position was different. They wanted someone from the outside with a new set of eyes to work with them. Hey, you can't win if you don't play, I say. So I applied, and prayed real hard. It was a lifelong dream to be part of the Space Program. I had spent the last forty years watching it work from across the river. I had seen rockets leave for space, and I watched Space Shuttle after Space Shuttle leave and return, always yearning to see it all from the inside.

Well, my prayers were answered. My dream came true. I was hired as a Safety Specialist to oversee all facilities for safety and perform facility safety inspections. I not only got to work there, but I got to see it all. I had the opportunity to walk up the Launch Pad towers, while the Shuttle Orbiters were on the Pad, standing only inches away from the ready-to-launch spacecraft. I inspected every floor and walked every one of the sixteen stair towers that took me up through the 500 foot high Vehicle Assembly Building (VAB), where I was able to enjoy the view from its rooftop. I could see all the Launch Pads, the beaches, the Shuttle Runway, and even all the way over into Central Florida. I visited the historical sites around the Space Center. I even saw launches from the closest location you could be for viewing. Some people who worked there never saw more than the location they worked at, but I went everywhere. It was absolutely amazing and beyond my wildest dreams.

But by the end of 2011 my life path was to change once again. The President had announced the end of the Space Shuttle Program. I was able to see it wind down and the Space Shuttle Orbiters begin to head to the museums. A sad time, yes, but I understood the plan for the future of space.

I decided to once again look for a contractor job overseas in hope of continued employment. Again, many nibbles, but no bites. Then, one morning, I received an email through the company I was working for at the Kennedy Space Center, for an overseas Safety Specialist position supporting the US Military. I looked it over closely. It was for South Korea. I never would have thought of going there. The pay was good, not nearly as high as the war torn countries, but it allowed family and pets. And they liked Americans and were not shooting at them. So I gave it a try.

Within a couple of weeks I had secured the position and would be heading to South Korea within the month. I never spoke much about it to friends, but this was another longtime dream that I had, to return overseas, to travel. I had grown up traveling with my family. My father was a soldier in the US Army until I graduated from high school. By the time I got to high school I had either visited or lived in fifteen different countries. My sister had been born in Germany and my brother in France. I really missed traveling around. I had dreamed for years of being able to do it again. In November of 2011, I arrived in South Korea, where I have been for eight years now, going on nine.

I love Korea. I love the culture, and I love the people. I also like Japan; I've had the opportunity to visit Japan twenty times since I have been living here in Korea. But, as a UFO/Alien Abduction researcher moving here, I saw no opportunity to continue my work. I felt alienated (no pun intended) from the field. I wasn't seeing sighting reports from Korea, there were no UFO groups, and no talk of alien abductions. I still had contact with my peers in the US and did frequent radio shows by phone, but it wasn't the same. I just did not see the same interest here as in the US, so I decided to find out why that was.

I worked with other American contractors here as well as Korean nationals. Most Koreans speak English as a second language. It's taught in all schools here. So I asked my Korean friends and acquaintances what they thought about the UFO phenomenon. Each time I would get the same answer: "I don't have time for that."

What did that mean? It seemed to be a strange answer to me. I felt maybe it was a translation problem. So I talked with my closest Korean friends, who are my Korean Safety counterparts, about it. They explained to me that the answer was correct, no translation problem. "But what does it mean?" I asked them. They told me how most all Koreans were educated on the UFO and Alien Abduction phenomenon from books in school, television shows, and movies from the US. But they really had no time to pursue the study of it.

Koreans are a very busy people. They have made leaps and bounds in their progress of modernization since almost total devastation 65 years ago during the Korean War. Many of the elderly are still surviving on farming, which takes up their whole day. The middle-aged Koreans are working long hours at a job or running a business to support family and pay for their children's schooling, which can get expensive. The younger generation goes to school up to 10 to 14 hours a day, striving to be the very best. No skipping school here in Korea; they know the value of a good education. Koreans are striving to not be the best in Korea, but the best in the world. They are focused on success, for themselves and their children. What free time they do have, they spend with core family and friends. And much of that free time is outside, as their favorite pastimes here are hiking and biking.

They don't waste any time on things that are not moving them forward to success, like UFO studies. Don't get me wrong, there is an occasional report of something seen in the skies, but it is rare. Less than thirty sightings in the past three decades have been reported. Then consider the potential of about 90% of them being misidentified, as the statistics show. There really is not much happening at all in Korea. And that just might be a good thing.

But after looking at Japan, I saw a little different story. With the many trips I have made to Japan, I made some good friends there. I had also asked them their perspective of the UFO phenomenon. There was considerably much more interest than in Korea, but nothing like the US or westernized European countries.

To me it seemed as though Japan was about three decades ahead of Korea in its status of reaching maximum progress. This is due to their fast recovery after World War Two, and that they were already ahead of South Korea prior to WWII. The Japanese people had acquired a decent financial stability, and were not so focused on material gain, and they could relax more and spend more time on things of personal interest, things outside of the norm, like the paranormal and UFOs. Because of that, you see a significant increase in the UFO reports coming out of Japan compared to the rest of the Asian countries. But again, nowhere in the numbers you see in the US or other westernized European countries.

Compare that to the US, where almost 500 sighting reports are submitted a month, (yes, per month) to the Mutual UFO Network for investigation. Compare that to a country where polls show that up to 2% of the American population is experiencing this so-called alien abduction phenomenon. Compare that to a country where people have fought to have a regular eight hour work day, where kids only go to school 7 hours a day, where everyone has much more leisure time to look at crazy things on the internet.

So what does this all mean when you put it together? Could it be that the number of UFO sighting reports is related to the amount of time on your hands? Now, that is an interesting observation, and a definite raised red flag, as far as I'm concerned as a researcher. It actually falls in line with what we found in relation to experiencers versus non-experiencers. Almost all experiencers were either asking to see or experience something, or they were unknowingly opening the door to the experience by dabbling in the paranormal or occult, or New Age metaphysical things (things the Bible told us not to be part of). Or they had the experience as children, where the open door to the experience had come from the parents.

Could it all be that simple of an explanation? That these deceptive spiritual entities can affect our lives if we allow them to, or unknowingly allow them to? It sure seems that way.

That takes me back to our original question that we put out there twenty years ago: "Are Christians being abducted by aliens?" And that's why we ended up with two answers, "yes" and "no." The devout, walk-the-walk believers in Jesus Christ were giving this UFO phenomenon none of their time or focus, whereas the talk-the-talk believers in Jesus Christ were still dabbling and spending time in things they should not be. Their full focus was not yet on Jesus Christ.

In the next section, you will find a question and answer section, which I hope will help you better understand the research and findings of CE4 Research. I will be going more in-depth into the way this all comes together.

Then, you will read the testimonial section, which contains the most powerful evidence in the world today concerning the true nature of the forces behind the UFO and alien abduction phenomenon.

Questions and Answers of CE4 Research Findings

As we were preparing this book project, it occurred to me to let those that have been following my work over the many years be given the opportunity to ask the questions that they may have, or think that should be addressed, in this book for others to see.

We used the CE4 Research Facebook page that I had established some years back for just that purpose. We pinned this announcement at the head of the page:

"Hello everyone, Joe Jordan here of CE4 Research. I would like to propose a project that you all can be part of if you want. I have always wanted to put together a book covering my twenty plus years of research into the so-called Alien Abduction experience. I would like to answer YOUR questions in this book, not just me giving a history of my research. What do YOU want to know from what I have found? I would like to take the best questions, if you have that many, and answer them for you personally. And if I use your question I will give you recognition in the book credits. This book will be a "not for personal profit" book. It will be to further spread the truth about the dark forces behind the experience. I want this book to be the HELP that so many hurting people have been looking for in this paranormal realm. Thank you for your support and God bless you all. You can post your questions here on this page, that way I can track who submitted them.

Please read through the ones posted so you are not asking one already asked. Thanks."

https://www.facebook.com/CE4Research/

The following questions are some of the ones submitted. Others will be answered in our upcoming second book. I have given credit, as promised, to those that submitted questions. And to them, I personally thank you for your support over the many years of research.

These questions will be answered by myself, with my own opinions or viewpoints, based either on my personal research findings of twenty five years into this strange phenomenon, or by using research or opinions or articles from other researchers that say what I want to say better than me.

I caution everyone that you may not agree with all of my answers or viewpoints as I answer the questions. My purpose is not to satisfy anyone's preconceived notion to a specific subject matter or interpretation of somebody else's research findings, or of any Biblical scripture. The answers are just my honest viewpoint, based on twenty five years of research.

Having said all of that, enjoy. And, if you, the reader, have a question after having read these submitted questions and answers, feel free to contact me personally and we'll talk.

Chapter 9

1)   From Mark Romaniuk:

I've had "sleep paralysis," where I was wide awake, but couldn't move at all. It seemed like a heavy blanket was on top of me. I was screaming in my head for my wife (who was next to me) to help, but no words came out. I became terrified and began screaming for Jesus. At first, I could only get a small mumble out of my lips, after about 7 tries I finally was able to say "Jesus." Once it became audible, I began getting control over my body one limb at a time. Finally, after about 10-15 seconds, I was screaming JESUS and rebuking whatever it was that was holding me down in terror. I stood up and chased and rebuked the entity out of my room and house and told it to never return in Jesus name. That was the first and last time something like this happened.

Question: What was this entity and where did it come from? What could have caused this entity to choose me to terrorize and paralyze? Lastly, why has it never returned??

Thank U Joe for your help and research and mostly your courage to stand firm in your field of work!!! God bless U

JGJ) Thank you for sharing, Mark, and those are very good questions. I guess I need to address some important things about these experiences right here in the first question so it can be considered throughout the later questions.

These experiences have been attributed to many different factors. Other researchers have found that people suffering from Frontal Lobe Epilepsy have similar experiences. Research has shown that high electromagnetics can cause the experiences. Then there is the concept that is held by many researchers that this is a "false memory" syndrome experience. But my research has shown, that whatever the cause of the experience is, if the experiencer makes this a primary focus in their life, they tend to look for answers that take them away from a focus on God of the Bible. They tend to look for answers to support their need to make it a real physical experience that happened to them, because the alternative to that is quite frightening to most.

This is where I think the real problem lies. Once the door has been opened by the experiencer, there is a realm of beings that are ready to give those experiencers answers or confirmation that will assist in their turning from Biblical truth. Those beings, I believe, are demonic beings, from what I call the spiritual realm. I believe there are two realms, ours and theirs. I've heard many terms or names given to these entities over the years. Personally, I call them demonic, deceptive beings from the spiritual realm.

Why did the entity choose you? I don't know without personally working with you and asking some very personal questions about your life and lifestyle to find that open door that allowed them to affect you, if there is one.

The secular researchers have been asking the question for years and years and years: "What causes people to have this experience?" And actually working in this for over 25 years, I've found a commonality amongst experiencers, and have been able to put my finger on an answer for that, one I believe would fulfill this question. It comes under 3 different forms. I have found through the research that people can have this experience because of one of three reasons or a combination of these reasons.

The first answer is that there are actually people that ask for this experience. And we've actually been at conferences and working tables where people come up and go, "You know I'd really like to have this experience to see what it's about." Be careful what you ask for, because you open yourself up to that experience wholeheartedly when you do that.

The second one is that people unknowingly open themselves up to this experience by dabbling in the occult, or New Age practices, or mystical things, in other words, the things the Bible tells us not to be involved with. These people are dealing with anything connected to the paranormal, not just UFO stuff, but also areas such as ghost hunting, studies, and experiences, involvement with psychic abilities, fortune telling, and they make themselves susceptible. Anything that's ungodly can open you up to this realm. It's like erecting a billboard to the entities, to say that, "You're welcome here. I'm looking for answers. I'm not looking at it in God's Word, but I'm looking at it elsewhere." And they are that elsewhere. They will come into your life and affect you in some form or manner. It's like the enemy has a million doors out there, wanting you just to pick one, whereas God says, "I stand at **the** door and knock." I have seen that most of the people become involved with this UFO experience because they have unknowingly opened a door in their lives that allows this experience to happen; they've been dabbling in areas that they shouldn't have. God tells us where to find answers to questions we may have; look at Jeremiah 33:3, New International Version (NIV):

> "Call to me and I will answer you and tell you great and unsearchable things you do not know."

The third one, where some experiencers were saying "I've had these experiences since I was a child," puzzled me. These children weren't openly asking for this, and they weren't really unknowingly opening doors to these types of things. They weren't doing other things that would unknowingly allow that to happen.

I started questioning them more about their lives and their past: what was your family like, what was your family life like, what were your parents into, what type of work did they do, what did they believe, did they ever talk about having unusual experiences, etc.? That's when I usually found an open door. And the open door wasn't caused by the child. The open door was caused by the family itself, the parents. And that opens it up to generational cycles of the experience, which secular researchers are seeing, though they don't have an answer to it. They always want to tie it back to, "There's some genetic trait that allows it to happen." Or it's the "blood type." No, it's not dealing with any of that at all: it's dealing with an open door. Similar to "the sins of the fathers," it's carried on to the next generation. But also keep in mind that the cycle can be broken at any time, and through that true belief in Jesus Christ and repentance, and taking the initiative to move on and get free from the experience. And then that will carry on through numerous generations, of being free from these entities' involvement.

There is one more possibility I have to add. It comes from a research peer and Christian Brother, Norio Hayakawa.

> "Norio Hayakawa (Japanese: 早川 弥生, Hepburn: Hayakawa Norio, born in 1944), is an American activist who lives in Rio Rancho, New Mexico. He is currently the director of Civilian Intelligence Central, a citizen oversight committee. He has appeared as a guest on Coast to Coast AM multiple times, and is most known for his UFOlogy investigations in and around New Mexico and the American Southwest."

https://en.wikipedia.org/wiki/Norio_Hayakawa

The UFO phenomenon seems to "pre-select" its observers!!
by Norio Hayakawa
CIVILIAN INTELLIGENCE NEWS SERVICE
February 8, 2020

The UFO phenomenon appears to me as a paraphysical intrusion into our physical dimension by an unknown intelligence or unknown sentient entities, paraphysically materializing themselves to a "pre-selected" observer (or a group of observers, whether small or large) and presenting to the observer as a physical extraterrestrial phenomenon and visitation for reasons yet unknown.

The "pre-selection" also seems to include a particular location as well as a particular time.

The phenomenon seems to be able to materialize and de-materialize at will and even seems to be capable of "transmogrifying" itself into any shape or form (as in the words of John A. Keel).

However, the phenomenon does not seem to be able to survive in our physical dimension except for a few seconds or a few minutes at a time.

Some researchers claim that the phenomenon seems to be able to temporarily affect our physical parameters (such as radar, etc.).

Yet the phenomenon also seems to be incapable of being photographed with clarity, if at all.

And on many occasions, it seems to me that these "UFOs" only deceptively appear (to the observer) to be utilizing some type of a propulsion system as they seem to take off into the distant sky at an unimaginable rate of speed.

Finally, by 'phenomenon' here, I would like to include both the 'craft' as well as the 'entities' and their seemingly paraphysical capabilities.

By the way, here is another of my favorite quotes from Dr. Jacques Vallee, the world's top-most authority on the UFO phenomenon in my opinion:

> "Contact between human percipients and the UFO phenomenon always occurs under conditions controlled by the latter. Its characteristic feature is a factor of absurdity that leads to a rejection of the story by the upper layers of the target society and an absorption at a deep unconscious level of the symbols conveyed by the encounter."

I am the first to admit that all of the above is purely my personal speculation, but it's the best that I could do, considering this sobering fact that:

Even though the UFO phenomenon seems to exist, it has not proven itself to be absolute, tangible evidence that we have been visited by actual physical extraterrestrial biological entities in any actual physical spacecraft of any kind. The term "UFOs" is misleading since we still do not know if they are really objects or if they are actually flying as we understand flying to be (as through the use of a propulsion system), as often mentioned by Dr. Jacques Vallee.

JGJ) To your third question of "why has it not come back", I truly hope it's because the demonic entities have realized you are, by the shed blood of Jesus Christ, a true child of God, who can no longer be deceived.

2)   From The Paranomalist

I had ongoing childhood experiences for several years that began almost immediately after my family moved to an old house in Massachusetts just after my fourth birthday. These were similar to the so-called "alien abduction" phenomenon (entities appearing in my room at night, etc.) but they were not the oft-reported grey alien type. They were short, stocky, powerfully built, entirely black, and had glowing or reflective eyes. Three years ago (some 40+ years later) I saw these same beings over two consecutive nights from 2:30 AM until dawn while out in the woods with two companions in the Northwestern USA. My companions saw them as well, as they appeared on the road entering our camp and stayed on the perimeter all night, watching us. No question in my mind at all that these were the same beings that I saw repeatedly as a child. I have come to believe that this is some sort of demonic attachment with which I am afflicted and that they were there for (or because of) me. The one gentleman, who I didn't know as well, camped in that spot often and had other paranormal experiences, but had never seen these entities prior to or after my arrival to this place.

My questions are: 1) What is your opinion of these beings' origin? and 2) Have you received reports of any such similar entities as the ones that I described? Or are they always the "grey alien" sort? Thank you, Joe. I admire and appreciate your work and I think you are correct in believing that these phenomena are demonic in nature. - John Carlson

JGJ) Regarding your first question, if you are truly dealing with a "spiritual experience", I refer to the entities perpetrating this experience as "demonic entities." I believe they are actually a normal (as opposed to paranormal) part of our God created reality.

The research findings show that this is not an extraterrestrial biological entity that we're dealing with. Rather, the research shows what we're dealing with here is a spiritual entity, and this is even what the secular realm is starting to see. They call it an "inter-dimensional" or "extra-dimensional" entity. Well, they're only one step away from using the word "spiritual." But they won't go there, because that would actually get them to accept the fact that if there's a spiritual realm then the Bible must be true. So they call these beings inter-dimensional, which I have no problem with, because we're actually talking about the same thing. From a Biblical perspective, we recognize there's only two realms. There's a physical realm, and a spiritual realm. And that spiritual realm, is another dimension to us. And these entities are from that realm.

I believe they are best described in the Bible here:

> "For our struggle is not against flesh and blood, but against the rulers, against the authorities, against the powers of this dark world and against the spiritual forces of evil in the heavenly realms."
> Ephesians 6:12, New International Version

This is the description of a demonic entity from the spiritual realm.

To your second question, no, they are not always of the "grey alien type" in appearance. They use the appearance of many different types of beings, which gives the illusion of there being many different races of alien (extraterrestrial) beings visiting Earth. But actually, I think the different appearances are just a part of the complexity of the delusion and deception these entities are perpetuating to deceive humanity into taking their eyes off of the one true God.

Author and Christian peer researcher, Ron Rhodes puts it this way, in an excerpt from The Truth about UFOs and Aliens: A Christian Assessment:

> "The winds of change are continuing to blow on the religious landscape in America today, and its effects should signal concern in the heart of every Christian. As the ominous dark clouds continue to gather on the horizon, with stories of UFOs and alien encounters continuing to surface,

many Christians go merrily about their way, oblivious to what is going on around them. Better to heed the warning of Jesus!

Jesus clearly cautioned His followers about religious deception in the last days: "At that time many will turn away from the faith and will betray and hate each other, and many false prophets will appear and deceive many people" (Matthew 24:10-11). Earlier, Jesus warned His followers to "watch out for false prophets. They come to you in sheep's clothing, but inwardly they are ferocious wolves" (Matthew 7:15). As I've demonstrated in this book, the so-called extraterrestrials seek to appear as benevolent "brothers," but in fact they are ferocious demonic wolves who seek to lead us astray."

Ron Rhodes, https://books.apple.com/us/book/the-truth-about-ufos-and-aliens-a-christian-assessment/id621244665

3)   From MaryAnn Owen

When I was newly saved I actually experienced paralysis, no speech and pressure on my chest and body. Being a baby Christian I didn't know who I was and that I had the authority to get rid of this huge thing. As all this was happening I was talking to the Lord in my mind and saying "Jesus, you said I would never have any fear if you were around what is going on?" I kind of figured it out for myself and started saying "Jesus, Jesus, Jesus," in my mind, until finally my mouth loosened and I was able to slowly say it out loud and that thing lifted up off me and out the wall. Before he lifted off me he said a few choice words and told me to keep my mouth shut!! This is no alien it is either Satan, one of the Fallen Angels, or a demon. They are deceiving many and I believe this will be the great falling away that the Bible speaks of. Joe, my question to you is if there any way I can help people who are going through this right now??

JGJ) Absolutely, MaryAnn Owen. The most powerful tool we have, next to God's Word, is our testimony of deliverance from the enemy's lies and bondage through God's Word. The secular realm does not accept these powerful, compelling research findings. I say to them, how many testimonies of personal deliverance is it going to take to convince you? Right here in this book there are over 100, and on my website there are over 100 more, and they still keep coming in.

You can help by sharing this research information any way you can. I freely share this truth through my website (www.ce4research.com) and through the many videos and radio show interview archives on my You Tube channel (CE4 Research). And I give everyone permission to share my research findings, website, videos, or radio shows, so others still under the delusion can know there is a Hope to this horrible life changing experience, something that no secular UFO/Alien Abduction researcher is offering.

4)   From Lori Eve

I would like to know more about what limits these entities. Where does the factor of "authority" come in? Why they are only allowed to do only so much to some while they seem to have free reign to hurt others much more? Does that make sense? Growing up I was "picked on" by them but knew on some level that they weren't supposed to actually touch me. I'm nothing special. My bloodline is nothing special yet they were kept at bay.

JGJ) Thanks Lori, but I'm not sure how to answer this question concerning their limits. I do not know for certain that there are limits they can go to when dealing with human beings. I do see that some people are affected in very horrible ways when others are not; I feel that may be due to how involved with them we become. My personal view is that they do not outright cause death, but instead go to every effort to convince us that God is not real, or He didn't really say what He has said, or mean what He has said. They want to cheat us out of God's gift, the ultimate gift of eternal life through His Son, Jesus Christ.

As for the factor of authority, let me try and explain.

In the beginning of my research, I too questioned the "authority" that the testimonies showed, of terminating the experience. I looked for the answer in God's Word for quite a while, but I just could not put my finger on it. I finally said, "Lord, help me, I think this is very important to the research." My understanding was that the sixth chapter of Ephesians was the Spiritual Warfare chapter for dealing with the lies and temptations of the enemy in our lives. I understood that verse 12 identified who we were fighting against.

Those that follow Jesus Christ are Christians, and Christians have access to the power in the name and authority of Jesus Christ. The name above all names. The testimonies you will read in this book give proof to just that.

What gives Christians that access? The answer is found in a mystery, a mystery that was once secret, but later revealed.

The mystery goes like this. The demonic realm has been running this world for quite some time. Then, Jesus is born into the world. They knew who He was (God manifest in the flesh on earth), and they knew there was going to be trouble. They knew the prophesies, and they were seeing them being fulfilled. During his time on Earth, Jesus did give the demonic realm a hard time, putting them in their place.

> "Then Jesus came to them and said, "All authority in heaven and on earth has been given to me."
> Matthew 28:18 (NIV)

So the demonic realm planned to turn the people against Him, to have Him eliminated. They thought that once He was gone, things would return to normal. So they influenced the minds of the people and they had Him crucified. But He rose from the grave on the third day. He defeated death, but He didn't stay. He rose to the right hand of the Father (God) in Heaven. The demonic realm thought they had won since He was gone.

But wait, Jesus had told His disciples something before He rose up to Heaven, found in Acts 1:4 New International Version (NIV):

"On one occasion, while he was eating with them, he gave them this command: "Do not leave Jerusalem, but wait for the gift my Father promised, which you have heard me speak about.""

On the day of Pentecost, in the Upper Room where they were gathered together, they received the promised gift from the Father, the indwelling of the Holy Spirit.

From that day forward, believers in the Lord Jesus Christ would all receive the indwelling of the Holy Spirit. Christ in you.

This, was the mystery revealed. Because every believer in the Lord Jesus Christ would have access to the power in the name and authority of Jesus Christ through the indwelling of the Holy Spirit. The power to defeat the demonic entities that come against them. And the testimonies that you will read in this book, will show just that.

This can be best seen, in the sixth chapter of Ephesians, the spiritual warfare chapter. Verse 12 identifies who we war against:

"For our struggle is not against flesh and blood, but against the rulers, against the authorities, against the powers of this dark world and against the spiritual forces of evil in the heavenly realms."
Ephesians 6:12 (NIV)

Verses 13 through 17 are about protecting yourself by putting on the whole armor of God in your daily life:

"Therefore put on the full armor of God, so that when the day of evil comes, you may be able to stand your ground, and after you have done everything, to stand. Stand firm then, with the belt of truth buckled around your waist, with the breastplate of righteousness in place, and with your feet fitted with the readiness that comes from the gospel of peace. In addition to all this, take up the shield of faith, with which you can extinguish all the flaming arrows of the evil one. Take the helmet of salvation and the sword of the Spirit, which is the word of God."
Ephesians 6:13-17

But you as human beings will tire, you will let down your defenses. Because of that, you have an offensive weapon that will put the demonic realm in its place. The most powerful weapon in the Universe. Those are verses 18 through 20:

> "And pray in the Spirit on all occasions with all kinds of prayers and requests. With this in mind, be alert and always keep on praying for all the Lord's people. Pray also for me, that whenever I speak, words may be given me so that I will fearlessly make known the mystery of the gospel, for which I am an ambassador in chains. Pray that I may declare it fearlessly, as I should."
> Ephesians 6:18-20

Let me break it down in simple terms for you. Prayer is a powerful weapon, especially silent prayer (in the spirit) to God the Father. Why silent prayer? Because the demonic realm cannot read your thoughts, but they will make you think they can. I do believe they can influence your thoughts though. This is warfare, don't give anything away to them.

Now look at verse 19, it says, "that whenever I speak," but speak to who? Remember, this is the spiritual warfare chapter dealing with the demonic realm. You are speaking, out loud, to the demonic realm. Why? Because they can't read your thoughts. But, they can hear your voice.

"Words may be given me," by who? The Holy Spirit, that indwells in the believer of Jesus Christ.

"So that I will fearlessly make known the mystery of the gospel." What mystery? The mystery I shared with you earlier. That we have Christ in us, through the indwelling of the Holy Spirit, and access to call on the power in the name and authority of Jesus Christ, the name above all names, the power over all the Universe and the earth.

"For which I am an ambassador in chains," I am a child of God, blood bought by Son of God, Jesus Christ, whom I follow, and are committed to sharing with others. And they have no power over you.

That, is the most powerful force in the Universe, able to break down any stronghold.

5)   From Andrew Gardiner

If you start researching UFOs and aliens, they start appearing and even coming in to your bedroom at night (sleep paralysis). My experience anyways. Jesus does work in dealing with these so they must be demons.

JGJ) You made a good observation, Andrew. It has been reported by many researchers in this field of study that many looking into this phenomenon actually become experiencers. Back to that open door idea I referred to earlier.

And Jesus does work, yes. And because He does, I too believe we are dealing with demonic entities. Why else would an (alien) being respond to that name the way it does?

Chapter 10

6)   From Rose Richardson

Joe, during a time of physical pain some years ago I had some "out of body" type experiences due to the lack of sleep and extreme fatigue. I floated up out of my bed, rotated like a chicken on a spit and settled back. During it I was GET OVER IT WILL YA! I was fully aware this was not demonic; it was due to my physical condition.

My question is this: how many times people put an exotic spin on a natural sleep disturbance? It does make you sound special to be in the abducted club rather than the exhausted club. This might be hard to weed out, but some folks might relate if someone talked them into it was abduction.

JGJ) Thank you Rose for your never-ending support over the past years. You make a good point that needs to be addressed. Even looking at the definition of Alien Abductions in Wikipedia, we find examples of other conditions that can lead people to think that they may have been abducted by aliens.

Alien Abduction
From Wikipedia, the free encyclopedia

The terms alien abduction or abduction phenomenon describe "subjectively real experiences" of being secretly kidnapped by nonhuman figures (aliens) and subjected to physical and psychological experimentation. Most scientists and mental health professionals explain these experiences by factors such as suggestibility (e.g. false memory syndrome), sleep paralysis, deception, and psychopathology.

Alleged abductees seek out hypnotherapists to try to resolve issues such as missing time or unexplained physical symptoms such as muscle pain or headaches. This usually involves two phases, an information gathering stage, in which the hypnotherapist asks about unexplained illnesses or unusual phenomena during the patients' lives (caused by or distortions of the alleged abduction), followed by hypnosis and guided imagery to facilitate recall. The information gathering enhances the likelihood that the events discussed will be incorporated into later abduction "memories". Seven steps are hypothesized to lead to the development of false memories:

1)   A person is predisposed to accept the idea that certain puzzling or inexplicable experiences might be telltale signs of UFO abduction.

2)   The person seeks out a therapist, whom he or she views as an authority and who is, at the very least, receptive to this explanation and has some prior familiarity with UFO abduction reports.

3)   Alternatively, the therapist frames the puzzling experiences in terms of an abduction narrative.

4)   Alternative explanations of the experiences are not explored.

5)   There is increasing commitment to the abduction explanation and increasing anxiety reduction associated with ambiguity reduction.

6)   The therapist legitimates or ratifies the abductee's experience, which constitutes additional positive reinforcement.

7)   The client adopts the role of the "victim" or abductee, which becomes integrated into the psychotherapy and the client's view of self.

Others are intrigued by the entire phenomenon, but hesitate in making any definitive conclusions. The late Harvard psychiatrist John E. Mack concluded, "The furthest you can go at this point is to say there's an authentic mystery here. And that is, I think, as far as anyone ought to go." (emphasis as in original) Mack was unconvinced by piecemeal counterclaims, however, and countered that skeptical explanations naturally need to "take into account the entire range of phenomena associated with abduction experiences," up to and including "missing time," directly contemporaneous UFO sightings, and the occurrence in small children.

Putting aside the question of whether abduction reports are literally and objectively "real", literature professor Terry Matheson argues that their popularity and their intriguing appeal are easily understood. Tales of abduction "are intrinsically absorbing; it is hard to imagine a more vivid description of human powerlessness." After experiencing the frisson of delightful terror one may feel from reading ghost stories or watching horror movies, Matheson notes that people "can return to the safe world of their homes, secure in the knowledge that the phenomenon in question cannot follow. But as the abduction myth has stated almost from the outset, there is no avoiding alien abductors."

Matheson writes that when compared to the earlier contactee reports, abduction accounts are distinguished by their "relative sophistication and subtlety, which enabled them to enjoy an immediately more favorable reception from the public."

Some writers have said abduction experiences bear similarities to pre-20th century accounts of demonic manifestations, noting as many as a dozen similarities. One notable example is the Orthodox monk Fr. Seraphim Rose, who devotes a whole chapter in his book Orthodoxy and the Religion of the Future to the phenomena of UFOs and abductions, which, he concludes, are manifestations of the demonic.

https://en.wikipedia.org/wiki/Alien_abduction

JGJ) It saddens me to see many who jump to the conclusion that it is all demonic. My research shows otherwise. We see from many researchers from many different fields of study, showing that the perception of it being an alien abduction experience can be caused by many different means. I believe some of these experiences possibly are demonic in nature, but not many. What I do see is the demonic attachment to the experiencer that comes to those who mistake this experience as alien, and end up pursuing that avenue for answers or support of the experience actually being what they pre-conceive it to be.

7)   From Mark W. Kirby

What is the best way to help an experiencer? What are key things to say and not to say to help guide them to the truth?

JGJ) First, show love and concern for what they are trying to tell you. Second, listen intently. Don't tell them they are deceived or wrong; the Holy Spirit will handle that for you. Third, ask them about things they say that don't make sense, this plants a seed of doubt in their head about their experience being real. Fourth, show them my research findings in CE4 Research. Show them many have found Hope for this horrific, life changing experience. Fifth, ask them if they would like to be free of the fear, the pain, the doubts, the shame, for good. Sixth, offer them the 8 R's to Freedom. Seventh, offer them the Eternal Hope and Peace through Jesus Christ.

STOP ABDUCTIONS - THE 8 RS TO FREEDOM

How do I make it all stop? How do I get free from this nightmare? How do I get my life back? Please, can you help me?

If you are asking these questions, we are glad you are here. Over the years we have been able to see many people whose lives were in shambles from these experiences get their lives back. We have seen many people have peace and joy again in their lives. To know they are no longer under the delusion of the enemy and his lying tactics.

I was given the book from Dr. Henry W. Wright to review. It was already a few years into the work of CE4 Research. I was told it could be of importance to the people we have been trying to help in this field of the paranormal. After reading it, and seeing the "8 R's to Freedom", I realized we had already been sharing similar information with people looking for help, but had not written anything down as far as a structure that they could easily follow. I decided to adopt Dr. Wright's proven method of helping people be free from the bondage and lies of the enemy (Satan). Please keep in mind, it is just a guideline for help. It has been very useful tool to those that have followed it in their fight with the enemies' lies in their lives. I do believe it can be a powerful guide for becoming and staying free.

Let's look at the 8 R's in relation to this phenomenon:

1. Recognize - You must recognize what it is.

The UFO/Alien Abduction experience is a powerful delusion from the enemy. The purpose is to take your eyes off the one true God. It is a war for your soul and the enemy will use whatever it takes for you to believe his lies.

2. Responsibility - You must take responsibility for what you recognize.

You must take action to stop this experience of the enemy now that you see it for what it is.

3. Repent - Repent to God for participating with what you recognize.

Repent for falling for the enemy's lies. Usually the experiences are from open doors in our lives that allow the enemy in. Even repent for not knowing what you had become part of. A lot of times we don't even know that we have opened doors.

4. Renounce - You must make what you recognize your enemy and renounce it.

Renounce any part of your life that is not of God. Anything not of God is of the enemy and it is our enemy.

5. Remove it - Get rid of it once and for all.

Remove all participation, involvement, research for information or answers, associations, books, charms, crystals, and anything related to the enemy's tactics of perpetrating the delusion or opening doors in your life to allow him back in.

6. Resist - When it tries to come back, resist it.

When it tries to come back? Oh yeah, he will, he used to own you, he knows your weaknesses. But keep in mind you now can see his methods and purpose, to destroy. But through Jesus Christ, the authority is given to make him flee.

7. <u>Rejoice</u> - Give God thanks for setting you free.

Free from the bondage of the enemy's delusion and having to live in fear.

8. <u>Restore</u> - Help someone else to get free.

We are told we reach the lost through the Word of God, and our testimony. Our testimony is the most powerful evidence, (proof), that God is real. The testimony of a changed life through the name and authority of Jesus Christ is the real evidence that exposes the lies of the enemy. When you share your testimony you give someone else the hope that they too can also be free. The enemy is defeated by your testimony of Jesus Christ in your life. The enemy does not want you to have or share your testimony of Jesus Christ changing your life. He knows how powerful it is.

You can find the actual 8 R's to Freedom by Dr. Henry W. Wright in his book;

A More Excellent Way
Be In Health, Dr. Henry W. Wright
Publisher: Pleasant Valley Publications; 7th edition (February 2003)
ISBN-10: 0967805929, ISBN-13: 978-0967805924

8)   From Catherine James

Do they keep coming back in different forms after you KNOW what they are? Do they ever give up (not asking for myself; I want to know what YOU think about that)?

JGJ) You always ask the good ones, Catherine James. The warfare never stops until we are received home by Jesus Christ. They can no longer deceive us in the facade they used before; we now know that truth. They may still harass us to try and make us stumble in our faith, but the same authority is always available to fight them.

9)   From Laura Maxwell

I've heard from people who used to receive communication from beings claiming to be Pleiadians, Arcturians, Sirians; beings from The Intergalactic Federation of Light and so on. Thankfully they discovered those so called light beings or aliens were actually demons, either because they'd lied to them or actually attacked them. Those folks received Jesus as Savior and had demons cast out, then the communication and attacks stopped. Sometimes when I've shared this with other channelers, they see he truth of it and find freedom in Jesus too. Other times, the channelers just can't see the link. What more can we say to them to help them see? Or is it more a case of prayer rather than merely sharing the facts with them?

JGJ) I believe so Laura. Real prayer, honest and earnest prayer for them. Then, just let them see the true signs of a Christian through you. Love them, because they are not bad people, only deceived. We, too, were once deceived. The seed has been planted. Let it grow.

A good friend and peer once told me to remember this: no matter how hard we try, some will choose the lie.

Chapter 11

10)   From Bruce White

Have you connected the aliens to demons yet?

JGJ) Bruce White, I am confident we have, yes. Not only from the testimonies of the name and authority of Jesus Christ stopping there activities, but also other evidence and red flags in this field. I'll let my partner in Alien Resistance, Guy Malone, cover this part. We have been doing this as a one-two punch at conferences for a couple of decades now.

This is from Guy's talk from the Roswell UFO Festival conference in 2018:

Not Against Flesh & Blood: The Rulers Over Roswell
By Guy Malone

So I'm not just a speaker, author, or even a religious nut activist or whatever you might want to call me - this is all very personal to me, because I'm an experiencer as well.

By that I mean that this "alien abduction" experience that many people speak of - famous names, published authors, like Budd Hopkins, and others like David Jacobs PhD, Dr. Karla Turner PhD, and Dr. John Mack of Harvard University have all researched and written extensively about this experience of someone being trapped in their bed or feeling paralyzed, while entities of unknown origin and seeming ill intent, "do things" to them, take them places, tell them things, and then return them to their beds and their so-called normal lives. Well, all of that was a part of my early childhood years. I had multiple experiences when I was pretty young, that most likely really shaped my psyche and my worldview at an early age. I also was not from a religious home, so the idea of my childhood alien friends being demonic - a topic being explored in this talk and in the film later today, honestly wasn't the first thing that came to my mind, and I didn't even consider that possibility for years.

Maybe, like I was, perhaps you're actually quite resistant to the idea in fact.

The first time I did this talk in fact, three people walked out on it, so don't think you'll hurt my feelings if that turns out to be you before too long. However, today I'm framing this talk, for the first time in fact, around what these findings - my experiences, Joe's research from working with literally hundreds of abductees, the conclusion of the *Alien Intrusion* film - I'm bringing this all home to what it could, or perhaps even should, mean for people who live here, in Roswell, and are Christians. So if you're not a Christian don't worry or think that I'm somehow targeting you with things you don't want to hear in this message, because not getting lynched by my own kind by the time this is done is really more of the goal today.

But stepping back in time first, it would be many years in fact before I would personally even consider the possibility that my experiences might've involved honest to God demons. And when I did arrive at that conclusion nearly thirty years ago after becoming a Christian, I kept it ALL completely to myself for many years. I was personally mortified and embarrassed that these things had happened to me to begin with, and I had no intent of sharing that information with anybody. Perhaps some of you here now can relate.

And if that's at least part of what drew you here today, I do want you to know that you're not alone in what you've gone through, or in what you're feeling.

But it has now been over 20 years ago, since I finally put my personal experiences and my earliest conclusions online as webpage back in 1997. At that time I was NOT part of the UFO Community, and I didn't even live here in Roswell when I was first publishing this in the 90's. Come Sail Away is still free to read on www.RoswellMission.org, and you can find the updated version Come Sail Away With Me as a book on Amazon, if you're not here in person, I mean.

So what got me to come out of the closet so to speak, was - while I was still living in Nashville, Tennessee, was the mass suicide of a group - most will say cult - known as Heaven's Gate in 1997....

This quote from the New York Times Company says the materials the group published claimed...

> "...Two members of the Kingdom of Heaven (or what some might call two aliens from space) incarnated into two unsuspecting humans in Houston... They consciously recognized that they were sent from space to do a task that had something to do with the Bible."

The idea that people would kill themselves based on something "aliens" told their group's leader about the Bible was quite shocking to me, and at the time it set me on a journey of using the internet and finding out how prevalent philosophies like this had become. I was pretty shocked, and ultimately concerned about what was happening to other people, who, like me, had experienced visits or abductions, and went looking online for answers.

By a vast majority, pretty much all of the information online - especially back then - was more likely to convince people to join a UFO cult themselves than anything else. And what's also kind of weird, and a large part of how this became a calling for me, is that I also felt a bit guilty about their deaths.

Because I thought that I'd already arrived at some of the answers these very people were looking for, but I was sitting on the answers, for years, too embarrassed to tell anyone what I'd experienced, or what I really thought.

I finally decided though, that I needed to share my views, to maybe help other people not fall for, or go to the extremes these people did. So as I said in my book, in 1997 "I got me a webpage and started writing". and I had no idea at the time that I'd wind up living in Roswell, much less being here doing something like this at the time.

So, you may be interested in knowing that way before I came on this scene though, one very famous, non-religious scientist put the idea in writing himself.

The idea of what researchers now call the demonic hypothesis (opposed to the extraterrestrial hypothesis).

Depending on your age, you may or may not remember Carl Sagan, anybody?

Carl Sagan was an incredibly well known but now deceased scientist and widely published author, popularly remembered today from his TV series *Cosmos*, but I'm old, and according to Wikipedia, that program *Cosmos*, was "the most widely watched series in the history of American public television, ...seen by at least 500 million people across 60 different countries. He also wrote the science fiction novel Contact, the basis for a 1997 film of the same name.

Sagan was no stranger to many ideas about aliens, is all I mean.....

He was also a member - still quoting Wikipedia "of the Ad Hoc Committee to Review Project Blue Book, the U.S. Air Force's UFO investigation project" from way back the 1960s. As said I'll get back to him later but real quickly I wanted to start with a quick quote from his book The Demon Haunted World, in which he very much down played the possibility of UFOs being true extraterrestrial craft - instead, he said

> "Think of how many other "explanations" there might be: time travelers; demons... tourists from another dimension... the souls of the dead... Each of these "explanations" has been seriously proffered."

I don't mean to imply that Carl Sagan personally believed or ever flat out stated that UFOs and aliens were demonic.

I do mean to say though, that as a non-religious scientist, he was just AS willing to have the idea of demons on the table, as he was aliens. And excuse me for being perhaps a little bit challenging, or confrontational here, but I want to stop and ask you to ask yourself - are you willing to consider that either one might be true, depending upon the evidence you uncover when you really research the facts of the matter?

Because to me, that's honest open minded inquiry. That's why I present his face first - and if you go yourself to the Wikipedia entry on Carl Sagan, scroll down to the section on UFOs there's a discussion that ends with "Some of Sagan's many books examine UFOs (as did one episode of *Cosmos*) and he claimed a religious undercurrent to the phenomenon." That says something I think, that the most famous credentialed scientist in the world at the time was noting spiritual, even religious, aspects were present in the alien phenomenon.

Now in contrast to Carl Sagan, I'll also mention just a personal anecdote, involving the very well-known and largely respected alien abduction researcher Budd Hopkins, now also deceased.

Hopkins was of course much more accomplished and way more famous in the field of alien abduction research than I'll ever be, and I met him only one time, and only briefly at a 2003 UFO conference in Las Vegas, Nevada.

He certainly wouldn't have known of me, I don't think, and I wasn't offering any opinions myself in this particular conversation, but for some reason he and I were in a very small group of people off in a corner for a few minutes where he was of course the center of attention. Someone asked him about alien abductions and my ears really perked up when he said something that struck me as kind of odd… He said "Well one thing's for certain, we know they're not demons…" One person - not me - asked him why not, and his reply was "Because there's no such thing as demons."

I have to admit that that just didn't seem very open minded to me. Imagine if I or anyone presenting here in Roswell were to say to you, "Well I'm not sure what's behind all these reports of abductions or things in the sky, but we can be certain that it's not aliens. Why? Because there's no such thing as aliens."

I'm just not sure that any honest research can be carried out, or any opinions can be honestly arrived at, if one possibility or another is ruled out from the very beginning. So assuming you stay till the end today, let me say thank you in advance, and I think it's really neat that you'd be here, and open minded enough to hear out this view out today.

Something's definitely happening, and I want you to know that many, many people out there are looking for serious answers. As some of you know about already from Joe's work, many people just want the experience to stop.

And I of course know that many people think the idea of aliens is just for fun, or just something we Roswellians can make money off of by selling T-shirts to tourists, but I don't want you to forget about people's felt needs, or how their experiences or beliefs about this topic shapes their world views, which can also once again, call the source of the experiences into question, and make the actual origins of the phenomena very relevant.

Another person whom I think you'll know, or know of, said:

> "One theory which can no longer be taken very seriously is that UFOs are interstellar spaceships."

That's Arthur C. Clark, one of the most famous science-fiction writers of all time! He wrote the book that led to the movie *2001: A Space Odyssey*.

I think it's fair to say he probably made a chunk of change writing about aliens visiting earth - as fictional - but it might surprise to find out here that he also honestly didn't think what we earthlings are currently experiencing actually was aliens from space either.

Someone you may not have heard of, but there's a book titled <u>One in Forty</u> referring to that percentage of the population that's experienced abduction that I mentioned earlier, by non-Christian author, Preston Dennit who says:

> "It cannot be denied that there is a connection between UFO encounters and psychic phenomena... UFO abductees have reported being plagued with all sorts of paranormal manifestations following their UFO experience.... objects moving by themselves, ... ghostly footsteps, apparitions, doors opening and closing by themselves, precognitive dreams, telepathy, telekinesis — the list is endless... Many ufologists ignore this aspect of ufology in an attempt to draw the subject out of the occult...They refuse to use all the evidence presented to make a theory

which explains all aspects of the reported phenomena. Instead they choose those aspects that would prove their theory, while ignoring the evidence that contradicts their theory... UFOs will never be explained until the psychic aspect of UFOs is also explained."

But back to real science for a minute, Dr. Vallee, is one of, if not "the" true pioneers of secular UFO research, and as for credibility, believe it or not, Dr Vallee actually presented his research and findings on UFOs to a special committee of the United Nations in 1978.

The entire speech he gave to the UN can be found as the appendix to his book Messengers of Deception, which is, I realize a highly suggestive book title. But again, he is not a religious researcher, it's just the wording he chose for what he observed as a scientific researcher to describe his findings. You can find the pdf of the whole book online easily, but here's an interesting quote,

"Although the UFO phenomenon is real ... I have failed to discover any evidence that it represented the arrival of visitors from space."

That's amazing, considering that Dr. Vallee himself witnessed a UFO, and he started out as a proponent of the Extraterrestrial hypothesis. He started out as a believer but his research brought him to another conclusion. He also worked partly with the U.S. government along with Project Blue Book's J. Allen Hynek. You might call Dr. Vallee and Dr. Hynek the founding fathers of scientific UFO study, and it's a shame that so many people in the UFO industry - yes I said industry - people in the UFO and alien merchandising business today completely ignore all of the work these guys did, because their findings don't add up to friendly space visitors - not by a long shot.

But in addition to being the author of a whopping 10 books on the scientific study of UFOs, Dr. Vallee helped coin the phrase in the 1970's "the inter-dimensional hypothesis" to explain UFO activity. The phrase "Interdimensional hypothesis" is actually a rebuttal, or an alternative, to the more popular belief at the time, known as the "extraterrestrial hypothesis" - meaning that what these scientists who studied UFOs and alien encounters for years on our government's payroll realized was that instead of being true extraterrestrials from space, the best word they could come up with to describe their findings was that they came from another dimension. Christians might say "spiritual realm" or "second heaven" or something similar.

In his report to the United Nations in 1978, on the same page I have punched up here, he continued to speak of the quote "psycho physiological effects" on the UFO witnesses, like disorientation, auditory and visual hallucinations, massive psychic reactions, disturbance of sleep and dream patterns, and so on.

He continues by saying the phenomenon was creating, quote: "a social belief system in all the nations centered on the expectation of space visitors."

He painstakingly notes that this belief system was contrary to what the physical evidence revealed, and that the general public was ignoring actual science in favor of this space visitor belief system. What he was stating before the UN, was that they were purposely tricking us into believing they came from outer space, but that the evidence showed otherwise.

He informed the committee that worldwide belief in aliens was resulting in new political and religious belief systems, and - for good or bad - he even noted that the global belief in "the expectation of contact with space visitors promotes the concept of the political unification of our planet."

In a separate interview, Vallee expressed that he thought some external force was causing in people what he called "induced hallucinations..." saying,

> "...It's quite possible that some of the stories that you get from people are essentially induced hallucinations in sincere witnesses – the witnesses are not lying. They really have been exposed to something genuine..."

It's not that the UFO witnesses were lying (he said) but that only they saw something that wasn't really there, at least in the physical sense it wasn't there. "Induced hallucination" - try to wrap your head around what that means if you can. That means that a non-physical, intelligent, outside force was present with the witness to induce the experience, The UFO wasn't there, but the experiencer really saw it.

In uhhh the Bible, that's called a vision.

Finally, author John Keel writes succinctly "The UFO manifestations seem to be, by and large, merely minor variations of the age-old demonological phenomenon..."

You can see by now how easy it is to make that argument with quotes from non-religious researchers and scientists who are just examining the data itself, but don't even have a spiritual - or at least a biblical - worldview.

Quite simply, the case for a demonic interpretation of alien contacts is often made quite well by non-religious researchers, presenting non-religious data.

So regardless of one's religious beliefs I want to point out that actual modern science still does not support that there's other life in the universe.

Science Fiction does, and the wishful thinking of many scientists does, but not science itself.

The book <u>Abduction Human Encounters with Aliens</u> by Dr. John Mack represents a decade-long study of over 300 men and women who claimed alien abduction. Dr. Mack is a Pulitzer Prize winning author, who, up until as his death, served as the Head of the Psychiatry Department at Harvard University School of Medicine, and he co-chaired a conference at M.I.T. that concluded that abductees weren't crazy, or lying, but that most showed symptoms of Post-Traumatic Stress Disorder, proving that something had indeed happened to them. And for the most part I believe them. And like I said, I am one.

After interviewing over 300 abductees, Dr. Mack finally summarized the aliens' messages by saying,

> "The information that abductees receive is concerned primarily...

> ...with the fate of the earth in the wake of human destructiveness."

"Scenes are shown...of the earth devastated by a nuclear holocaust, vast panoramas of lifeless polluted landscapes and waters, (folks these are images actually flashed directly into the minds of abductees, that they have to live with the rest of their lives) and apocalyptic images of giant earthquakes, firestorms, floods, and even fractures of the planet itself are shown by the aliens. These are powerfully disturbing to the abductees, who tend to experience them as literally predictive of the future of the planet. Some abductees are given assignments in this future holocaust as it is displayed, such as to feed the survivors, or are told...that some will perish while others will be taken to another place to participate in the evolution of life in the universe."

Extensive research by Dr. Mack, Karla Turner Phd, David Jacobs Phd, Budd Hopkins and many other prominent abduction researchers bears out that visions of the end of the world – or at least some massive future apocalypse – is one of, if not THE MAJOR THEME that contactees experience in their interactions with aliens.

Now it's pretty well known that Christians have our own versions of the end of the world, but here's the catch - in speaking with contactees and abductees, they also often speak of how the aliens will help mankind survive this period.

Dr. Mack relates this conversation with an abductee named Ed:

"I asked him what is called for, what he has been told is to be done. He answered personally... "She's telling me, showing me that I have the tools within me to survive. I have this extra dimension. I have the choice of listening to it or not... I am to listen to my inner, something deep inside myself, and listen to the earth."

Some abductees are told the key to surviving the Last Days is in themselves, while others are told the aliens will save them:

"It will be the time when the disasters are at their peak.

It will happen when people will no longer be able to stand the disruptions and the chaos. The remainder of the people who are living will be picked up by spacecraft and be taken to safety the planet Saturn. Here they will be cared for until the Earth is once again ready to be inhabited… You are all in the hands of the Space brothers, and the sooner you realize this, the better."

Are you starting to see why Christians call this stuff the doctrines of devils?

In Romans 10:9, The Bible says clearly, that it is only Jesus who saves, and that whoever shall call upon the name of the Lord will be saved! Not Sananda, not Ashtar…

Aliens routinely promise that THEY will deliver their believers from the disasters foretold in the Bible in the End Times, in a variety of ways depending on exactly which aliens you're talking to - including but not limited to cloning, reincarnation, and/or by lifting those who "follow" the aliens off the planet just in the nick of time.

Those friendly aliens really seem to have all your bases covered don't they?

Or do they? Is it possible that they're lying about these things? Is it possible that they're being intentionally deceptive?

I know that nobody can ever point to an exact passage in the Bible that says there's NOT life elsewhere… I'm simply asking that if you're a bible believing Christian, that you to let your faith rest entirely on what God does say to settle this for you, at least as it pertains to what you teach others. In short, I'm asking you to take what IS said in the Bible, and draw the most likely conclusion, based solely on what God's word actually states …

Whether you're a Christian pastor, or just a Christian who might get asked by somebody what THE BIBLE SAYS about life elsewhere, I'm simply admonishing you to not let your imagination take you beyond what is written.

> "Casting down vain imaginations, and every high thing that exalts itself
> against the knowledge of God" 2 Corinthians 2:5

As Christians, I simply think we have a responsibility to teach only what God's
word does say, and nothing more. God can do anything yes, "nothing is too hard
for God" that's biblical. But when it comes to teaching, we are compelled and
constricted to impart God's word alone.

> "For my thoughts are not your thoughts, neither are your ways my ways,
> declares the Lord. As the heavens are higher than the earth, so are my
> ways higher than your ways, and my thoughts than your thoughts."
> Isa 55:8-9

That's Isaiah 55, the passage that ends by saying His word will not go out and
return void. Our words will return void. Words that come from our imaginations
will not bear fruit. So what I'm hoping to send you out with today - is what His
word says. And here's what The Bible does say is absolutely true, no conjecture
required.

The only stated purpose of the stars is to give light to the Earth and to mark the
seasons...

> "And God said, Let there be lights in the firmament of the heaven to
> divide the day from the night; and let them be for signs, and for seasons,
> and for days, and years: And let them be for lights in the firmament of the
> heaven to give light upon the earth: and it was so. And God made two
> great lights; the greater light to rule the day, and the lesser light to rule the
> night: [he made] the stars also. And God set them in the firmament of
> the heaven to give light upon the earth, And to rule over the day and over
> the night, and to divide the light from the darkness: and God saw that [it
> was] good." Genesis 1:14-18

Only the Earth is stated as "created to be inhabited." (This is not said of any other
planet or star.)

"For thus saith the LORD that created the heavens;
God himself that formed the earth and made it; he hath established it,
he created it not in vain, he formed it to be inhabited: I [am] the LORD;
and [there is] none else."

"He who fashioned and made the earth, He founded it; He did not create
it to be empty, but formed it to be inhabited"
Isaiah 45:18 (NIV)

The Bible states that God populated the heavens with angels, which are not
biological entities.

"Thus the heavens and the earth were finished, and all the host of them."
Gen 2:1

"And suddenly there was with the angel a multitude of the heavenly host
praising God, and saying, Glory to God in the highest, and on earth
peace, good will toward men. And it came to pass, as the angels were gone
away from them into heaven, the shepherds said one to another, Let us
now go even unto Bethlehem, and see this thing which is come to pass,
which the Lord hath made known unto us." Luke 2:8-15

Those are all true statements, and they are all sound doctrine! The Bible exhorts us
to speak sound doctrine, even though in the latter times many people will not
endure sound doctrine.

As individuals, you and I can believe whatever we want; it's arguably true that
we're all entitled to have our own personal opinions on some things. There are
indeed what the Bible itself calls disputable matters, and I will argue for your
liberty in most cases, every time. It's a demonic ruler, or power… it's a very
powerful principality, just like Ephesians 6:12 teaches.

Guy Malone, www.RoswellMission.org, https://youtu.be/LrbCWYWHxqs

11)   From Simon Watts

What are the most common concerns, irritations, frustrations and topics "aliens" address with abductees?

JGJ) Simon Watts, I think Guy Malone best answered that above. Thank you for your question.

12)   From Kate Akers Beeman

In all your years, have you encountered many spiritual deliverance ministries/ministers who have been there as a support for people working through their stories? I myself have gone through sessions for prayer sessions in various occasions - some totally off base and ineffective, and some very God sent, true freedom occurred - so it has been a journey. But in my experience, these ministries are very few and far between. I am interested in hearing if you have come across effective folks who do deliverance prayer over the years - and if so, do you feel there is a need for more called to deliverance ministry to step out into this community affected by those who have gone through these experiences?

JGJ) Good question, Kate Akers Beeman. I have encountered many of these spiritual deliverance ministries/ministers who have been there as a support for people working through their stories. But only a few able to make a change.

If an experiencer is totally relying on an outside deliverance source like these ministries you speak of, they will continue to have issues. Deliverance comes through a true personal relationship with Jesus Christ. If the experiencer does not change, repent, close the open door, and stop dabbling, then these entities will come back.

Chapter 12

13)   From Lisa Sumner

Aliens or demons. Explaining this would be good.

JGJ) I think once you see it all put together here in this book, Lisa
Summer, you will be able to make that call yourself. But for me, I'm leaning
toward a "spiritual" experience perpetrated by deceptive demonic entities. I will
also share with you a good friend and peer's view on this. This is from Ian Juby.

> "Ian joined Mensa in 1994, and was interested in joining a Special
> Interest Group (SIG). Much to his surprise, he found out there were
> actually very few SIG's in Canada - and certainly not one on Creation
> Science. When he first tossed the idea of a Creation Science SIG around
> amongst other creationists, a group of interested Mensans congealed
> almost immediately (the original "fab five" as he fondly refers to them).
> Only one other member was Canadian - and he was leaving the country!
> So Ian pursued international status for the SIG to accommodate these
> members, and was granted recognition as an International Mensa SIG in
> 2004. Today, the SIG has members in Canada, England, the United
> States and South Africa.
>
> Ian Juby is a young earth creationist who hails from Ontario, Canada.
> Juby is the director of the Creation Science Museum of Canada, as well as
> a member of Mensa — Juby is known for using his "high IQ" as an
> argument from authority when promoting creation science under his
> YouTube alias Wazooloo."
> https://ianjuby.org/

Aliens and Evolution
By Ian Juby

You might wonder how on earth a young earth creationist wound up on this topic. I come from a background with a strong interest in anything science and tech (and teaching it since I was 16 years old) and Christian matters (as my Christian faith literally saved my life). I wound up in itinerant ministry for ten years speaking on the creation/evolution controversy. I toured all over North America with my traveling creation science museum with fossils and dinosaurs in the back of my van and eventually, even a bed back there. The bed only had about 18 inches of clearance to the roof of the van, but considering I spent the first two years on the road sleeping across the front seats, that bed was a huge blessing.

I lectured on the topic to all ages and after every session I would have some time allotted for questions and answers. Q&A was always a favorite time for everybody and invariably I would wind up with questions about science and tech that had nothing to do with creation or evolution, nor the topic I had just spoken on. Not that I minded, because I loved science and tech anyway and usually had some knowledge on the question posed.

For the first 6 years or so, the single most common question I would get during Q&A sessions had nothing to do with creation or evolution. It always pertained to questions about global warming. Being Canadian and wishing for that global warming, I had my answer practiced down pat, as you could almost guarantee I would get a question about global warming during every Q&A.

It was also interesting yet strange the insight that Q&A sessions gave me into the current cultural questions. Over the years I watched the most common question change and as a result, I had my finger on the pulse of North American culture and particularly Christian culture as I was mostly speaking in Christian settings. I stopped speaking tours in 2012 and switched gears to producing my weekly television show, Genesis Week. But Genesis Week was a show focused on current events and I took questions from the viewers and addressed them on the air. So even though I switched gears, I still had a finger on the pulse of the North American culture through the most common questions of the day. In fact, the culture spectrum broadened as the TV show brought in a lot more comments and questions from the non-Christian and even anti-Christian cultures.

For the first six years I was in Creation ministry, the most common question related to global warming. Interestingly, it was perhaps about five or six years ago at the time of this writing that I watched the most common question change once again to the flat earth topic. I was on a live call in show in Alberta four years ago and during the preparation discussion with the show host, I predicted (correctly) what questions we would get from callers and specifically told him "You mark my words, someone will ask about the flat earth theory." Sure enough!

But it was back around 2006 or 2007 during my speaking tours that my Q&A sessions took a very unexpected and rather dark turn. Virtually overnight the most common question changed from "What about global warming?" to questions about aliens: "Is there alien life on other planets?" "What does the Bible say about aliens?" "Have aliens visited earth?"

The questions almost never directly referenced UFO's, although UFO's were kind of presumed to be part of the questions as most people did not differentiate between UFO's and alien encounters.

While these questions about aliens came primarily from teens, I even had children as young as eight asking these questions.

Of course I had my own thoughts and opinions on it at the time, but I was admittedly pretty ignorant on the topic. The question came up so frequently that I felt I had to study it further. This was especially triggered at one teen Bible camp I was speaking at one summer. In the space of about two days, I had around eight different teens come up to me privately and ask my thoughts and scientific opinion about aliens. About three of those teens were in the space of a half an hour on the second day. Some of the questions showed genuine concern, not just curiosity.

I got down to prayer that afternoon, praying and asking my good Lord Jesus to teach me. Give me wisdom and insight into this topic so I may know what to say.

To this day, I'm still a little shocked at the information overload I received on the topic within the next 24 hours. Especially considering I was in a remote place with extremely limited internet access, and essentially no access to a library or books on the topic. Let's just say the Lord answered my prayers! I learned so much in that short space of time that there was even quite a bit of that information for which I can now no longer provide the source, because I have since lost the source of the information and never found it again!

This was the start of this journey of learning which was simultaneously fascinating to me, but also had many dark and disturbing turns. CORE Ottawa (Citizens for Origins Research and Education, a charity focused on creation science based out of Ottawa, Ontario, Canada) had taken myself and the Genesis Week show under their wing. CORE's secretary, Rev. George Desjardins, had previously mentioned aliens in passing conversation. Because of these past conversations, I first called him and he basically just made a blanket statement that aliens were demons and that people encountering them should invoke the name of Christ to get rid of them.

Fair enough, but this was far from answering the questions that were in my mind. I continued to call around and try to research what I could on an incredibly bad internet connection.

I do not even recall how I stumbled upon the next piece of information, although to be fair there was so much information that came to me in less than 24 hours that it truly was like drinking from the fire hose. But I do recall that the next revelation came in the form of statistics that suddenly answered why the question of aliens had become so prevalent. I can't even give you the source because I do not know where it was I first stumbled upon these statistics. I had either found or was given some brief statistics for which I could neither verify nor refute the authenticity or accuracy at that time. The statistics were that some 1 in 15 people surveyed believed that they had seen a UFO. 1 in 40(!!!) believed they had had an encounter of some kind with an alien, and that encounter was usually the "alien abduction" phenomenon.

So considering the teen group at the Bible camp that week numbered around 100, statistically speaking there was probably 2 or 3 of those teens that had been abducted by aliens. The alien abduction experience is traumatic and confusing, and thus it's understandable that the abductees would have nagging questions.

At that time in my life it was fairly common to find myself speaking to crowds of three or four hundred, and usually two to three times per week when I was on speaking tours. So just statistically speaking, every week I was unknowingly interacting with probably 25 or so people who believed they had been abducted by aliens. It suddenly becomes no wonder why questions about aliens came up so often.

After encountering these statistics (which I have since found they hold true) and crunching some statistical numbers in my head, I started calling friends of mine across North America in hopes they might give me more insight and wisdom. I was floored when multiple friends, many of whom I'd known for years, confided in me that they had been "abducted by aliens" at one point or another. I was blown away to say the least. Just my small sample group was showing that if anything, the statistics I had received were too conservative. Those friends were all Christians now and were able to relate their personal stories of how, after becoming Christians, these "aliens" eventually left them alone, although sometimes only after directly confronting the "aliens" and invoking the name of Jesus Christ.

But these friends also unanimously shared one other statistic that quickly became apparent: 100% of those who had had encounters with alleged "aliens" had been involved in the occult in some way: either they themselves or their immediate family (mother or father). Now, some 15 years of research later, I have found that particular statistic still holds true. I have yet to find an exception. Furthermore, for people who were 'raised in Christian churches,' the numbers of alien abduction encounters appears to drop to zero. There probably is some person out there who was raised in a Christian church but was "abducted by aliens," I just haven't met or interviewed them. Regardless, just based on this anecdotal evidence alone, I think it safe to say that the alien abduction statistics drop significantly within the Christian community.

Because my interest has always been scientific and specifically approaching this topic from the perspective of our origins, I started dealing with the "aliens" question from the creation / evolution / science & the Bible approach. When Joseph asked me to contribute to this book, I felt I should stick to this area as it is my area of expertise. I have never experienced the "alien abduction" phenomenon, though I have interviewed many people who have, and who escaped that horrible, traumatizing experience. I have even helped a few people escape it. But Joseph and the others contributing to this book bring far more experience and knowledge to the table with regards to dealing with what I think you will discover is a spiritual phenomenon. While I had had encounters with fallen angels previously, they had never attempted to present themselves as aliens. I knew who they were, and they knew that I knew. These beings did not try to hide their true identity. But our modern culture has made us ripe to receive "aliens," and these notoriously deceitful beings know this and play into it.

Our society has not only been prepared to embrace "aliens," but has actively looked for them. The prolific references to aliens in pop culture have made belief in aliens quite common and normal. And I admit, sci-fi would be pretty boring if it weren't for aliens. But step back and think about it: how many references to aliens have you heard this week? Probably more than you realize, primarily because of pop culture. How many book or movie titles do you recognize in this list?

War of the Worlds, Star Wars, Star Trek, Spaceballs, Contact, 2001 A Space Odyssey, 2001: A Space Travesty, The 5th Element, Abbott and Costello Go To Mars, The Hitchhiker's Guide to the Galaxy, Alien, Aliens, Predator, Mars Attacks, Lost In Space, Superman, Ender's Game, Men In Black, Thor, any of the Avenger's movies, Close Encounters of the Third Kind, The Last Starfighter…. I could go on for a very, very long time.

Even music with Styx's hit song "Come sail away" references aliens, but ironically (profoundly?) first refers to them as angels.

But remember the children asking about aliens as well? Hey the kids aren't left out either! How many of these movies do you recognize? E.T., Aliens in the Attic, Monsters Vs. Aliens, Muppets in Space, The Cat From Outer Space, Planet 51, Mac and Me, even the Dr. Who television series.

While aliens in fiction have been around since the turn of the last century, it has only really taken hold since the advent and acceptance of Evolutionary theory. In fact, the theory of Evolution is the foundation for all things E.T. How? Because once you accept the idea that life arose by natural processes, then it only naturally follows that life could have arisen elsewhere in the Universe. After all, if it happened here, then surely it happened "out there" as well!

In fact, this has become a truism in pop culture, sci-fi and popular science. It has inspired major scientific research projects like SETI (Search for Extra-Terrestrial Intelligence) and SETI@home. Pretty much all of sci-fi and pop culture alien references have the subtle assumption of evolution. I can only think of two exceptions: both were books written by a creationist. This includes Johannes Kepler's science fiction Somnium in which the character Duracotus is transported to the moon by non-human inhabitants. Of course I'm being very open to include Somnium in my short-short list because if you actually read the book Kepler even calls the non-human inhabitants "demons." The point being, the acceptance of the idea of aliens is actually rooted in the Evolutionary paradigm.

In the book of Genesis, it tells us "And God said, Let there be lights in the firmament of the heaven to divide the day from the night; and let them be for signs, and for seasons, and for days, and years:

> And let them be for lights in the firmament of the heaven to give light upon the earth: and it was so." (Genesis 1:14,15 King James Version)

The stars in the heavens were created for the inhabitants of earth. To be for signs, seasons, days and years. The stars weren't created to be home to Zoltar the space alien. When Christ the Savior came, he came to Earth, not planet Eurocolypse. He died and rose again to save the human race from its sins. In fact, He didn't even die for the sins of the animals on Earth.

Nowhere in the Bible can you find a hint of extraterrestrials of any kind – save for the inhabitants of the Kingdom of Heaven, and those inhabitants who were cast out of heaven, down on to earth. And all of those beings would technically be outside of the natural realm – extra-natural, not extra-terrestrial. The inhabitants who were cast out of heaven were the fallen angels who followed Lucifer in his rebellion and attempt to overthrow God Himself. Hell was not created for people, rather it was created as punishment for Lucifer (now renamed Satan). This was made clear by Jesus Himself when he spoke of judgment day and what would be said to those who were not redeemed:

> "Depart from Me, ye cursed, into everlasting fire prepared for the devil and his angels." (Matthew 25:41)

And Satan is certainly not some guy in charge of punishing those in the lake of fire. No, the punishment was fashioned specifically for him.

My point though is that the concept of intelligent aliens on other planets comes from the Evolutionary paradigm, and not the Biblical account of Creation. The Biblical Creation account most certainly does speak of non-human intelligent life, but it's not extra-terrestrial aliens, but rather extra-natural beings.

One of the great ironies of this whole controversy about our origins and intelligent alien life is that the SETI project uses the scientific tool of intelligent design to identify intelligent design in signals from outer space, while denying that the scientific tool of intelligent design could be used to deduce that the SETI scientist's brains were intelligently designed by a being of mind-boggling intelligence (pun intended).

Nevertheless, from a scientific perspective it's important to ask questions like "Could life arise by natural processes, without any outside, intelligent intervention?"

Spoiler alert: Not. A. Chance.

There are very few laws of science and nature. A scientific law only becomes a law because the observations have been consistent, repeated numerous times, never failing and with no contradictions. There are two scientific and natural laws which specifically address this idea that life could arise from natural processes: The law of biogenesis, and the laws of thermodynamics (specifically the second law of thermodynamics).

The law of biogenesis came out of research conducted by Louis Pasteur in 1864. It was his experiments that led to the Pasteurization process we know of today. Basically, the law of biogenesis is that Life only comes from life, and that like begets like. We have never seen an exception to this scientific and natural law. So any process that produces life from non-life is neither natural, nor scientific because it defies this well established, scientific and natural law. Such a process would be, by very definition, an extra natural / supernatural process! A miracle.

So congratulations, whether you believe we were created or you believe we evolved, you believe in the supernatural. This should make the uncomfortable discussions of supernatural entities undertaken in this book much easier for you.

There are very good reasons why life only comes from life. The only way life can arise from a rock sitting in a pond is imagination. Let me give you a quick example of why that is, pointed out to me by my good friend, Stan Lutz, many moons ago.

The cells in your body and brain are composed of, and even controlled by, proteins, the basic building blocks of life. Some proteins act as building blocks, others as enzymes, still others act as hormones. These proteins are built up from smaller components called amino acids. There's about 20 different amino acids to choose from and you can think of them like Lego™. You have 20 different Lego pieces to build with, and what you use and how you assemble them radically changes the design and shape of the final construction. In fact, if you get one wrong piece or even the right piece put in in the wrong way, you may not be able to complete your construction. It's the same way with proteins.

If you put two amino acids together and you have 20 amino acids to choose from, how many different combinations can you make?

20 x 20 = 400 different combinations. It's calculated as 20^2 – 20 options, and 2 in a sequence. If you add a third amino acid to the construction, and it too can be any one of the 20 amino acids available, then you can have 20^3(written out that's 20 x 20 x 20) = 8,000 different combinations to choose from. Add another amino acid to the construction and you have 20^4 = 160,000 different combinations. And by the way, during this construction you have to get the correct combination all the way along. You have to add the correct piece out of a choice of 20 pieces, add it in to the construction in the right sequence, over and over again. Or else, like our Lego construction, you will be unable to successfully build the construction.

You can quickly start to see where Sir Francis Crick, co-discoverer of the DNA double helix, gets his numbers in his book Life Itself. (1) He used a smaller protein of only 200 amino acids long as an example. The number of combinations is simply written as 20^{200}. This equates to approximately 10^{260} different combinations. Written out, that's
100,000,000,000,000,000,000,000,000,000,000,000,000,000,000,000,000,0
00,000,000,000,000,000,000,000,000,000,000,000,000,000,000,000,000,00
0,000,000,000,000,000,000,000,000,000,000,000,000,000,000,000,000,000
,000,000,000,000,000,000,000,000,000,000,000,000,000,000,000,000,000,
000,000,000,000,000,000,000,000,000,000,000,000,000 different
combinations of amino acids you can achieve.

Effectively, only one of those combinations is the correct one.

To help you grasp the sheer astronomical size of that number, it has been estimated that the total number of atoms in the entire Universe is around 10^{80}! (Yes, someone with apparently too much time on their hands actually sat down and figured that out.)

The universe is claimed by the naturalists to be around 13.8 billion years old – give or take a week or two. I don't believe that number, but let's go with it. 13.8

Billion years x 365 days X 24 hours x 60 minutes x 60 seconds means the universe is 435,196,800,000,000,000 seconds old.

So you have 435,196,800,000,000,000 seconds in which to try out all 10^{260} different combinations. So dividing 10^{260} different combinations by 435,196,800,000,000,000 seconds means you have to mix and match

2,297,811,013,316,274,384,370,473,312,303,800,000,000,000,000,000,000,000
,000,000,000,000,000,000,000,000,000,000,000,000,000,000,000,000,000,000,
000,000,000,000,000,000,000,000,000,000,000,000,000,000,000,000,000,000,0
00,000,000,000,000,000,000,000,000,000,000,000,000,000,000,000,000,000,00
0,000,000,000,000,000,000,000,000,000,000,000,000,000,000,000,000,000,000
different combinations of amino acids every second, for 13.8 billion years to be guaranteed you'll arrive at the single correct combination of amino acids to construct one protein.

And that was a short protein.

Do you know how many proteins you ate for breakfast this morning?

Your body produces at least tens of millions of proteins every day, so you can like, keep on being alive and stuff.

This isn't a simple formula of odds or chance. What I've shown here is what would be required of a process unguided by intelligence to produce one relatively short protein. This is not at all like the seemingly impossible odds of a major lottery. The odds of winning the lottery can be exceedingly small. But someone, somewhere will win in spite of the exceedingly small odds.

Our protein-formed-by-chance doesn't even have a chance. The odds are not exceedingly small, they are literally zero. You cannot win this lottery for the simple reason that the lottery cannot be set up with a draw and a prize. It's physically impossible. There are literally not enough atoms in the universe to make the lottery – the "natural" process by with which to try the astronomical numbers of combinations you need to try for the chance forming of the correct combination. And then you'd need to repeat that process at least dozens of times more just to make enough proteins to make some basic components of a single cell. And even then, you still do not have "life."

It is a literal, physical impossibility for life to arise from unguided processes. It has to have been assembled by a higher intelligence. So to make claims like "Hey, life evolved here, surely it evolved somewhere else!" is not only a non-sequitur, it's a nonsensical statement. The impossibility I just described is for the formation of one protein in our entire known universe. So the "odds" against alien life are now infinite x 2 because you will need to accomplish the impossible not just once, but twice within the same universe.

No, life could not evolve from non-life here and so therefore could not have evolved elsewhere. That is a major, scientific reason why we can confidently deduce there is no intelligent, alien life on other planets.

I know, boring.

The conflicting origin accounts of evolution or creation really do exhaust all other possibilities. The Raëlians are a religious group out of France, founded by its leader, Claude Vorilhon now known as Raël. Raël claims that there is a third option for the origins debate:

"In "Message from the Designers", Rael presents us with the vast amount of information that he received during his UFO encounters in 1973 - a third option: all life on earth having been created by advanced scientists from another world."(2)

I disagree. They have not presented a third option, they have dodged the origins question. They have simply sent the origins question to a far away, distant planet and we are still left asking the question "Ummm… did these alien scientists evolve? Or were they created?"

The Raëlians believe these alien scientists to be natural beings when I've already demonstrated the first life had to have been supernatural.

Ironically, though creationists acknowledge the supernatural origin of the first life, the creation model still follows the law of biogenesis: we still claim the first life on earth came from pre-existing life. We just have that pre-existing life, our Creator, as being from outside of the natural realm. In fact, He created that natural realm and the laws of nature imposed upon it. You know, those laws which dictate that life cannot arise from non-life? This is precisely why you do not see a rock giving rise to living cells.

So then if it's scientifically impossible for there to be alien life on other planets, then what on earth is going on with all these alleged alien encounters? Think about those statistics for a second: 1 in 40 people have had a horrible experience of being abducted by these "aliens," and when you hear the testimonies, you'll notice it's never a pleasant experience. Think of 40 different people you know. At least one of them has been abducted by an alien. Those are staggering numbers. Think about how many people are in your little town, or big city. Now start dividing that number up statistically. That's an incredibly high number of encounters with alleged "aliens." If you'll please pardon a second pun, what on earth is going on there?

These descriptions of these "aliens" are also very consistent and these "aliens" seem to have a penchant for expressing their religious views and are very anti-Christ. Their message is quite consistent:

Alien: The end of the world is nigh. We want to help you help yourself. We want to help you bring world peace by establishing a one-world government. You should explore the occult. Christ and Christians must be removed from earth before we can help you to help yourself.

Me: Wait, what? You just traveled fifteen bazillion light years to torture me and say you want to help me? You came all this way to preach your religious views and discuss spirituality with me? And what's your beef with this Jesus guy anyway? Did He come visit you on your distant planet? Here, show me on this doll where He hurt you.

Look at the influence on major occults that have arisen out of conversations with these "aliens." I already mentioned the Raelians, just have a look at their writings. It's all there. The Heaven's Gate website is still maintained, decades after the group's mass-suicide, so you can go and read for yourself *why* they did this.(3) It was because of their communication with beings claiming to be aliens coming with a spaceship in time with comet Hale-Bopp. These beings convinced these people that leaving earth for the "Kingdom of Heaven" was the next step in their *evolution.*

Can you start to see a theme here?

If we were created by a supernatural, hyper-intelligent being, then we should ask the question "Who is that Creator?" It's important. There's only one person ever to visit planet earth who claimed He was the Creator incarnate. Who demonstrated his supernatural abilities in front of countless witnesses, including multitudes of hostile witnesses. He demonstrated his ability to go between dimensions, even walking through solid walls into a room, startling those who were gathered there (John 20:19). He was the only one to say "...I am the way, the truth, and the life..." (John 14:6) and then demonstrated his authority to that claim by defying scientific and natural law and doing what the combined sum of all of our best minds on planet earth cannot do: He rose from the dead.

If Jesus Christ is our Creator (and I would contend He is), then the things He said become of paramount importance. He described angels both in heaven, and those cast out of heaven, to earth. (Luke 10:18) We know from the things Jesus said and also the testimonies of multitudes that these angels are extra-natural beings who can take on different forms in our natural world. If the "aliens" visiting planet earth are simply fallen angels, then suddenly everything makes sense. Their distinct hate-on for Christ would make sense, as He is the one they rebelled against and tried to overthrow, only to find themselves hurled out of the Kingdom of Heaven down to earth. They can't hurt Christ directly, so they instead hurt those whom He loves: the human race. They still want a kingdom for some strange reason, and so they deceive people and try to start their own kingdom here on earth. Hence their strong interest in a one-world government which, interestingly, the Bible discusses at great length in the final book of Revelations. That book tells us this one-world government will happen, headed by the "anti-Christ." If Jesus is the Creator, and these alleged aliens are simply created, fallen angels, then He has power over them. This explains why the "aliens" respond to the name of Jesus Christ when people who have repeatedly been attacked ("abducted") call upon Him to save them.

It's simple, really. These "aliens" are not extra-terrestrials, but rather extra-naturals who have the ability to transit between our natural world, and the extra-natural world we are in but cannot see with our natural eyes. But we have an advocate who really does love you and I, and can also transit between our natural world and the extra-natural world. As you will hopefully see in this book, Jesus can defend you.

---

1) Francis Crick, Life Itself – Its Origin And Nature, 1982, Publisher Simon & Schuster, pages 51-52
"If a particular amino acid sequence was selected by chance, how rare an event would this be? This is an easy exercise in combinatorials. Suppose the chain is about two hundred amino acids long; this is, if anything rather less than the average length of proteins of all types. Since we have just twenty possibilities at each place, the number of possibilities is twenty multiplied by itself some two hundred times. This is conveniently written 20^{200} and is approximately equal to 10^{260}, that is, a one followed by 260 zeros. Moreover, we have only considered a polypeptide chain of rather modest length. Had we considered longer ones as well, the figure would have been even more immense. The great majority of sequences can never have been synthesized at all, at any time."

2) From the website preview page of Rael's book "Intelligent Design – Message from the Designers" Caution-https://www.rael.org/download.php?view.1

3) http://www.heavensgate.com/ From Heaven's Gate website: "The joy is that our Older Member in the Evolutionary Level Above Human (the "Kingdom of Heaven") has made it clear to us that Hale-Bopp's approach is the "marker" we've been waiting for — the time for the arrival of the spacecraft from the Level Above Human to take us home to "Their World" in the literal Heavens."

Chapter 13

14)   From Tony Breeden

Is the name of Jesus the ONLY way to stop an "alien abduction"?

JGJ) Tony Breedon, a $1000.00 question for sure. Simply answered, no. Secular researchers will tell you that there are many reported ways to stop an alien abduction experience. I agree. But does it terminate the experience entirely from their lives? That is the question.

The only way I have ever seen it terminate completely from a person's life, for a real spiritual experience from deceptive entities, or the opening up to the UFO paranormal realm, is through a personal relationship with Jesus Christ, and through the name and authority of Jesus Christ. No other method leaves a person with Love, Joy, Peace, Longsuffering, Kindness, Goodness, Faithfulness, Gentleness, and Self-Control, all the fruits of the Holy Spirit indwelling in a Christian walking with Jesus.

15)   From Damion Jones

How can I contact you Joe by email or phone?

JGJ) Damion, My web page is www.ce4research.com. I can be reached at ce4president@yahoo.com. You can also reach me through my Facebook page at https://www.facebook.com/CE4Research/. If anyone would like to talk by phone, just send me a request by email and we'll work out a time.

16)   From Frank Johnson

Just how common are abduction experiences in the general population?

JGJ) Good question, Frank, and one that definitely needs to be included. I'll use this article below to answer that for you:

"The "abduction experience" is characterized by subjectively real memories of being taken secretly and/or against one's will by apparently nonhuman entities and subjected to complex physical and psychological procedures. The number of such experiences has been estimated by Jacobs (1992) as 5-6% of the population, and by Hopkins, Jacobs, and Westrum (1992) as 2% of the population. More conservative estimates may be derived by counting the actual number of cases that have been reported by investigators. For example, Bullard's (1994) survey of 13 investigators yielded 1,700 cases. Whatever the number, few aspects of ufology have attracted as much attention."

https://nexusnewsfeed.com/article/consciousness/the-abduction-experience-a-critical-evaluation-of-the-theory-and-evidence

17)   From Rose Richardson

Have you seen people who have confused medical conditions with abduction symptoms? For example, I was on a medication for a time that caused some sleep disturbance, bad dreams, and buzzing in my ear. I even prayed in Jesus' name during the experience and it didn't help so I really felt bad until I put it together and asked the pharmacist!

This leads into my other question: are their reports of prayer in Jesus' name not seeming to work? To me that points to something else of course and could lead to the confusion that I felt until I put it together. Thanks for your research!

JGJ) A most important question Rose Richardson. Being that there are so many varied reasons for people thinking they have had the Alien Abduction experience, the method they choose to stop it (as calling on the name and authority of Jesus Christ) might not be suitable for the actual cause behind it. You gave a great example yourself, prescription medication side effects. It could be because of a mental disorder like frontal lobe epilepsy. Or it could be just a false memory in the first place. But, as a believer in Jesus Christ, prayer may give you the answer you need get to a real cure, or method to stop it. Not all recalled alien abduction experiences are a deceptive spiritual experience by demonic entities. That should be the last option looked at after all other simpler explanations are exhausted. If you don't work in that order, you will end up with discouraged and disgruntled experiencers left in worse shape than when you met them.

18)   From Eric Wheeler

Since there is so much talk about saviors from or going into the heavens, has this fueled more sightings?

Also how would we explain certain knowledge-based presumptions the past peoples have had that modern day society has just now discovered to be true.

JGJ) Good questions, Eric Wheeler. Not only has it fueled more sightings, it's even bred new religions out of it. Here is an article from my friend and research peer Gary Bates on that subject.

UFOlogy: the world's fastest-growing 'scientific' religion?
By Gary Bates and Lita Cosner
Published: 12 May 2011

Many people wonder why we write about the UFO phenomenon. Isn't it just a 'side issue'? But in fact, it's so important to oppose this particular belief, because ET belief is quickly becoming the world's most scientifically acceptable false religion and a major stumbling block to Christianity. And although some of its adherents are serious followers, the reality is, that polls show that belief in UFOs is mainstream and held by the average 'Joe' in the street. For example, a CNN/Time Magazine poll in 1997, found, among other things that;

- 80% believe that the government is hiding the existence of extraterrestrial life forms
- 64% believe aliens have contacted humans
- 50% believe that aliens have abducted humans
- 93% have never been abducted
- 75% believe that a UFO crashed near Roswell

So, in one sense, the majority of the population believes that UFOs are real physical craft piloted by beings from other planets. Does that make them adherents in the religious sense? The purpose of this article is to sound a clarion call that such beliefs make people vulnerable to further and possibly deeper deception. This is why it is important to place all of our thinking on the Bible, and not be misled into thinking that because the universe is so big, that there must be extraterrestrial life on other planets. Our view that God did not create life on other planets has even made us relatively unpopular among Christian friends. However, as this issue affects the veracity of God's Word, and is indeed, a salvation issue, we have been careful; drawing a strong, exegetical, and historical picture from the Bible. Many are worried that real ET visitations might falsify the Bible if we are wrong. While such motives might be sincere, we should not be concerned that the Bible should be falsified as to its truth claims—particularly if we are claiming it is the very Word of God.

Unlike Buddhism, Islam, etc., extraterrestrial belief has a veneer of scientific credibility. Arguably, the world's most famous scientist, physicist Stephen Hawking, has even stated that he believes aliens probably exist. And the world's most famous atheistic evolutionist, Richard Dawkins, as anti-theistic as he is, has no problem with aliens' theoretically seeding life on earth, provided that somewhere down the chain of creators, there's a life form that arose via evolution. Antichristian scientist, and co-discoverer of the DNA molecule, Sir Francis Crick, similarly proposed that life came via panspermia (life seeded by aliens) as a possible explanation for the mind-boggling complexity of the coded information on DNA. As atheists, mainly due to their evolutionist beliefs, they claim there is no evidence for God. However, they have no problem resorting to 'unseen' aliens as our creators. Design, apparently is not the problem. It's God being the designer that they have a problem with.

When people see an Unidentified Flying Object in the skies or come into contact with beings who claim to be from 'a galaxy far, far away', it has added credibility in the minds of the experiencers because so many scientists believe in alien life.

When people see an Unidentified Flying Object in the skies or come into contact with beings who claim to be from 'a galaxy far, far away', it has added credibility in the minds of the experiencers because so many scientists believe in alien life. In addition, science fiction, which is massively influential, creates futuristic worlds where highly technologically advanced aliens can overcome the laws of physics to visit the earth from star systems billions of light years away perhaps. As such, the majority of people, including most Christians tend to gravitate towards the idea that they have just seen or experienced something otherworldly.

Seemingly more credibility was added when NASA launched an 'Astrobiology' program, dedicated to studying "the origin, evolution, distribution and destiny of life—wherever it might exist", it gives added traction to the idea that there actually is life out there. Why would SETI (The Search for Extraterrestrial Intelligence Institute) be scanning the skies, using many millions of radio frequencies every second, for broadcasts from intelligent beings if they didn't believe they actually exist? New Scientist (NS) recently reported that Seth Shostak (Director of SETI) was confident that within 24 years we would detect an alien civilization. He said,

> "There are maybe 1021 Earth-like planets out there ... Believing there aren't ETs is believing in miracles."(1)

NS said "He bet the audience that we'd find ET within our lifetime or else he'd buy us a cup of Starbucks."

As we wrote in "Prepare Ye the Way—the aliens are coming", the ET religion is not only a subset of the origins issue, it provides a complete replacement theology for Christianity. The Raelians are only one example of a cult that has evolutionism and UFOlogy at its core. They believe that the Elohim were our extraterrestrial creators, but don't know where they came from. Were they likewise created, or did

they evolve from mindless matter? And if they were created, who created their creators, and their creators' creators? Although they think they have solved the origin of life issue—even advocating intelligent design—each creator race only moves the question back one step, to a different planet and no ultimate answer.

Part of 'salvation' in the ET religion often involves evolving to the level of our ET benefactors. Its origins are found in the satanic 'you will be like God' deception that emanates from the Garden of Eden. If the ET deception has the same source, we shouldn't be surprised at the parallels.

Doctrine of UFOlogical religion

There is also a soteriological (doctrine of salvation) aspect to UFO religion. Our 'space brothers' are said to be older and more advanced both ethically and technologically. This is a bizarre claim given the brutal and sordid nature of some alleged abduction encounters. Often, 'New Age' religion is strongly intertwined with UFO beliefs. The ETs are going to save us from global warming, etc, and show us how to live in harmony with our planet. Earth as an organism figures in as well, a theme popularized by the film Avatar.

Part of 'salvation' in the ET religion often involves evolving to the level of our ET benefactors. Its origins are found in the satanic 'you will be like God' deception that emanates from the Garden of Eden. If the ET deception has the same source, we shouldn't be surprised at the parallels.

Sometimes ETs also act as judges. Raelianism claims that there is a panel of judges who will get to decide who gets to be cloned again to eternal life, and who doesn't. This is based on works, like all other false religions such as Islam, Mormonism, etc. But in the absence of an omniscient God, who decides what's good enough? And what authority do mere men have to decide whether someone is good enough—are they themselves 'good enough' and by whose standard? This problem is common with the redemption aspect of most false religions.

There is also an eschatological aspect. In some beliefs, the ETs will come and take away all the people who refuse to let 'Mother Earth' evolve, either destroying them or taking them to someplace else. For instance, New Age, ET channeller, Barbara Marciniak writes in her book <u>Bringers of the Dawn: Teachings from the Pleiadians</u>:

"The people who leave the planet during the time of Earth changes do not fit in here any longer, and they are stopping the harmony of Earth. When the time comes that perhaps 20 million people leave the planet at one time there will be a tremendous shift in consciousness for those who are remaining."(2)

This is a not-so-subtle take on the Christian pre-millennial view, in which Christians are raptured, that is, taken away by Christ, before the time known as the Great Tribulation. There are also views that ET believers will be taken away by spaceships to a planet called Heaven, which in some iterations even features a golden city much like the New Jerusalem. Channeller Thelma Terrell, who also goes by the 'spiritual' name 'Tuella', writes:

"Our rescue ships will be able to come in close enough in the twinkling of an eye to set the lifting beams in operation in a moment. And over the globe where events warrant it, this will be the method of evacuation. Mankind will be lifted ... by the beams from our smaller ships. ...

" ... Earth changes will be the primary factor in mass evacuation of the planet. There is method and great organization in a detailed plan already near completion for the purpose of removing souls from this planet, in the event of catastrophic events making a rescue necessary ... . The Great Evacuation will come upon the world very suddenly. The flash of emergency events will be as a lightning that flashes in the sky. So suddenly and quick in its happening that it is over almost before you are aware of its presence ..."

This is strikingly similar to 1 Corinthians 15:51-52. However, we should not be surprised. The enemy has always been a counterfeiter and we are warned that he masquerades as an angel of light (2 Corinthians 11:14). In others, the aliens will herald in the apocalypse. Some types of ET belief have alien/human hybrids as an integral part of end-times scenarios.

Farrakhan's Nation of Islam's link to UFOs

In <u>Alien Intrusion: UFOs and the Evolution Connection</u> (p. 298) we revealed that
the founder of the 'million man march' and current leader of the Nation of Islam
(NOL) was a former UFO contactee. As a young man, Louis Farrakhan, claims he
was taken aboard a UFO where he met Master Elijah Muhammed (the former
leader, then deceased). This was kept under wraps for years, probably due to
credibility problems that such claims would have, but apparently not any more.
Farrakhan and his followers apparently believe that Armageddon is coming and
that the spaceships will return again someday. On reporting about a recent
convention in Chicago where over 10,000 followers gathered, Fox News reported
that belief in UFOs is:

> " … one of the group's more misunderstood–and ridiculed–beliefs,
> something organizers took into account when planning the convention
> …. 'There's enough evidence that has been put before the world and
> public,' Ishmael Muhammad, the religion's national assistant minister,
> told The Associated Press. 'There have been enough accounts and
> sightings and enough movies (documentaries) made, I don't think you
> would find too many people that would call it crazy.'"(3)

Indeed, by embracing popular belief and incorporating it into their religion, NOL
might increasingly be more attractive to many trying to fit UFOs and aliens into
their religious worldview.

Sacraments and 'holy places'

Some people get so involved in the ET phenomenon that they actually start
'channeling' supposed 'space brothers'. Sometimes they claim that the aliens
actually communicate through them. But how can a physical being be channeled?
Some alien beings claim to have evolved beyond matter, to a spiritual existence. It
seeks to provide an atheistic, evolutionary mechanism to justify that the aliens are,
in fact, really spiritual beings, who can replace the ultimate spiritual being of man's
construction—God!

'True believers' point to crop circles as a major physical evidence of alien
visitations. They claim that the designs are too complex to be man-made. Groups

like Circlemakers amply disprove the claim that crop circles have to be created by beings with advanced technology (in fact, traditionally crop circles are easily made with planks and ropes). But this does not mean that even indisputably man-made circles aren't relevant to the UFO phenomenon. People involved in the construction of crop circles often report strange phenomena surrounding these sites:

> *"Our crop formations are intended to function as temporary sacred sites in this landscape.* While constructing crop formations in the fields we have experienced a series of aerial anomalies including: small balls of light, columns of light, and blinding flashes. All apparently targeting us and our crop formations. We are unsurprised at the numerous visitors who have reported a diverse assortment of anomalies associated with our artworks. These have included physiological effects, such as headache and nausea. Healing effects such as one report of a cure for acute osteoporosis. Physical effects such as camera and other electronic equipment failure. *We are certain that our artworks are subject of paranormal forces and act to catalyze other paranormal events."* (4) (emphasis added)

Demonologists expect that when people dabble with the occult, even as a joke or a prank, evil spirits will usually jump at the opportunity to deceive and gain control over people. But Circlemakers may not be entirely innocent in this regard, as our book <u>Alien Intrusion: UFOs and the Evolution Connection</u> documents:

> "A little-known fact about Circlemakers is that before they entered the lucrative commercial market, they called themselves Team Satan. This is a very bold name and might be suggestive of their intent. ... Indeed satanic worship continues to be quite prolific in the world today, and many are drawn into it by its allure and mysticism. Have crop circles become modern shrines of occult worship? Most certainly, Team Satan is not ashamed to publicly draw attention to the 'supernatural side' of its work and, perhaps deliberately, draw more folk into the dark world of the occult using the curiosity factor." (p. 218)

What does the Bible say?

The Bible doesn't specifically mention aliens or UFOs, and we shouldn't expect it to. The Bible was written for all believers in all cultures, but it was written to specific people in specific cultures, so we should expect the text to conform to those cultures somewhat (though God's word in every case also transcends that culture). Talk about little green men would be incomprehensible and nonsensical to the first-century Jew; it would be completely outside his worldview. But, although the Bible does not speak specifically about aliens, it is not silent about this issue.

God's creation was anthropocentric, in that the goal of creation was to produce mankind in His image; to have eternal fellowship with Him and produce a bride for Christ. This goal was so important that even mankind's sin didn't cause Him to abandon us; instead the Second Person of the Trinity sacrificed Himself for us so that we could be brought back into a right relationship with Him.

First, the Bible is clear that God created. In fact, one of His core attributes is that He is the uncreated Creator. It is the vital difference between Him and the lifeless idols created by human hands (Isaiah 40–44). And His creation was anthropocentric, in that the goal of creation was to produce mankind in His image; to have eternal fellowship with Him and produce a bride for Christ. This goal was so important that even mankind's sin didn't cause Him to abandon us; instead the Second Person of the Trinity sacrificed Himself for us so that we could be brought back into a right relationship with Him.

Second, the Bible states that there are spiritual beings called angels, 1/3 of which rebelled against God. The leader of this rebellion is called Lucifer (literally meaning 'being of light') or Satan ('accuser'). His primary trait is that he is a deceiver, and we can see this in that his first recorded act in Scripture is that he deceived Eve so that she sinned and persuaded Adam to rebel as well. His mission is to spite God, his creator, by taking down as many human beings as He can. Satan hates humans because we are made in the image of the Creator, who he hates, and because God loves us.

These angels can appear in a variety of forms; the ones who are obedient to God always appear as males, but not always like human males (see the angelic descriptions in Ezekiel and Revelation, for example). Many believe that at one point in time fallen angels cohabited with human women, producing the Nephilim. But these angels are confined in a special prison awaiting judgment, so this cannot be repeated (2 Peter 2:4–5).

Signs and wonders

The Bible indicates that the last days will be characterized by an intensifying of supernatural 'signs and wonders' designed to deceive the world (Matthew 12; Mark 13). (Lest anyone think that we're advocating one eschatological view or another, the Bible seems to refer to the time where the Church exists on earth as the 'last days', which has lasted for nearly 2,000 years and counting, so we're using 'last days' in the biblical sense, not the sense of any particular eschatological view.) Revelation is even clearer, saying that the false prophet will do signs and wonders to draw people to the beast, also known as the antichrist (Revelation 19).

The devil is a counterfeiter, so we should not be surprised that just as Jesus' signs and wonders were designed to point people to Him and the truth of His teaching, the false signs and wonders also serve to deceive people into believing lies. When Paul refers to this in 1 Timothy 4, the context makes it clear that he is talking about a certain heresy making the rounds in the Asian churches, which seems to be a form of proto-Gnosticism. But 'doctrines taught by demons' also seems to apply especially well to the teachings, actually a whole alternate theology, taught by the alleged aliens.

A heads up

It is a mistake for Christians to be uninformed or to ignore the alien phenomenon. Belief in aliens is so prevalent that the church will be seen as irrelevant in this area if Christians can't address the 'reality' for the culture on this topic. Its 'scientific' bent has an allure not readily found in other false religions. We regularly dialogue with people who morph Jesus into an advanced extraterrestrial; who's advanced technological prowess gave him the ability to perform seeming miracles and even raise the dead. Such ideas are challenging traditional Christian belief. In most churches he visits, one of the authors [GB] regularly meets individuals who have seen something in the sky that they can't explain, or even had an encounter with a being that claimed to be from another planet. Often they have never spoken to their pastors or others in the church about it for fear of ridicule. As such things escalate due to the ongoing conditioning of the culture we should heed the warning of Jesus in Matthew 24:24-25:

> "For false Christs and false prophets will appear and perform great signs and miracles to deceive even the elect—if that were possible."

Gary Bates and Lita Cosner, https://creation.com/ufology-scientific-religion

---

JGJ) To answer your second question, I think this is what all the interest in Ancient Aliens is all about. Even Jacques Vallee recognized what could happen in the future.

> "I think the stage is set for the appearance of new faiths, centred on the UFO belief. To a greater degree than all phenomena modern science is confronting, the UFO can inspire awe, the sense of the smallness of man, and an idea of the possibility of contact with the cosmic. The religions we have briefly surveyed began with the miraculous experiences of one person, but to-day there are thousands for whom the belief in otherworldly contact is based on intimate conviction, drawn from what they regard as personal contact with UFOs and their occupants."
>
> Jacques Vallee, https://www.azquotes.com/author/33226-Jacques_Vallee

---

1) Exoplanet findings spark philosophical debate, 10 March, 2011. www.newscientist.com/blogs/shortsharpscience/2011/02/practical-and-religious-implic.html

2) Marciniak, B. Bringers of the Dawn: Teachings from the Pleiadians (Rochester, VT: Bear and Co, 1992), cited in Bates, G. Alien Intrusion, 2nd ed (Atlanta: Creation Book Publishers, 2010), p. 319.

3) Farrakhan's Nation of Islam to Argue UFOs Are Real, www.foxnews.com/scitech/2011/02/25/nation-islam-convention-include-talk-ufos/?test=latestnews, 10 March, 2011.

4) 'Circlemakers', www.circlemakers.org/press.html, 10 June 2003. Cited in Alien Intrusion, p. 216.

Chapter 14

19.   Have you found any other name of a religious personage that stops the experience?

JGJ) We have heard of only a handful of such cases. But never with the life changing evidence that comes with using the name of JESUS CHRIST. It seems the Alien Entities allow this to give the impression of another name working. The real evidence comes from a true life change of being set free from the oppression that comes with the experience. No evidence is shown that the "spiritual" experience can be terminated completely from their life except through the name of JESUS CHRIST and a personal relationship with him.

20.   Would you explain what is meant by "good cop/bad cop" in relation to abductions?

The experiences that these abduction experiencers have with these entities are very traumatic in nature: medical examinations, sexually oriented experiences during the experience. And they seem to continue for a good period of time.

But there are cases, many cases, where the experience changes at some point, and there's a different entity involved. One that seems more angelic, or adds higher spiritual motives to the experience. And what we're seeing here when that happens, is more communication between the entities and the experiencer themselves. And that communication comes from this second entity that becomes involved with the experience.

What we're seeing here is referred to as Stockholm Syndrome in the UFO community. These experiences that the abduction experiencers have when they first start out are very traumatic, but somewhere along the line, you recognize that these experiencers have become messengers for the entities themselves. And that's when you find out that there's been that second level of experience come into their lives. And, in other words, they've sided with the enemy.

That's what the Stockholm Syndrome refers to. It was first termed after observing recently liberated prisoners of war. These prisoners were actually saying the same thing their captors were saying. They had actually sided with their captors, after all they'd been through. They were siding with the ideology of the captors. And it confused the military when they first encountered that; they didn't understand how that was possible. And as psychiatrists and psychologists started looking at it, they saw how that worked, and recognized that it's a brainwashing effect. What you're actually seeing here is a portrayal like we see in TV shows of "Good Cop, Bad Cop." You got one cop that is beating you down during interrogation, and the other cop is in the same room with you, and he's trying to be the nice guy to you. But keep in mind, they're both cops, they're both after the same thing. And that's what we're seeing with this abduction experience. Even though the experience starts out traumatic, they have an agenda to bring you to another level, to where you become a disciple of them, and you actually are their messenger here on earth. And that's what their main agenda seem to be, to turn you into that particular testimony for them. And you see the same thing in people that have become involved in cults. Whether it be UFO cults, or Bible-based cults, or whatever; there's a brainwashing that goes on.

21.   If I don't believe in JESUS CHRIST, why should I believe your research findings?

JGJ) Our research has shown us in the many cases we have worked with that It does work, and we can help you stop the experience also, if you truly want it to stop. That is called "repeatability." And there is nothing else in the entire UFO phenomenon today that is repeatable. You can't have a UFO sighting and say, "I'll make it happen again in a few minutes." Or have an abduction experience and say, "I'll make sure it happens again tomorrow."

The evidence stands by itself, whether you want to accept it or not. That choice is yours to make. The question we have asked all along is, "How many cases does it take for you to see that what we have found is the truth?" If you need more than the many testimonies we have posted for you to read or hear, you only need to come back later to see or hear more. We still have them coming in all the time.

22. From Lucette Banas

There are some who have been found to have chips inside their bodies after being abducted. When the chips are removed, what materials are they made of, and can scientists discover their origin? Are they made of unknown materials or can they be traced to have been manufactured here on Earth?

JGJ) Thank you, Lucette Banas, for your important questions. Trying to answer your question of so-called "alien implants", I've included an article I did some time back with my friend and co-researcher Paradox Brown.

"ALIEN IMPLANTS"

By Joe Jordan and Paradox Brown

This article intends to focus on the topic of "alien abduction implants" from various Christian perspectives. A basic assumption taken here will be that "alien abductions" are actually caused by fallen angels or demonic entities. This assumption is based off of the numerous documented cases of "alien abductees" which testify that their abductions have stopped in the name and authority of Jesus Christ, using spiritual warfare methods. (1)

There have been numerous reports from "alien abductees" of receiving from "aliens" what the UFO research community commonly calls "implants".

Implants are said to be small solid foreign objects of earth-based materials, usually of metal or ceramic, found imbedded in an abductee. Sometimes, though not always, abductees will say they remember a medical procedure in which the area of the body implanted in was the target of the procedure. These procedures, when remembered, are often said to be quite painful, involving long needles or drills, and no anesthesia.

Perhaps the most recent Christian research into the mechanics of an actual abduction experience, caused by an evil spirit, is that these experiences are real-seeming visions. These visions are completely real-seeming to the bodily senses in many cases. That these visions are mental can be established in the fact that there are documented cases that abductees can have an abduction experience, while a witness present sees the abductee does not go anywhere nor physically experience what the abductee later recounts as having happened. In the Bible, angelic visions are described in such a way that it seems they were often completely real to the bodily senses. As such, fallen angelic visions have a Biblical precedent for also being highly realistic experiences.

In some of these encounters with evil spirits, there is a perceptible level of physicality to the experience. This is seen in that injuries, such as bruises, cuts, puncture wounds, etc. are present on the abductee after the experience. Sometimes the person does not remember they have had an abduction experience, but still will notice unusual unexplained physical injuries that they cannot account for. These injuries likely are attributable to the same evil spirits causing the vision experience of alien abductions. There are cases in the Bible of angels causing physical injury to people; perhaps the most notable is the case of Job, in which Job was inflicted with boils by Satan.

And then there are the small foreign objects that have been taken out of people who have had the "alien abduction" experience; commonly called "implants". Usually these implants have no entry wound or scar, but in fact appear like the object materialized under the skin without passing through the skin.

What should Christians make of "implants", coming from the perspective that "alien abductions" are actually caused by fallen angels?

Assuming that a metal or ceramic object has been removed from an abductee, the first question is whether or not fallen angels actually did implant this object into a person. It would seem that fallen angels are capable of doing this. But do they? Is this the only option?

Doctors do report that sometimes objects can become embedded in a person accidentally, without the person being aware of it. If this was the case with an abductee, there stands a possibility that fallen angels might just play off of this sort of unknown embedded foreign object. A fallen angel could tailor the vision of an abduction experience to include the deception of a medical procedure to implant an object, which has already been present for some time in the abductee through normal circumstances. (2)

It is interesting that of all the supposed implants that have been removed from abductees, none seem to be technology, but rather are inanimate bits of metal or ceramic of a normal earthly composition. This is just the type of object composition one would expect to find from accidental embedding during the normal course of life. There are no documented cases of implants having any technological purpose or intelligent design to them. These objects are inanimate, and benign in their effect on the body. (3)

As this is the case, for an abductee or former abductee, it is rather impossible to tell whether or not the fallen angelic abduction experiences actually are the origin of any such foreign object found, or if the object may have appeared through natural means.

There is also the case in which an abductee may perceive that they have an implant, seeming to feel some hard object under the skin, having heard such is common among abductees. Without x-rays or other medical scans of that area of the body, no one can say for sure if such is a foreign object. There are many sorts of hard growths that can occur naturally in the body. These can include polyps, cysts, tumors, calcium spurs, small bone growths, and many other things. This kind of thing should be checked out by a doctor, to see if it is benign, and to see if it requires treatment. Sometimes growths like these will go away on their own. (4)(5)

For those abductees that do have an unidentified foreign object under their skin, if it is a biological growth, that's appearance coincides with a recent abduction experience, there is some possibility that fallen angels may have caused the biological growth. There is also the possibility that the growth would have occurred naturally, whether an abduction experience had taken place or not.

For abductees, there can remain unanswered questions as to the nature of hard growths, or hard objects, found or perceived in their body. There is little way to tell for sure as to whether an evil spirit responsible for an abduction experience is responsible for these objects or not. Many people which are not abductees, have hard growths under the skin, or find embedded objects in themselves accidentally. These things happen to everybody, including people who have never had a single abduction experience

As such, there is no need for abductees to claim that they have "implants". This is a belief that is not, and summarily cannot, be supported by actual proof. While abduction experiences do happen to people, these are deceptive experiences. As many non-abductees experience hard growths and objects unknowingly embedded in them naturally, it is entirely possible that those evil spirits responsible for abductions simply deceptively play off of what are natural occurrences.

http://www.alienresistance.org/ce4implants.htm

1) www.alienresistance.org/ce4testimonies.htm
2) http://weldingweb.com/showthread.php?p=293489
3) http://www.susanblackmore.co.uk/journalism/ufo97.html
4) http://www.webmd.com/skin-problems-and-treatments/guide/cysts-lumps-bumps?page=3
5) http://en.wikipedia.org/wiki/Torus_mandibularis

"It wasn't enough to stop the dreams. They only stopped when I began to realize in my own dreams what I was seeing was a dream. It gave me a very weird sense when being asleep and knowing in every thought that you are asleep and dreaming. It's made me more aware when I do sleep and dream."

From an anonymous experiencer

"Still another way of looking at this sighting pattern is that the reporting of high-strangeness experiences whose nature falls just outside the parameters of being susceptible to empirical proof suggests that the UFO phenomenon may lie in a realm that Hutson Smith calls the "middle kingdom" – a different realm than the terrestrial but related to it, where "enigmatic energies of some kind seem to be at work, but…it is the very mischief to verify them or identify what they are." The controversial association of UFO phenomena with the idea of this scientifically unverifiable middle kingdom is the subject this volume has addressed."

The Lure of the Edge, Scientific Passions, Religious Beliefs, and the Pursuit of UFO's - Brenda Denzeler 2001

"For the weapons of our warfare [are] not carnal, but mighty through God to the pulling down of strong holds; casting down imaginations, and every high thing that exalteth itself against the knowledge of God, and bringing into captivity every thought to the obedience of Christ."

2 Corinthians Chapter 10:4-5

The CE4 Research Findings

The Most Powerful Evidence in the World Today Showing the True Nature of the So-Called Alien Beings of Ufology

The Testimonials of abduction experiencers who have terminated their experiences from happening again through the name and authority of Jesus Christ, and choosing to have a personal relationship with Him

The testimonies you are about to read were sent to CE4 Research over the past few years. They are but a few of the many testimonies that have been received from experiencers, which can testify to the name and authority of Jesus Christ, terminating the horrific experience from people's lives. They have been kept as much as possible in their original sent format. So please excuse their miss-spellings, grammar, and punctuation. It's the content that's most important.

1.   I wanted to share a couple testimonials but the first might not be what it seems. Would you consider an abnormal out of body experience an attempted 'abduction' or just a conscious drifting? As I was sitting on a porch one summer some 10 years ago in my teen years, I kind of got lost in my own thought, you know when you day dream and have that empty stare into nothingness? It felt like that, I don't remember what I was thinking but I know I was reflecting for some reason and concentrating on my thoughts, I started to notice I wasn't inside of my body anymore, I was floating upwards but watching my body on the porch below starting to get smaller as I went higher and it was so vivid that I could make out familiar houses as I looked down on my neighborhood and the tops of the trees from above. I wasn't going just straight up either I would say more at a 65 degree angle and in an instance I was on the porch looking up in the direction was just travelling, leaving, drifting I don't know what to call it.

The second isn't as much as an abduction as what I couldn't describe at all and until I read Whitley Strieber describe an experience of his own in his book "Transformation", pg. 181 which was "I felt an absolutely indescribable sense of menace, it was hell on Earth to be there [in the presence of these entities], and yet I couldn't move, cry out, couldn't get away. I'd lay as still as death, suffering inner agonies. Whatever was there seemed so monstrously ugly, so filthy and dark and sinister. Of course they were demons. They had to be. And they were here and I couldn't get away."

I had experienced this twice in 2012 while incarcerated at the Yakima county department of corrections. I felt an overwhelming sense of dread, I mean sincere, genuine fear, out of nowhere, nothing happened I was handcuffed walking back to my tank and I told the officer on my floor I couldn't go further, I was standing but my legs wouldn't go forward so I leaned my forehead against a wall and all the sudden start crying in anger and told him if he put me back where I was I would hurt someone. They took me down to the loony room with padded walls which had I known that's where I was headed would not have confessed that bit to him, so they stripped me naked and put me in this padded room with a hole in the floor (their version of a toilet) and a few hours later put me in an enclosed holding cell still naked except for a smoke 'to protect me from hurting myself' they say where I stayed for a week and a half with a black towel over the window with no shower so one night I was bathing in a sink, bird bath we called it, no bigger than a kitchen aid mixer bowl when I heard screaming. So I stopped to concentrate on that and as it got more intense I leaned against the wall to get a better listen and as soon as I touched the wall I took my hand off and backed up. I could feel something in that cell with me, I looked all around, saw nothing but thought to myself, "this place is pure evil", in fact I call it the devils' playground. I could feel something so much stronger than me that I backed up again until the concrete bed hit the back of my legs and I tripped ending up sitting down on it. I was basically frozen in terror and could still could hear the most heartbreaking screams that I won't ever forget. They could not have been a delusion this person was in more than I've ever heard, begging for someone there to stop, pleading and I was trying to yell but I don't think anything was coming out. After a bit I scooted back into the corner covering my ears as tight as I could, trying to think and take myself anywhere else mentally, telling myself "it's not real and it's in my head". Trying anything not to hear her and nothing would muffle her torturous cries, I couldn't do anything, go anywhere, talk to anyone and I clenched my jaw so tightly while covering my ears that I choked and nearly threw up a few times. I don't know how long this went on for but I remembered one of the guards gave me a plastic Spork for cereal so I got it and broke it. Then began digging at my left wrist because I was trying to leave the only other way possible, so I'm tearing up and down at my wrist right where the artery is supposed to be and sure I bled but wouldn't bleed out. I started to get frantic when it didn't work and I started praying, pleading to God to deliver me and I surrendered myself 100%, my pain, my fear my entire essence saying sorry over and over for trying to leave in such a cowardly way and just then a train rolled by and sounded its horn, loud and long and something told me it's not meant for me to go yet. Not verbally but mentally told me and I knew that was my horn of salvation accepting my plea because the screams stopped and I cried tears of joy. My pleas were heard and I get somewhat emotional when I relive the experience just by thinking about it, I haven't mentioned it to anyone in two years but I need for people to know that there are forces out there beyond ourselves and our understanding that torment us and deliverance if you ask for it from the pit of your soul. I never felt more alive.

The guards came to move me back to my cell some days later and found what I did to myself in their protective care unit, no one believed anyone gave me that Spork but I still had it, they claimed I snuck it down there and I refused to leave the cell. I felt the wildest most irregular sense of security that I the guard went and got another two guards and still I would not leave. Finally 5 guards came back with a stun gun and I had already been tazered twice so I accepted defeat and went with them. They took me to the medical floor and the second that door clanked behind me I snapped, I mean I was engulfed with absolute and uncontrollable rage, yelling as loud as I could to go back, slamming my fists, elbows and knees on the door, the bed the metal mirror, the toilet, kicking the door. It was the most childlike tantrum a grown man could ever have. The final straw was when I slammed my head into the door, that sent me back in a shock kind of and I backed up, snapped back into my normal controlled self within an instance, holding my forehead of course, but that was not me in there a few seconds ago by any means in that cell. It was not. So I was back in control again after recovering and went to look at the window as if I could see out, they're painted grey of course to gain the whole sensory deprivation affect, and I closed my eyes to pray and when I finished apologizing for my actions I opened them and the grey window was sky blue and I was watching little illuminated dots of orange/yellow lights dance around as if they were lights in the sky. This experience could have arguably been the result of my assault on the door I know, but dancing lights were not there before I prayed, only after and faded away as the window started to appear grey again.

Harry

2.   Please forward to Mr. Joe Jordan.

My name is Joe. I live in Cape Coral, FL. I am 38 and I am a medically retired police detective out of NC. I spent ten plus years on the job before my injury stopped me from staying in law enforcement. I subsequently left in October of

2007. I moved to Florida in 2008 where I simply spend time with loved ones and care for my two children. In that I believe a person's word is everything in this life so I say that to share some things in hopes of helping with answers not just for me but for many people who wonder about this life. I have had a full life so far and can honestly say I have had experiences some of which I can only explain as supernatural. I never share this stuff but I was compelled to do so.

Sir, today, 1st, I was watching a video I came across on YouTube from I believe 2009 with Mr. Joe Jordan. Mr. Jordan was sharing stories of his time with MUFON on UFO's and alien abductions. I believe it was at a church. Now I must admit I rarely ever watch things on UFO's or UFO abductions because as a Christian my belief is the UFO phenomenon is connected to either the military, unexplained weather anomalies, or if legit fallen angels and evil in some way. I am no expert by any means but I almost fell over when I heard a story from this conference on UFO's. It was related to something that happened to me in 1996. Mr. Jordan was telling a story of an abduction from 1976, the year I was born, on a man who was in bed with his wife when he felt paralyzed and wound up being lifted above his bed. The man had been assaulted with a pole in his rectum and the assault stopped when he called on the name of our Lord Jesus. I nearly fell off my chair, and even getting ready to type the next paragraph am shaking a bit. Is this that common?

I guess I am sharing this to say I know what that is like. In 1996 I was living in upstate NY. I was living in a duplex with my parents on one of the Finger Lakes. At that time in my young life I was just starting to get into watching TBN at night and found myself searching for more on why we're here. I recall asking a lot of questions like why we are here and who God is for us as humans. I had had some experiences as a kid that I could not explain so I always felt like something more was around me and my family. I was not on any drugs by the way either. One fall night I saw an ad on TBN for a youth March in Washington DC called Washington for Jesus. This was for teenagers all around the world to go there and be with likeminded youth. I felt a very strong urge to go to this upcoming march so I called in to the station and was hooked up with a local church to go.

The following night I was laying in my bed in the mostly dark room watching the shadows of the trees blowing in the wind outside. I heard my name whispered very abrupt but faint sounding. I tried to sit up but I started feeling tingles all throughout my body and all of a sudden I couldn't move. I became very afraid and at that moment I started lifting up off my bed towards the ceiling. I felt like I was being pulled. I was in a state of pure fear as I began floating while still on my back towards the doorway going out into the hallway. Everything seemed almost misty, as if I was in a black and white movie or even in a bubble of some sort. I initially cold not speak at all but somehow I was able to say out loud, Jesus, please Jesus help me. I began slowing down even though I made it to the hallway it felt like I had stopped moving almost. I then yelled loudly, in the name of Jesus stop. All of a sudden I was pulled back into my bed, it nearly collapsed my frame. I laid there and though I felt I could move I was almost in shock so I just laid there and stared upwards. Somehow I eventually passed out and when I woke up my bed was all thrown about. I sealed that story of what happened inside and this is the first time I have put it out there.

I was able to go to the march that following month and while there I became a born again Christian. The months that followed that were both amazing and scary. I had a few more events, one of which was similar but this time I was warned by something shadowy in my room of an upcoming event and to be ready. That next day I was involved in a horrific accident in my car, but several miracles happened because of that car crash and it has shaped me as a believer to this day. I would be happy to share further but I had to for now share that event with Mr. Jordan. I do believe it was not a UFO, or an abduction from an alien from another planet, but in fact I felt as if it was a demonic attack. An attack that I believe people mistake for alien abductions.

I did not realize that specific type of event was connected to what people think are abductions so I would be happy to share this or more if you are still interested in this phenomenon. With my previous experiences and career perhaps I can also be of some assistance.

Joe

3.   Joe,

I saw one of your videos on YouTube and thought I would share some experiences that I and my family have had with aliens, demons or inter-dimensional creatures of some kind. My story is as follows:

Location: Alabama, Date: 1989 – 1997 It's a long story.....

The time surrounding this particular series of events began around July 1989. This is not to say thatJuly1989 was the first time I had paranormal activities in my life, but the things that I'm going to relay to you now, began around that time... And although the things that I'm now telling happened over a long period of time, I feel they are related.

It began with an evening at an American Legion, in Alabama.

I had went with my brother and his 12year old son to the local American Legion, where they had open dart throwing contests. Not actual tournaments, but just open games where anyone could enter the competition. I don't throw darts (if that is the correct phrase), but my brother had bought a nice set of darts and so I was there with him. After an evening of mediocre games at best, we felt it was time to get back to his house, so that his son could get ready for school the next day. Also, the American Legion closed at 10:00 pm, so there was actually no other choice.

We left the American Legion at around10:05 pm and made a quick stop at a convenience store. After that, we drove to his house, which was approximately 8 miles away. He lived in a rural area that is very sparsely populated and the road to his house had no houses for miles. About half way there, we stopped to use the bathroom, which is something most country boys in Alabama do without even thinking twice. The "bathroom" consisted of a patch of weeds on the side of the road with no traffic. I'm sure there are many out there that understand exactly what I'm saying. Anyway, I add this bit of information only to establish a relative time frame for the trip from the Legion to his house. The trip, including the stops at the convenience store and the weeds, should have taken no longer than a half hour, at most. (I went back over the route the next day and it took less than 25minutes.)

When we arrived at his house, his wife came out and asked why we were so late... We didn't understand what she meant, until she said it was after 12:30 in the morning! (12:35to be exact) -We both said that was impossible, until we checked without watches... She was right! Not really understanding any of this, I departed and went home.

The next morning, as I was putting my socks on, I noticed a pink "scar" on the inside of my ankle, about the size of a small pencil eraser. I looked at the other ankle and there was another one, identical to the first in shape, size and location (except on the opposite foot). The marks looked like "scars", but I had never seen them before. They appeared like two small "gouges" of skin had been "scooped" out and had now healed. (Although they were NOT there before!) The marks were approximately 6 mm in diameter and 2 mm deep- 'cup' shaped (like a crater).

Still not believing the time 'lapse' the night before, I got in my car and immediately re-traced our trip from the night before, stopping at both the store and the side of the road, re-enacting everything we had done the night before. There is no way the trip could have taken over 25 minutes. But it was evident that over 90 minutes were MISSING! (Not including the stops and actual driving time.) I went over all the details with my brother, his wife and his son... there was no deviation in accounts of the trip and times of events. This was perplexing, but there was nothing we could do about it. At the time, there was no reason to do anything.

A few nights later, I had a very vivid dream of three tall "beings" (doctors) standing over me, examining me and several smaller "things" watching. I was on a metal table with platforms so my arms could be outstretched at 90degrees and be supported (like a flat metal cross). There was a table of sorts, to the right of my head. I was lying on my back and the three tall "doctors" were to my right, while there were several shorter, darker beings seated behind a small two feet tall wall to my left. The distance from where I lay to the small beings was around eight feet.

There was a strong light above me, but I couldn't actually see a "light". One of the tall ones (to my right) said, as if instruction to the smaller ones, "This would normally be terminal". -- That's about all I can remember of that now.

Fast forward a couple of months...

I found a beautiful house for rent on a bluff, overlooking several miles of the Tennessee River, between Scottsboro and Guntersville, Alabama. The house was beautiful, but very isolated. There were only a few (3) houses within a quarter of a mile. It was about an eighth of a mile down a little gravel drive that dead-ended at the house. There was nothing around the house but woods and a cliff, overlooking the river.

(This is the house; a new house has since been built right beside it and another near it, but at that time it was only one house, the lower one.

There is a cliff below the house that give a great view of the river, one mile below.

The house had not been occupied for a long time (which I found strange, because of its beauty and location) and a little work was required. The view of the Tennessee River (5000feet below), was blocked by several small to medium trees that had grown up between the back yard and the bluffs (cliff). One of the first things I did was to start clearing those trees so that we could see the beautiful view of the river from the 2nd floor deck.

I cut one of the wild cherry trees that fell to the ground, but was evidently in a bind and I didn't realize it. I was going to cut the tree into small pieces so I could move them away from the cliff. When I made the first cut, the trunk sprang back and struck me in the chest. I was knocked to the ground and almost unconscious. Immediately upon getting back up, I realized that the impact with the tree trunk had broken some ribs on my left side. I went to my doctor, who confirmed that I had broken two ribs, over my heart, about an inch to the right of my left nipple. He also said that because of this, I would inevitably get pneumonia... When I asked "why", he said that because I was a smoker (then), I would favor those ribs and not cough, causing a buildup of phlegm in my lungs, causing pneumonia. I then saw that he was right, because I hadn't coughed much since the accident. [I know this is dragging on, but I promise, there is a purpose to all this. ;-)] Because of what the doctor said, I 'forced' myself cough often after that.

The night after the doctor visit, I was asleep in my recliner in the living room (I couldn't bare the pain to lay flat in a bed), when I awoke during the middle of the night and went to the bathroom. On the way to the bathroom, a 'LOUD' sound scared me so bad, I jumped at least four feet. The sound was like in the movies, when a spaceship takes off! It "whirred" a few seconds, then faded off, straight up! (The weather was pleasant outside, so the windows were open.) I first wondered if I had been dreaming, but the dogs barking outside told me that if it 'was' a dream, the dogs had the same one. After slightly composing myself, finally got to the bathroom to complete the mission that woke me up to begin with (go pee).

Standing there, I knew I had to cough, so I prepared myself in the now familiar fashion of folding my arms around my chest and braced for the excruciating pain. I coughed and-...NO PAIN! I coughed again and... NO PAIN! This was wonderful! I must have coughed twenty times!

As soon as the elation died down, I began to wonder "why" there was no pain. I looked down and saw a small hole, "burned" into my shirt, directly over where the broken ribs 'had' been! I always carried a pen in that pocket and upon further inspection, I found that the burn had gone through my shirt pocket and into the "Pilot V" pen. Not all the way through the pen, but deep enough that I wondered why it wasn't leaking. (I still have the pen with the melted spot in it.)

I don't know what healed me, but it did! It burned a hole through my shirt and into the pen in my pocket- and mended my ribs! I still had the calcification lumps caused by the breaks in the ribs, but they were now healed!

After that "healing" encounter, strange things began happening on a regular basis. My wife and children witnessed many events that, had I not been there, I would have a hard time believing.

Once, my daughter said there were "men" outside her window (which was on the ground floor) with "flashlights" that shown through the curtains and into the room. (This room over-looked the bluffs.)

My 8 year old son (at that time) said that "little men" led him out during the night and showed him their spaceship. He drew the "ship" that he said was in the front yard.

He said that as they were leading him out, they passed by me and that I was sitting up in my chair as if in a trance... my eyes were open, but didn't react or "help" him, as the beings lead him outside. I found him asleep on the floor by an open door (downstairs) the next morning.

My wife "dreamed" that beings (other than human) transported her to another "place". I would regularly "dream" of interaction with aliens.

I set up a mini tape recorder that used the small cassette tapes (before the time of solid state memory) and set it on "Voice Actuated" record, so that it would automatically record when a sound activated it. The next morning, there was a strange noise at the beginning (like dishes breaking), then 60 minutes of white noise. I tested it over and over and it always turned on when there was no sound.

We began seeing lights outside at night. There were no other lights around anywhere, so any light could be seen easily. The lights would travel at very slow speeds to very fast speeds with no sound. These lights were within a 3 to 5 mile radius over (and INSIDE) the Tennessee River below. Approximately 5 miles across the river below us, was another mountain, the same height as the one we lived on. It was on these mountains and their slopes, where the 'lights' occurred.

On the mountain directly across the river, was a small town and community called "Fyffe". That is in a different county (DeKalb County) from the one we lived in (Marshall County), but we could see the activity from our mountain side.

There are documented events in Fyffe, where even the sheriff of that county saw a UFO. (Google "Fyffe Alabama") Anyway, that is about 5 to 7 miles from the house we were in (as the crow or UFO flies), so we could see some activity that even they couldn't, because it was on the slopes or on and 'IN' the river. I watched some of those lights go down to the river, then go beneath the water. You could see a dim light when they went under, but sometimes they would come out and sometimes the light would disappear.

One morning, after a real busy night of light activity, there was an army helicopter that came up the bluffs, as if searching for something, and when it got within hundred yards or so, we could see right inside, because it was at the same level as our house. The men (soldiers) inside acted like we weren't even there... that was all. After that, the local television station reported people seeing a black helicopter right before several cow mutilations. This happened several times. I don't know what ever became of that. My brother brought a couple of psychic people up there that couldn't wait to get away. People coming to visit would say they could "feel" a difference at our house. When things got quiet (like at night), I could hear an extremely low-pitched rumble that sounded like a bulldozer underground.

Humming birds flocked to that house. One even built a nest right by the second floor deck and I watched as she raised two little babies. There were hundreds of bats that roosted in our attic. In the evening, they would dive out of the attic, above the sliding glass door (so we could count them), and fly into the surrounding woods. Several of their babies fell out on the deck below their exit. It seemed that all types of wild life (including spiders and scorpions) were drawn to that house! This "activity" continued for several years, until I finally had to move in 1997 because a combination of deteriorating health (mental and physical) and deteriorating family.

Well, that's my story... or least the 'part' of it that I can now remember. I really "can't" remember everything, but I know there was more. A LOT more! Since then, my family has dissolved! My daughter joined the Air Force and refused to come home again! My son began taking drugs and began to get straight F's at school, then dropped out (I don't know where he is now.). My wife left and now lives in a different state. There is something hanging above all our heads that haunts our memories and our dreams. It has destroyed my family and has almost physically destroyed me! Once considered hypnosis to quit smoking, but refused for fear of remembering "things" that I don't want to know. I'm sure that if my son, daughter or wife were here, they would say: "You're not telling half of what happened", but that is all I 'can' tell - for now. It's more than I've been able to talk about for over eighteen years. I honestly believe that if I had not been a Christian, much worse things would have happened to me. I rely upon my Lord Jesus Christ every moment of my life and for everything in my life that is good.

Then and ever sense, I have used "holy" or blessed oil and water to anoint above all the doors in my home, for I never want anything to do with any of that, ever again.

You are the first person that I have shared this with (outside my family); I posted this in a UFO type forum years ago and never received a response, but I think that website closed.)

Sincerely,

Ronnie

4.   Hello, and thank you for providing a forum for believers in the powerful name of Jesus. My name is Tim Davidson. I came across your website (or the concept of your website) from a YouTube video called "Age of Deceit". I would like to tell you my experience. Actually, I have had two minor 'unwanted encounters'.

The first time I was accosted was when I started reading the 'Left Behind' books. I was working as a security officer at the time. The books piqued my interest in all things Heavenly and I was becoming more and more focused on learning about God. I was raised in a Christian church, so I had heard many stories, but this time it was personal. Then, one night, I was sitting in the chair at work and suddenly I couldn't move. I worked in a guard house by myself. Yet, I was sure there was something (not someone) behind me. I didn't get the feeling that it was something terrible that was trying to harm me. Instead, it seemed like something was trying to test me, to see what I would do. I was unable to move or form actual words. My lips stuttered as I quietly uttered the name Jesus. Immediately, the sensation left me and I was able to turn around (although it took me several minutes to muster the courage to do so).

The second time it happened to me came after I had been baptized and made sin-free for the first time in my life. I felt clean inside. I felt like I had been spared. It was a great feeling. Like a ton of guilt and burden had been lifted from my shoulders. I was still working as security at this time and I worked nights. I made it home one morning and decided to lie down on the sofa and take a nap. As I eased into a slumber, I felt a total body paralysis. This time, it felt as if something was restraining my entire body, from head to toe, and preventing me from moving or speaking. Having experienced something similar before, I quickly called on the name of Jesus and the sensation left again. I told my experience to my coworker a few days later. He was / is not a believer in Jesus, but more of a believer in political and occult phenomenon. He explained away my experience as 'sleep paralysis'. I was tempted to believe him, but he had no explanation for me ending the attack by calling on Jesus.

To date, I have had no other experiences. But I make sure to keep the name of Jesus on my lips so that anything listening or watching knows I'm not alone. My wife often tells me that she gets spooked by what she says looks like a person in the house or a shape of a being at first glance. Or a noise or even what sounds like my voice coming from another room when I'm at work. I tell her to call on Jesus and use His authority to claim her (our) house. I believe what didn't work on me is trying its luck on her. I will continue to pray for her and me. And I will pray for your success as well. Continue promoting Jesus and His authority.

Sincerely,

Tim Davidson

5.   My name is Richard and I stumbled on to the CE4 from watching videos on YouTube. I heard on the video something that i had experienced and wanted to detail to others. I'm also a believer of Christ and has accepted him as my savior but being 21 and still a young I haven't been the best Christian. I was attending college a year ago when this happened, I was staying with my parent's. My parents are good Christians and like many struggle to be. We would have daily bible readings and this helped us try to understand the scriptures better. Being in the new age I tried to peace and puzzle things that are happening now in society and incorporate them with the word. I believe in UFOs and had an understanding that they were extra dimensional beings. I also believe in demons but never really tried to put 1&1 together and realize there the same thing. It started when one night I went on the front porch and smoked a cigarette and looked up at the stars like I did for weeks. I had noticed to thing fairly odd in the sky that night. Off about a mile away there was something moving in the night sky. Living in Texas out in the country there's not too much static to make me see something I didn't. This ball of light was moving sporadically above a corn field. Maneuvering up and down and left and right. As if it was a laser pointer. I call my sister and brother to see what I see. They came outside to witness what I was seeing. They saw it and wanted to go and see if we can get closer. We drive to where we saw it. I kept track I saw it the whole time but the others didn't. I saw it move down behind the tree lines like it was going to the ground but I could not investigate because the others were sacred. We go back home and the others go inside but I stay outside to smoke another cigarette from excitement. I looked back to the spot in the sky were I had first seen it, all of a sudden I see it again doing the same thing. I said out loud "I see you". I took a couple more drags then something else caught my attention, footsteps. The footsteps were on the roof walking slowly. It wasn't a cat or any other animal because living in the country one can distinguish the difference. But what I heard were to feet steeping cautiously towards the porch. While listening to the footsteps I began to feel the felling of fear. Every step that got closer I cringed. I called for my cat thinking it was him. He would have at least meowed with acknowledgement but kept coming closer. I yelled and hit the side of the house but nothing. Finally I ran inside and looked the door and sat on

the couch and listened for anything, but nothing. Everything had stopped. I was waiting for the door knob to jiggle as if it was a horror movie but nothing. So I heard that same sound several Times and every time was mind blowing. I had feared was that they knew I saw them and they would get me. I had dreams of tiny aliens coming in my sleep and taking me. But I just though my mental was getting the best of me. Till one night I was trying to go to sleep and felt something grab me. I sat up and didn't see anything but darkness. I brushed it off and tried to go to sleep. Then all off a sudden I hear a loud crunching mixed with high pitch frequency noise in only my right ear, which was facing towards the ceiling. I gutted it up and went to sleep, I wasn't going to be scared. The next day I told my mother the experience and she told me that it was just demons and the devil messing with me. Making sense because the devil has been after me my whole life I told my mom that I wasn't afraid of the devil and I wasn't scared. Later that same night I was sleeping and had no problems going to sleep. I later was awoken. Not physically but mentally awaken. My eyes were closed but my senses were not. I first felt the felling of fear like I had felt on the porch the exact felling, an evil felling. Then I felt my upper body being raised off up out of my bed as if something was drawing me closer to themselves. I couldn't open my eyes and I believe that the Lord didn't want me to see the being or they didn't want me to see them. But as soon as they lifted my upper body from the bed I said out loud "Lord Jesus Christ save me". I soon as I said I was let back down gently, not roughly but gently, and went back to sleep not waking up one bit. I told my friend who is a good Christian the story when I saw him and was amazed with the story but also with the fact that I cried for the lord while not even being awake. I learned that these beings can touch you as in my case but I know they can hurt you. You just have to call on the Lord and he will save you like he saved me. That's my story, sorry its long but I had to make you understand me a little and I hope this will help. You can use this for your website and hopefully you do so others can read.

6.   I have recently watched your video on "Alien Abduction".

I am grateful for your putting the perspective of demon activity to it.

I am 58 yrs. old and have been walking with Christ since January 1993 when I committed my life to Christ. I have had many trials and tribulations through these years that has taught me much about the relationship Christ has chosen me to have with Him and others. I understand spiritual warfare and have been involved in it many times. The occurrences I wanted to share are not those of being a Christian, but the earlier days of when God was first revealing Himself to me.

This is my first attempt to document the occurrences, but my memory on these incidences has been kept very clear over the years.

The first that I recall took place when I was 16yrs old. I lived in an apartment, my brother had just moved in and my abusive husband out. Found that I was pregnant again and was pressured into an abortion.

Shortly after the abortion a friend took me out for miniature golf. I remember it was difficult for me to stay awake. It was a strange form of sleep I had never known and kept me deep in its hold. It was what happened the next evening that was more disturbing. I had gone to sleep but awaken by a presence in the room. I felt paralyzed. As I looked around the room there were strange colored lights in different patterns flowing through the room. I remember fixing my eyes on the lamp in the far corner and the patterns of colored lights seemed to pass through it as if it was not even there. I also began to feel my covers being tugged off. I began to panic but couldn't move or yell out to my brother. It was then I sensed I was no longer in my body, but fighting something for it. I couldn't tell you what I was fighting. Just a force that I battled with. I somehow began to believe that if I didn't win, I was going to die, and that this force wanted my body. I felt I had to fight with everything I had. I don't know how but with all my strength, with great intensity and force I fought back and suddenly it all stopped. I realized I was in my body, lying in bed and screaming at the top of my lungs.

My brother rushed in and I tried to tell him, but he thought I was having a breakdown. The next day I stayed at the apartment, not sure what to make of what happened when I had a knock at the door. A friend of mine whom I had not seen for some time was there. He had never been to my apartment and it puzzled me how he knew where to find me. As I asked what he was doing here, he simply stated "God sent me!" It was then I told him about what had happened to me and he told me about Jesus. I began to know Jesus as Savior, but had not been disciple or made a life commitment to Christ. I don't think I understood all that yet. I read the Bible and wanted to learn and took a firm stand for Christ in my life at that time. I also relocated to Florida and in just a few months from that incident, I would have another.

My sister had a friend who practice witchcraft. She painted her home in some gruesome paintings and had a large witches wheel painted on the wall of her kitchen with two large iron candle holders on each side. She was willing to let me rent her home very cheaply and I needed a place. I lived there with a boyfriend for a short time and felt Christ would take care of me and I didn't need to fear demons. But one day I felt a strange sensation something was near. A presence. I went to bed that night and all was well. It was the next night however that it happened. I left a card game early from our neighbors home, feeling tired, leaving my boyfriend to continue to play. I relaxed in bed to sleep with nothing really on my mind at all. I awoke to a presence suddenly and felt paralyzed again. Through the window to the right of my bed a face appeared distorted and of a strange light. It crossed the walls of the room until it was directly in front of me. As it appeared to start coming straight at me, I felt a sudden attack of something through the window on my left beside me. I remember trying to scream with nothing coming out. Again I found myself wrestling with a being spiritually that I could only describe as a black panther like being. My boyfriend appeared in the room through the door, looked at me closely and then took something out of the night stand draw and left the room, all the while I was trying to scream to him to help me. When he had shut the door, I knew I had to fight this thing again and with a strength and force, with all that was in me, I fought back and suddenly found myself in bed, in body and screaming. My boyfriend came running in to find me in hysterics and asking why he didn't help me. He simply said, "You were asleep". I then told him what he did in the room and knew I had gone through something strange and terrifying.

It would be at least another year and a half before I would have another incident. I moved in with a man I would marry later on. He was a sci-fi person and got me interested in sci-fi movies and books. It was evening and we had just finished watching, "The Stranger Within" that Barbra Eden played in. As I laid in bed, I felt that familiar presence again. This time I prayed and asked Jesus to help me and protect me. I then fell into a peaceful night's sleep. In the morning I was in the kitchen fixing coffee when my future husband came down and I welcomed him with a cheerful good morning, but he was troubled and look still tired and I asked what was up. He said he felt like something was banging on him all night trying to get inside of him. I realized what had happened. It had come for me and couldn't through Christ, so it turn to him.

Many years later we separated and I met my third husband in Colorado and he was very on board with me in seeking Christ. We dedicated our lives together to Christ at a small local church in January of 1993. I would then do allot of ministry work with pregnancy centers, helping women and training women to help others.

The only spiritual incidents I have since are in Christ. And they have been incredible! That bad presence has not terrorized me since I prayed that night to Jesus Christ to protect me from it.

My husband passed on three years ago, and I continue to walk in Christ and evangelize where ever possible.

You have permission to use this testimony if it can help in your ministry. It seems strange to have written about this after so long a time has passed. If nothing else, I would like this to be an encouragement to you for the work and ministry that you are doing that many can learn from the things God has brought to you. I have several people into this "alien thing" that I plan to share your videos with.

Thank you again, in Christ

Denise

PS. The women who practice witchcraft would often talk with me back then. She would talk about what she believed and I would talk about Christ. I heard from my sister that she had become a Christian because of those talks. It's awesome how our God works, even thru our ignorance.

7.   Joe,

I accidentally stumbled upon your video on YouTube last night. After what I and my mother experienced over a 22 years ago, I have been searching for answers. I had suspected my answers were correct, and when I saw your video I didn't need any more proof.

I agree that alien gray's and all the rest of them are 100% demonic, and I can tell you a story that proves it. What I am about to tell you is real, and pure truth. I have never told this story before in this great of detail, so you are the first person to read this since it happened 22 years ago.

It was 1992 and I was at home in Tacoma, Washington. I was 14 years old. At this time my family was always arguing, and there was a negative vibe throughout the house. Whatever this entity was I didn't know, but I met it on 3 different occasions over about a 6 month time span. Each of the 3 occurrences increased in severity as time went on.

Encounter #1

I was alone in my room and sleeping one night when I suddenly awoke and was terrified. I could feel an evil presence near me. All I wanted to do was get out of bed and run upstairs to get away from whatever it was. It was pitch black and I couldn't see anything. I went to get off my bed and there was a shelf that was at the foot of my bed blocking me (these shelfs were against the walls and away from my bed, that's where they always were). I pushed the shelf with my hands but something was on the other side pushing it back against me. I became extremely terrified and moved to the left side of my bed where I found the 2nd shelf blocking my escape, so I moved to the right side of my bed and there was the 3rd shelf blocking my escape. Now I'm really scared and my heart is pounding. I feel my way in the dark back to the shelf at the foot of my bed (at this time I am aware that this is a demonic entity) and I began pushing really hard to knock down the shelf, but each time I pushed the shelf would come back because something was on the other side pushing it back at me. I knew there was only one way out of this situation so I jumped over the shelf and slammed my knee into it in the process. I ran to the wall in the dark and I remember flipping on the light as I ran out of the room. I didn't look back to see what was there, I just ran out of there and went upstairs. I did not sleep in that room for a couple days.

Encounter #2

After about a month or 2 I had completely forgotten about what had happened to me. One day I was skipping school and was alone at home in the day watching television upstairs with the dog. It was about 10am in the morning. My parents and siblings were all away at school or work so it was just me and the dog. I was sitting on the floor in front of the TV when I heard and felt a loud bang on the ceiling right beneath me (something was downstairs below me slamming the ceiling). The dog jumped up with its ears standing straight up and we both looked at the floor. About 1 minute later I heard/felt another loud bang below where I was sitting. This time I banged on the floor once, and a few seconds later the entity banged on the floor once. I banged on the floor twice, and the entity banged on the floor twice. I banged on the floor 3 times, and the entity banged on the floor 3 times. The dog was with me waiting for the banging too and the dog was alarmed at what was downstairs banging at us. I banged on the floor 4 times and about 10 seconds passed, then whatever was downstairs banged on the ceiling beneath me so hard that I jumped up to my feet and me and the dog ran outside. I was terrified and couldn't come back inside the house for hours. I eventually went back inside and it was gone, and I eventually forgot about it until the 3rd occurrence happened.

Encounter #3

One night about a month or 2 later, I was alone in my room getting ready for bed. I got in my bed and turned the lights off. As I lay in bed I could see where the walls were, and where the window was (it wasn't 100% dark, it was late but I could still see in the dark). I could see where the air vent was, and where the walls started, where the small window was, etc. I had completely forgotten about the 2 previous encounters. As I lay in bed I saw that the room was growing black, and I could no longer see the air vent, where the wall was, etc. It was like a pitch black cloud overtaking me. At this moment I could no longer move my body. I was paralyzed from my neck down. The only thing I could move was my head, and I could speak, I could only think and speak and move my head (this is also the reason that I believe our soul is in our head). It didn't have total control over me. I'm moving my head looking around and wondering what is happening and thinking this thing is back! As soon as I understood that these demons were here I became terrified and started praying in my head and I was saying out loud "Oh my God, what is this?" "What is this?" "Oh my God!" I knew there was only one way to get rid of these demons, and that was the word "Jesus Christ". These demons kept me from speaking any words, so I began to pray in my mind. I prayed to God to just let me say His name, I prayed that I could just utter the words Jesus Christ. About 5 seconds later I was able to speak and I said "In the name of Jesus Christ I command you to be gone!" At this exact moment it was gone and I could move my body and everything was ok. I felt very safe and not scared anymore. As I looked around the room I caught a glimpse of something outside my window (the pitch blackness had gone away). It was a small creature that looked like an alien gray, he was crouched down on all 4 limbs and looking through the small window at me before it vanished. I few seconds later I fell asleep so peacefully and woke up the next morning with the Holy Spirit strong inside me. When people ask me how long I have been a Christian I say "Since 1992".

Years went by without me ever mentioning this to anybody. One day I asked my mom if she ever had anything weird happen to her in that house, and she described the same exact thing -except she only had the encounter similar to my 3rd encounter. She also commanded the evil away using the name of Jesus Christ.

Since then I have seen 1 UFO in Tacoma, and 3 UFO's in San Diego where I live now. They let me see them from time to time and they now know that I am untouchable because Jesus Christ walks with me. I don't fear them at all anymore, as I now know that it's not aliens coming from other planets -its Satan's demons pretending to be aliens.

After I saw your video last night, I prayed to God and thanked him for putting this video in front of me. I felt very warm as I prayed and I knew that God was with me. I have never told this story in this level of detail before so you are the 1st person to know about it. In this story the demons mock God, they used 3 shelfs to attack me, it banged on the ceiling 3 times, and there were 3 encounters, 333. I had to email you this story. You can use this story on your website but all I ask is that you hide my name. If you have any questions I can be reached here at this email address.

Thank you for reading and God Bless, in the name of Jesus Christ, Amen.

Jeremy

8.   To whom it may concern,

My name is John, I just turned 28 years old. I am a licensed full-time Youth/Associate Pastor and currently majoring in theology and apologetics at Liberty University. I come from a Pastor's family and have been raised in a Charismatic church my entire life. The reason I am writing you this is because I came across your site via YouTube. I had an Alien encounter that i have very rarely opened up about when I was just 12 years old. While most 12 year olds were wanting to have fun all the time, I was always a "deep" kid. I loved to ask my Dad difficult theological questions and frustrate my Sunday school teachers (typical cocky pre kindergartner lol). Anyways, when I was 12 years old, we went on a family vacation to Pensacola, Florida. Little did I know, i was going to have an encounter there that, even as I type this, still impacts me to the point that every hair on my body is standing right now. We were visiting a church down there,

Brownsville Assembly of God. Revival had come to Pensacola and my family and I were eager to get a taste of it.

When we arrived, I remember being blown away by the beautiful condo we were staying in. It was right on the beach, I remember leaving the balcony door open just so i could hear the sound of the waves as they crashed to the shore. The first day we were there, it was like any other family day at the beach. Sand castles, sea shells, and the occasional soaking of my sister which always had me running away.

That night, however, my beach experience was about to change...indeed...my life was about to change. I slept out in the living room with my older brother that night. There was a pull out couch and unlike me, my brother could sleep just about anywhere- anytime. We had all been watching a vas copy of: "Gilligan's Island", my brother fell asleep about an hour or so before the rest of my family went to bed. After the show ended, we all said our goodnights, and I laid down to go to sleep. After being asleep for about three hours, I woke up-wide awake- and felt an extremely strong presence in our living room. I remember trying to wake my brother up just to have the comfort of not being alone, but he was out cold. Finally, i decided just to "mind over matter" what I was feeling and go to sleep. I remember as i laid my head back down, realizing that it was storming outside. I didn't mind storms, i actually enjoyed them, still do in fact; but something eerie was going on and I just couldn't put my finger on what I was experiencing. As i laid facing the balcony, I felt a presence on the other side of me. Even as I write this i am reminded as to why I am apprehensive about sharing it... it sounds crazy. Anyway, I slowly rolled over and standing next to the pull out couch was what appeared to be an Alien. I was immediately paralyzed with fear! "These things don't exist!" I thought, and I literally pinched my arm to make sure I wasn't dreaming.

Just then, I heard the most god-awful scream come out of that thing...but not from its mouth...from its stomach! I will never forget this as long as I live. I stared right in its eyes and remember mustering up all the strength/courage i had to stutter out...Je-Je-Je-Je-JEEEEESSSSSUUUUUSSSSS!! The scream got louder but instead of a sinister scream, this time it was a terrified scream! I watched as this being literally looked like it shattered into nothing right in front of my eyes! I ran into my mom and dad's room woke them up, but did NOT tell them what happened. For some reason, I felt like i couldn't. My parents usually believed me, I was always an honest kid, but i could hardly believe what i experienced myself. Sure enough, I told them i had saw something and their response was that of any adult: "oh honey, you just had a bad dream." and that was the end of it. The story doesn't end there, however, the next night at the Revival...God was going to heal me from what I had just experienced. The pastor at Brownsville (Pastor John Kilpatrick) came down at the end of the service and was praying for literally thousands of people. I remember pushing through the crowd, I needed prayer, and I needed it badly. Let me back up real quick. The day after my experience, i was terrified...in fact I was traumatized. I remember not wanting to go anywhere even out to the beach, and the beach was and is my favorite place on Earth. I was a mess and could not grasp what had happened to me. I asked my brother if he had heard anything last night, NOPE! Of course not, i was alone, and telling the story would surely seem like effrontery..."terrified little John took on an alien by saying the name "Jesus"...yea...ok...sure." So once again, i told no one. This had not been a nightmare, i had nightmares. I was awake, i was awake and thinking. I was awake and trying to wake my brother up before i ever saw it. Then, to top it all off, I pinched myself...which come to think of it, problem even confused the demon (alien) lol.

Okay, back to the Revival service. I'm pushing through the crowd when suddenly, Pastor Kilpatrick reached between two people in front of him and put his hand on my shoulder. The two people, moved so he could get through. I wasn't crying or trembling, but i wanted to tell him what happened but before I could...HE TOLD ME! He came up to me, got right in my ear and said: "Last night you witnessed something that terrified you, didn't you?" What did he say?!? I was in as much disbelief as when i saw the alien. Nodded my head aggressively, he said: "Don't worry, God is going to heal you from that experience right now..." he placed His hand on my head and in an instant the fear, terror, and trauma, were all gone. I slept like a rock that night, and being a fearful kid, that would have otherwise been impossible. So here I am, 16 years later. Married, working hard at church and in school aspiring to be a pastor/professor, and I have witnessed an Alien (demon) and the power of the name of Jesus. Not only that, but i have witnessed the healing power of our savior. While I have rarely shared that experience, and even when I have it has been pretty vague and something I wanted to avoid. I feel like now is the time i should share it. Thank you for listening, and thank you for letting everyone know that there is NO other name by which man can be saved, no other name but JESUS! Amen.

John

9.   Hello, sorry for the lengthy testimony, but I feel all is relevant to this research.

While watching "Breaking News, UFO, Fallen Angel video" on YouTube, I came across the part about alien abductions. Since I was a kid, I have battled these episodes while sleeping where I would wake up on a conscious level but my body would be paralyzed. I was always filled with terror and felt an ominous presence around me. I would try to scream and shake myself awake, but I never could wake till the episode was over, taking, what felt like 20 minutes to an hour of real time.

Sometime during my early 20's, after failing at life and living in sin I decided to go back to church like I did as a child and was baptized and became born again accepting Jesus Christ as my Lord and savior and into my heart. Shortly after this I experienced an influx of these "night terror attacks" I would call them where I felt like I was fighting for my soul. I had a bible on the nightstand next to me and I instantly brought my mind to the bible and started praying "I love you Jesus Christ, please help me" I awoke in about the time it took me to say this in 2 or 3 repetitions, matter of a minute or 2, with such a violent fashion that my heart was beating out of my chest.

After a few months of battling these episodes which seemed to be almost nightly, the episodes just stopped. I am 40 now. My faith has backslid thru this time, watching shows like "Ancient Aliens" and "The Universe" I started reprogramming my brain on how I perceive creation, life and the spiritual realm. A few years ago, I was telling a colleague of mine about my "waking up in my sleep" and being paralyzed episodes. He said his father was a sleep doctor and said that for people with sleep apnea it is very common for people to "wake up" while still asleep to consciously force themselves to breathe. Now, ever since I have heard this, I no longer feel like I am fighting for my soul, but for my life and I feel a great weight on my chest trying to suffocate me. I struggle again to what feels like 20 minutes to an hour, I scream in my head and shake, no help. I even try to force will myself awake by sitting up and just waking up. I get so close to waking up, then just get pulled right back down again. My oldest son has been complaining of the same episodes in last year or so, about the time he turned 13.

Which brings me today on why I was watching YouTube videos on these subjects and why I am here. 2 nights ago, my kids and I where downstairs watching TV and we heard weird noises coming from upstairs perhaps in the walls, these noises went on for 20 minutes or so, we could not locate the source. We wrote it off as maybe an animal in the walls. The next day, the kids and I were talking about how creepy it was, I said I hope it isn't Satan. I then in a loud commanding voice said, "Satan you are not welcome here in this house and' ,'In The Name of Jesus Christ our Lord I Command you to leave this house.' 'This house is protected by Jesus Christ!" Soon afterwards my dog started growling and showing his teeth in a viscous manner at something up in the air looking towards the steps. It FREAKED us out trying to figure out what the dog was growling at, as he is a happy loving dog who has been fixed since a puppy and never has shown aggression like that. I put 2 & 2 together and I know what it was or who even. This is why I am here and watched quite a few YouTube videos, from illuminati, new world order, Christ, and all other kinds of videos linked to these pages. Searching for some conviction to my faith I have so far strayed from.

Next time I have one of these episodes, I will make sure to call out for Jesus Christ for his assistance. When I was in early 20's I awoke pretty quickly when calling out for him. For some reason I feel that it will work again.

Daniel

10.   I had my first experience when I was 18 and burnt my face lighting a stove. I took a pain pill and laid down and almost immediately I began having a tingling feeling in my toes and it started to move up my body and when it reached my upper body I suddenly became terrified beyond comprehension I couldn't move and I felt as if something horrible was standing over me. The next night I took another pain pill and laid down and it happened again and the next night it happened once again, only this time it was different. I was laying on my stomach with my head on my arm and I couldn't pick my head up and I wasn't in my bed I was in the living room on the floor and I could hear my mother's dog running around me and I heard my mom let the dog out and I struggled and finally was able to jerk my head up and I was still in my bed and everyone was asleep. Once I was in bed with my wife and I saw 2 red eyes at my door and became extremely terrified I screamed trying to wake my wife up but I couldn't move or open my mouth, at this point it got Real weird and my bed began to melt and i fell to the floor I stumbled and got up and fumbled my way 2 the bathroom and sat on the toilet and again the toilet melted and I fell to the floor I struggled to get up and couldn't open my eyes or control my body then I suddenly managed to open my eyes and I was in my bed. This happened several times over the years and when it happens I always try to scream and get somebody's attention but I can't open my mouth or eyes or move my body. A few times it happened it wasn't a scary experience but I felt like I was floating and I started to experiment with what I could or couldn't do inside these experiences and I could float up to the ceiling and fall slowly to the floor I once actually floated thru the house. I still had the ones that gave me the overwhelming sense of fear and after reading some of your studies last night I told myself I was going to try it next time it happened and as I started to doze off it happened I also forgot to mention that when the scary ones happen I get a sharp pain n the side of my rib cage almost taking my breath away and it happens in waves it comes on very strong then fades away and then it happens again and fades away and it continues to do this over and over. Well last night It happened and it caught me so off guard it was a little more terrifying than

usual and I immediately began to say in my head Jesus Christ, Jesus Christ, Jesus Christ. It stopped immediately and I peacefully fell back to sleep. For 15 yrs. now I have been powerless to do anything during these experiences but roll with them and hope they stop soon but this worked I don't know why it worked I don't consider myself a Christian or even a religious person but it worked. You have permission to post this email.

Thank you!

Wayne

11.   Dear Sirs;

I wrote this about four times. My computer kept erasing parts of it. I think this will go through, I hope it will.

My Dad, now deceased, was a "Star Trek" fan. He loved everything space alien, UFO and all that jazz. His father was a 33 Degree Mason. My Dad was disowned and abandoned when he was very young because he refused to join DeMolay. My Dad's mother was institutionalized for "epilepsy" in an insane asylum. He never met her. She died while he was in Korea during the war. My father also had undiagnosed seizures. He would have "spells" where he would just check out.

In 1963 I began seeing "creatures" in my bedroom occasionally at night. I had always had dreams of something sinister grabbing me by the ankles in the hallway and dragging me through my bedroom door into another dark room, not my bedroom. I have never slept well at night, I still don't, and there is too much going on.

In 1964 my sister and I were playing with two neighbors in their back yard in Boise, Idaho. I saw a little black spot in the distant sky coming toward us. It loomed larger and larger. You will laugh, but it wasn't funny then or now. It came to a stop directly over the back yard not 25 feet off the ground and hovered there.

It looked like a gigantic lazy boy recliner with a white sheet draped over it. The sheet was undulating in perfect waves all around the bottom edge. I have never been able to recall what the very bottom looked like. I ran. The other three children stood mesmerized. I ran around the lilac hedge for my house and my mom. She had locked the screen door so we wouldn't run in and out. She wouldn't come look, she was busy doing something. I looked back around the hedge several times and continued to scream and pound on the door. Finally she came. It was gone. This chair was at least ten feet square and probably twelve feet tall. My sister remembers it too but will not talk about it. I have never contacted the other two individuals. It just vanished.

In the late 70s and early 80s I was introduced to marijuana, other drugs, and alcohol through "friends" and relatives. I want to point out that I was NOT a heavy drug user by any means. You need to be aware that drug use, weird movies, weird books, and drunkenness, sexual activity, pornography, anything at any level in defiance of God can open a door which you cannot shut.

My second son was born in the mid-80s with a heart defect that required surgery. One day at home alone pondering these things Jehovah showed up and asked me what I was going to do. I stood there and argued with the God I claimed didn't exist. The irony finally dawned on me. I didn't own a bible or read the bible. A thought occurred to me, "harden not your heart as they did in the desert in the day of provocation". I didn't know where that came from but I did know that He was telling me this was the last, the dead last chance He was giving me to submit. I was afraid. I submitted. I was converted and baptized that same day. I don't know how or why I know this, but this was the Father and not the Son.

My second daughter was born mentally retarded and having seizures; at least 85 seizures a day to be accurate. We had to eventually put a football helmet on her to prevent serious injury. Every do-goody-good on the planet told us she had a barbiturate deficiency and needed mood altering narcotic drugs to control the seizures. I read in the bible that a man had a son with a demon and it could only be cast out by prayer and fasting, I fasted every Monday for 5 years. One day Jesus showed up and said, "Okay, I'll do that". She hasn't had a seizure since and she is now 24.

In the early 90s I was in bed trying to sleep. There have always been little dark clouds around on occasions. This night a different kind of black thing came into the room. It was a higher authority, middle management. I don't know how or why I know that, I just do. It was blobbed in shape, had eyes blacker that the rest of it, it was completely opaque, had long spindly misshapen arms and legs, huge hands, and three inch spike like claws. It also had a stupid flat top Spanish style hat that seemed to be part of its head. It was not funny, then or now. It jumped on my chest and pushed me to the bottom of the water bed. I don't know why my wife didn't slosh out the other side. It put its right claw on top of my head. I could feel the claws penetrate my skull. It was going to kill me and take over whatever was left. I tried to say my wife's name, tried to touch her. I was paralyzed and couldn't speak. I did finally utter a harsh raspy, "JESUS, HELP!" He did. He didn't do anything or say anything to that little creep but it immediately let go of me, jumped back the length of the bed, paused and snarled and the shot out the door. I wanted to chase and kill it. Jesus said, "No, not now." I argued, "But it's getting away:" Jesus said again, "NO, NOT NOW!" and then He left too.

In the mid-90s we moved. I was in bed trying to sleep one night when my wife woke me up muttering. There was a little dark cloud next to the bed.   I have always had occasional dreams of floating and flying. Some of these dreams are addictive, they are very much like some of the drug experiences I have had in the past. One night I was having one of these dreams. It is so easy to enjoy them; they are warm and fuzzy, and feel so wonderful . . . they are dreams within dreams within dreams. One night in the early 2000s a particular dream was deep, deep, deep and I was finally sleeping so well I didn't want it to stop. I was finally relaxing and sleeping, really sleeping. A voice said to me, "Why not let go and see what happens?" It was not my voice or my idea. That startled me and I screamed, "NO!" and it was over. Guys, I have been saved for almost 30 years.

I have seen stars within known constellations in the sky move; Stars that are not on the star charts. I have seen the lights shooting across the sky at unbelievable speeds in formation, I was not asleep. I used to be fascinated by this UFO garbage, but now I don't find any of this Hollywood and internet junk very entertaining. I still look at some of the news surrounding these phenomena but I believe it is all a conditioning step for a great deception. I began telling my children this 25 years ago. I have never told them about all of my encounters. I don't think very many people would believe me. Most would say I need to see a psychiatrist. These things are not aliens. They are demons and devils and evil spirits and whatever else is out there. They are pretending to be whatever they think will convince you to give them control. I know I don't remember everything that I have experienced and honestly I don't want to.

I disagree with this websites pronouncement that the name of Jesus alone is sufficient to stop an attack. There were in the Bible some guys running around trying to cast out demons in the name of Jesus who Paul teaches. The demon said, "Jesus I know, Paul I know" and then proceeded to beat the hell out of them and send them running bloody and naked. The name of Jesus should not be used as a talisman or magic bullet. Be careful, in my personal experience it was Jesus Himself who drove off the demons when I called upon Him. He is the ever present help in time of need. Don't just start throwing His name around or you may get a rude surprise.

I would like you to publish this. I think there is something in here that someone needs to read. I am old now. My name is Nathan. If you do publish it would you do so with only my first name?

Nathan

12.   Hello. My name is Jose, from Spain, February 6, 2014.

I give permission to publish my testimony.

Read some testimonials from those of you on the page I realized that my case is similar to what you are posting.

I traced to 1990, when I was not yet born again Christian , I had a life like any ordinary human being and normal, one night while asleep in bed with my wife I woke up middle of the night would be four five in the morning I do not know because you do not look at the clock, saw a great light in the hallway of golden color, the room door was open, and very curious that I noticed that the glow did not go to the room ran to the door of the room , then the logical thing would have been to have happened that light inside the room too, but it was not , in this happened a being floated as a 1 m from the ground gray how 1m 80 tall and with a sort of crown on his head , that being, was floating slowly as when we walk slowly, went to the foot of the bed where we were sleeping and stood next to me , because I was sleeping beside contrary to the hall door .

I then in those days was a Catholic , but not practicing , I thought it was the Virgin Mary who was appearing to me , then to see that being put into position next to me was crying in my mind to and mother me 'rosary ; ! by putting up with me that being, I find the gut ran through my head and body inside , while a tremor as if electrocuted , and it came out through the anus , being gone, I woke my wife and she to touch me realized that I had a cold sweat all over my body, I told it the experience I had had an experience that could not stop , experience that filled me with fear , experience which came other experiences ,one day I was in the morning lying in bed just awake, the room door was closed, through the door of a grotesque demon form and came toward me with her hand over her and came back to my and with his little finger touched one of my lumbar vertebrae that left me to this day , the pain you gave me left me for three days lying in bed, I could not do anything to avoid that experience.

I was terrified when night came, he said goodbye because what you had to create night?

A consequence of all this, I suffered from depression, and I hated the night, as it was when these entities were manifested.

The house lights melted alone and sometimes came on alone.

Two years after suffering several meetings he could not avoid or stop, while I was at work, a colleague of mine was born again Christian, I preached Christ and I thought he was the solution to my problem, then I started reading the Bible and understand what it was that I could protect myself from these attacks that I and my family were suffering, I realized that invoking the name of Jesus Christ I could stop all these unpleasant experiences.

At the time I was baptized in the name which is above every name (Jesus), in my house there have been some more demonstrations but was unable to stop naming the name of Jesus Christ.

The next year after being baptized, receive the gift of the Holy Spirit with the efficiency of speaking in other tongues, one morning I woke up at about six in the morning, I saw down from the sky a bright light that came through my head, my mouth moved one speaking a language I did not understand, but I knew it was the Holy spirit that was baptizing me.

Acts2:38-39 Peter replied, 'Repent and be baptized every one of you in the name of Jesus Christ for the remission of sins, and ye shall receive the gift of the Holy Spirit. For to you is the promise, and to your children, and to all that are afar off, even as many as the Lord our God shall call.

One night while fasting , I got out of the body, i.e. my body was in bed and I was outside him out of the walls a demon gray grabbed me by the shoulders me shaking left right and threw me into my body and I turned to get inside, the experience received could see that he no longer had the fear that I had those things, because now I was privately owned , i.e. Christ , so I knew that what I suggested I was because God had made it possible for me to learn to use the authority that had been given me as the body of Christ we are.

A month ago I had written this testimony , was sleeping in my living room, I had another body experience , i.e. I turned to leave the body , would can walk down the hall of my house and in this I saw another being of these ,looking human person, when I saw him , I fell back scare but I got value because the word says it is stronger that is in us than there are in the world , then I went to that being to grip his shoulders and said, (IN THE NAME OF JESUS OUT OF HERE) that demon disappeared instantly to pronounce that name and with power and authority .

Now I 'm ready to exercise the authority that the Lord has given us when we pronounce his name.

For we wrestle not against flesh and blood, but against spiritual wickedness in high places.

You who are reading this testimony and his life is a mess for such demonstrations do not doubt for a moment move closer to that is mighty to save him from all that, and you will find rest for your tired life and power to be able to defend all those aggression.

God bless you for the good work they are doing with this new ministry that the Lord Jesus Christ to set up.

13.   Dear Mr. Joe Jordan,

I'm originally Hungarian, and I saw your video on YouTube just right now. I was amazed and in the same time shaken. Something is strange and bizarre around your theory and I have the same feeling about all the people in the video. I miss something to complete all of that. However I would like to share something, maybe it can HELP to people, who had same kind of experiences and feel in trap, living in fear.

My experience is no exactly the same as the others I could ever read, or seen on videos. In the same time 99% of the elements are exactly the same ones.

Since I'm kid I was extremely scared that "one they will come back for me from space and will bring me home". I could never explain this feeling. I have never seen before this feeling any sci-fi movie, neither my parents they have never talked me about this kind of things. I felt like this is originally with me, since I have been born. I had studies about philosophy of religious (what strange step in my life) as I was scared somewhere deeply, continuously scared. I wanted answers and I was searching any escape of this fear.

I never could sleep without light in my bedroom until the following event of my life.

I had dreams that one day I have sold my soul, and I can never be free again...(concrete dreams with their symbols images would be too long to share through an email), but for today I have understood that it was a kind of feeling like You can read in Dante's divine Comedy. (by the way that was the most scary epic poem I have ever read- made me depressive through years in my teenage years).

After when I was about 22-25 years old, I was laying in my bed, just falling asleep, the TV was still on. My boyfriend was in the same room, a bit more far on the bed: sleeping. I felt the bed shaking, like it was earthquake. I awoke. I asked my boyfriend if he felt the same. He became angry not to let him sleep, as he felt nothing. I t was strange, I was so sure that the bed was shaking! After it happened 3 times again, but I could awake, before anything else could happen. The TV was still on, I still remember it was a scientific documentary about Silicon Valley, and the new generation of scientists. They were talking about computers. So I heard very well the TV, during I felt asleep again. In my brain in my head each time I heard strange noises, before the bed started to shaking: a noise like when we turn the button of the radio here-and-there. And suddenly a "click", when an old type-writer machine ends to the edge of paper, and before you have to push it to the next line. It was so scary. I felt like something happens to me, that never before, and it is not me who control the things.

At the last time still at that evening, I was too tired, so I did not awake, and i started to feel like after the noises in my head, and the bed shaking, that my body starts to fly up from the bed. My eyes were closed, but I was sure that I'm flying. I felt so light and weightless. I wanted to open my eyes, or to move any part of my body, but I could not. I was completely paralyzed. I started to see a kind of plastic globe, or glass globe above me, with 2 person inside. just shadows, yet, but clearly they were human look like figures maybe a woman and a man .And at that moment my fear became extremely huge, and I "get back to myself in my brain" and I thought NOBODY and NOTHING will rule me. I will NEVER let it happen. As before on TV it was a documentary about computers: I have imagined a keyboard, and I "pressed the ESC"...and strangely I could open my eyes!!! I could move again!!! What was strange only, that i was sitting (not laying) in my bed... My boyfriend noticed nothing from all of that...

I could not tell this story to no one (even my boyfriend was laughing at me, and said I'm foolish), but one day a friend of mine explained almost the same experience. Also she told she went to someone who helped her to step over on this... she mentioned someone, a woman (spiritual-karma cleaner or whatever she called herself) who could help her. I have visited this woman, even if I was extremely sceptic. She was coming from Serbia, or Slovakia, I do not remember that well. Anyway she drove me through a kind of "trip", where I could meet with some human look like creatures, and instead to accept an agreement in the past, I destroyed that kind of documents. It was a karma-travelling. She said. I HAVE NEVER BELEIVED IN ANYTHING LIKE THAT, I was hesitating a lot to visit this woman, but I had to realize that ALL MY dreams, fears has been STOPPED after this "imaginative-trip" ...Completive information: I am Christian - but I never believed as a Christian believes. The woman who helped me, she is Christian, too and she believes. I made studies about religion, mostly about Buddhism, specifically how meditation can affect the brain, and how faith can reflect and create physical changes on the body. I'm not scientist at all, but I can say that my studies and interest was/is a bit more than laic. I'm nobody to make conclusions, and all I'm too small to have answers for all of that. But I believe that most of these experiences are NOT real, and real in the same time. Phenomenon's, playing with us.

And we can REALLY STOP IT, if we BELEIVE that we can stop it, or if we DO NOT LET IT HAPPENS!

I'm sorry about any grammar mistakes or typing mistakes.

Kind regards,

Ms. T.

14.   Hi Joe, my name is Brandon, I am 23 years of age, and have been a born again Christian since the age of 18 even though being raised in my Christian family home.

I would like to give permission to CE4 Research to publish my testimony, I feel no shame or fear in sharing my experiences to assist others.

Growing up as a child, I have been prescribed all sorts of medications.

I never did agree with taking them and they all resulted in a side effect with behavior even though behavior was the reason I was taking them. I was very impulsive, and at a young age was given an IEP in school, labeled ADHD, OCD, and possible bi-polar. Today, I am listed as having OCD tendencies, small amounts of hyperactivity, not bi-polar, but slight ADD. The IEP in school states that

I have a mental disability, greatly affecting relationally and learning capabilities.

As a young boy in church, I've always wondered growing up, always struggling difficultly with how to have my relationship with Christ Jesus. It perplexed me, as I grew up in youth groups and bible camps. Today, I believe He is who He said he is, but have difficulty reading the bible and prayer (Maintaining my relationship with The Lord over everything else). I had strong understanding of the Word, but I wrestled with it in my heart. I could understand mentally but my heart was "hardened" if you will to where I was still lost. At the age of 16, my Grandfather passed away, who I looked up to all my life. It was the turning pointy for me. I began to rebel, first with cigarettes, which I still find myself fighting against, but moved onto the drug scene and further down the road, into this screen of being a member of the "Juggalo family" who are associated with Psychopathic record company that produce demonic music 100%. It's dark, sick and twisted and evil.

I began roaming streets for drugs with face paint on like a clown, intimidating others, and causing conflict.

To this day, because of what I have sown, I am still rebuilding relationship between my families that I had burnt down at the age of 17-18.

But, while engaged with what I was involved with, I had experiences where I had been choked with no one around besides my friend, loss of mobile ability while still moving, and thoughts projected into my head. I hadn't known what these things were, and usually because I was with my drug buddy, he was around when they would occur.

Later down the road, at the age of 18, I had been living on my own, lost my apartment due to drug addiction, and a Christian family took me under my wing, led me to Christ, filled with the overwhelming joy of the Holy Ghost, and went through deliverance of the things I had opened the door to.

After staying with this family, I was allowed to return to my parents where I began witnessing to my old buddy, who in turn had seen things himself as well and also experienced. One night I was invited to stay the night there, as he was actively asking how to close the doors opened by our actions. We engaged in conversation for a very long time, got rid of things he removed that we were aware he wasn't supposed to have after being led to Christ.

At 2am, April of 2008, I was explaining how careful we must consider to be. I continued to explain how it can be possible that some card games that are played or video games, tv shows or movies, drugs and music we listen to can be an open door. After I finished the sentence, and before I explain that, let me go ahead and explain the setting.

We were in Tim's bedroom. His family was asleep with all doors closed except for his grandmothers. His grandmother was very aggressive, always agitated, and creepy in a sense. Anyways, Tim was lying on the mattress on the bedroom floor and I in his brother's bed against the wall and window. All lights were off except the light from his grandmother's television peeping through underneath his door as her bedroom was down the hall. It was dark since we had his door shut, as we didn't want to disturb the other members of his house while we talked.

And now, back to where I am going.

As I finished explaining those actions could be the result of an open door, we could hear the opening theme song of the X Files from his grandmothers room. And when I heard that, I instantly remembered nightmares I had experienced when I was a child when observing that show when my parents watched it. So I used that as an example explains to Tim that even a corny show like the X Files could open the door. I remember that even the smallest clip viewed by my eyes would result in a horrific nightmare. After explaining that (by the way, Tim was cooperative in asking questions, answering and listening) his attitude became hardened and he told me bluntly "whatever". And while lying on his brothers bed, I questioned Tim, "what, where did that come from" (meaning his response towards my example).

After I stated that, the entire bedroom filled with this heavy sense of dread, an extreme paralyzing fear that was completely overwhelming to the point where I couldn't speak out loud and I couldn't move. My face was sideways with my eyes open looking down at Tim, and he immediately pulled the covers over himself, and was also feeling the same experience as I was as he began to cry.

This feeling I knew was evil, no doubt in my mind and had changed the way I see spiritual warfare today.

As we were experiencing this, I was able to turn my head facing the ceiling where I could sense the feeling manifesting.

As I saw, and the only way I can describe it, was a spiraling, heinous, black cloud hovering above my head just below the ceiling. At that moment, I was petrified with fear, and called out to Jesus in my mind.

When I called out in my mind, the Holy Spirit filled me, and I able to recall remembering who I was as a believer.

"The Lord is my strength" I remember thinking and was instantly able to move. So I sat up still feeling this demonic presence, stood up, walked in front of Tim, and began speaking in another language. I have an idea of what I was saying (thinking that it has no right to be here as we are believers). When I began speaking in another language, a large impression was imprinted on the comforter Tim had over him, and to me it looked as if a great force was pushing on him.

That's when I began speaking in English "we are covered by the blood of the lamb, and I stand militant before my Christ Jesus!"

In an instant, the cloud, the intense feeling of heavy fear vanished. The imprint on Tim was removed. Being frightened about the incident, we spent the night at my grandmothers instead.

Since that time, I haven't gone through any paranormal, demonic experiences, extraterrestrial if anything. But I have had very, very, real dreams since then, of great natural or manmade disasters of soon to come, and here in America.

I have seen some that hold too much detail, as I have written them down, waking up feeling as though this life here on earth is fake compared to the dream itself.

There are also dreams of being levitated up by an enormous draft of wind carrying me upwards that shrieks with a frightening scream when blowing, unable to move, and unable to speak. Thinking in my dream "rescue me Jesus", and the dream stops and I awake in a panic, sweat, and nervous and to what is happening because they are so real.

It has been at least a couple months since a dream like that, but the most recent that are more realistic than this life are the ones involving future events, some sort of war, or maybe just a invasion of indifferent, hard to describe helicopters coming from the north, and they are of very large numbers. Multiple dreams being different all having that same thing in common.

I'm a guy who dislikes creepy films, refuses to watch anything, listen to anything, or even be near anything I feel uncomfortable around like those such as horror flicks, secular music, etc.

I am also trying to get back to my relationship with The Lord, where when I was 18, filled with the Holy Ghost and experienced Gods overwhelming love for me. After ridding myself of drugs, past relationships that should have been cut a long time ago, and getting my life on track, i still feel unconnected like I was before as a new born believer.

I feel that maybe I'm not committed enough, and ponder at this. I know that someone I need in my life is a Christian man who I can learn life skills and/or Christian life skills to mentor under which with the church today, and me growing up at church as "a problem child" it becomes very hard to find someone with availability or with the heart to want to. That's something I have been praying for a couple years now.

At the moment, I am homeless staying at a shelter downtown in Phoenix. Actively looking for employment, and trying to interpret the word of God as best as I can on my own.

As I conclude, I would like to thank you for your time.

Thank you again Joe Jordan for everything you have been doing in your ministry.

Brandon

15.   Hello, my name is Emily. Right out of high school I spent the next 10 years of my life receiving a formal education. I was working to become a lawyer. With the process of becoming educated, I began to question everything, and became conditioned by academic critical thinking to use deduction to come to concert conclusions about anything. The sheer amount of information I reviewed,

read, and memorized contributed to a growing doubt in my religion, and in particular my belief in Jesus. I grew up in a Southern Baptist family. I had attended church most of my childhood. For many years I did not go to church. Instead, I went to school full time and couldn't afford to miss work on Sunday. Between 2008and 2010, I started attending a church again. I wasn't there so much to worship, but to research, and to either debunk or confirm the truth behind religion. My once strong beliefs in Christianity very slowly being pulled apart, and by the end of 2010 I had totally rejected Jesus and all other religion. I held on to a belief in a God and have always had powerful spiritual experiences, but religion had no creditability to me anymore. My conclusion was that religion was true only when an individual believed in it. Since what we ultimately believe to be true is reality, and since reality is perception, if you believe it, it's true. And I left it at that. Religion was nothing more and nothing less than the collection of systematic beliefs that were contradictory, open ended, and unbelievable to me.

I felt a lot of guilt for losing my faith, but in my search I had found no evidence that gave me any other choice. There were so many times that God had answered my prayers in the past, but this time he did not come to my aid. I would pray for God to show me the truth, and to give me the information I was seeking because I wanted to believe, but the information just didn't add up anymore. I had no divine interventions or answered prayers related to the existence of Jesus during this time. This then confirmed for me that religion and Jesus were a hoax. For two years I lived without Jesus. I had a close relationship with God, and he answered prayers for me, but I did not pray to Jesus. It was my view during those two years that Jesus was unworthy of prayer because he was not actually God himself, and was likely nonexistent all together. I thought i had it all figured out and had moved on spiritually.

But In December of 2013, I had a very bad cold and had taken some Alka Seltzer. An hour or so after taking the medicine, it became very hard for me to breathe. I felt very much disoriented and foggy minded. I laid down on my couch in my living room and the longer I laid there, the more I felt as though I were dying. And I believe I might have. There is simply no other way to see what I seen, in the realm we live in. Maybe it is possible but I've never seen anything like the figure I seen that day anywhere. What I seen in my living room in front of my fireplace, was a full figure in white robes with a crown of light above a man's head. It wasn't until my eyes meet his that I knew exactly who it was. There is no doubt in my mind that the man I saw that day was Jesus. He did not say a word, but every day since then I have believed in him. That experience has changed my life forever, and in so many ways. So many, that I don't think I even realize all it has done to change it quite yet. I do know this, God finally answered my prayers when I asked for proof of Jesus, and I can firmly say God has never let me down. All that one can do is have the patience to find the answers, and in time, all prayers are answered.

Seeing is believing but this is not the reason I have been lead to your collection of testimonies or your cause. The reason I am writing this is because of the events I just described to you. After seeing Jesus, I have been hearing the word, "testify," over and over. I do not know where it is coming from or why, but I am here today because of it, and because of what I am about to tell you, and because I have been called to give this testimony on behalf of Jesus, and despite looking crazy, I am doing it because no one in their right mind would dare defy God, and because I believe it can be helpful to other's to know that just by calling Jesus Christ and believing in him, he can and will deliver any human from evil.

This is my testimony on using the name of Jesus Christ that saved me from the presence of evil.

Since I was a teenager I have had dreams where I wake up inside my dream and walk around my house. I have lived in 3 houses why whole life and have experienced dream walking in all 3. When I awaken inside the dream everything is the same visually in the houses. The same pictures are hung on the wall, the floors, curtains, furniture, and the layouts of the house are exactly the same. The only difference is the feeling of terror I get, and the colors are duller because the lights are never on. On one particular night, I got up out of bed and tried to turn on the light and even though I flipped the switch, the light did not come on. I can see my family members sleeping and my pets. They cannot see me, but I can see them.

The medical term is called Sleep Paralysis. I've done a lot of research on it, but I've come to only one common dominator about it. In every account I have read and heard, the experience is always dark, and the feeling of sheer terror is always present. The medical condition known as Sleep Paralysis depicts it as a natural function in human sleep. The theory in a nutshell is when in a deep sleep our bodies release a hormone that paralyses the body so that we do not act out our dreams, end of story. It does not explain the dark presence people are feeling nor does it explain how it is possible to walk around if you are paralyzed. That theory could hold up with me if I were paralyzed every time I wake up within the dream, but this is not the case. There are times that I cannot move any part of my body except for my eyes, then there are other times where I feel like i float out of my body and i assure you, I walk around my house. I can think just as clearly as i can right now and i am capable of the same emotions, the same senses, and even problem solving. I have the same sense of consciousness and awareness as I do now. While I am walking around my house, I always see something dark and evil and feel fear in some way or another. My last experience with dream walking terrified me. I was so scared. I have never been so scared. I mean, things in this reality do not have the power to scare you like this. I believe it is a fear only felt by those who experience the true depths of hell and its followers. Being extremely afraid I found comfort in knowing I believed in Jesus at this time and I said out loud Jesus Christ, and then said it once more, I heard a booming sound and I was back in this reality again sitting up in my bed.

When I saw your website and read some of the testimonies, I felt a pull to let you know that not only are you correct that "UFO" abductions are demonic spirits, but that they attack people in other ways such as their dreams too. The fact that by saying Jesus Christ could banish the darkness tells me that they are demons, or else Jesus Christ would not be so powerful against them. These experiences have shown me that death is transformation, devils use trickery and deception, but God, Jesus, and Angels have real power and in comparison the Good has real power where the dark only mocks a copy of the real power and is weaker than the most evil human being, because as I walk through the valley of the shadow of death, I will fear no evil.

Do what you will with this information. Share it and help those who need help fighting the demons that chase them. God was the Creator, and in his image, we are the creation but also we are all creators.

Emily

16.   Hello Mr. Jordan,

My name is Chuck, and I have been experiencing "sleep paralysis", "old hag dreams", or what many view as alien abduction phenomena since I was about 12 years old. With a rough calculation I determined I could have experienced this over 600 times in my life.

The experience would always involve a presence in the room, the inability to move or speak, and would be accompanied at times by deep, guttural voices speaking languages unknown to me, a strong forceful pressure on my perineum that at the time seemed very real. I remember incredible pain and pressure that would stop when I would finally come to.

I was raised a Pentecostal Christian and so I always believed it to be demonic and malevolent, (scary voices speaking different languages in your room pushing on your body will have that effect on you) but I also knew there was power in the name of Jesus, and I would struggle and fight to say His name. As I did the experience would stop, there would be no pain, just the fear of what had happened.

As I grew older it did not stop, but actually continued until I was 41 years old. I have become a part of a deliverance ministry, and being a part of that strengthened my understanding of my authority over the demonic. The last night that I had a full blown episode of this something notable happened.

The presence came in my room, I couldn't move, and I planned to just go through the same old pattern that had gotten me out of it thus far, to say the name of Jesus. But before I could say His name I heard another voice speak to me. I recognized it as the Lord, and he said something to the effect of "No, this time fight it, command it to leave in My name." So in my mind I said "In Jesus name, I command you to leave me!"

I felt the presence pull back, he seemed almost shocked. So I said it again, but with more boldness. "You wicked spirit leave me NOW!!" I could sense the spirit fly up from me.

We live in an apartment and I actually heard the young child that slept in the room above us cry out when that demon would have gone through his room. I prayed for his protection and that he would never experience what I did. So in my experience, the name of Jesus stops the episode, but understanding your authority, facing the demon behind it and commanding it to leave takes care of it for good. I wholeheartedly agree with the 8 R's to freedom, and Gods desire is not for you to just "get through" the episodes, but to overcome the spirit behind it. This is not something you have to live with.

Thanks for hearing my story, feel free to post it, I want people to know there is freedom in the name of Jesus.

~Chuck

17.   Greetings Joe Jordan and Team...

I'm a 'lifer'... my experiences started at (according to conscious memory) 4 years old.

My story is in many ways similar to status quo, but my reluctance to come forward in the past has been because some of the experiences I have had - I have never found anyone mentioning it or coming close.

I have never had any study done on me...I have never been part of any UFO group or community...

I did however...over a looonngg period of time, learn how to break free.

I broke free through the power of Jesus Christ - even before I was a 'true believer' in Christ I would call on Him when I was in fear... and it would work.

I didn't become a true believer in Christ in walk and life until 4 years ago - but I can testify that through the power of Jesus Christ not only do 'they' lose their power over you - a true believer actually holds more power than they do, and that is their biggest fear - that we will figure that out.

After I freed myself from 'abduction' they changed their tactics...

My testimony is going to be a long one. I feel that if I am going to tell my story, I must tell all of it - or at least, as much as I can remember. I feel as though it may turn out to be quite autobiographical seeing as though the abduction phenomenon ends up becoming the abductee's lens through which they experience life.

I may have to send you a few emails, with my story written in episodes and I already know at the get-go that just talking about will open up the proverbial can of worms in my subconscious memory...so I am positive a lot that I don't know I've avoided will come out too.

I aim to be as thorough and open as I can be... So here I go…

I was born is the western suburbs of Sydney Australia. My family is of mixed racial origins, including Dutch, Belgian, Polish, French, Greek, Irish and Indigenous Australian. I was the youngest of Daughters to working class parents. My parents struggled financially and I grew up compared to others as pretty poor - despite both parents holding respectable jobs. My parents separated when I was 8 and from 8 on I lived solely with my Mother. My Mother never re-married.

As a child I attended the Church of Jesus Christ and attended Sunday school and all other Church activities however my parents did not attend. Neither of my parents walked as Christians. My Mother used the Church as a means of having a break from 4 young children. The Church would pick us up by bus and drop us back off. Christ was never discussed in our home, yet my Mother will say she believes in Christ, but refuses to this day to actually read a Bible. As I child I had the 'awe' in Christ…I couldn't get enough. I found Jesus to be amazing!

First experience I can recall:

I was four years old and I was sleeping on the bottom bunk in a bedroom shared by my eldest sister. She was 10 at the time. I was awoken by light coming through the window that was slightly higher than my head and behind the bed head. I had to sit up and turn around and peek out the window on my knees. As I looked out the window the bright white light was blinding. The light was growing larger and larger as it moved closer and closer toward my window. The light encompassed my whole yard and the yards around mine. As the brightest part of the light (in the center) came down over the yard (less than 6 foot of the ground) I went 'somewhere else'. The next thing I knew I was on the top bunk and shaking my sister to wake her up. My sister asked me crankily what my problem was and I told her about the light. She told me the light was a falling star and to go back to sleep. In the morning I actually went outside to find the falling star because this 'star' had come down in my yard… it wasn't until I got much older I realized what a falling star was and what happened that night were not the same thing.

After this event I met 'mermes' and 'macomba'. Mermes and Macomba were my not-so-imaginary-friends. They we not figments of my imagination, I remember them as clear as anything else. In fact, I used to say they were 'more real' than people. Mermes and Macomba would teach me, instruct me and get me into lots of trouble. I began to 'know' things I had no way of knowing. I would be reprimanded for speaking of things that were 'too adult' and knowing details of what people had done, were doing, or going to do. I got in trouble for this all the time. Not only did I get in trouble; but I was rejected and bullied by relatives. At the time I didn't understand it. I didn't realize I was 'aware' of anything that others were not aware of. This strife occurred at school also and it resulted in a lot of negative experiences. I longed to fit in and I longed to be loved, but these two things eluded me for most of my life. I can't be sure how long Mermes and

Macomba hung around 'visually'... but I do know that even when they were no longer visual they were still around me telling me things in my head.

I also recall that I would fall asleep tightly tucked into bed by my Mother and wake up suffocating with my head at the foot of my bed unable to get out. This happened sooo many times that even to this day I refuse to tuck in my bedding.

I was plagued by nightmares and being awoken to beings outside my window and was never comforted nor given any explanation... there was a lot of 'bizarre' activity that would occur during the night in our house. My siblings never mentioned any of this happening to them...in fact my whole life, even now, my family considers me weird and strange.

When my Father left, my Mother feel into a deep depression... One strange experience I can recall was during this time I came out from the hallway calling my Mother. My Mother was standing at the front door, looking out the screen door in a daze. I kept trying to call her but she wasn't listening. I somehow - without explanation - found myself as though I was inside my Mother. I saw what she was looking at, I felt what she was feeling and heard what she was thinking. I couldn't comprehend it, because I was 8 - but I know it happened...someway somehow, I was shown all of that.

A similar experience had happened when I was about 4... I had cut my right heel open to the point it was literally hanging off... As my Mother drove, My father and two of my uncles had me lying across their laps as my father hugged my shoulders my uncles were holding my leg in the air to try and slow the loss of blood. I realize I must have been in shock, but at this time I felt nothing, I only felt and knew what my Fathers thoughts and feelings were.

When I was 12 I began having a reoccurring vision that I would be in a car accident. Some visions more detailed and vivid and others less so, but the story was the same.

While I was 12 I was in a car with a friend and an older 16 year old. He was showing off in front of an ice skating rink and attempted to do a burn out. He lost control of the car and the car spun out of control...I was behind the passenger side (Australian, left side rear) and I time slowed down...I could see a light pole coming closer and closer to my door. While time was slowed a voice said 'not yet' and the car came to a stop. The light pole was less than 2 inches from my door! I do not lie!

After that incident the dream continued. I became nuts with telling people to drive carefully and began to speak candidly about my dream. It was no secret.

Through my teen years things were really hard for me emotionally. It was at 15 I finally realized that I knew information that others did not know. I discovered the hard way that not everyone just 'knew stuff' they were not told or learned about. Friends would tell me stories and leave parts out...they would gossip and complain and I would let's just say, fill in the blanks. They started to question how I knew the 'blanks'. It was an uncomfortable experience... It was isolating.

In my teen years I also began having conscious 'out of body' experiences where I was 'taken' someplace else and shown things. At the time I had no conscious knowledge that all these different experiences were connected. I felt very uneasy and constantly watched...I began to feel 'oppression'. Meanwhile, the reoccurring dream continued.

In 1997 I had a really vivid OBE in which I was taken and shown a past-present-future vision. I fought the presence that had me and said I didn't want to die...I was fearful and angry. I could hear a song (I forget the song now) playing in the background. I was 'pulling' (energetically) away from these beings (they were invisible to me but I was aware they were there and spoke telepathically) I was pulling so hard and then I violently 'fell' back onto my bed. I immediately 'came to' and the same song was playing on the radio in 'reality'. I was 18.

At 19, on March 28 1999 I was involved in a fatal car accident. Out of 4 passengers, one died, one was uninjured. The driver (My eldest sister) died at the scene but was revived using the paddles...the shocked her heart as she was still sitting trapped in the car. I was thrown from the car at an impact speed of 240kph. (The car sped up because my sister lost consciousness)

I should have been dead! The car accident occurred in slow motion (for me) what occurred in 3.5 seconds for me felt like at least 10minutes. I had no fear, I knew what was happening…and it was until I register 'we are going to hit the petrol station' that I felt as though I was 'sucked up' out of the top of my head. Where I went…now that the interesting story… while my body was being flung through the air, my consciousness was soaring above Sydney having a conversation with what I thought then was God, and what I believe now was an angel of the Lord.

I was told that I could choose to live and serve the Lord or I could die. I choose to live and do the 'job I was born to do'. I woke up on the ground of the service station unable to open my eyes because they were filled with class. I was not breathing at some point and given CPR but I was not clinically dead at any point. My sister on the hand was.

I suffered fractures to the c3, 4 and 5, and L3 vertebrae. Miraculously I did not sever my spinal cord. I kept my legs! I was put in a halo brace and began a long recovery (however I never fully recovered).

The crash investigation team said there was no scientific explanation of HOW I could have gotten out of the car the car was crushed like a tin can. I was told over and over it was a miracle. And it was.

Throughout my ROUGH and painful healing process, I was visited repeatedly by a being that kept identifying himself as arch angel Michael. He took me on many sojourns in the Spirit. He took me to my old home (my childhood home) and held my hand (I was as a child again) and we watched the house burn down. I can't remember much more.

I continued to have strange experiences. The accident cause closed head injury that resulted in frontal lobe damage. The frontal lobe is the epileptic center of the brain. The epileptic center is responsible for psychic phenomena - meaning it's the part of the brain that those experiences work through. So it's no surprise that after the accident I was spiritually hypersensitive. I was seeing things, hearing things, feeling things. People began to call me psychic and began acting very strangely around me. The biggest thing I could tell - was when a person was lying.

These experiences led me to look for answers…I tried to attend Church(s) but had very negative and traumatic experiences. I church hopped from 19 to 21 but found no understanding, no compassion and no help. I met with rejection and disapproval. This led me to find answers on the internet and the internet lead me to the new age explanations and philosophies. I didn't realize it at the time…but the worst was yet to begin.

From the year 2000 I was in hell.

And this was when I began to understand WHAT was happening while I was meant to be sleeping.

I hope I am writing this 'right'… smiles.
Leanne

18.   Hi,

I am 50 years old and have been a born again Christian for the last 17 years. All my life I suffered from depression, panic attacks, OCD, post-traumatic stress disorder, etc., etc. Over the last 20 years, I have struggled with knowing this "stuff" was not "me".

After reading some of the testimonies and watching some of your videos, I realize that some of my childhood experiences resonate with what others have experienced. What a relief to know I haven't been crazy all these years!

As a young child, I experienced visitations in the night by evil forces. I was paralyzed during these experiences, neither able to move or make a sound, and would lie awake in my bed tormented, tossing and turning all night. As well, there was so much tension and fear that my face would tense up which led to permanent squinting that has only been recently alleviated. As well, I know I was violated rectally and believe that something was implanted in me at that time which has taken over 40 years to "dislodge" using extensive detox methods and extended periods of all-out spiritual warfare. This process continues to this day. I have had spiritual ministry, deliverance sessions repeatedly over the last 17 years, and have been told by several people that my case has been the worst they have encountered with demonic interference.

Along with this, I very vividly recall dreams/visions of an apocalyptic nature. In one of these, I woke to total devastation around me and with the knowledge that I was alone in the world, with all life on earth destroyed except for me. Needless to say, this was terrifying to me as a young child.   In addition to this, I would have repeated dreams of being thrown up in the air and falling, always awakening in a cold sweat before I would hit the ground. This dream would occur 2 or 3 times a week. (I'm not sure of the significance of this, but know it was evil).

I was led by the Holy Spirit to make detoxing a way of life several years ago. From piecing together the wisdom I've asked for and received from the Holy Spirit, I believe that the physical, demonic energy that was implanted in me as a young child has been very acidic in nature, and the energy itself very dark, both in nature and in physicality. After years of detoxing, I expelled dark sticky material that would stain my bathtub severely and was extremely difficult to clean up. This dark energy has been buried very deeply in my tissues as evidenced by the amount of time and effort it has taken to get rid of. As well, I remember dark matter staining my body, toes in particular, when I was a child that just got passed off as dirt, but I now believe it was this foreign, dark energy. So acidic has this matter been in my body that in releasing it, I was off my feet for 7 years due to the amount of stuff that was in me being expelled that my body struggled to handle.

I continue on my journey to total freedom and regaining my own personality (which is pretty fantastic, by the way!).

If this can help anyone else, by all means use this story. More keeps being revealed to me as I go along, and perhaps one day I'll know exactly what happened to me all those years ago. I am grateful to God that He never gave up on me, when most other people did. Thank you for sharing this information!

God bless you!

Jennifer

Ontario, Canada

19.   Dear Joe,

My name is Sara I am from Texas. I am 29 years old. I am contacting you because I watched the video online called May 3 2012 Breaking News UFO Fallen Angels New World Order. And you are featured in the UFO section. And I felt you could be the best person to help aid me in understanding my experiences. I too am Christian. And I do believe that the things we come in contact with are fallen angels. While living in our family home which we shared for 20 years. My mother and my sister and I had the same encounter one night. Which we all saw as a dream at the time until we realized we shared the same dream. Down the very small details. For me the dream took place in my bedroom as it did for my mother and sister. I was standing at the window in my bedroom that looked out towards our backyard. Everything was very illuminated. There was a tree to my right under it was what would seem to be a child's large bouncy ball. But it was glowing and there were shapes and animals jumping out of it. The one I remember the most was the tiger. We all has this same dream on the same night. We all remember different details about it. I suppose because we all were watching from our own view of it. But all of our stories fit together as one story. That's just what happened in mine. What is interesting about this is. We all had the vision from the same window in our home. That part was a large part of it for all of us. That this window was showing us something. Around the same time something else happened to me. I am a very light sleeper. I wake up to anything even a shift of air in the room will wake me. One night I had a dream that I slept walked to our backyard. Which was an acre long with our neighbor's back yards surrounding ours on our city block. I remember getting out of bed from my top bunk bed. Going outside all the way to the back yard. The night before bed I was wearing my favorite necklace at the time which was a snow globe with Santa inside. I stopped at what appeared to be Christmas lights in my neighbor's back yard. Now this is odd because it was not the season for this. I just happened to like that necklace and wore it all the time. So the lights caught my eye. And as I stared at them I noticed they seemed to be moving upwards. Upon seeing this I was afraid dropped my necklace in the grass and ran inside the next morning I woke up thinking "Oh what a crazy dream". Until I went to hop down from my bed and realized my feet were all dirty, and my necklace was gone. I went outside hoping to not find my necklace laying in the grass. But it was in the grass. Right where I dropped it in the "dream". We remodeled the bedroom we stayed in. And we took the window out. Nothing like that happened again after the window was taken out of the bedroom. I don't know what relevance the window has or if there is any correlation between the windows being present and then not being present. To my knowledge my sister and my mother have not had any more experiences after this. But I have. Over the past couple years I have had these night terrors. And then I feel the worst fear any one can imagine. There are these beings. But I would not say that look like what we call aliens. They look like shadowy figures. And I believe being a person of faith. That they don't feel the need to disguise themselves. I see them in their true form. Being an odd child I was obsessed with horror movies. When I have these dreams. The only thing I can think to say while I realize I have some sort of control over what is happening is the quote the exorcist saying "The power of Christ compels you ". Sometimes even making the sign of the cross with my hands. While watching the video and hearing your part in it came to me. Maybe they are still trying to communicate with me. I had never heard of someone being "abducted", but not leaving their home. In these dreams when I do defend myself by saying those words it stops almost immediately. My question to you is.... Are these bad dreams. Or could they be something that others have reported. And if you found anything in your research that may tell us why they are trying to communicate with certain people. I hope this letter finds you well. God Bless you.

Sara

20.   Hi CE4 Research group

My name is Maricela I'm from Costa Rica, Central America. I saw your video by chance.

I was always passionate since I was a little girl from the UFO subject, now I have 39 years.

When I was 19 years old, one night at my house, I was ready to go to sleep, the light in my bedroom was off, but some light was coming from the Street. I saw a shadow on the ceiling, then this shadow came into my body and I was paralyzed, could not speak, scream or move. I felt I was dying or going out of my body; like I am Catholic I thought the only one that could help was God.

I said to God "remember me please, if I'm going to die today", and the entire experience was over immediately. I was afraid, and I could not sleep the other night.

I leave this experience in my memory, I said it to my mother, I think that the other persons can't believe me, but when I saw your video I understood that I was not the only one.

Thank you for your video and testimonials.

Excuse my English.......!

Maricela

21.   My name is Jeremy. I am a Christian. I am also a combat veteran and fear nothing. I proclaimed Jesus as my Lord in January 13 2002. Before i was a Christian I had what I call an episode. At age 13 I and a friend went camping behind my house in Indian Head, M.D. I was an experienced camper and a boy

scout for many years prior and during this episode. There are 200 acres behind my house. Our tent was set up, it was mid-summer, on a hill were hunters had set up a camping area with a fire pit and so on. I would say 1 meters from my house. We were in the tent facing out the screen watching the fire. Then what we thought was a helicopter was flying towards us. The next thing we remember is the fire being out and our body's half out of the tent. We both woke up at the same time. We couldn't understand what happened so we grabbed the flashlight and ran back to my house leaving everything there. Reluctant we returned at daylight to retrieve our camping equipment. I believe it was around 3 or 4am when we left the camp site that night. Nightmares and dreams plagued me for 2 yrs. after till i said enough. After that year I returned to N.H. to live with my mother. The dreams and nightmares followed. In my house in N.H. was where I said enough. Before I moved from M.D. I did see a creature in the woods that I would have to explain in person or another email. Not sure if it is related. Last but not least I had an episode with my father camping in Maine were we were camping on a lake. The water was babbling, crickets chirping and wind blowing. All the sudden it was silent. I could hear my heart beat. I and my father stopped to listen. A nocking sound came from the north of us and a second nock from the west of us. Then as quickly as everything went silent it was loud with nature again. The water was babbling, crickets chirping and wind blowing. Not sure it is related. What plagues me the most is the camping trip at age 13? I also drew a picture of the creature I saw a few weeks later. I went to Iraq in 2005 to 2006. 13mnths. You would be surprised at the things you see in the sky that is unidentified. As I said before, I fear nothing and have complete faith in the Lord Jesus Christ. I fear no evil or man or any unworldly things. I am curious if under hypnosis to find out that faithful night when I was 13. I hope this helps. Feel free to email me if you have any questions. I am 36 yrs. old now. This is the first time of writing about what has happened to me. Thank you for your time.

Jeremy

22.   Dear Joe Jordan...

I have come across your work. I would like to share with you my personal testimony of an experience I had when I was 17 years old, (I am now 36) before I begin reading the testimonies on your website to find similarities. I would also like to thank you for the work that you have done in this area because the UFO/Alien phenomenon was a big hindrance to my personal relationship with Jesus and His Word when I was younger. There was just not enough information that told the "Whole story".

I was a junior in High School and my bedroom was on the second floor of our home in Toledo, Ohio. I had been interested in UFO related material and occult activity but participated reluctantly. I had tried Astral Projection (according to the Time/Life series of books) with no success except for a strange feeling which caused me to give it up. I had used Ouija boards with an attitude that if there were spirits... they couldn't touch me and had a very strange experience years before. (Which I attribute to the following testimony) My family had a menial Christian faith but not really walking with God or really believing it. Luckily my grandmother had always talked about Jesus as if she knew Him personally and had a great influence on me later.

I had gone to bed around 10:00 on a weekday night and was 10 minutes into sleeping when my sister turned the hall light on and woke me up. I am an extremely light sleeper so I got out of bed and slammed my bedroom door shut so that I could sleep. About 20 minutes after falling asleep, I felt a presence enter the room and what appeared to be a shadow move towards me... I screamed and pulled the covers over my head. My heart was pounding and I was telling myself that I must have been dreaming. It was only a dream. I tried to rationalize so I could calm down and about 5 minutes of heart pounding and breathing, I felt something sit, or jump onto my bed. I had a water bed back in the 90's and I KNEW that I was awake at this point. It felt fairly heavy and it began to pant... the most wicked thing I've ever heard! I was so scared that I said out loud, "In the name of Jesus, Get OUT of here!" Whatever it was became totally silent and I didn't know if it was waiting for me to do something... I didn't feel it move or leave. After 20 minutes of cowering under the covers, I slowly reached my hand out and turned the light on above my head. I looked and there was nothing there. I cowered the room and looked in every closet and hiding place to see if my dog or cat was in the room but the door was closed that there was nothing there. I went down stairs and the dog was sitting next to my dad watching TV. I asked him if he heard me scream and he said no... He was oblivious.

Years later I became a Christian and really understood what it was to be a disciple of Jesus, I began to understand the significance of what took place in my room in 1994. The name of Jesus had stopped something from taking place and I thank God that it was HIS name I relied upon and not my own belief, not knowing at the time how powerful HIS name really is.

I don't know what came into my room but I do know that the name of Jesus stopped it from going any further. If you find this story of any relevance, you have my permission to use this to help somebody else. Thank you once again for your research and God bless

Matt

23.   Hello,

I was drawn to write you my testimony, so long as it might be I think you will find it very rewarding for your purposes in its content and instruction. Here it is;

I was born into an atheist family yet at the age of 13 I came to Christ through the help of 2 rebels, well those whom the world would have seen as rebels yet were rebels for god defying the new order of things, defying the new way and breaking the "norm".

Within one week of being brought into the light I was shown visions almost if not every night. The Visions were all of things I had never heard of, read about, seen, believed or ever thought of before. These were of a blood moon, fire raining down from heaven, a bright star falling to earth and by myriads of flying saucers bringing our false salvation, the greatest earthquake the world has ever known and the sky receding like a scroll with winds that shook upon the face of the earth.

During all of these vision I somehow knew these beings were not "right" and that they were "wrong" because I had Gods love within me and I felt that they sought to destroy me and all men, whilst pretending to save them in order to destroy them even faster (what a perfect plan).

Now being shaken by this idea, this prophecy, the pain, the power and suffering I witnessed I was forever changed and knew a truth that would never leave me, a truth that would guide me away from deception and would serve me well. Within days of learning truths of the age we live in and of the desires of angels and men working for Satan I warned all those I knew of about a coming deception that the sci idea of aliens which all my young friends found to be a wonderful idea were not aliens, they were the demons of old and that they would deceive man and destroy gods people, and that they need to know this and that they need to turn to god and trust him. Every single person (bar 2 - the 2 rebels) all laughed and said that this idea was the most stupid thing they had ever heard and that aliens are "real" that aliens are not demons and that they would save us not destroy us.

So It seemed that before I had ever heard of this idea, god gave it to me, I preached this idea to this day and have convinced some but most still rather the alternative idea, the one without god.

Now as for my many experiences in which I stopped their menace, within days of telling all I knew of these ideas I was woken from my sleep and saw a darkness hovering above the end of my bed, it was not space and was within, within, within darkness, it was like a black hole, a vortex or a portal. I then felt a power so menacing that I was confused and troubled. I felt it was alive and real and the moment I was aware of its presence it pushed me into my bed.

I was wide awake I assure you as I heard the springs of the bed being pressed in and my eyes could move so I looked to my side and I was pushed deep into my bed and the bulk of the pressure was upon my throat, being new to god I did not think to call upon him but I screamed for my father but all that came out was air, my voice box would not work only air would pass through it and my lungs lost more capacity with every attempt. Soon after when I thought all was lost and that death was here, my heart pled with god for help, then I heard a voice, a great and terrible voice, it said, MICHEAL (slightly confused in authoritative tone), MICHEAL!!!! (In anger) and then the way I felt,,, I felt, that the being who made me feel that way now felt that way in regards to this greater voice.

To this day I am certain that one of Satan's advocates was sent to stop me because I was never seen in his plans because of my upbringing, It was a gift from god that I was saved and shown many secrets and Satan was not pleased especially that I did not fear to speak of god of Christ or of the deception.

Over the years I have had many experiences with Satan's Angels / Saturn's Aliens (LOL). I have found that in the earlier times the name of Christ being called upon whilst living a fulfilled life or at least trying to live a fulfilled life the demons/aliens as most men now think of them would leave or would stop and be gone.

I do have one thing to say also in regards to this, Christ, God or other angels are all helpers, yet I have met things which even with the name of Christ would not leave, those things are allowed to be here under contract with Satan and with god, as they still speak and makes deals, until the day he is cast to earth. Now since being saved I have become corrupted, not of mind or soul but of flesh, the desires of the flesh have destroyed me and since this has occurred I cannot receive help from god when they come, it is entirely up to god if he chooses to give help, he might give me a millionth chance or he might say no, you have made you bed sleep in it.

All in all CHRIST is not a magic word, nor is God, Gabriel or any other name above the other names, what will save you is being saved and living a saved life, then if you are attacked which you will be, you have God's blessing, gods armor and gods power. I have been attacked while saved and had POWER OVER these beings but when corrupted I have NO POWER over these beings, which tells me one thing, ALL POWER COMES FROM GOD, GOD IS POWER AND WITHOUT GOD WITHIN YOU, YOU HAVE NO POWER OVER THESE THINGS.

Blessings to you all and please pray for my soul, for I am lost. Be blessed and live a saved life so that you may not be destroyed or deceived by these powers.

If you decide to use this on your web page or for any other use, I Simon Alan Lutze grant CE4 Research web page and organization full use of this testimonial and to quote my email name or any other details required as a means to educate others of Gods power over this evil.

Regards

Simon

24.   Hello Joe,

My name is Frank and while watching a video concerning the new world order agenda, fallen angels and their connection to alien beings, clips from your research caught my attention in a manner I didn't quite imagine before and this is the idea that alien abductions are none other than demonic beings in the guise of extraterrestrials.

I have experienced several encounters from what I have considered demonic oppression instead of alien abduction ever since I could hold a memory as a child but I believe that my perceptions as such have been because of my Christian upbringing. I also do remember being around occult practices as a child and at times all of us neighborhood kids who were part of the same crowd would sometimes mimic the rituals we would hear from grownups around us. Although I never experienced a spaceship hovering over me, I did have a recurring dream of two demons and by demons I am relaying what I thought I saw at the time. I was around 4 years old then where I would become conscious of lying flat on my back completely nude on what I sensed was a clinical bed in the presence of what appeared to be two women at the first, one at the foot of the bed and the other at my head. What happened next was perplexing to me then absolutely horrifying. The two women were naked too. The one at the foot of the bed mounted my groin with hers and as soon as I became aware of what I felt to be extremely uncomfortable and in fact sadistically invasive against my being, the woman at my groin immediately turned into a terrifying grotesque looking demon whose female parts would almost simultaneously constrict on male parts and the one at my head would follow suit quickly and mount its female part on my lips and constrict on my lips. The grip their parts would have on me was overwhelmingly captivating, dominating and completely paralyzing so much so it felt so physically real and I could not move or breathe worth anything. Then the dream would leave me just as quickly as it came.

Now, later in my young adult years I started having an in body and spirit experience with a non-human entity in my sleep, as I would be half conscious at the time these experiences would take place. I would be so consciously aware of my surroundings that I could see the objects in the room around me in its most minute detail whenever this other entity would visit me. Out of the blue again, this overwhelmingly evil and completely captivating presence which I couldn't see although my spiritual eyes would open as I could see my physical surroundings yet all I could move were my eyes but very slowly. This demonic force which felt like a gruesome slithering snake would press upon my groin and abdomen causing such a gravitational pull on my whole being, mind body, soul and spirit. I felt completely nailed to my bed. The excruciating pain I felt was deeply painful yet purely spiritual. The life in me was literally depleted out of me. The experience felt countless times worse than a weighted down free fall ride. I couldn't open up my mouth to scream but I did a lot of screaming in my mind begging God to help me. It seemed like God was nowhere to be found and that thing would leave me as freely as it came upon me. As it was leaving, my spiritual eyes would close as I was fully aware of my physical surroundings, while still in a dream state, my physical eyes would slowly open as everything around me was intact and I was in the same position; whatever position I would be in at the time of each visitation. It wasn't until I wanted to fight back because this tormented me throughout my life that I got my first breakthrough. This breakthrough began, both, mentally and spiritually. And by finally using the command, "In the mighty name of Jesus get away from me you freaking devil!", in one of my encounters that I was able to move one of my hands and grabbed the snake like texture on my abdomen and groin. The effect of it rushed through my hand straight into the heart of my being into that part of my brain which the core of fear like a viciously biting electrocution (much like when I got electrocuted by a 120 volt outlet while standing in a mud puddle when I was 6 years old. In fact, that's how the evil presence always felt in the physical sense.) But I held and maintained my ground even though it was painful and terrifying. Finally, it succumbed to my resistance and broke away. As it broke away, I felt it slither along my abdomen up along my chest and as my spiritual eyes were closing I caught a glimpse of its frogish green arm. Transparently my physical eyes opened just after I saw it disappear under the bed. Again, same position and surrounding details. I later hand an encounter where a much bigger demon attempted to subdue me. I invoked the powerful name of Jesus and my spiritual arms responded and got a hold of two of its large snake like fingers which thickness felt the diameter of middle section of a standard baseball bat. I was much stronger by then and as I held my ground while I was prying him off of my abdomen he retracted instantly after I drained the life out of its fingers and broke them like what felt like hollow pretzel shells. What was also puzzling to me was when I saw my spiritual eyes leave my physically arms, I was on my back with my arms crossed and I saw my spiritual arms rise up while I could still see my physical arms still in the crossed position. Ironically after the battle when my spiritual eyes closed and physical eyes opened, my arms were crossed completely and painfully dead asleep. I quickly realized that I never brought my spiritual arms back before I woke. It took a minute or two to wake my arms up. Since then I have asked the Lord that if I was allowed to suffer my whole life like that for Him to give the opportunity to make a much greater stand if I gave to meet up again in their realm. Alien demons is what they are and I strongly believe our spirit can fight them in their own dimension, God grant us the right of passage in the mighty name of Jesus Christ the Righteousness of God the Father. Amen!

Yours truly,

Frank.

25.   Hi, I want to give a report about my experiences with sleep paralysis. Weather it was alien/demonic in nature I don't know, but the name of Jesus helped me each time.

Each time it was like some kind of sleep paralysis and there weren't any beings around me I could see but I could feel some forces, intense fear and weight pressing down on my belly. I could barely move or speak.

The first several times I experienced this was very terrifying but I never thought it had anything to do with aliens or demons. Two years ago my sister began reading the Bible and became a Christian through her boyfriend. I, being very inquisitive, became interested in the Bible. Though I tried, I couldn't take the organized religion part of it seriously (the ritual and dogma) but I found myself agreeing very much with the spiritual teachings of Jesus, but I still didn't really believe in him or that he is there protecting us. I read online about some ways to cure sleep paralysis then and one of the ways was calling upon Jesus name. I decided to give it a try and the next time I had a sleep paralysis/attack, I immediately was released and woke up upon calling Jesus' name. I couldn't still believe it really worked and for a time I thought it was some kind of autosuggestion thing. But then it happened a few more times and each time, it worked, although the last few times I had to call the name of Jesus several times until the things disappeared. I figured whatever was attacking me was very intelligent and tried to trick me into believing the name of Jesus didn't work and tried to stay with me as long as it could bear, so I would doubt, but as I wouldn't back down - in the end it had to leave.

Since then I only had one more experience where some child-size being hugged me and tried to restrain me from behind while sleeping in my bed with my boyfriend and I just shook it out in half sleep and when I woke up I was really freaked out because at first I thought it was my boyfriend - but he was lying in front of me!

After that I went deep into the study of the occult, aliens and spirituality and there is definitely something going on vamporizing people's energy - demons, vampires, aliens, extra-dimensional beings, malevolent thought-forms, I am convinced it's all essentially the same thing. Furthermore I believe they are our creations in a way and that this is why we, by virtue of our higher mind (when we are not in the state of fear), have authority over them. Those things are parasitic as they do not have their own source of life energy and as such they are weaker than us in every aspect. That is why they cannot attack us openly but only when we let our guard down and using energy technology using mind tricks and appearing more powerful than they truly are.

By knowing we are the divine children of God and under the protection of Jesus Christ/Christ consciousness, we can stop being a victim of these buggers forever and be free of fear.

There is another part of this and I want to explain this quickly without going into too much detail and I hope you keep an open mind on this because it may seem that it has nothing to do with this -but it definitely does. Nothing can enter our space without our permission. When we consent to being represented by our governments, our government has the right to enter us into contracts. The governments of the world signed contracts with otherworldly beings which bind us to whatever the contract contains - as long as we accept the jurisdiction and authority of our governments. Understand that these contracts are more spiritual than material. When you revoke your consent to be represented by a government, you revoke false authority and nullify all contracts the government has made in your name - it's place you have to accept only true authority which is the authority of your Creator (whatever you believe your creator is) as true authority implies true authorship! This way, you get all your birthright and power back in this world and the spiritual world! This is ABSOLUTE PROTECTION from all evil entities for all eternity. So what do you have to do to get it? NOTHING! Just know that this is the truth and it is so: No one has authority over you but your creator - who would never harm you. No one else CAN have authority over you without your consent - so DO NOT CONSENT!

Hopefully, this helps you.

J.G.

26.   Hi, I just want to say that I heard about you guys via a YouTube video that I am in the middle of watching this very moment.

When it got to the part where you are talking about how people were able to break the "abduction experience" by calling out the name of Jesus Christ, that's when my eyes lit up. I never thought anyone else may have had the same experience or had done something similar. I had something very similar happen to me a few years ago. It's something I'll never forget.

One night I was lying in bed in my room alone at my parents' house. During this period of my life I remember that I was very interested in UFOs and the supernatural. In fact I have always been interested in such things. But I remember prior to this particular night I had been researching in great detail about astral projection of all things. I remember reading about how the best time to try to leave your physical body was during that point in time just as you are about to drift off into a dream state. It is then that you want to try and sit up outside of your physical body. But I could never do it. But not too long after reading about all this i remember waking up in the middle of the night. It felt like it was about 2 or 3am. I knew this because even with closed eyes it was extremely dark and the air was cold as it is early hours of the morning. And there was absolutely no sound or activity heard at all. I became fully conscious in my mind yet my body was still "asleep". My eyes were closed. And when I realized that I was conscious and my body was still in slumber immediately I thought to myself "Hey this is it! Maybe I can leave my body now. I'm sure this is the state I need to be in!" So I made sure not to try and open my eyes or move my physical body at all. Instead I began trying to will my spirit up out of my body. At first it was a very fascinating feeling. I remember ensuring to myself that there was no rush. Just savor the moment and try and wriggle my way out of my physical body somehow. I think about 30 seconds later I noticed there was a slight "electrical" sound about my ears. Like static or something. The static was only subtle so I thought nothing of it at that stage. Now I begin to try and sit up straight. Ever so slowly to be sure that my physical body wouldn't follow suit. Once I felt like I had successfully sat up off the pillow about 5cm the static in my ears began to get stronger. The higher I tried to sit up the stronger the electricity became in my ears and at the same time it prevented me from going any further.

I remember the more I tried to push against it the more intense the electrical sound became but now the intensity was becoming painful. So now I quickly lay my "spirit" body flat down on the bed again to alleviate some of the pain. But to my surprise that same amount of intensity remained and I could also now feel this static in my abdominal muscles. It was beginning to really hurt now. At this point I became very afraid. I tried to open my eyes now but I found that I couldn't. In panic I tried to get my physical body to sit up but that resistance intensified more. The harder I tried to get up the more painful this "electric shock" became. It got to the point that I could feel my abdominal muscles tensing as hard as possible and it was preventing me from breathing. I remember I tried to scream or cry for help but nothing was coming out of my mouth. It felt like I was very much paralyzed and this feeling of static in my body was just increasing more and more. I was so afraid I really thought that I was going to die right there. At the point that I thought that this was going to be my last breath I remember trying the only thing that I could think out of fear and panic. I cried out within myself, and with ALL my heart and soul, Lord Jesus! Help me please!! Lord Jesus!! And IMMEDIATELY it stopped, I sat straight up! I was covered in sweat, trembling to the very core and it was day time! I couldn't believe it.

At that moment I didn't know what shocked me more. That all this had just happened, or that it went from what felt like 3am instantly to the middle of the day in the absolute blink of an eye! I sat there for a few minutes going over what had just happened, whether it was a dream or something. But I knew it wasn't a dream. But how can one ever really convince someone else of the reality of it all. All I know is that it really happened, I'll NEVER forget it and the only reason in my mind that I survived it was because the Lord heard me cry out to Him and He saved me.

That was the only time in my life that I have experienced that kind of thing before so I can't say whether it would have otherwise turned out to be a so called "alien abduction" experience because He saved me before it got that far. But I know there was something there in the room with me. Something dark and strong. Nevertheless, stronger is He that is in us than he that is in the world.

That's my true story. If it suits you to use it as a testimony then I would be most happy to approve if it might help others in similar situations.

Thanks for taking the time to listen. Take care and God bless.

Kind Regards

Kaiwa

27.   Hi, from around the age of eight until seventeen, was on a fairly regular basis (say every few months on average) being visited by spiritual beings. To give more depth and understanding I will describe several encounters (not near all of them, there were way too many) and what I did to make them stop.

I was about eleven years old and had just gone to bed, it was about nine pm. For some reason I woke during the night with a chilling feeling so I sat up and turned my light on. When I gazed around the room, out the corner of my eye I caught the sight of movement. What happened next was clearly the work of some cross-dimensional being? I looked down to my right only to see my soccer ball next to my bed spinning in a circle about one ft. in diameter. I lost my breath in shock, I couldn't understand what was happening. I suddenly screamed and pulled the covers over my head. I yelled to my parents as loud as I could but they never came which was so strange because they would often come down the hall at the slightest hint of noise to indicate I was still awake.

A year or so later I had developed a hobby of collecting and reading books, strange for a kid at that time but I'm better for it. I would often stay up late and very quietly read my books, with the door closed, a towel at the bottom of the door to stop light going through and only my bed light on. Next to my bed was one of those 'Far Side' calendars and every day when I would tear them off I would scrunch them up in a very strange but unique way that even to this day I haven't seen before. At about ten pm I switched off my light and laid down to sleep, when a piece of paper hits me in the face. I immediately turn on the light, there was never a noise, and the door was still closed with the towel firmly pressed against it, still shocked I look down at the paper on my lap. I see that I have scrunched this up, it was a Far Side calendar page, what is stranger, it was twenty days old. This also was not long after an Ouija Board experiment.

I had since moved house and had little harassment from these spirits or whatever you wish to call them when one day I was alone in the house, watching T.V, when I looked over to the kitchen to find a person standing there. I stared for what seemed forever and then suddenly, poof, it shot off into the laundry. It had until this stage not shown itself to me; this was an advancement in its methodology and it truly was freaking me out.

I had many other experiences between all that I have mentioned, often ones involving being woken up frozen in bed or being touched, but this is just a snippet.

I told my friends mum, with what I admit to be some pride, that I had been consistently visited by spirits since I was a kid and told her a few of these experiences. She was horrified and instructed me to not engage these beings, only do so if I wanted to get rid of them. She told me to say, "Get out of my house as it and my soul belong to Jesus Christ". I shrugged it off and that was that.

About six months later I was at home, it was night and I was walking up the stairs. I got to the top and a spirit ran straight past me and touched me then slammed the door after it. My parents yelled at me for the door slamming and then realized something was wrong when they saw I was frozen and looked as white as a ghost.

Later that night I went to go through that same door from the other side. I had left the door open half way so I had to open it a bit to get out. As soon as I put my hand on the handle there was an almighty pull from the other side, it was so strong, so much so that I had both hands on the handle and was using my body weight to pull. After about ten seconds of pulling the door all of a sudden gave way and I fell backwards (Please keep in mind the windows were closed and there was absolutely no draft.... and not even a draft could do that).

I told my brother this story and he also told me a few, one of which was the constant slamming of the cellar door of which had to be lifted from the ground up and weighed about twenty kg (approx. 38lb). I told my friends mum about the recent events and she reminded me of the previous conversation we had on the topic. The spirits are evil she said; "if they are acting in secret, if they hide from you and demonize you then they are not of God"!

I took the advice seriously this time and when I got home I prayed for the Lord to rid the spirits for my house, to take out all that is evil. I then commanded in the name of Jesus Christ for anything not of God to leave my house as it and my soul belong to Jesus! That was when I was seventeen, I'm now twenty four and haven't had a visit since. I'm a born again Christian and worship on a daily basis. Jesus is my Lord and savior and since that moment when I was only seventeen he has led me through other tough times. Without Christ I would cease to exist in my view. I would be nothing more than a lost, deceived, tortured soul, walking the earth only prolonging my Hellish fate.

This e-mail is intended for public display and as such CE4 may display it on their website.

Kind Regards,

Scott

28.   Dear Joe...

A man named Tim on you tube did a video about you today and it got me thinking I should tell you about my life! I don't know if you have ever heard anything about what I am going to tell you, but I might be able to answer a few of your questions or at least help you understand why... I am very much a believer in Yahuwah and Yeshua, and I know for a fact they are real, alive and always around!

I don't tell to many people because it is hard to believe, it's hard to think something like this can happen and how awesome He is when it comes to protecting what is His! Many put Yahuwah in a small box of beliefs and tell me, I am of Satan or a demon is inside me. It hurts to hear this on many levels! It is hard for some to hear truth, to believe it is possible.

The verse of John 10:27-29 will have more meaning to you after you read this email, you will understand more of how this verse applies! I am sorry but it will be a long email so please get comfee, open your mind and remember "Anything and Everything is Possible with Yahuwah!!" There is NOTHING He can NOT do!!!

All my life I have been stubborn, I have always been strong willed. I never really fell into peer pressure and I always over analyzes situations, it is more, of listening to each side and figuring out the right way. All my life, I have a sense of things that are going to happen, to explain: years ago I was in a custody battle with my ex. I was on the phone with him, heading to work, and I told him "I will get her back!" he got mad an asked, "What, you are going to take me back to court?" I told him "no, I will not have to." A few years later, I did get my daughter back without going to court... that was about 10 years ago.

Another time, I was at work, and I looked around my office and thought, "I am going to de-personalize my office. So I took down things, boxed stuff up, I left the box there that night, and my co-worker was leaving, she asked if I was quitting, I told her no. I took all the pictures I had on the wall with me. The next morning, I was fired.

All of my life, I have always been right with the sex of an unborn child. With my own kids, I knew as soon as I found out for sure I was pregnant. With my son, I never looked at girl names, my daughter was the same. With my youngest sister, I had a feeling she was a girl, but I knew she was going to be born on an odd day, she was born on Nov. 21, 1985. A co-worker was having a hard time getting pregnant, I told her she needed to lose some weight and she would have a little girl, about 3 years later, she lost weight and had a little girl. It has to be with people I know, not just anyone am I able to tell. Years ago a co-worker said she wanted a boy, I told her he was a boy…

For many years I stopped being so close to Yahuwah and Yeshua because of religion… But one day, I heard a Trumpet (it was more like a shofar). I was outside when it blew, it was nothing like our musical instruments we have here on earth and you can tell it was coming from above. That was my wake up call, to come back to them! As you read my story, you will understand what I mean. If you search you tube, people have recorded this sound and put it on the internet. I have always been a servant, I just have not always had Him in my life, but I never stopped believing He does exist, because I know for a fact they do. I was more like a child who is upset with her father, and didn't want to talk to Him for a while. When I was a child, I was very close to them, but when things happened, I didn't understand. I would talk to preachers or pastors and they would not believe me or give me short answers that did not make sense! I would pray but never got answers until after I heard the shofar! He has opened my eyes and ears to all His truth! I know who I am and why I am here! John 10:27-29 will give you more understanding!

All kinds of things have happened to me all my life, I have had dreams come true, I can sense the kind of person, and people are. I have been called an "Angel, Christian, a God sent, etc." all my life. My family always called me "special", even thou I did not feel that way and I did not like being called that. I have always lived with the motto, "Everything happens for a reason, we may not understand the reason at the time, but the answer will eventually be revealed." I tell my kids this all the time and also, "if it is meant to be, it will happen perfectly."

My Story, My life…

As you read my story please keep an open mind, and it is up to you if you believe me or not. I know some people will be able to relate to my story, others I know will mock me. My kids found out about it a few years ago, they don't really believe me because they have never experienced anything like this. I just want people to know that Yahuwah, Yeshua, angels, fallen-angels, demons, heaven and hell do exist, it is very real. It has taken me many years to open up and tell my story.

Like most people, I have gone through a lot in my life and have asked why me?! What did I do to deserve this hell of a life? When I asked a pastor or preacher these questions, I always got an answer like, Yahuwah gives us trials because he knows we can handle it or it is a test to your commitment to Yahuwah. Well, now I understand but then… I had enough of these test and trials, I just wanted my life to calm down and live in peace just for a little while. So for a while I did lose my way, and got angry with Father. When I heard the Shofar, something inside just woke up and has brought me back to Him. I will always be extremely grateful to Him for waking me up and bring me back to Him.

Things happen all over the world that cannot be explained, and like my kids, will not believe until they experience something like this. My kids grew up not having Yahuwah or Yeshua in their life, because of me. When they were young they went to church but over time that stopped. I blame myself for not having Yahuwah in our home, or in their lives, because I was angry with Yahuwah and I did not want Him in our house. Now that has changed, I am trying to get them to believe that there is a life after you die. They have the same beliefs as Steve Hawkins. He believes, we just cease to exist, that there is just nothing after we die. I know for a fact that is not true, which I will explain later. My son knows humans are energy, and that energy has to go somewhere, where, he does not know. He believes there is a creator but not man made religion. He is right to a point, man has messed up religion by allowing Satan to influence them.

Yeshua said in Revelations 2:3-5- Without growing weary, you have persevered and endured many things for the sake of My name. But I have this against you:

You have abandoned your first love. Therefore, keep in mind how far you have fallen. Repent and perform the deeds you did at first. But if you do not repent, I will come to you and remove your lamp stand from its place.... He also said-Psalm 119:115- Depart from me, evildoers, That I may observe the commandments of my Yah. Our first love is Yahuwah and His word. We all should be following His word, His laws and not the way church leaders have changed His ways. Man has corrupted His word.

Yahuwah's word in Psalm 91:9-12 - (KJV) Because you have made the lord, who is my refuge, Even the Most High, your dwelling place, no evil shall befall you, Nor shall any plague come near your dwelling place; For he shall give His angels charge over you, To keep you in all your ways. In their hands they shall bear you up, lest shall dash your foot against a stone.

Years ago, I don't remember how old I was but my mother dropped me off at a day care and I was placed into this room with other little kids. What I remember the most about this room was not so much as the other kids but what was flying around in the room. I don't remember how many but there were several of them... Demons. To explain what they looked like; if you have ever watched the movie "Ghost," when the demon's come out of the dark to take the evil soul, they looked a lot like them. They were black, I could see a head (no type of face), arms, and a form of a body but not shaped like humans, with no legs. I didn't hear them, I could only see them. They kept circling me and left the other kids alone. I remember being scared and wanting to get out of that room but the door was locked.

When I was about 6 years old my mother married this man named Mike, he was in the Military. I thought he was a great guy but over time, I realized he wasn't that great. We were living in Oceanside, California in an apartment on the second floor. The steps were made out of cement and there was a little bit of an enclosed patio at the top where the front door was. I started to sleep walk and getting dizzy spells. When I would walk down the hall way, I would run into the walls, or fall down. When I sleep walked, I would wake up outside on the porch or on the steps, my mom had to put a lock at the top part of the door to keep me from going outside. When my mom was pregnant with my brother, Mike and I had a bet on the sex of the child, I was right but I asked him if he would be black or white. I was young and didn't understand how all those things worked, but anyways it pissed him off. That was the first time I saw any meanness in him. We had another bet when my mom was pregnant with my sister, I won the bet.

I use to walk all over Oceanside on my own. I knew I was protected, and I didn't worry about being taken or worse. Thinking back now, that was really a stupid thing to do, with all the evil people in the world, but it was also during a time when those kinds of things were rare back in the 70's.

We moved back up to my home town, a few hours away. One day when we were moving into the home. Mike picked me up and slammed me into the wall and told me to take a bath. That is the only time I remember him physically hurting me. I don't remember having anymore sleep walking or dizzy spells but I started having nightmares. One day my mom got me a cross and told me to ware it. She said it would protect me and when I lay down to go to sleep, to picture myself standing in a white light, and as long as I was in that light, nothing could hurt me. I didn't understand why she told me this until years later. During this time my family was not really religious. They believed in Yah but didn't go to church and the only time we prayed was during the holiday meals.

A few years later, we ended up moving into the next town, closer to the Military base. The house (which is still there) sit's just off the main highway. I think it use to be a motel because there are several small apartments behind the house. I started to go to church every Sunday and I was told how Yeshua was going to come back on a cloud, to get all of his people. As a kid you think that is the coolest thing in the world. So I started to like clouds and kept looking for Yeshua. I still look at the clouds wondering if I will get to see him coming on his cloud; I think I will, and what an awesome sight that is going to be.

My nightmares continued, but I started to try and commit suicide, I realized later that I was being influence by spirits. I was about 8-9 years old the first time I tried. I tried to cut my wrist, while I was in the bath. Next I tried to hang myself in my bedroom. I tied a rope around my neck and around the light that was above my bed, when I jumped off my bed, it broke. Yahuwah was watching over me.

Any time I wanted to go into my mom and step-fathers room (which was not very often) I would run into the room and jump onto their bed and before I would leave, I had to look around the bed, then jump off and run out. I felt like something really evil was under the bed and it would come after me. I did not like that room.

The mornings when we had to go pick up Mike from the base, it was always just before light out and I would always see these demons following us. They looked just like the ones at the day care. One day I told my mom about it and she said it was the bogeyman. I didn't understand really what a demon was but I knew what the bogeyman was.

I need to explain a little about this house I was living in. If you were standing in front of the house, my bedroom, my brother and cousin's bedroom was in the back of the house. My room was on right side and theirs on the left. We had a Jack-n-Jill closets. (In other words you could go room to room through the closet) It is an old house and the windows were small and high off the ground. There was no carpet in our bedrooms, so the doors were a few inches off the floor.

One morning, when it was still dark out (I was wide awake when this happened, I need to stress this point, "It was NOT a dream"). I was woken up and given instructions. I was told to go and get my cousin out of his room and bring him back into my room. While I was standing at the front door to my room, I looked back and ask "what about my brother?" I was told he will be fine, go now and be fast, he's almost here. I went into their room and my cousin was on the top bunk, I woke him up and took him back to my room. I was told to close the doors and to put my dresser in front of my closet door, because my cousin (who is 3 years younger) was not strong enough to hold the door and to have him push on the dresser, so nothing could get through. I was told to hold the main door closed to my room, not to touch the handle and to stay there until I was told to let go. I was facing the door with my palms flat on the door, my body and feet were close to the door and I was told to move my feet back, so I was in a arch position. The next thing I know the door knob started moving and I could feel pressure on the door, I looked down and saw like fingers coming from under my door. They were not human; they were long, skinny, and dark in color (I don't remember how many) the best way to describe them: They looked similar to E.T.'s fingers. The fingers disappeared, I was told to let go and then my cousin and I was standing on my bed looking out the window, the light was just coming up and I was told we would be safe.

A few hours later we went around to the neighbors and asked them if they heard any voices this morning and no one did. My mom, brother and sister (she slept in my mom's room) were all fine and slept right through it. I went to church and told someone about it. He said that angels watch and protect us from evil and he told me how an angel helped a friend of his. I knew Yahuwah protected my cousin and I.

After we moved out of that house into another, that house stay empty for years. About 5 years later my mom went to see a friend that lived near there and I walked over to that house and looked into my old room, I got really scared and left fast. Anytime I drove by that house I look at it. There are people living in there now and have been living there for years. I asked them once if they had any problems with the home and they said no and they loved the house. I have never been back inside that house.

I was around 10 when we moved into another house. One night I was really sick and I must of had a nightmare, because Mike came to my bedroom door and stood there, when I looked, all I saw was this black figure, and I started screaming and trying to move as far away from him as I could, the next thing I remember is my head on my mom's lap and her comforting me. They got a divorced and when he moved out, my nightmares stopped.

Because I was a tom boy growing up, I use to play with lizards, snails, snakes and frogs. I got a lot of warts on my hands, they were huge. Other kids at school would always pick on me, and I tried to use wart remover but it did not work. Then one day, they just disappeared, all of them. I like to think Yahuwah got rid of them, but I don't know if He did or not.

When I was about 18-20, I finally told my mom about what happened. She said that when we were living in Oceanside Mike had to leave for a few weeks training in another state. He met a girl who was very much into White Magic, which he started doing also. My mom said that night could have been the night she tore off the pentagram he had around his neck. A few years later, I was on the phone with Mike and I asked him about the White Magic. He said they were looking for the missing links in the bible. So I told him what happened, and also asked about the pentagram. He said he remembered my mom removing it, but he said, that thing should have never came after me or my cousin. He didn't know what is was or why it happened.

When I was pregnant with my son, I was worried because I was told never to have kids because I was born with Spinal Bifida. So I called a psychic, I just wanted to know if we were both going to be okay. She told me yes, you will both make it through the pregnancy and delivery just fine, then she said "but, you have this black figure following you." When she told me that I knew what it was about. Throughout my life, I have always felt and saw the demons around me but I knew they could not hurt me. Think of it like this: There is a force field around you, people call it an "Aura," but it is the protection of Yahuwah. Demons can get through once something has disturbed your field. People, your own doubts, and the closer you get with Yahuwah, the stronger your force field will be. In 2 Thessalonians 2:6-7- And you know what restrains him now, so that in his time he may be revealed. For the mystery of lawlessness is already at work; only he who now restrains will do so until he is taken out of the way. The Holy Spirit is the restrainer, which is also your force field. It will be removed, Yahuwah's people will be or are marked, but man can invade your field. I still see black figures following me but I just go on my day like it was not there. Other times I have seen gray figures; a shape of dog, cat, child and adults, but they never feel evil to me, not like the black figures.

Yahuwah says in 1 John 4:4 (KJV) - You are of Yah, little children, and have overcome them, because He who is in you is greater than he who is in the world.

Yehshua says in Matthew 18:3 & 4 (KJV) - Assuredly, I say to you, unless you are converted and become as little children, you will by no means enter the kingdom of heaven. Therefore, whoever humbles himself as this child is the greatest in the kingdom of heaven.

Mark 10:15 (KJV) - Assuredly, I say to you, "whoever does not receive the kingdom of Yahuwah as a little child will by no means enter it."

Children are born in the most pure of heart (even thou they are born into sin.). They are loving, trusting, hopeful, silly, and they believe anything is possible. Some or all are able to see, hear things that adults can't. Animals are the same. When a baby is looking off in a direction and starts laughing. Doctors say it is spontaneous reaction, they have no control. I never believed that. I always felt it was a family member that has passed, playing with them. Or your dog just starts barking at nothing in the corner, I believe, they are seeing something most humans cannot see. Have you ever taken care of a loved one that is getting close to death? Have you noticed they start seeing or talking to people that have passed away or did you just brush it off as if they were crazy?! I believe the veil is over our eyes and ears only during a period of time in our lives, or maybe it's because we get told when we are children that none of it is real, then we put the veil up our self's?! Kind of like when you believed in Santa Claus, then you were told he was not real, so you stopped believing in him. Some people, the veil never covers them. They are able to see or hear the spirits throughout their lives. I am one of them!

When a child is scared of the dark or believes there is a monster under their bed or in their closet; you might want to ask questions and learn more. See if they can describe and explain why they are so afraid. Have them imagine they are in the light. Reassure them that Yahuwah will protect them. Let them have a light on in their room during the night. I was scared of the dark, even with a light on, because there still was dark areas in my room and I knew the demons were there. If they have an imaginary friend, don't dismiss it and say they have a wild imagination.

Learn more about their friend; just because you don't see them doesn't mean their imaginary friend is not as real as you are. Make sure Yahuwah is in your lives and in your home. He will protect you! He is the light! John 1:5- the light shines in the darkness, and the darkness has not overcome it. 1 John 1:7 - But if we walk in the light, as he is the light, we have fellowship one another, and the blood of Yeshua the Christ His Son cleaneth us from all sin. If you read about the light in the bible it tells you all you need to know what the light does to save you! Matthew 5:16 – Let your light so shine before men, that they may see your good works, and glorify your Father which is in Heaven. Who is the light? Palms 27: 1 – Yahuwah and Yeshua is my light and my salvation; whom shall I fear? Yahuwah and Yeshua is the strength of my life; of whom shall I be afraid? Yeshua is the light, the truth and the way!

Do you understand why we should see ourselves in the light? Nothing can hurt you when you are of the light! You don't have to call on His name, you can also picture yourself in His light! I watched a movie on Netflix about a man who was able to see a person's aura, angels and demons. The movie is called "Wake Up." The man's name is Jonas... People have their choices to be good or bad, to walk with Yahuwah or with Satan... This choice affects your aura... When you walk with Yahuwah your light becomes bright as the stars the closer you get to Him! Very few people can see this aura, this force field around you. The more you walk like Yeshua did, the stronger your light becomes! If you want to call them "Aliens" you're more than welcome to, but they are demons and fallen angels! Demons cannot take a physical form, fallen angels can! When you walk with Satan, you have no light, and in the spirit world it can be seen! We are told this throughout the bible!

After my mother's death, I was laying on my bed crying, I felt her sit down next to me and start playing with my hair like she did when she was alive. When my grandfather died it was around 1 A.M, I was asleep dreaming about something and he came into my dream, told me he loved me and I woke up. Then my phone rang, it was my aunt telling me he died, I told her, I know. My cousin, his wife and son were on a plane, when his son said "dad there's granddaddy" that is how he found out he passed away.

When my grandmother was getting close to dying, she asked me if I was the person that was there to take her away, I told her no. And the night she died, I was sitting outside with my aunt. She was on the phone. I felt a hand on my shoulder, and was told "it is time," I told my aunt it was time, as I walked into the house where my grandmother was at, I watched her take her two last breaths.

I use to have this small Geo Metro car. It is a small, compact vehicle. I was driving, my son was sitting behind me and I had a friend in the passenger seat. I was at a signal, it just turned green, but I heard a voice tell me, "Stop, and look." I saw an 18 wheeler truck coming, he was speeding and ran a red light. If I would have gone, we all would have been killed. I don't know how many times they have tried to kill me... but with Yahuwah and Yeshua grace and love... I am still here!

I have heard YHWH's voice on more than one occasion. It has been a few years since I have hear his voice, but I will always keep my ears open, for whenever he wants to talk to me again. As our Lord Yeshua said in John 20:29-Jesus said to him, "Thomas. Because you have seen Me, you have believed. Blessed are those who have not seen and yet have believe." And also, Luck 8:21- "But HE answered and said to them, "My mother and MY brothers are these who hear the word of Yah and do it."

When I felt that hand on my shoulder... Every cell in my body woke up! I could feel this over whelming love and warmth! Nothing I have ever felt before or since! I did not hear the words like if someone speaks in your ear! I felt the words. This voice was different than the other times. This voice was Yeshua! John 14:17 – Even the spirit of truth; whom the world cannot receive, because it seeth him not, neither knowth him: but ye know him; for he dwelled with you, and shall be in you. John 14:3 – And if I go and prepare a place for you, I will come again, and receive you unto myself; that where I am, there ye may also be.

Satan, fallen angels, demons are able to influence, take over humans and more. The people who are evil, the unbelievers their soul will be tortured. But what I fear is Revelation 9. The bottomless pit will be opened, the locusts will torture everyone who does not have Yah's mark, for 5 months. John put it in a nicer way, these things are worse than any nightmare movie our brains can think of. People need to realize every word Yahuwah has told us about Satan, is very true. I had a small taste of these things when I was young and by our Messiah grace He protected us, but what is coming, NO ONE THAT IS NOT MARKED BY YAH, WILL NOT BE PROTECTED FROM IT, IF YOU ARE STILL ON EARTH.

Other things have happened in my life that I have not written down. He has been protecting me all my life, I am here for a reason, and some of these other people might be for the same reason, but I don't know that for sure. Very few will be raptured out before tribulation, but some will return to help bring in the harvest. I am a harvest worker and that is why I am being protected! Mike may have opened the door but Yahuwah wasn't going to allow them to hurt me! Just so you know, I am not a Christian, I do not follow their ways… I follow the way of Yeshua…I follow the whole bible! I am a Natsarim!

Thank you for taking the time to read my email…

Jeannie

29.   While I hesitate to reveal this account, I do so willingly for one reason and one goal; to help free others who are lost in the mystery of their own experiences and lost in the finding meaning of it. It is my hope that someone will benefit from my story.

In 2017, I walked away from a lucrative management position with a major outdoor industry company and set out to engage in something more fulfilling (though I did not know yet what that something was). I felt led to write a historical account that might help people better understand our past as a nation. While researching for my manuscript, I stumbled into many rabbit holes and had a number of "interesting" crumbs dropped into my lap. However, it was not until I stumbled onto a video (Age of Deceit) that I had my own personal world shaken to its core. In the video, I heard an account from Whitley Strieber and his abduction experiences. I nearly fainted as I listened to his descriptions of his experience in his books Communion & Transformation. What did all this have to do with me personally? For that, we must time travel.

In the spring of 1997, I became saved by the grace and blood of our Lord and Savior Jesus Christ. However, I—like so many had no mentor or anyone to guide me through my new faith. That fall I went to college as a theater major (Acting) where my subsequent years were heavy laden with new age spirituality hyper-homosexuality, and eastern mysticism. Some of the activities conducted during many of my classes were subtly substantially misleading at best, spiritually harmful—though I was not aware of it at the same. In January of 2000, I had an experience that to this day (almost twenty years later) I cannot explain. While sleeping in my girlfriend's apartment one early morning, I had a dream. In this dream, I became possessed by......something. I had never dreamt such a dream ever before. I awakened frightened and shaken. However, many moments later, I had calmed myself and struggled to return to sleep. I was not prepared for what would happen next. The entity that had robbed me of myself in the dream...took me over in reality... Frightened and terrified do not come close. Eventually, the 'experience' would end but I would never be the same again. I struggled for years to make sense of what had happened to me in that room that day. I recounted what happened to my mother who I had always esteemed as the most spiritual person in our family and my rock of faith. She admitted to me that while my father attended seminary in Washington D.C. during their engagement days that he had attended several Church of Satan meetings while "researching a paper". Whether this has anything to do with what happened to me that day I do not know. (But interestingly, I have since heard of the "lascivious" spirit that Solomon supposedly conjured up in the Testament of Solomon chapter 71. What's so curious is it claims to possess men whom it cannot destroy with a demon who causes them "to devour their own flesh"... Every male in my immediate family (including myself) have chewed our finger-cuticles which was a habit begun from our Nana and her mother's Nana (my father's mother and grandmother). I just discovered this text less than two weeks ago.)

What remained so peculiar about my experience is, for a long time, I did not know what to make of it. I had heard about sleep paralysis and the scientific explanation of what the body and mind are capable of however the details (as you will read in a minute) and timing just did not satisfy. You can imagine my astonishment then while listening to Whitley Strieber's detailing of his abduction experience my shock and horror realizing what he was describing was—for the first time ever, over eighteen years later—the exact same thing that had happened to me. It makes no sense until one realizes that the two (alien abduction/demonic possession) can be (or are) one in the same. I had never seen or experienced any "extraterrestrial" before or since that morning. But as I heard Strieber utter these words, the color must have left my face. This is his account of his alien abduction, "I became entirely given over to extreme dread. The fear was so powerful that it seemed to make my personality completely evaporate… 'Whitley' ceased to exist. What was left was a body and a state of raw fear so great that it swept about me like a thick, suffocating curtain, turning paralysis into a condition that seemed close to death…I died and a wild animal appeared in my place." (Communion, p. 25-26) I couldn't believe what I was hearing. Someone was describing—exactly!—what I had felt that day all those years ago.

Then, in a later book called Transformation he wrote, "Increasingly I felt as if I were entering a struggle that might even be a struggle for my soul, my essence, or whatever part of me might have reference to the eternal. There are worse things than death, I suspected… so far the word demon had never been spoken among the scientists and doctors who were working with me… I felt an absolutely indescribable sense of menace. It was hell on earth to be there [in the presence of these entities], and yet I couldn't move, couldn't cry out, couldn't get away. I'd lay still as death, suffering inner agonies. Whatever was there seemed so monstrously ugly, so filthy and dark and sinister. Of course they were demons. They had to be. And they were here and I couldn't get away." (Transformation, p. 181)

As I sat listening to his describing this phenomenon, I got absolute chills running up my spine. My event occurred on January 24th 2000. I dug out an old journal where I knew I had written the account of that day. The following description is what happened to me:

January 26th, 2000 (it had taken a couple days for me to process before writing).

I had gone to bed that night late, and throughout the night had a dreams that were all unusual by nature. One dream I had dreamt involved my father and I at a dinner table. The subject or environment I can't recall but I remember becoming angry towards my father because he wanted his way concerning the conflict. I "told him off" and he got up and left—end of dream. The following dream, I was playing tag with a young woman in my father's old church. Her identity still alludes my memory. After I drifted back to sleep, I found myself in the rafters of a cross between another (or the same) church and a large theater-house. My girlfriend and I had just seen the musical 1776 (mostly male cast) that night. There was one man on the floor (of the stage) calling places for each character in the show on an individual basis. (Not the way it usually works) I was looking down at this "stage manager" and other members of the cast (all male) whom all stood 20-30+ feet below me (in the rafters). As I began to worry about where I was, I started looking around for somewhere I could go to be 'in place' when my character's name was called out. I then spotted this 3 1/2 -4 foot tall glass door and I knew that that was where I was supposed to be. I crawled over to it and could see inside the door lay a small cubicle. The walls were white and the glass door had a small wooden boarder around it. The cubicle was approximately 4 foot in depth, 3 and a half foot wide, by 4 feet in height. I looked and saw that there was a 2 ½ -3 ft. gap between the rafters and the landing of the cubicle. I cannot remember if the door had been opened or closed when I first saw it. I stepped over the gap and into this cubicle. Sat down, crossed my legs (Indian style); at that moment when I sat down & the man on the floor called out my character's name (which I don't know or remember) I felt an energy explode & fill me like water rapidly filling a glass. It felt like a thousand fireworks exploded within me simultaneously. As the presence of it infected me to its peak, my eyes grew inhumanly wide. With these huge eyes that within a second were not mine or under my control, I looked very slowly at the men on the floor who were once ignorant of my presence in the rafters were looking at whoever/whatever I was. With two very stiff fingers (index & middle) it pointed and pressed against this glass door, it slowly pushed the door open. Looking at the men it opened my mouth and in a voice I had never heard from myself that was an eerie, ear-piecing, but not high in pitch and somewhat nasal voice, "Hello there." "You know who I am?"

I—at hearing/feeling that voice—was aware there was an evil inside me that was not expected. I became frightened and horrified. I told myself to wake up in the hope of it all just being a dream…. I opened my eyes… it was just a dream. <Whew> I was back in bed with my heart still racing from when I had heard the voice. I became calm & at peace at the realization of it just being a dream. I rolled over from my stomach onto my back. Closed my eyes. Started to feel myself slip back into a slumber when I felt the presence from the dream fill my body with just as much quickness and efficiency. I opened my eyes at the first awareness of it. I was in the bed. I was laying on my back in bed. It felt as if my whole body was stretched out and pressed down into the mattress. How could this demon from my dream cross over from my subconscious into reality? It made no sense. But it was 100% real! My eyes were opened big in fear again, yet they didn't feel like mine like before. I only existed in the immeasurable depths of my mind. A tiny small voice inside of a huge cathedral. I knew what was inside me even though it never revealed itself to me for the 20 ¾ years I have been on this earth. I was being possessed. I tried to speak the piece of scripture I had always (growing up a pastor's kid) held close to my heart, Psalm 23—but couldn't find any of the words. At my loss, I found that not only could I not open my mouth, I couldn't even feel my mouth. I tried to cry out for my girlfriend who lay next to me fast asleep. I tried praying in my own way pleading the Lord to rid me of the powerful presence inside me. My prayer as I tried to find the words felt like it was being battled with the presence who fought to keep that voice inside my head mute. I began to recall the Lord's Prayer. I said it as fast as I could inside myself when I reached the part "…and deliver us from evil…" I found myself repeating that over & over & over "Deliver me from evil!" "Please oh Lord—deliver me from this evil presence" As I made my plea, I very slowly felt the tight grip on the nap of my neck release, hold, release, & hold again. I could feel a battle being fought. I repeated the line from the Lord's Prayer. Like sands falling from an hour glass, the presence floated out of me. I could feel my body again and my inner voice became bigger and louder. My heart, which I could not feel earlier was beating faster than that of a small bird. I thanked and thanked and thanked the Lord for coming to my rescue. I, still in a great deal of shock, began to become confident that whatever was inside me was gone. This experience was very fresh and weighed heavily on my thoughts in the day that proceeded my getting out of bed. An experience I pray never happens to me again. No one should ever have to feel fear of that magnitude. Ever get lost as a child? Know that horrifying fear that overwhelms you? THAT, is just a small degree of the terrifying fear I had felt that morning......"

To this day I am haunted by that dream and that partial-possession, sleep paralysis, whatever you want to call it. Sleep paralysis can explain some of it but not all. Since hearing Whitley's account I have read Chris Smiths book Sleep Paralysis and that has also served to confirm my deepest suspicions of what may have happened that day, though it is still somewhat shrouded in mystery. Though I have had many similar trace-dreams I have never had anything like it since. Seeing the movie the Exorcist in my twenties was startling as the only voice I have ever heard like the one from my dream was the voice of the demonically possessed girl from the film. The latest dream I have had was approximately three months ago when I dreamt I had seen 3-4 very tall luminescent blue beings walking several hundreds of yards away from me when I spoke, they stopped (they were walking very slowly with the same gate as the cloners from the star wars prequels), and turned their faceless heads toward me when I began to levitate into the air slowly but increasing enough to fill me with a sense of fear. I simply knew whatever it was, was trying to "take me". As I climbed ever higher, and higher still—being level if not above the Bitterroot Mountain peaks by my home, I began to pray ardently for Christ to end the experience. I woke up and prayed for peace for the rest of the morning. I have learned to start praying more when plagued by such dreams. I don't know how any of this could be of any assistance to others. But if my story can help bring understanding then so be it. I have never felt my spiritual self-squashed down to the smallest speck of my being while something else toyed around with my physical. I will be soon (as soon as my manuscript is finished) going through my old college files as I am suspicious if a particular acting exercise (while playing King Claudius in Hamlet) may or may not have correlated in the timeline of events. This particular exercise consisted of me going into a blacked out basement classroom with the objects strung out everywhere. Per the professor's instruction, I had to (in my blinded state) make it to the other side and back. He had my classmates play the role of "little demons in the dark" taunting, harassing, and toying with me—psychologically—the entire time. I do not know what to make of it but I am nearly certain the two happened relatively within the same six months of one another. The best way to lose, mislead, and destroy a newly saved Christian is to send them to an American college campus. May God bless those who read this story, as I am still somewhat lost about what it all means, why it happened, and what I am to make of it.

--Lee

30.   It was sometime around 1980 to 1982. I was between the ages of 5 and 7. If I had to guess, I would say I was closer to age 5. I lived in a little suburb of Detroit, Michigan.

My sister and I shared a bedroom. She is 3 years older than me. We each had a twin bed that sat against opposite walls on either side of a window that looked out into the backyard. She says she has the same memory as I do regarding this incident.

One night, I awoke for an unknown reason. I was suddenly wide awake. I looked over and saw my sister waking up too. I knew it was the middle of the night, but was confused because it was very light in our bedroom. The light was coming from outside the window. We both stood up on our beds and peered out the window.

The light was a strange light. It was super bright, yet had a blue tint to it. As I looked out the window, I remember being amazed at how far I could see. I saw into the backyards of neighbors many houses down. It almost seemed like I should not be able to see that far with such great detail. I was so confused because I knew it was the middle of the night, but it was almost as bright as middle of the day.

I do remember talking to my sister. I asked her where the light was coming from. She said she didn't know. I then tried to identify the source of the light. I remember looking out the window toward the sky. It seemed as though the light was coming from above, but I never identified the source.

The last thing I remember of that night was standing on my bed, looking out the window, and my sister was also standing in her bed looking out the window. I do not remember lying back down in bed to go back to sleep.

The next thing I know, I woke up. I did not think anything about the night before. A little time had passed, and I heard my dad (technically, step-dad) yell for me and my sister to come to the backyard. It was a nice day. The grass was very green and the temperature was mild. As we went toward my dad, I saw him kneeling on the grass in the middle of the right side of the backyard.

He was not happy…actually he was pretty angry. As we approached, he asked us if we had been playing with matches. He then pointed to the ground at what appeared to be a perfect circle (more like a donut shape) that was burnt or dead brown grass. It was about 12 inches in diameter. The weird thing was that the center of the "donut" was perfectly green. It seemed as though the brown area was not burnt away, but kind of lying flat; there was still length to the blades and they were intact but brown.

I motioned to my sister immediately and said, "Do you remember that light?" She said that she did. I then tried explaining to my dad about what had occurred the night before. He didn't want to hear it. We got grounded for playing with matches.

Right around the same timeframe (unsure if before or after), I had a "ghost" experience. I know it was around the same timeframe because my bedroom was set up the same way as it was when I had the "light" experience (we moved furniture around frequently).

I woke up in the middle of the night to what sounded like a party going on in the living room. I heard voices and the clinging of my parent's roach clips tapping the ashtray (a common sound in my house). I got out of bed and went into the living room. The whole house was dark. (We lived in a small 3 bedroom ranch approximately 1000 square feet.) I heard voices and commotion, but didn't see anything. I stood in the living room and rubbed my eyes to make sure they were open...nothing...I saw absolutely nothing.

I proceeded to the kitchen. It seems as though the voices had stopped as I walked toward the kitchen. As I got to the entry of the kitchen, I turned on the light. I noticed the cupboard immediately to my left was open. I looked into the kitchen toward the dining table, and there was a box of Pops cereal that was spilled over onto the table. I remember thinking how odd that was because my parents kept an immaculate house...nothing was ever out of place.

Suddenly, I heard my parent's bedroom door open and I heard the dog come out. I freaked out because I didn't want to get into trouble for spilling the cereal on the table. I ran as fast as I could back into my bedroom and jumped into bed. Then I heard the clock in the living room ding 2 times. It was 2 o'clock in the morning.

Next, I heard my dad exit his room and I thought my heart was going to beat out of my chest. I thought was going to get in trouble for spilling the cereal. To no avail, my dad went to the back door (through the kitchen), put the dog on his leash, and left the house. I eventually fell asleep.

The next morning I tried to tell my parents what happened, but they minimized it. I then looked at my dad and asked him if he took the dog for a walk a 2 in the morning. He said he had.

I am thankful we have freedom in the Name above all names, Jesus Christ!

Signed,

Dee from Detroit

31.   Hello, my name is Britney and I've been a Christian for about 10 years now. Even though I always believed in God, I didn't grow up in a religious household so I never really knew Jesus at that point in my life. When I was a

teenager, I began experiencing pretty severe sleep paralysis. At the time I didn't yet know Jesus or the power that his name held but that would soon change.

I was experiencing these sleep paralysis episodes quite regularly to the point that I truly feared sleep. As someone who did not yet know Jesus or the bible, I just assumed that these were just nightmares. Now, I truly believe that they are demonic attacks. In my dreams, I was constantly being attacked by a female demon. She always had the classic scary face and she always appeared wild. The scenario sometimes changed but I always just knew that this evil thing wanted to hurt me. I could never move during the attacks and I could barely speak although I tried to scream from the depths of my soul, whatever I could do to get this hideous thing off of me.

One time during an attack, I knew that I couldn't get away and I knew that I was trapped during the dream yet somehow it came to me to say the name of Jesus. At this point, I did not know Jesus or the power of his name yet, somehow I knew I needed to say his name. I managed to get it out and I instantly woke up.

Around that time my cousin invited me to church with her and I went. I was baptized and wanted to get to know this Jesus that freed me from my terrible nightmares. During that time, the sleep paralysis stopped. I was a teenager at the time and kind of put Jesus on the back burner again and lived a sin filled life. It wasn't until I was in my early 20's when became pregnant with my daughter that I knew that I had to again pursue my relationship with Jesus.

I wanted a different life for my daughter. I wanted her to grow up in an entirely different environment than I did as a child. I wanted her to know Jesus at a young age. I wanted a life of peace and hope for her. My husband grew up in the church and his family worked in the church so it really just all came together. We attended church regularly and I even started working at the church daycare (where I learned so much about the bible and who Jesus was and is). Since my daughter could talk, she has made up worship songs about Jesus. She loves Jesus wholeheartedly and loves learning about all of the amazing stories of the bible. She goes to a Christian school and loves to go to chapel every Thursday. She's on the worship team at church and just has the biggest heart for Jesus and for people. I am truly blessed that God gave me her. Through her, he has changed my life.

Fast forward to 2018, I'm now 28 years old and a mother to two. I go to church regularly and have a fire for learning all that I can about the bible and Jesus. I actively pursue him in every way that I can. I have only had a few episodes over these last few years but I instantly know to say the name of Jesus and I wake up.

I also want to include that I have always had dreams that have come true. I dreamed about my daughter even before I knew that I was pregnant with her as well as my son. I have dreamed about deaths that happen exactly the way that they actually happen in real life. And there is much more. A few years ago I had a dream that felt apocalyptic in a sense. A woman, who I think was possibly an angel asked me if my country was a God fearing country to which I responded no. She told me to pray for my country. She then took my head and bent it down and began to speak something into the back of my head. She spoke another language that I knew that I could understand but chose not to out of fear. It was a message, something important but I chose not to understand it. I woke up crying and felt this weight. The weight of the importance and urgency of the message. The weight of what it meant for the world. But most importantly the weight of letting fear keep me from listening to what she had to say. To this day, I don't know if it's significant but felt that I should include it.

On June 17th, I was at my parent's house celebrating father's day. My entire family was there (my mom, dad, 2 sisters, brother, my husband, my nephew and my two children). We were all just really enjoying each other's company as we don't get a chance to all get together very often. You could just feel the peace and happiness amongst us. My dad was looking up and saw something right above him. Eventually I came over to see what he was looking at. At first I could not see anything. I was standing exactly where he was and could not see anything. Then suddenly I began to see a reflection from something almost metallic. The longer I watched it, the more this metallic orb became visible. We had binoculars with us so when we looked through them, we were blown away. With the naked eye, it appeared solid and metallic. With the binoculars, it was transparent, almost iridescent in color and had a pulsating plasma in the center that had beautiful light. I didn't feel scared or threatened. I was freaking out at the fact that I couldn't identify what I was seeing. I could just sense that it wasn't some sort of technology, but it was alive. My brother ran over to see and at first he couldn't see it, like I couldn't. Then slowly it began to reveal itself. As he was looking at it, another one smoothly and very controlled, came gliding in from the left of our view. My sisters came over to see but could not see anything. That day we saw 3 total. They didn't make a noise. They didn't leave a trail. They just seemed to be watching us. Then they just disappeared. Since then, I have seen them 4 times in total in the same location only. They don't often come very close except for the first and last time. The last time, which was in October, they were in a cluster as if they were morphing and they were very clearly visible to the naked eye. They were coming in from our right. This was the only time that I recorded them. I never intended to but my dad insisted that I did I think as proof to ourselves that we were indeed seeing something. They don't appear the same on camera as they do with my eyes. On camera they just appear as a small white lights. In person it's a pretty incredible show.

I never believed in UFO'S or aliens. When I was younger, my dad loved Sci fi movies but they always scared me. Specifically Close Encounters of the Third Kind. That was one of his favorite movies but it scared me so bad. It made me think of a haunting.

As a child I always have had trouble falling asleep. I would literally sit up in bed hyperventilating because of fear. We didn't really have any restrictions as far as what we watched on TV and my family has always loved scary movies. I always just wanted to believe that things like UFO's that abduct people didn't exist in real life. Especially being a Christian, there's really no room for the idea that there is life outside of earth. So as you can imagine, my perception of the reality that i thought that I had known was rocked.

People suggested making a report to MUFON, which I did. An agent was assigned to my case and asked to have a phone conversation with me which I agreed to. He was very intrigued by my story and had no explanation as to what I could be seeing. He promised to keep in contact and update me with any news. Unfortunately I didn't hear from him again on his own account. I was seeing reports of these things daily on Reddit, YouTube and MUFON. I informed him of this and he asked me to forward any reports to him and he would share anything he comes across with me. Unfortunately he never did. To my knowledge the case is still open or at least I haven't heard otherwise.

I have shown video to a former Boeing employee and a former Airforce member who also had no answers for me. I have no doubt in my mind that what I have been seeing is not of this world.

In hopes to find my own answers, I began reaching out to other witnesses. I have begun to notice a pattern. We all consider ourselves to be spiritual individuals. Most even say that they identify as Christians. We all have had experiences with the paranormal (I don't particularly believe in ghosts, I believe that they are demons as the bible doesn't say that our souls hang around on earth after death). Most people say that they have always seen ghosts or like in my case with my sleep paralysis, have had demonic attacks. What's interesting is that we all seem to be genuinely good people who love people and want healing for humanity. We all agree that there has been almost a sudden urgency in our spirituality around the time of sightings.

One girl that is close to me in age has become almost like a long distance friend. She is also a Christian. She has also experienced paranormal activity. She sees the same thing that I have been seeing but much more often. She sees them everywhere and all the time. She has pictures and video backing her claims.

I have begun to notice a theme with all of this. From research that I have done on my own and from my own experience, I have come to the conclusion that what I am seeing, what people all over the world are seeing, is spiritual rather than extraterrestrial or technological and others agree with me. They are telepathic. They seem to have a hard time staying in this physical realm (which is why they fade in and out from view). People can "summon" them (which sounds demonic in itself). Some people report an increase of paranormal activity after seeing them. The girl that I have been talking with says that they want her attention and when she doesn't give them enough, they really put on a show for her as if to say that I am real (her words). The big trend with these orbs seem to be the new age movement. As someone who has been saved by the blood of Christ, I know that the new age movement is not truth.

I must admit, at first, I started questioning my beliefs. How can I be seeing something physical that's not mentioned in the bible? Is the bible real and if so, then why are these otherworldly beings not mentioned, especially if I am seeing them with my own eyes. However, if anything, this experience has made me cling even harder than ever to Jesus. We have faith as Christians that there is more than this earthly realm but it really solidified my belief SEEING that there's something more.

In the bible, not much is mentioned as far as the spirit realm. Not much about angels or demons or heaven or hell. But I believe that there's a purpose for that. God tells us not to contact psychics or mediums etc. And while I know that it's because it says that they employ demons for their "knowledge" I also believe it's because we're meant to live an earthly life for a reason. Our souls are put into human bodies for a reason. The spiritual realm, other than what we receive from God, is supposed to be hidden from us.

I can't help but think that there is a reason why I have seen what I have seen. I have prayed and prayed about this but I haven't gotten any answers. My soul tells me that it probably isn't good. But if that's the case, then why a sudden increase in sightings? I have looked through the bible and have not found anything that talks about mass demon sightings. Is something big happening? What am I to do with this information? In cases where I don't know what to do, I would turn to my church family or spiritual leaders for guidance. However, I know how crazy I sound when I talk about this. I have a lot of ties to my church and I don't want them to think I'm crazy. Even talking with my own family, I know that they think I'm crazy.

After stumbling upon a YouTube video that talked about your website I came to check it out. I read Joe Jordan's testimony (I can't find it again) but I instantly felt similarities when reading. I was becoming obsessed with all of it. I was losing sleep over all of it. Evey time I went outside I looked for them. I was starting to be open to some of the new age ideas but because of Jesus, my soul knew it was wrong. While I still do want answers, I have taken a step back and remembered to put God first when looking for answers and known to guard my heart. I am remembering to continually make it a point to pray daily over my family, myself and our household. I will wait for God to reveal what he wants and when according to his timing.

At this point, I can't just move on. I have tried but something pulls me back. Especially now after becoming friends with this girl, I feel like I have to help her as well. I have told her where I'm currently at and about your site. She currently believes that some of the orbs are good and some are bad. She believes that the some are demons and some are angels sent to protect her from the demons. But I know in my heart that this is bigger than just our isolated incidents, especially after seeing the surge in sightings and how open the world has become to them (most are still under the guise that they're from another planet). It's becoming so mainstream that even the news have been reporting sightings.

I know how the story ends. I know that God ALWAYS wins. I'm just wondering what role I play in this. What does God want me to do? I know that you can't answer that but I do believe that God brought me to your site for a reason.

After reading so many testimonies on your site, I realized that my sleep paralysis does seem to be connected. The night before I came to your site, I experienced once again another episode. In this dream, there were two demons, it's only ever been one. The dream was trying to convince me that the name of Jesus didn't hold any power there. But I KNEW otherwise. I pressed on and tried probably the hardest that I have ever had to try, but I said the name of Jesus and instantly woke up. I have no doubt that it was connected.

God continuously tells us to look up (per the bible) and look for signs and wonders in the sky. I've looked up and I've seen something. If there are demons in the sky, are there angels up there too? One of the times that I saw them, I asked God for a sign. A white dove flew by which is incredibly uncommon for where I live. Was that a sign? Is something major happening? Are these the signs that the bible tells us about to warn us of the end of times? I do not know.

Thank you for combining both the topic of Christianity and UFO's. There's not much out there on the matter.

I also want to add, I have not been abducted or have any signs of being abducted. I have not had any other experiences other than seeing them and my sleep paralysis. The girl that i have been talking with has had loss of time. She has had marks on her body that even the doctor apparently couldn't explain.

Anyway, thank you for taking the time to read what I have sent.

Britney

32.   Not sure where to begin.

I just watched a video that was talking about things I often experience. They named your website as ones who have other experience. I've only told one or two people about these things but I frequently experience them.

I have these dreams where I can't move and it's as if I'm watching myself from above. Things then emerge from the darkest points in the room. Tall dark entities with no particular shape just the blackest black imaginable. Usually 2-3 the most 4. And they surround me and I can feel them pulling. Not on me physically but as if they're trying to take everything I have and am. Only when I cry out in Yeshua's name do they stop.

My father was a world religions professor and an ordained pastor but an evil man. He died in prison three years ago. My entire life I've had these experiences and have been told by many they don't think I'm human. I see to know things about and I can't tell you how I know them. My father told stories of how his father saw things and my father himself often had dreams of demons. Strange things always happened around the house and he'd always say "it's your demons coming to get you". My brother sees things as well but he only speaks to me about these things. No one knows the extent to which I suffer. They see the outside and I make up lies and excuses. I rarely sleep these days. I've gone in stents of as long as 10 days with no sleep. Right now I'm on day 5 of no sleep in one of my stents. My family witnesses it and I make excuses. I assume they probably think I'm on drugs which I'm on no drugs or medication of any kind.

In the dreams I have where they don't come I never dream about myself, ever. It's always third person dreams where it's as if I'm watching a movie of what people did that day or at some point. I often fly in my dreams and dream in foreign languages I don't know. In the dreams I understand everything but I wake up and am clueless. Some nights when I dream about other people, people have told me they dreamed about me. The most disturbing case being, I had this dream I was in an old run down house. There was this most freighting noise. Almost like a gasp or heavy inward breath, mixed with a hiss, and a low pitch but distinct sounding growl at once. I followed the noise up a stairway to a room. I get to the door and it's cracked so I pushed it open and inside it's dark with only a rocking chair. His incredibly disfigured not even human looking old man with a deep wrinkled face, long white hair, tattered clothing and again an incredibly disgusted almost non-human looking face looks up. Directly at me. I stood at the door way and noticed he was holding and infant wrapped up in cloth on his lap. So I take a step into the room. While he's staring me down with eyes I can't even put into words, he makes the terrible noise again as if he's angry but short of break. When he's done inhaling all he said was "wake up". And I was immediately awake. I woke up terrified and didn't know what to make of it. I called my friend who is often have spiritual talks with and told her I had a crazy dream. She told me to tell her so I told her everything I just told you. As I'm telling her the dream she starts crying. And when I finished telling her she told me she had a dream with me in it the same night. That since she was a child and she had been visited by the same old man I described. For 20 years she had been visited by him. And that she'd often, even being in her 20s end up sleeping in the room with her parents. And that they had tried praying over her and having pastors and everyone else try and nothing seemed to work. But that night she dreamt he had her cornered in a room and just as he went to get her I opened the door. She said I then came in the room and took her by the hand and flew off with her. As she was telling me I was shaking and speechless. I still don't know what to make of it. We've spoken about it since then and it's now been over 5 years and the old man has never visited her again.

I feel different from other people. Like there's something in me that keep me separate from others. I often question if it's my bloodline itself and if we have been corrupted. I quit school in the 8th grade for reason yet seem to have knowledge beyond my understanding in most things. But when it comes to the spiritual it scares me the things I could tell you. I always joke when people ask how I can function with days without food or sleep. In which my response it always to throw on a fake smile and laugh and say "I don't know, I guess I'm an alien". In which people respond by telling me they wouldn't be surprised.

I have dreams of things to come. And sometimes I physically see things while I'm awake. I've had countless encounters and visions that have literally saved my life and that others can verify. In those situations I usually end up going into a trance like stage. I start speaking about things and at times have even said things that were about to happen to myself and the people I'm with when they question me about what I'm ranting about. In which it happens and they freak out again all this can be verified by others. I've encountered people I know that were possessed and even the people who are with me say the people were. I also have encountered people I know that aren't people. Where as soon as they walk in the room we've never met or seen each other but my whole body will being to shake out of freight and I will get a feeling inside I can't describe. In these times the person also sees me and always comes over to me and approaches me as if they know me. I've even had situations where I've been told "look who we have here...I know you, I know all about you" and again the person and I have never met, seen each other, or heard about each other and in those situations I usually have a feeling that tells me to flee. And I end up making excuses to leave. And more than once it has turned out where if I had stayed I would have been killed. Where people were plotting against me and I didn't know or where something terrible happens after I leave.

I feel like something is wrong with me and it scares me. I feel like I can no longer connect to people and often I wonder if my bloodline is corrupted if I can be saved, or if I have the same fate as the giants in the book of Enoch. They knew their demise was at hand and asked for Enoch to speak on their behalf yet he told them they couldn't be saved. Am I like them? Can a corrupted bloodline have salvation? The word says children suffer for the sins of their father. I never met my father's father but have been told by family I'm a lot like him. My mother's side also has an odd connection to the spiritual world I can't explain. And they have told me stories of when my grandfather came back from WWII. He NEVER spoke of anything that happened over there to ANYONE EVER. He was in Paton's 3rd army and was in every major battle from D Day across Europe into Italy. By all accounts he came back a different man that left. But they tell a story of being at the dinner table. And a cousin named Converse which who was close to my grandfather and the family. Who even taught my uncle to play piano as a child out of the blue at the dinner table just started asking my grandfather if he remembered things that happened in the war. Converse never went and my grandfather never told him what happened. Yet Converse went into explicit detail of things that happened talking about deaths of my grandfather's friends and different things. They said my grandfather kept telling him to stop and started yelling at him to stop and the kids were made to leave. Converse happened to acknowledge and accept and know what was going on. He wrote a book that's published called "Ghosts of Concord" by Converse Nickerson.

What can I do? I know the word, I read it, I believe it. But my whole life I just have this feeling that I'm different and that my time is yet to come. By all accounts I am different. I've always conducted myself different than others and seemed to see things in a different way and light than everyone. As far as I can remember. I have had things I can't explain and a lot I won't talk about at this point in my life. Things I see and feel and know and I can't and never have been able to explain it. I've decided even if I can't be saved I'm not going to live improper. I pray the father will be able to judge my heart and maybe I can break this family curse. I've lived a spiritual life my entire life and faith and the Bible and fellowship has always been there. But there's always something in me that's makes me stand out among others. That seems to draw people to me but not good people or good things. I guess I've said enough for now and this is the most I've ever said to anyone. Is there hope for someone like me? I know everything is spiritual at this point and I know the days are numbered and things are about to begin. They already have begun but the blinders are being removed and soon things will be visible but people will be blind, deaf and dumb to what they're actually seeing. They will put their faith in wrong doctrines as they already do, they will believe things are not what they actually are and they will continue to be fooled. Even just an acknowledgement that you read this and that I haven't wanted my breath would be greatly appreciated if nothing else. Please.

33.   Hey there

I have always wanted to share my experiences with UFOs and sleep paralysis with someone who would be able to understand what I was experiencing.

My testimony might not exactly be about stopping an abduction experience but I do think you will find it interesting and that is does testify about the power that is in the Name of Jesus Christ our Lord and Savior!

To Start: My name is Andrei, I was born 2 October 1988 in South Africa, Cape Town, I still live in Cape Town.

My fascination with aliens and UFOs started at a very early age, about the age of 10 or 11. As a young child I used to take out all the books on aliens and UFOs at our library and I was very much sucked into believing that there is aliens out there and that these UFOs were actual manufactured crafts from some alien race.

As I got older I got interested in the occult and satanic music, I do believe this opened more doors for the devil to work in my life.

My sleep paralysis

One thing I struggled with for many years, since I can remember, was sleep paralysis, I absolutely hated this, I never saw anything but I would wake up at night unable to move or even utter a word and it always felt as if something was bending my head backwards so that my throat wanted to burst open. It was horrendous! I was told by many people that is normal, that is just means my body is asleep and my mind awake. I believed this lie for many years.

My UFO experience

Somewhere in the year 2011 or 2012 (I really can't remember the exact year) I started getting back into UFOs and aliens, I started watching documentaries and videos about the latest UFO sightings on regular basis again as well as getting into stuff by guys like David Icke. During this time I started going outside at night, always a cloudy night, I then started to see these blue lights above the clouds, usually about 6 or 8 lights. These lights would hover in different patterns, then they would all seem to turn into one light again before splitting up again in many lights. It started to become to a point where it felt like I can make them appear every time when it was cloudy outside during night time.

I suppose I stopped looking for them eventually.

I got saved in 2014 - During this time I found your website and read some testimonies, I was blown away that people could stop these abductions by using the name of Jesus, it made total sense and the fact that these beings and UFOs were all demonic also made total sense to me now.

Here is how these testimonies helped me with sleep paralysis.

After I got saved I cannot remember that I ever struggled with sleep paralysis again. This was till 2017 when I was in a bit of a bad spot spiritually, I started watching a series called American Horror Story, I used to watch this when I was not saved, this series was extremely satanic and I could not watch more than 3 episodes. Not long after watching this I woke up one night, totally unable to move, say a word, over taken with fear, a demonic presence, and it felt as if I was being chocked. I immediately remember how the name of Jesus stopped the alien experiences and I knew that it will also stop my sleep paralysis, I just said in my mind JESUS and just like that I was free! Never had another experience again.

After this I read about many more people that also stopped their sleep paralysis by calling upon the name of Jesus. I now know that sleep paralysis is demonic, this and the alien abductions are one and the same spirit at work.

Last UFO sighting

This year (2018) June or July, me and my girlfriend was walking outside at a park when my eye caught something in the clouds, I did not look up and we continued to walk, I eventually looked at the clouds after a while and noticed these exact same blue hovering lights that I saw a few years ago. I told my girlfriend to look up at the clouds and she also saw them, they did the same thing as they always did, the patterns and then turning into one light and separating again. We just ignored it and walked away. Never saw these things again. I know I am protected by the blood of Jesus Christ and they cannot touch me!

This is my story, thank you so much for bringing hope to so many people! I know it helped me get free for life from the sleep paralysis that torment me for so many years! All glory to God All Mighty!

May the Lord bless you!

Kind regards

Your brother in Christ

Andrei

34.   Hello, my name is Scott Richardson and I have had experiences such as out of body experiences, sleep paralysis and what I believe to be demonic encounters. Every time I invoked the name of Jesus it would stop the encounters.

Now I don't think that these experiences are similar to "alien abductions" but if you're saying they are one in the same, well I just wanted to get this out there and maybe get more information?

Just to note I have never tried to go into these states. They just seemed to happen but as my faith grew the experiences have stopped and only when I'm in a bad place will something happen. My experiences have shaped my life and I am close to God and am familiar with the bible. I guess I just want to share and maybe find some info that I haven't found myself.

Subject: My story

(Usually floating out of body and projection happen 1st)

This has happened ever since I was a child, the fear usually starts before going to bed for me. Once asleep I begin to hear the fan in my room making a slow "whooshing" sound, like it's beginning to slow down. This is the start of my sleep paralysis, then three demons slowly approach, their deep growling gets ever louder as they get closer. One materializes near my window, door, and closet. Intense fear and dread overcome every fiber of my being. One screams so loudly in my left ear, extremely haunting sound (always the left side corner of my eye), while the other 2 observe from a slight distance. My eyes are open, but I cannot move. As I try to peer at this beast, it always manages to just stay out of view. No face, just pure darkness. The fear and complete evil is unexplainable in words. In my mind I call out to Jesus for help, they immediately stop and de-materialize and screams and fear fade quickly. Sometimes when I can't use my thoughts to get them away it continues to grow, and I feel like I'm going to die. I've never told anyone about this, as most people would think I was crazy. I'm just now starting to talk to other about this experience which has helped me greatly. After I put the pieces together,

I then realized that spiritual warfare is real, and there is only Jesus, my savior! I fell away from the lord for a while as I was deceived/and thought it was a hallucination or an alien abduction. These experiences have opened my eyes to what's really happening and I'm ready to die for my lord and savior Jesus.

Subject: My abduction experience

As a caveat I must say that when this experience occurred I was rediscovering my Christianity after having abandoned it in the past.

My experience began while I was asleep one night. At first I thought it was a dream but that the dream was very lucid. I quickly began to realize that my consciousness was very clear except that my vision was fuzzy and I slightly groggy and time felt as if it were moving slowly than usual. The effect was the same one I had experienced before as that of being sedated for surgery through spinal epidural.

I found myself in a room that was a half circle with a cushioned, couch-like, seat lining the majority of the circular part of the room, above which was a small window which appeared to be looking out into space leading me to understand that I was on a spacecraft. The other part of the room was a straight wall that seemed to be splitting a full circle construction. On the seat sat a handful of human beings which gave me the impression that these were powerful men from Earth in positions of leadership and power. I felt as if being forced not too looked at them directly and their faces were blurry. Through only the sensation of impression I could identify one man, by name. I will not mention him here out of fear of reprisal. These men were not in charge of what was happening but we're seemingly in allegiance with whoever was. They were casually talking about me as if I was being assessed for the selection of something.

Suddenly I was in another room. This room was some sort of operational room. There were what seemed to be drugged humans sitting behind consoles which were recessed about 3 feet lower than a walkway which separated them on their left side, with one group being on the other with a total of 3 groups that I notice up to now. The drugged people were grouped into small sections and we're distinguished as separate groups by colored shirts. One group wore red, another yellow and another blue. These distinctions seemed to indicate their work responsibilities. It had an eerie similarity to Star Trek. I was looking at this from the aspect of standing on the catwalk like walkway and noticed that a tall alien being which appeared almost identically to the Slender man character but proportionally normal. Almost as if a human that was 8-10 feet tall but with grey skin, no face and wearing what appeared to be wearing a black suit. The being walked toward me and turned away from me, toward a wall which I could not see. He said to me: "what do the interpreters say?" I almost instinctively turned and started walking towards a group of 5-6 "drugged" humans wearing grey shirts and sitting side-by-side in a juror-like box which sat about a foot above the level of the walkway. As I was getting closer in what seemed to take longer than it should because of the slowness of time, I began to sense dread and danger and suddenly, in my mind, I instantly knew that if I spoke with this group and repeated it to the alien being, it would be as if I acknowledged and accept the beings power over me and would be trapped. As I was walking, the thought of prayer came into my head almost as if out of nowhere, but I was panicking so much by now that I couldn't think of what to pray so I did the next best thing and began reciting the beginning of the the Bible, Genesis 1:1. "In the beginning GOD created the heavens and the earth…" I emphasized GOD. While saying this I began to think in my mind: "Jesus help me, Jesus save me!"

Almost in an instant the experience stopped and I began to feel my consciousness being funneled back into my body as if it was water going down a drain. Immediately I sat up in my bed, wide awake, and to this day can recall in detail the experience as if it was a memory from reality.

35.   Dear Mr. Jordan,

For the past two weeks I have — for the first time in my life — been researching Christian ufology, and — for the first time — am now extending an open mind to it. Prior to these past two weeks, Christian ufology was only ever something I had heard about in passing, and which I readily dismissed as a fringe phenomenon of the emotionally unstable and the intellectually irrational.

But I am now reconsidering that position.

In my web searching, I came across your site "Alien Resistance" (among other sites) and decided I would like to contact you.

To keep this e-mail as brief as possible, I will succinctly say I believe I have a life history of low-level visitations. In my use of the term "low-level" I am spontaneously (and perhaps clumsily) coining a phrase here in this e-mail to try and convey the idea that my visitation experiences were of minor significance and also of lesser trauma than what I have been reading about in the internet testimonies of other victims.

My visitations have included 1) dreams and 2) out-of-body experiences. The dreams, which were very rare (a few times a year at the most), started when I was around seven years old, and were always about creatures, or monsters, or outright aliens (usually only one entity per dream, not multiples) who would come to me during the course of the dream, often hurt me, and when I awakened I would still physically feel the pain that they had inflicted upon me in the dream. Never once did any of the creatures/monsters/aliens in these dreams speak to me or engage in any other type of communication. The out-of-body experiences began when I was about four, were very rare (again only a few times a year at most), and stopped for the duration of my teen-aged years, but then returned again for a very brief while after I had reached adulthood AND after I had become a born-again Christian. But when the out-of-body experiences returned during my new life as a Christian, I spoke to some women in my church who prayed for me, and the out-of-body experiences stopped. They have not happened again since then. In 1992, I went on a short-term summer missionary trip to Ireland where I believe I was literally attacked in my sleep while staying at a Christian woman's house in Dublin, and the validity of the attack was corroborated by two other Christian women in the house (the Irish hostess, and the other American woman who also came as a missionary for the summer).

At this stage in my life, I believe these visitations have probably ceased. It has been many years since I have had any such dream at all. I spent probably the first eight years of my Christian walk experiencing occasional dreams which I was too embarrassed to tell anyone about, and which I couldn't help but think had to be MORE than just dreams because they were the only dreams I had where I would get hurt in the dream AND ALSO awaken still experiencing the sensation of literal pain and discomfort from the dreamt injuries. A solid correlation emerged: dreams that "hurt" always had a monster, and dreams with monsters always "hurt". But I never got "hurt" in my any of my "normal" and "monster-less" dreams where I perhaps fell down a set of stairs or got hit by a tidal wave or crashed a car. I even had a "normal" dream once when I was in college in the middle of final exam week, and in that dream I tripped and fell face-first onto the sidewalk and broke all of the teeth out of my mouth from the impact. And then I stood up in my dream with broken teeth all over the ground in front of me and I had blood gushing out of my mouth, and then I woke up at that exact moment of standing up with a bleeding mouth, but even THAT dream did not "hurt". But in all of my "monster" dreams, which began at the age of seven, I have experienced any of the following assaults: I have been punched, choked, stabbed, dragged across the floor, thrown against a wall, and had many other violent things done to me. Some of the assaults were sexual, and ALL of them "hurt". And whenever I awakened from any of my "monster" dreams, the echo of the pain from these traumas remained as a conscious and unignorably physical sensation for up to half an hour after waking up and walking around (I believe this might technically fall under the category of what medical science refers to as "phantom pain").

The only explanation I can offer as far as the cessation of this life-long bout with what I shall call "painful" dreams is that I did learn over the years to call upon the name of Jesus in my dreams, and perhaps that has been the difference to cause them to finally stop. I can't assert this correlation with any certainty, nor can I claim that my initial practice of calling on Jesus' name brought an IMMEDIATE cure. It was actually several years from the time I started to do this in my "painful" dreams until such dreams stopped. Perhaps it took several years for me to get adept at it — to achieve a high enough level of dream-state cognizance and alertness to utilize Jesus' name with deliberacy and with immediacy and (most importantly) with consistency. And perhaps then it was only after I displayed such consistency that "their" efforts with me were abandoned.

I write to you today as a Christian woman who believes her entire life has been "vandalized" by demonic forces. I have spent most of my Christian life (I was saved in the late 1980's at the age of 19) wondering if a demonic presence in my life was responsible for much of the grief I have endured in my daily living. Even other people around me (Christian and non-Christian) have commented that they are stunned at the amount of grief my life has passed through, sensing my portion of troubles surpasses what the laws of averages dictate I should get. But whenever I tried to research the possibility of demonic influences in my life, I always recoiled in horror at the blatantly unsound theology I found in many books and teachings on the subject. I was leery of immersing myself into what I sensed was an odd and unstable corner of the Christian sub-culture where I would be consulting with people who saw a Communist behind every bush and a demon under every doily. So very many of these deliverance-from-demons ministries insist that a truth-seeker must repent of witchcraft and occultism, and to even repent of any witchcraft or occultism that parents or grandparents might have engaged in. And to my knowledge neither I nor my parents nor my grandparents have ever engaged in witchcraft, but I'm supposed to repent of it anyhow. How can I be convicted of a sin the existence of which I'm not even convinced? But ALL of those demon-deliverance ministries insisted that repentance of such hidden occultism was prerequisite to deliverance. So I felt like I was walking on very unstable ground whenever I looked into these teachings, as if the proponents of these ministries were asking me to invent transgressions that never existed, or manufacture a sin history (either in myself or in my family) that was pure imagination. Self-delusion is not something I embrace readily, even if a promised reward of happiness and blessings are offered for doing so. I only want the truth.

The Christian ufology movement is admittedly the very last place I expected to find something that made sense to me. But it was only after reading the internet testimonies of various people on your web site (and other web sites as well) that I began to sense that perhaps this movement has some solid grounding in actual truth, AND that these truths related to me and my circumstances. My dreams and my out-of-body experiences fit more into the alien visitation model than into the witchcraft model. I know of no occultism in my family, but after spending the past two weeks reading these Christian ufology web sites, I do believe there is a history of visitations in my family. So I am infinitely more comfortable concluding that I am a visitation victim than a witchcraft victim. That conclusion in no way invalidates the testimonies of those who claim to be victims of occult abuse, nor does it try to play down the severity of witchcraft's sinfulness as spelled out in Scripture. If anything my conclusion only lends credibility to the idea that Satan has MANY avenues through which he conducts his campaign of deception, and the UFO-lie is one of the latest.

I have a great deal more to read about in this topic. But I believe I am able to read further on the subject matter without the same recoiling-in-horror reaction I have always had with demon-deliverance ministries.

In conclusion, I really would like it if you could connect me with someone I could pray with about this. There's no one in my church who would be even remotely tolerant of any such notions. So if you could help me network to a counselor, I'd be very grateful.

Regards

–Eileen

36.   There is a book by David J. Hufford called The Terror that comes in the Night. The sub-title of the book describes the contents: "An Experience-Centered Study of Supernatural Assault Traditions." Dr. Hufford is a sociologist and university professor. According to his research about one sixth of the population experiences the phenomenon described in his book yet almost no one talks about it. The experience Hufford describes is similar to what has become known in our culture as the "alien abduction" phenomenon, yet differing in some aspects.

According to a Roper Poll done in 1992 at least two percent of the adult population in the United States has experienced what they call "being abducted." It is difficult to get an exact number since it is believed that many people completely repress the experience and many others just don't talk about it.

The Roper Poll used a sample of 5,947 respondents corresponding to the equivalent number among the 185,000,000 ostensibly represented by Roper's demographically balanced sample. The margin of error is + or − 1.4 per cent. The poll excluded everyone under 18 years of age and all residents of Hawaii and Alaska, as well as all residing in dormitories, hospitals, etc. When respondents were asked if they had ever awakened paralyzed with a sense of a strange "presence" in the room 18 per cent said "yes." This percentage with a + or − 1.4 margin of error represents 33,300,000 people.

In 1973 my husband Coleman and I and our two baby boys lived in Virginia. Coleman was working for Christianity Today as the advertising manager and I was a stay-at-home mom doing some freelance artwork. One night I awoke with a start. My eyes flew open like a close-up in a horror movie when the dead person comes back to life. I was totally awake with the sense that something was very wrong. That sense moved very quickly to terror. I was paralyzed, unable to move anything except my eyes. To my left, over my husband's sleeping body, I could see three figures gliding into the room. Their feet, which I couldn't see because a monk-like robe covered them, never touched the ground. They were coming out of a walk-in closet bedroom and my first thought was, "How did they get in there?" It was communicated to me in some fashion – I don't know how – that they had come through the large second story window in the nursery, glided down the hall, gone through the wall into the master bath, and from the bathroom had glided into the closet. I knew they were very, very angry with me for some reason, but I didn't know why. They communicated to me, without speaking, that they were going to levitate my stiff body, slam me through the window above our bed and drop me on my head killing me. They wanted me to know that my husband would be blamed for my death.

I had no doubt that they were capable of doing this and my terror escalated. I tried to scream at Coleman to wake up but I couldn't. My vocal cords were paralyzed. Then I began to pray. I tried to call out, "JESUS." Again nothing would come out of my mouth other than grunts. Once more I tried to say "JESUS." More grunts. Finally a garbled "Jesus" came out. At the name of Jesus the beings dissipated into the air into little triangles just like a visual effect.

I immediately woke Coleman and told him what had happened. After comforting me, the inevitable question came. He said, "Are you sure it wasn't just a bad dream?" Irritated, I replied, "Yes, I'm sure. Because if it was a bad dream I'm still dreaming. I awoke before it began and I have not awakened since. Besides I just KNOW it was real." At the time, neither one of us knew what to do with this experience, so I just filed it away and didn't talk about it again for over 20 years.

Then over twenty years later Coleman was writing a pilot script for a television series that was supposed to be about all sorts of strange phenomena. He gave me a book on alien abduction and asked me to read it and see if there might be any story ideas in it that he could use. As I read the book it struck me how similar these people's experiences were to mine. Then I came across a drawing of one person's alien abductor. It was eerie. He had drawn the same beings that had come into my room.

At the same time, I was reading a book about several different missionaries who had gone to a variety of Third World countries to tell people about Jesus. The book was titled, Demon Experiences in Many Lands and it was published by Moody Bible Institute in Chicago in 1960. In the preface we find this statement by the publishers: "It has been many years since any serious study of demon experiences has been published, and possibly never before a compilation from competent observers in many parts of the world. The reason for this omission is not clear, but the result has been a feeling on the part of many Christians that these strange (to us moderns) phenomena were only valid in Bible times." Several of the missionaries had this attitude themselves when their strange experiences began. Most were totally unprepared for the assaults that they and their new converts confronted.

Several of these experiences were very similar to the ones described in Hufford's book and countless alien abduction books. A conclusion from Hufford's book is that people unfamiliar with any notion of what he calls an "Old Hag Tradition" describe their symptoms precisely in accordance with those aware of such a tradition. Hufford never called these experiences "demonic." But all of the missionaries came to that conclusion. They believed that they were dealing with demons and they looked to the Bible to learn how to overcome them.

As I began to form my own opinion about my night terror experience, I went to the Internet to see if any one beside myself had had a similar experience. Was I the only person who had used the name of "Jesus" to end a night terror or alien abduction experience? I found an article from Florida Today magazine that appeared on August 17, 1997, written by Rita Elkins concerning alien abduction and it's similarity to demonic oppression. She quotes Joe Jordan, a director for the Mutual UFO Network (MUFON) a clearinghouse for UFO related research. When he is not checking out UFO claims for MUFON he works in product development and engineering for Sea Ray Boats. He and his partner Wes Clark, also a member of MUFON, who is a quality control engineer at the Kennedy Space Center, have, through their work at MUFON, come across several people who have been able to stop their abduction experience by calling on the name of Jesus. He shared a taped interview with Elkins for her article in Florida Today:

Jordan told Elkins that other secular researchers had had similar cases. They had not revealed this because they felt it would hurt their credibility, especially among the folks that invite them to speak at UFO Conventions. I certainly can understand this. A number of years ago Coleman and I went to a UFO Convention in San Francisco. Most of the people there were defiantly New Agers and didn't seem to be open to traditional religion at all. In spite of the fact that abduction experiences are described as horrible, brutal and denigrating many believe they are done by good aliens and are somehow beneficial to human kind. So my question is, "Do you really think our alien 'space brothers' are assaulting us or could there be a demonic connection to these experiences?

You may be wondering why I have decided to share my night terror story with the world on the Internet. I am sure that there are many who will just think I am a total wacko. Some of you who know me may think I am farther gone than you realized. But if there are people experiencing these assaults who want them to stop I can offer way out.

Few years ago, my son was taking a college class at a secular university. The teacher of this class, which was a language class and had nothing to do with what we are writing about today, began asking the same questions that were asked in the Roper Poll. After a few questions one girl raised her hand and began to tell the class about her abduction experience. When she had finished my son said to her, "There is a way to stop these experiences if you want to." The teacher interrupted," No, there is no way to stop them!" "Yes!" my son replied, "They can be stopped." "No they cannot." At that point the teacher went back to the curriculum.   I want people to know that my son's teacher is wrong. There is a way to stop these experiences. Please don't think that I am saying that the name "Jesus" is magic. It is not magic, but it does have Amazing Power. The Creator of the Universe knows his children. The Good Shepard knows his sheep. Surely if he was willing to die for our sins, He is able to protect us from the Evil Ones. If you want His protection, put your faith in Him.

If you have experienced a night terror I would like to hear from you. Please write and tell me your story.

Carel

37.   Hi Joe, after looking through your website and several Christians experiences with the deceiving abduction experiences from demons, it was chillingly similar to something I experienced when I was a child too living in South Australia. I reluctantly will talk about it both because people don't believe me, think I am crazy or believe I was dreaming, and because of how frightening it is to think about it.

Seeming you share the same belief as me, that 'aliens' are really demons here to deceive us away from Jesus I will tell you my own experience. I was a very scared child for some reason when I was young, I never wanted to sleep by myself and always wanted to sleep with mum in her bed because of this fear, and I know all kids are scared but for some reason I just knew there was something always there when I was by myself.

One night, I believe I was about 7, around 1987 sleeping next to my mum on the right, I had my eyes shut but knew something was standing there looking at me. I felt fear like none other, but I was not paralyzed so I opened my eyes bravely. And there it was, this wrinkly leathery brown, with the moonlight reflected on it, demonic being with dark eyes (and I knew it was demonic on the basis of the fear I felt from it) looking upon me. In fear I ducked own under the covers and started shaking my Mum who was asleep but said I was just having a bad dream – however I knew what I saw. I slowly looked out from over the covers and whatever it was, was gone.

The next morning I woke up and noticed dark markings on the carpet where this demon had been standing.

Anyway, I at first believed this to be a monster of some sort because I didn't know anything about aliens. I must have known it was evil as when I went to Sunday school I told my teachers about this experience. My mum also had a friend who told me that she believed aliens were demons when I told her my experience, but years after that, I didn't move away from God, but I was certainly deceived by believing I had seen an alien due to what society had dubbed this so-called phenomena happening worldwide. I didn't think it could be a demon, I just had to force myself to believe it was an alien.

It was only after I started praying and really have gotten to know Jesus the past few years I have felt the truth in my heart, what I had truly witnessed as a child. I ask myself why it happened to me as a child. But then I remember how confused I was after, and then being influenced to believe it was an alien and not a demon, it is all part of the devils trickery to deceive the nations that there are aliens, not Jesus.

And to think this is happening to children worldwide (just recently saw a YouTube documentary on kids who witnessed an alien at their school and were very frightened), it is a very surreal scary thing especially for children when Jesus said 'suffer the little children to come to me....'

But then as a child, I know what I saw with my own eyes, but I often question why this thing did not take me anyway as many people say they have been. I think because I did go to Sunday school the devil did not have complete control over me, and the fact that my mum is a very good person and Christian as my brothers are, so my home was always a Christian household. I personally think this is why kids have to go to Sunday school or at least be taught about Jesus early, because you are open to evil at all ages no matter what. Unfortunately I think part of this 'alien' demonic deception plan is to start with children…

Although I believe I have never been 'abducted', and the experience I felt when I was younger I was protected entirely by Jesus as I was not abducted, but ever since I will admit I still often feel fear at night. I have also had dreams, very scary dreams of this horrifying 'tickling' thing demons seem to do to their hostages where you can't move but you feel as if you are being tickled, but I believe that again is the devil tricking me as I know in my heart Jesus would never let that happen to me.

I have prayed and Jesus knows in my heart how frightened I can be, and therefore I do believe has shielded my sight from these demons, and the devil for that matter, and I guess what I mean to say is believe Jesus can do this to all of us simply by saying 'Jesus'. He knows what is in our hearts, and what we can take both physically and mentally. Often at night if I feel afraid for some reason, I just say 'Jesus' out loud over and over and I know whatever is there cannot touch me or make itself known to me. I do believe Jesus can shield your whole house and if only people with current horrific abduction experiences knew this, it would literally save them as there are so many. And also importantly their children who are being subjected to this.

Anyway, I just thought I would share my experience with you despite my reluctance talking about it as it is not something I like to remember. But now that

I know the truth and I see how Jesus protected me even when I did not know him very well, I will uphold his name to the ends of time and I pray for all the children out there who are going through worse experiences than I did because they do not in any sense know Jesus and their parents dwell in sin. Pray for them constantly.

Regards,

Jasmine

38.   Hello, you have my permission to use my written testimony on your website. Please only refer to me as Marie.

This is my story:

My first experience began when I was staying in a motel with my husband and 2 sons. It was one of those creepy motels you would see in a scary movie. We were all having a conversation and I felt tired so I fell asleep. I dreamed as if I continued the conversation with them and had never fallen asleep to begin with. I felt an uneasy feeling and went to sleep (in my dream). I then looked up and into the open doorway of the bathroom and was scared, waiting for some figure to appear in the doorway, but nothing appeared. I laid back down and pulled the covers up to my head and immediately felt the weight of something hovering over me. I was terrified and couldn't will myself to see what it was, so I tried to call to my husband, but no words came out and I was completely paralyzed. I said, "Baby" three times and then screamed it, but nothing came out! Finally, in my head I said, "God, unlock my tongue." and this time when I said "baby" it actually came out. My husband asked me what was wrong and I told him I had been calling for him. He said that I was sleeping and I hadn't said anything at all during my "nap".

Another time I had a dream that Satan himself was attacking me and trying to hurt me. He was all green (like a pale green) and had very long and skinny arms and legs. I could not see his face because he was wearing some sort of robe or cloth. I kept saying over and over "I rebuke you in the name of Jesus" and he would disappear and then reappear. He just kept coming after me trying to get closer, and I kept rebuking him until I woke up.

As I began to read the Bible more, I started to become more spiritually attacked. In fact, nearly every night (and this is still ongoing) I hear footsteps up and down the hallway. Sometimes the footsteps are regular paced, and sometimes they're running up the hallway towards our room. It happens at all hours of the day, but most of the activity is at night. I've started to have dreams about our hallway. The first dream I had I was walking down the hallway and there was a green alien in my kitchen. It was a light color green and had the alien face, but the body had long, skinny arms and legs. It had a twinkle (or flash of light) coming out of its eyes. It started to do a seductive walk towards me, but I woke up before anything could happen.

The last dream I had is probably the worst. After reading this website I started to say "may the lord Jesus Christ rebuke you" to any bad spirits in/around my house. Well, I had another dream about going down my hallway to confront whatever was making the sounds of the footsteps. In the dream, I was seeing out of my own eyes, but I was much taller (almost to the ceiling and sort of looking down). The lights were on, but there was no VISIBLE entity that I could see. I could still feel something there (and I was scared to confront it), so I said, "Be gone in the name of—" and I could not say Jesus. Whatever it was had blocked my speech before I could say the name of Jesus. I woke up terrified and said "Jesus" over and over again.

When I hear the footsteps I start to pray and ask in the name of Jesus for it to stop. The last 2 nights it's stopped right after I've prayed and I've been able to sleep peacefully. I hope my story can encourage other people going through the same ordeal.

39.   Hi Joe

I have just watched one of your presentations and feel the need to contact you and provide you with my testimony regarding Sleep Paralysis.

You have my permission to do with this information what you wish and I hope it may benefit someone in the long run.

I hail from Melbourne, Australia I am 48 years old and have had a history of what you may call strange visitations at night since as a young child. I do not now and have not ever belonged to any religious group although I have always had leanings to Christianity and like some of the ideas behind Buddhist teachings, cause and effect and the role karma play's in that. My earliest memory of childhood was having an imaginary friend who I remember looking different to us and my memory is that it used to hover over me.

I had an accident when I fell down the back steps at home and suffered a hairline fracture of the skull at about 31/2 years old. That day was important in many ways as according to my parents, from that point on I began to suffer night terrors and was extremely afraid of the dark and had to sleep with a light on, this fear of the dark lasted right into my twenties and only in my late twenties did I begin to sleep with the light out.

As far as my memories serve I was in my early teens when I began to experience vibrations in my legs as I drift off to sleep and a sense of falling that sometimes woke me and other times I would go back to sleep. I sometimes in the night heard horses clip clopping yet I lived in the suburbs and no one else heard what I heard. I would also have these strange night terrors where I would feel nauseas and all I could see is this grey ooze, it generally would wake me from my sleep and naturally I would be panicking and seek comfort from my parents.

For some reason around 1990 the sleep paralysis got worse, I was having nightly visitations and after working all day I would struggle to keep my eyes open after getting home, I had one encounter where I fell asleep watching TV and the rest of the family had gone out to dinner I was awoken with a start and on TV was a strange face staring back at me and behind him was an empty grave, this being began to choke itself in front of me. I thought it was TV and tried to change the station but it was on every station. I began to panic and thought I had actually died. I started to pray to God and apologize for anything I may have done wrong and gradually I got my senses back and looked at the TV and it wasn't even turned on.

The sleep paralysis continued and my younger sister who was about 23 and was a closet wiccan (young girls in 1990 LOL) thought she could stop the sleep paralysis by asking it to leave me alone and come to her instead. She would never do that again as that is exactly what happened and I got a good night sleep. She told me how she couldn't move or talk and felt a pressure on top of her with a terrible smell in its breath.

This is what I endured most nights, years later I would read about the old hag syndrome or incubus/succubus but it wasn't always like that. Other times it would be a strange little white being with red eyes and a bloody mouth sometimes it was a rotting corpse either way I am sure I was being attacked by demons.

In my mid to late twenties my mother decided to contact her cousin who was a catholic nun, within weeks these attacks stopped and didn't begin until in my mid-thirties after my mother's cousin had passed away. I had begun working night shift and was having these strange attacks during the day from time to time, I would get a sign of what was to come I would hear a horn like sound in my left ear and I would struggle to stay awake, try as I might I would fall asleep and experience the leg vibrations, the feel of falling and then there it was pressure on my chest, paralysis and the feel of something in the room with me. It was around this time I began to meditate and found that asking the angels and God for guidance and protection these incidents became few and far between.

In about 2005 I had a slight breakdown, I couldn't bring myself to go into work on night shift and started crying uncontrollably, I drove out of the car-park and drove about 150 km's. Where I stopped and rang my wife and told what had happened, she said come home and we went and saw a doctor the next day. I was diagnosed with depression and put on anti-depressants Effexor XR, I wasn't allowed to work for six months and began seeing a Psychologist.

I began meditating again and combined with the meds started having some very strange insights and much lucid dreaming. In one of the dreams I met the white creature with the red eyes and mouth and asked it what it wanted, it said its name was Pookah and upon research I found it to exist in Irish folklore, I actually beat it up in a dream and it hasn't been back since.

During these meditations I actually contacted my higher self who calls himself Ezekiel, but not the one from the bible just happens to share the same name. This higher self during meditations told me to pray to God and ask for protection whenever sleep paralysis would ensue and it has worked. He also said that he lost contact with me when I had the concussion when I was young and only with the help of the medication and meditation was he able to get back in touch. He has told me that organized religion is wrong and being controlled by evil forces but the Ten Commandments are true and to have faith in Jesus but not necessarily organized religion which has been corrupted for a very long time.

Also the bible is in essence many stories put together, not necessarily the true word of God. Many of the stories left out have as much relevance, and that the body of work as a whole is mightier than the bible itself. Everything my higher self has told me has worked in my favor in more ways than I choose to go into now.

He has also told me that the Aliens and the demons that have plagued me are one and the same and use the persons fear against them. They are parasitical and drain the victim of life force or energy. This explains why I never had much energy after an attack.

I agree it is interesting that they are fearful of God, I think there is more to the biblical teachings than meets the eye. Possibly they are fallen angels and prey upon humanity, it just happens that Alien attacks are the modern version of the old hag syndrome.

Two years ago I had a dream where I was taken into a spaceship and was put on a metal table. Again I couldn't move or speak and the grey implanted something into my left foot. For months I felt there was something in my foot, at times it caused pain, other times it was just uncomfortable. About four months after the dream I had another dream where a human looking alien had landed his ship and walked towards me. I remember this being had a brown beard and appeared Caucasian but his face seemed to be scarred by acne or something. He said there is nothing to fear and I must admit I was panicking, he fired a beam at me and all around me seemed to be like a small tornado and I could feel tears coming out of my eyes, this all stopped and said now you are fine.

I don't remember much more only to wake up and for the first time in many months my foot felt fine, no discomfort and no pain. I still have many lucid dreams and many dreams where I myself am actually flying without any mechanical help. What that means I am not sure. I will just finish with a dream of two nights ago. I am in the street and looking up and see a black pyramid shaped craft hovering, it has an almost marble texture it and the marbling is light and seems to be moved all around. I wave at it and it begins to move away but at the same time I am being lifted towards it. I am then immersed in what I would call a beautiful golden light and i feel absolute joy at this and amazement at what I am seeing.

I then find myself in the craft and see many other dumbfounded people all asking the same thing what we are doing here. At that point a middle aged man walks up towards us and says welcome and tells us to be calm and that everything is OK. He then begins to tell us that we have been deceived by the government of this world and that he is offering us a chance to have our spiritual DNA repaired as it has been changed in such a way that we can never leave the reincarnation process and that we cannot remember passed lives and experience because of this. He went on to say that we have been unfairly imprisoned and that they were there to help.

He said that with the DNA adjusted, you will remember past lives and live until at least 1000 years old.

In order to do this we must be willing to leave our loved ones behind, at that point I looked down a corridor to the left and could see soldiers marching. These soldiers were dressed like roman centurions from the movies only all in black. He noticed that I had seen this and told me not to look as I was not ready for this yet.

I was then asked what I wanted to do and I said I have a young family and they need my support, I then woke up. Would I have woken up if I agreed?

Vivid dream yes, also very weird. Something strange is a foot and I do believe these aliens are mostly demonic by nature and that there is a war going on for our souls and they are doing anything they can to get them. It seems their favorite mode is while we sleep through our dreams.

I hope some of this is interesting to you and that it can in some way help others.

For me the Journey is far more important than the destination, it's more important how you choose to get there than how far you may go.

I believe all answers reside in ourselves there is too much disinformation and lies around us, the truth lies in ourselves and God.

Kind Regards

Ian

40.   Hello,

My name is Eric. I'm 23, a Celebrity Jewelry Designer and Fashion Major. That's just a little bit about me but actually God brought me to this video of your brief description of an abduction and I cried my ass off. My brother and I have had similar dreams for the past 4 years, well my brother's dream happened last year. By the way don't mind you using any of my information because I believe it is for the Glory of God that I tell these things. You have no idea how it feels to not be the only one who has had these dreams. My brother told my mom about his separately and I told my mom hours after it happened, so she put the two together and said we had similar dreams. We even started to be skeptical that it was GHOST! I didn't read any of the testimonies yet so that you may know my experiences are genuinely my own. I will read them after this email.

First I would like to tell my brothers. Briefly he told my mom that he was asleep and he had a dream that the covers were snatched from his bed leaving him vulnerable I guess or visible so to speak. Then he heard growling in his ear and he couldn't speak nor move. Then he managed to say Jesus and woke up. After that night he switched rooms and never had the dream again. He assumes it was a ghost only in that room. When the dream occurred to me, I wasn't aware of what happened to him. Only my mother and they had never spoken to me about it. Well 4 years ago we lived in another house and I had that exact dream. I never talked about it because it only happened once. Well this time it happened again and it changed my life

I was practicing Buddhism trying my best to find God. Raised as a Christian so I never stopped believing in Jesus, I just wanted to be more spiritual. Then I stumbled across and Internet site that spoke about a book on different religions. "The True Light" I found out that chakras are actually against the works that Jesus Christ does. They bypass asking for forgiveness and does away with Jesus Christ authority. Then I found out that Satanism uses chakras as well. I read about Satanism and his supposing to be the Real God and Bringer of Knowledge. Like he was trying to free us but I knew in my heart it was all lies. So at this point I was more confused on which path to take. Continue with Buddhism or go back to Christianity. God knows I was trying my damn hardest to find him, but instead he came to me.

TESTIMONY:

I had a dream I was standing outside the Gates of Heaven. There were two young boys crying so I walked over to them. I asked, "What was wrong?" They said that someone was taunting or haunting them. I then said as a being walked next to me, "Here is my friend, he will protect you! Just call on him when and if they return".

This was the (HOLY SPIRIT) He had no face but he had a physical presence. He wasn't neither light nor dark….but he was there. They immediately wiped their eyes and started to walk away. I had a feeling like I passed the test or I did what I was supposed to. The "being" then put his hand on my shoulder and told me to come walk with him. We turned around and walked into what I think is the Kingdom of Heaven. There were Angels everywhere, & people. There were also some who couldn't walk so they were carried by two different beings. The being then walked over and sat in a chair. There were three chairs. He sat to the right. Next to him, without a doubt, was Jesus Christ. Next to Jesus was a third man who didn't look my way. I asked the being (Holy Spirit) If I could speak to him (Jesus). He said yes, if he will hear you.

So I walked over and the third man remained looking in another direction. So I turned forward to the middle chair and sat Indian style in front of Jesus. I KID YOU NOT he leaned forward directly in front of my face and smiled. I saw him as clear as day and felt his presence/comfort and stability. I was SAFE! I asked him if I was allowed to ask him questions. He said to me, "You may ask me anything." I asked did he see what I was doing. He said I see all things on Earth. I even see your Earrings and they are beautiful. Then I asked how the Kingdom of Heaven is and he said, "It is good". At this time I was comfortable and I started looking around at all the surroundings. The Angels and the people. I heard voices…I then asked while not looking at him but at the others, "Can I ask another questions?" He said. "Yes if time permits… but be Hasty." Then I heard growling…like a beast of something coming from the distance. I knew the devil was near or what I thought it was. Jesus then reached out and touched my arm, I looked directly into his face and he gave me a name like Charisma. It sounded like Charisma but I know that's not what it was. I still cannot figure out what he actually said but he tried to tell me before I woke up, or when I appeared to be awaken. After he spoke I woke up in my room. Exactly how I went to sleep, the room was just the way I remembered it before, but I wasn't awake. Even though I thought I was because it seemed so real. I was instantly paralyzed in the bed and when I tried to speak I would mumbled every word. Then they came. It was more than one, maybe two or three. They played with my covers around my feet and legs and then blew wind in my face. Then they growled in my ear very loudly and yet I never saw them. Then something crazier happened that never happened before. They took both of my arms and twisted them completely around with my palms touching both sides of the wall. Then they took my head and turned it completely around and my entire body was distorted. I still mumbled and couldn't say what I would normally say, "Satan I rebuke you in the Name of JESUS CHRIST!" Then my sister came in the room and screamed. At that moment I spoke, "Satan I rebuke you in the name of Jesus Christ!" I woke up, heart beating, scared, afraid and crying. I went to my mom and she said it was amazing my brother and I had the same dream. I know for a fact I met Jesus that night and he showed me his realness and being so to speak. & now after watching the video like an hour ago I'm astonished and amazed that others are experiencing the same things. I believe even more now than ever. I thank you and God for doing this for me. I know I have a special relationship with God and the fallen are either trying to scare me or they are trying to know why I am selected by Christ! This is an Amazing night. I apologize for all the grammar errors but I wrote it all out in one take. Again you can use any information and I hope this helps. Thanks again for allowing God to use you and brink comfort and knowledge to my life!

-Eric

41.   I am Joe S. and I can confirm with confidence that there is power in his name; Jesus name, that name saved me from certain death or insanity—I will attempt to explain. In spring 1997 I was an antique and collectibles dealer, selling at the Rose Bowl flea market in Pasadena every month, and hitting up estate sales and thrifts stores collecting my wares in my hometown Bakersfield. At that time, the "Greatest Generation" or WWII population were passing away in large numbers across the country in what I imagine was a peak point in history. Every weekend that Spring I filled my truck with vintage clothing, furniture, and what had become a hobby, collecting rare books. Due to our location, and its proximity to both Edwards Air Force Base and China Lake Naval, a good portion of residents had careers in the Skunk Works, Northrup Grumman, etc. and I

acquired a notable collection of fairly sought after esoteric and "secret society" publications, due to the fact that most of the deceased were lodge members, as well as the fact there was a Theosophist Society, Odd Fellows Hall, Lemurians, and Bohemians. Selling at the Rose Bowl introduced me to the major "niche" collectors from all over the world and I was struck by the degree of persistence from certain rare book collectors as they called my home and showed up around town, this after I had started selling some of my collection. One in particular, had always been friendly and was like most people in L.A., a name dropper whose connections to the movie industry and New Age, even went as far as Hillary Clinton as his spirit leader did vision quests, was an American Indian, and even worked for the FBI.

Here I was a Christian and I was spending my free time reading these writings, of which some were hundreds of years old, about subjects that I knew were evil; but, I ended up reading the Bible for the first time. Along with all the garbage I was reading, I ended up reading the Bible twice front to back with a new understanding. It seemed like everywhere I went these rare occult books started just falling into my hands and I was getting paranoid and started having visions (while not asleep) and thoughts of events that seemed to be setting what I would later discover, were a precursor. I didn't know if it was delusions and madness from the items; but, I became paranoid fast after I concluded that some of what I was "falling" into was no coincidence and instead purposed. Strange people hosting estate sales that had this cult like feel, the spirit guy who was always inviting me to do his "vision quest" or Kabala with stars, was now living in Paso Robles, taking care of a ranch and calling and coming to town trying to get me to hang out. I later learned that the "ranch" he was caretaker, was also the residence of L. Ron Hubbard where he died.

I had started having visions of airplanes and nuclear explosions and other what I thought were WWII spirits, which until then I never would have believed in, when after a series of events that I later discovered described to a tee in an art project called "Agrippa" that a cyber punk writer had done in 1992 in NYC called transmission about memory, his grandfather, and a poem that described the events that happened in 1997-2001; some of which I will attempt to describe.

Footsteps on the roof and a large impact would lead to the discovery of a WWII era slug being found when we went to see what had hit the house. I had not slept for 2 days due to intense paranoia after I had finished reading some material from the 1800s that was pivotal at my complete understanding of just how nefarious the grand design was in its effect having signs that were everywhere, I was going insane, and at least I thought I was. When the police arrived it was clear that they were not interested in the planes that were flying low for the last few nights or the SOS signals of lights being a constant theme; they inspected the bullet we pulled from the roof and said "what bullet? And focused on me with cryptic interrogatives that ended with an odd tow truck driver showing up to change their tire and then towing one patrol car and leaving in another. They said they were not from here and alluded to the Men in Black toying with their flashlights mentioning I must have pissed the wrong people off and was I ready to do a confessional.

Nonetheless, I was subsequently arrested the following morning after spending the night driving a few hundred miles and back again, my plans were to contact authorities in Fresno as no local office existed locally at the time (FBI). I was tackled and handcuffed in a small town 15 miles from my home that morning after visiting the film location of "Joyride"; which, my mother had told me there was a giant Boeing 747 wrecked in a corn field that looked like the scene at Universal Studios. All I found was a few signs that had the movie name and an arrow; no plane. Later I would see the movie, about some lunatic who goes crazy after some phone pranks. It was not a popular film domestically and Wikipedia has changed the information since I read this; but, it was a hit in other countries. One was Israel, where it was titled "Never Insult an Arab", and it was under a different name in Europe, I never knew that films had different names in other parts of the world; but, one thing is certain: there was nothing about a plane or a crash in the movie. To this day my mother who has never lied sticks to the fact that she saw the broken plane spread across the field.

So I am in the back of the Sherriff's car and I notice a film crew as we drive away and the van they are driving has the words "Industrial Lights and Magic" across the side. I am thinking that this is some psy ops and that they are planning to kill me so when we arrive at the jail I begin resisting and screaming to which the staff place me in a segregated cell with only a urinal, sink, and telephone. I pick up the phone and make a collect call to the FCC whose number I memorized along with others I had been calling during my madness. A woman accepts the collect call and I tell her about the radio station that was playing in my head and how the airplanes were crashing and she tells me that they had been reorganized and no longer had an interest or jurisdiction with radio broadcasting, she explained that they were focused on the internet now (again this is 1997). She then asks me where I was calling from and she says how I reached her in NYC and proceeds to say her building was near the antenna, and the line goes dead. I noticed a buildup of deputies appearing at the door to the cell through the shatterproof glass. Suddenly, they storm in (goon squad) and there must have been 10 of them, they had me in a five point hold, one on each leg and arm. Right then one of them pounced on my back and must have weighed 300 lbs., all of my air just pushed out and I was being suffocated. I was trying to yell but couldn't, I had no air left in my lungs and I could see my life flash before my eyes. I thought I was dead, I can't explain the feeling of being crushed and not being able to draw air into my lungs; while my mind is trying to say "you're killing me!" What seemed like an eternity and felt the person move off my back a little and my belt being undone and pants yanked down as I looked back, a man in a white scientific/nurse coat is holding a needle and everything just goes black. I still had not taken in a breath before losing consciousness.

I am not sure about when exactly but my next brain activity is this full audio/visual that was like the tunnel vision that I had left with as it was unable to see anything to the left or right and was disoriented. It was the brightest white light that I could even imagine and like nowhere found on earth, it was foggy and bright reflecting like a white wall; but, as if your riding on the wing of an airplane with the wind pressure and the noise. Then I was restrained, pinned lying down looking up and felt like I was slowly waking up as if asleep. In my mind I could see now, in like

360 degree vision as if I had a periscope because I was incapacitated still and yet seeing and above myself lying there motionless. I had this new sensory, like an ability to hear the thoughts and those were two other conscious that were like confused by my presence. Suddenly, the entire structure seemed to come alive and a wall of lighted controls (the two were facing at the time) made this loud emergency warning alarm and I hear these as thoughts of confusion and many other thoughts they were consulting, which I could only tell that they were not prepared.

I instantly noticed these two were Phoenician Priests, like the type in Egypt that had those catlike ears and I felt as though it was a threshold or transition ritual they had planned. I could see the scales and a human heart being weighed and a census being taken, and the crossing on a floating barge they wanted to get across with us. Right then, like a camera switched on my above view is that of my neighbor, who is also in an egg shaped enclosure filled with a gas or fluid? He is a fully armed and armor wearing soldier and I sense he is awakening, even though he hasn't moved yet. Now I can sense just as they had become aware of my brain activity and the ship we are in is alive, like an entity separately in control that is losing power. The Egyptian huge head and half beast looking pilots start into a frenzy as the soldier is waking up.

This feeling of the most impending fear just hits me where all that time awakening I was not afraid the least bit, now I sense the feebleness and ineptness of the two who are paralyzed as I start calling out Jesus name. I just keep repeating his name over and over and the ship and the lights are just flashing and alarm ringing. I keep saying his name and feel this overwhelming feeling as the two Phoenicians are just powerless and don't know what to do.

Next thing I know I am back in the foggy bright white and then I look up from the ground and see that I am in a cell hogtied and handcuffed to the floor. I continue saying Jesus, Jesus, Jesus and I hear this growling noise and it's a female trustee who is like being escorted through the walkway outside of the cell and she says "I hate that name" in the most evil voice. At this point I am begging for water and have no idea that I was in that cell for almost 48 hours and they had forgot about me. The officer returns and opens my door giving me a Dixie cup with a mouthful of water. I said thank you and he said I would be moved to booking soon and i asked where the evil women went and he said "I sent her back because that voice freaked me out". When he loosened my leg cuffs and the arm cuffs he said "they forgot you were here and there is no record of your arrest." I ended up staying another two weeks under evaluation and was never even taken to court. I can tell you that I went home and burned every last book and to this day there is a charred mark on the concrete where it always reminds me: and have only told a few others about this.

42.   Hi Joe I am from South Africa, Johannesburg, and I what to share this with you and hope it helps. I'm 40 year's old and have been fascinated about aliens for my whole life and started research on it for the last 20 years. A lot never made sense to me for I was not saved, the year 2005 I give my life to Jesus Christ and the Lord started to show me things. Around 2008 the Lord revealed a lot of information to me and I started to go into to shock for its was too much information for me and fear started to take over my life and family, I prayed to the Lord I don't want to know any more He must take it away (let me forget or show me how to overcome this). That night something else happened, it was so real and I don't know what to do with it at that stage. As we were asleep I woke up and I experience a UFO over my house and I felt this is bad and wrong in so many ways and it's like you can hear there thought's as they speak and they said they came to take me and my family for I know too much and I'm not allowed to share it with the world. I got my family together in one room me, my wife and 2 daughter's. As they were coming into the room (the greys) as some people call them I just heard a voice that penetrated my being and it was not from the GREYS. It felt like it came from somewhere else, it almost felt like it came from inside me for my whole body shake when the voice spoke and I just knew it was the Lord Jesus Christ. And the voice said put your trust in Me and I just scream out, I'm under the protection of the Lord Jesus Christ you have no authority here, please help Jesus and at that moment they just walk past me and my family as off they could not see us and

they just left, (disappeared) instantly. As they were gone I was still shaken full of fear I heard that same voice again and it said, Don't be afraid For I'm and as long as you are in Me no harm will come to you. I fell to the floor and just cried. No one can remember anything but me. My wife said maybe it was a dream and any one I tell it to. Dream or no dream but it was so real and vivid, but one thing I know is it was Jesus that spoke to me and the moment I shouted His name everything change and felt peace and they (the greys left)   Yes Jesus lives and He is King over all.

And yes Joe you are welcome to share my testimony on your website just not my contact details but you are welcome to contact me.

Kind Regards

Heinrich

43.   Joe Jordan, I wish for your permission to give my testimony.

I have experienced these visions of entities through self-inducing myself with a psychoactive drug and brought myself to a completely alternate reality/realm. I knew there have been cases of people talking to entities in this chemical and found "spiritual enlightenment". This wasn't the case for me, instead I wanted answers and what the answers I found was alarming. I truly did get into contact with this entity and I will explain this it all in full detail. I have been intrigued with the new age mumbo jumbo that we live in a simulation and spiritual awakenings are happening all over the world. Well this new age teaching is blurring the lines of the curious people and distorting the truth between what is right and what is wrong. Hermeticism is now called quantum physics. Science is the new religion... More back to my story. I took the drug and began hallucinating and fell into the dream world and began to hear mumbling of someone. The voice could not be determined if it was male or female. I was aware I had its attention and "it" had mine. It had no real form but I could still tell it had reactions similar to speaking to someone else. I spoke out "Who are you?" "It" pointed at itself and said "Who am I" and looked like I caught "it" off guard to how normally it is spoke to I assume from other visitors or abductees. It had a very alien feeling as well. Like I was being observed as well. "It" point back at me in a somewhat sly manner and said "I am you!" I shook my head and said "NO, You are not me... you are lying." I somehow knew it was lying. It was deceiving me. You see I somehow knew what this was about and I realized this was the spiritual battle we are all born in the middle of. The choice of whether or not you follow God or you follow Satan. This entity was not of God's will and I said "God made me, he made all of us individually." "IT" began to scowl at me and threw its arms in the air and spoke back in defiance "We made God up to hide you from us." I grew up in a Christian family and had been taught in the truth and the life of Lord Jesus Christ. I fell away from that lifestyle as I got older, taking drugs and abusing my life with sex and partying. But for some reason I remembered a dream I had when I was a child that God showed me his realm and that his gates were closing soon and someday I will be faced with something and you will know your place after you face it. My faith is what saved me from the deception. I never rebuked the Lord from my life but I questioned his existence. "IT" resumes it's deception on me and said "Don't you want to be one? You are me, I am you, you are her, and you are him. We are all one. Don't you want that?" I said "No! Because I've seen the truth and the light and God IS real! You are lying!" I realized it wasn't an entity anymore but a demon. The demon spoke back to me, "God doesn't share his light with anyone. LOOK AT ME! Why do you think I am here? Why do you think YOU are here?" I knew everything that demon was saying was a lie I said, "You are lying, I don't want any part of this/your reality because I know there is a better realm. Better than this and God wants us to love him and that is our key." The demon turned from me and the entire hallucinations absolved into nothing. I knew what I saw was real. I know that I know that I know. There is a real battle going on. From then on I am a soldier in God's great army and I will continue to serve in the name of Jesus. Please use my story as a testimony, to reach out to others and show them that this is very real thing and people need to know the God is the truth to and rely of this. I sought truth in all the wrong places and I am so fortunate to remember what I was taught as a young boy. That God is really in charge of it all.

These demons have no hold over you, they can lie to you but as long as you have faith and know God is there for you, he will never turn you away. The demons cannot read your mind either but they can sense sinful thoughts. I have gained so much knowledge about them I can write a whole novel of this experience. In fact it wouldn't be a bad idea to do it. Use my testimony as a tool for others.

Sincerely Josiah

44.   It stopped them

It was 1992, I was staying with my cousin in San Diego. I had minimal experiences before. This night was different. My sister called the night before from Toronto sharing her abduction experiences. She told a story about her phone making these weird musical noises. The next night a ball of light fly over the sky while I was sitting in a hot tub at the apartment complex, another man in the hot tub seen it too. A bit later I was up in the apartment, the phone rang, it was my cousin calling from Tijuana, and he was having car problems and would be late getting back. At this time the call waiting went off. I told him, so he hung up. I picked up the other line and there was these strange musical noises. The hair stood up on the back of my neck, I knew what was coming. As much as I did not want to go to sleep, I did. I had a huge window in my room. I felt them come in. Three of them, small beings with small eyes, the beings were tan in color. I was taken, I remember seeing through the bottom of the ship, it seemed like glass, I could see the city of San Diego, and Tijuana. They were telling me I wouldn't remember. I argued with them and said I would. They seemed aggressive and getting agitated with me. I finally started repeating the Lord's Prayer, then said I am protected by the body and blood of Jesus Christ. I repeated that statement. They were not happy with me, I was brought back, can remember floating back through the window and floating down to my bed. I was never bothered by them again. I moved back to Michigan after that. I did have more back home, not those beings. I did repeat the same things, but these beings that I did not see were tougher. It was always a fight between my words and them. I know a couple of times after that

I would just give in and allow them to take me. I did again repeating Lord's Prayer and that I was protected by the body and blood of Jesus Christ. I have had no more experiences. I do feel one time I was taken by some people. I had printed up some info on things to this day have happened. I won't say it here. But at this time I was back living in San Diego. I was an exotic dancer. Papers were given to me from a DJ I worked with. Once I copied them a few weird things happened. First one is i went to Rubio's for fish tacos. I was in Pacific beach. Out of nowhere this young man who was close to my age at the time. I was 23. He started talking to me about UFO's, and that his mom was the president of the San Diego chapter. He then asked what I was doing. Told him I am going shopping. He walked with me into buffalo exchange. I grabbed a shirt, he offered to pay. Of course being a dancer I was fine with it. Then he asked what I was doing later. I think I responded I was working... That was it... about 4 or 5 years later I was watching a show about some hotel downtown, they showed a restaurant that over looked the bay, all of a sudden I had a memory of being there. Everything came to me, men sitting at a round table, and that young man was there. I wanted to get away, I said I have a headache, I want to go. The men got agitated that I wanted to leave, I remember getting to the parking garage to my car. The next memory was being in my car in ocean side, 30 minutes north... To this day I am unsure what had happened. I feel the men were not men, they were something else. To this day I know I had something in those papers and should not have made copies. It is strange to have no memory of incident until I saw that hotel and restaurant on that travel show.

45.   God bless you all for your work.

The devil is a deceiver & father of lies. Demons are real. Ephesians 6:10....

Jesus cast out demons. Acts Ch. 16 a demon was cast out of a psychic lady.

Deuteronomy Ch. 18:10-12 warns us about dabbling into the demonic occult.

Sadly sin is rampant via abortion crime drugs family break up, suicide, porn fornication adultery, evolution lies, Idols, pride, cults/false religions, & the occult/witchcraft & in all it's 100's of forms...Ouija board tarot cards astrology Wicca new age Satanism astral body travel sleep paralysis ,UFO, charliecharliechallenge, on & on...

I once did astral body travel but after Jesus saved me it stopped!!!

Once got a very good Christian themed article in a major newspaper. At 3:30 am an invisible devil / demon presence came into my bedroom. I spoke in the name of Jesus for it to leave. This evil presence that felt like Evil x 1000 fled from the room immediately. Hours later the newspaper hit the streets with the powerful Christian testimony story. 1/2 page long.

Once in my life I felt my body get paralyzed as I laid on the bed. Suddenly felt a pointed object trying to push in my bum area. No one was in the room but me.

Held my bum as tight as I could & silently prayed for Jesus to help me.

After about a minute the encounter stopped!!!

I witness a lot to strangers & many kids teens adults have told me of having sleep paralysis events, using Ouija boards, being involved in Satanism...

With all the Harry Potter books movies, occult themed movies, TV series Lucifer & ghost reality TV programs, psychics on TV, on & on ...people are going to dabble into the luring occult practices with is all 100% fueled by Satan & demons.

95% of pastors have no idea of the reality of the works of evil spirits at work in our community. They talk about God & ignore the other supernatural powers at work Satan & demons. If they bring up the subject most will say "the enemy" but do not use the word devil or demon.

Somehow they think talking about the devil reality detracts from the reality of God's Almighty power. Sadly by ignoring the reality of Satan's devices in our churches had resulted with a near zero warning for the lost unsaved from dabbling in the occult.

Many times an unsaved person being demonized by using an Ouija board goes to Christian churches for help. Sadly most pastors have no idea what to do for the person. The demonized person walks away still under demonic attack & is forced to get help from MDs. & psychiatric help which in turn uses medications to treat the person. The pastors should be holding major media events warning the public not to use Ouija boards & avoiding any occult involvement as it's all a hot phone to the pit of hell!!!!!!!

God bless you all in Jesus Name.

Al

You can use my story on your website if you wish.

46.   Joe Jordan, I wish for your permission to give my testimony.

I have experienced these visions of entities through self-inducing myself with a psychoactive drug and brought myself to a completely alternate reality/realm. I knew there have been cases of people talking to entities in this chemical and found "spiritual enlightenment". This wasn't the case for me, instead I wanted answers and what the answers I found was alarming. I truly did get into contact with this entity and I will explain this it all in full detail. I have been intrigued with the new age mumbo jumbo that we live in a simulation and spiritual awakenings are happening all over the world. Well this new age teaching is blurring the lines of the curious people and distorting the truth between what is right and what is wrong. Hermeticism is now called quantum physics. Science is the new religion... More back to my story. I took the drug and began hallucinating and fell into the dream world and began to hear mumbling of someone. The voice could not be determined if it was male or female. I was aware I had its attention and "it" had mine. It had no real form but I could still tell it had reactions similar to speaking to someone else. I spoke out "Who are you?" "It" pointed at itself and said "Who am I" and looked like I caught "it" off guard to how normally it is spoke to I assume from other visitors or abductees. It had a very alien feeling as well. Like I was being observed as well. "It" point back at me in a somewhat sly manner and said "I am you!" I shook my head and said "NO, You are not me... you are lying." I somehow knew It was lying. It was deceiving me. You see I somehow knew what this was about and I realized this was the spiritual battle we are all born in the middle of. The choice of whether or not you follow God or you follow Satan. This entity was not of God's will and I said "God made me, he made all of us individually." "IT" began to scowl at me and threw its arms in the air and spoke back in defiance "We made God up to hide you from us." I grew up in a Christian family and had been taught in the truth and the life of Lord Jesus Christ. I fell away from that lifestyle as I got older, taking drugs and abusing my life with sex and partying. But for some reason I remembered a dream I had when I was a child that God showed me his realm and that his gates were closing soon and someday I will be faced with something and you will know your place after you face it. My faith is what saved me from the deception. I never rebuked the Lord from my life but I questioned his existence. "IT" resumes it's deception on me and said "Don't you want to be one? You are me, I am you, you are her, and you are him. We are all one. Don't you want that?" I said "No! Because I've seen the truth and the light and God IS real! You are lying!" I realized it wasn't an entity anymore but a demon. The demon spoke back to me, "God doesn't share his light with anyone. LOOK AT ME! Why do you think I am here? Why do you think YOU are here?" I knew everything that demon was saying was a lie I said, "You are lying, I don't want any part of this/your reality because I know there is a better realm. Better than this and God wants us to love him and that is our key." The demon turned from me and the entire hallucinations absolved into nothing. I knew what I saw was real. I know that I know that I know. There is a real battle going on. From then on I am a soldier in God's great army and I will continue to serve in the name of Jesus. Please use my story as a testimony, to reach out to others and show them that this is very real thing and people need to know the God is the truth to and rely of this. I sought truth in all the wrong places and I am so fortunate to remember what I was taught as a young boy. That God is really in charge of it all.

These demons have no hold over you, they can lie to you but as long as you have faith and know God is there for you, he will never turn you away. The demons cannot read your mind either but they can sense sinful thoughts. I have gained so much knowledge about them I can write a whole novel of this experience. In fact it wouldn't be a bad idea to do it. Use my testimony as a tool for others.

Sincerely Josiah

47.   Joe Jordan, please know you have my permission to use this information if you wish to post this testimony on your website.

I would like to share my experience with you regarding 'aliens being demons'. I had just returned to Christ, and I want to emphasize this, that I was a returned 'new believer' who had been steeped in the new age for over 30 yrs., yet I was not well versed in the subject of UFO's or aliens. When I returned to Christ I also wanted only Him to teach me, only Him and the Holy Spirit of truth, as I saw and was shocked at how the new age has crept into the many churches I visited, for I recognize what I used to teach.

While in prayer one day the Lord showed me the following;

Jesus came to me while in prayer in July of 2013 and showed me the following... he opened a door it was dark within, there were these beings...small, grey, slimy, very disturbed looking, all huddled together in darkness...chained. He said to me "this is the face of fear, they have chained their hearts with their thoughts for where fear exist there can be no light". He then closed the door!

I recognized immediately their appearance as being that of the 'greys', the aliens known to many from drawings that exist. I also knew the Lord was showing me demons and felt I was being warned. I was aghast I didn't know why this had happened, or what it meant but I was soon to find out.

Now this is quite difficult to put into words but I will try my best. Not long after this one morning upon awakening, I saw only what I can describe as beings which were small and grey, not anywhere in my room, but within my mind. Just briefly upon opening my eyes and nothing more. I immediately recognized them as the 'greys'. I thought it odd and brushed it off continuing to get ready for work. However there seemed to be another being, tall, that looked like the others, but was not grey being much lighter in color. There seemed to be telepathic communication going on here with me that stopped me in my tracks. I heard it say "I'm not going to hurt you I love you! This seemed unreal tome, and thankfully it then dissipated. I then realized these were the same beings that the Lord had showed me! Demons. As I was getting dressed I noticed and was quite alarmed to find what I can only describe as a black/blue mark quite large at the right lower quadrant of my abdomen. It had not been there when I went to bed. I was perplexed as to how this could have occurred. It eventually dissipated but unlike a usual bruise did not turn lighter, but stayed the same dark color eventually fading.

In hindsight If I had heeded the Lord's warning I could have avoided this situation but I was still 'new to Christ', still hanging on to other philosophies which in time thankfully I would discard. Only later was I to find reference to what the Lord showed me in 2 Peter and Jude. I tell you I almost dropped my bible when I read it! For indeed the Lord was showing me those fallen ones who were bound in darkness!

Another time later I heard a voice in my room as I went to sleep stating 'here she is'. I felt nothing but fear, paralyzing fear. I immediately called out 'Christ Jesus help me! At which time I saw a ball of light within and then that fear, then that presence was gone instantly and has never returned.

I know it was the name of the Lord Christ Jesus which removed them from my presence!

Regarding the 'dragon' and those who serve him the Lord would tell me the following;

10/02/16 I was praying and suddenly was taken to what I call the throne of God again. Again I saw Christ and the Father who was sitting on His throne. Christ was standing, his back was to me. I was behind him. There was the dragon watching me outside the throne. Suddenly Christ raised his hand and the dragon turned away. Christ said to me 'he rejected the Father to such an extent that his appearance became grotesque and those who worship him worship him in such an image'.

It is Christ that we are to call upon 'not ourselves' to subdue the Dragon...and those who worship him.

Praise to the Most High God, the Father I Am, whose breath gave me life. Praise be to the Son of God Christ Jesus whose cross, blood and resurrection free me from sin and death. My prayer is that many be saved from any more of these encounters by calling on the name of Christ Jesus.

Thank you for taking the time to read this and God bless you.
Megan

48.   REQUESTED TESTAMENT, FRANK

Hi Joe

My story is a bit different from what you are used to getting I suppose, but here it is. I used to be interested in astronomy and had a 12 inch reflector telescope that I used to check out the stars and planets, and I love to watch the skies at night. I was into the new age and having a catholic upbringing I totally rejected the Christian religion.

So anyway, I was watching this documentary on UFOs in the late 80s and I wondered why I have never seen one...so I went outside one night to have a quick look at the night sky not expecting to see anything but one flew over the top of me below cloud level as a bright orange glowing ball...this really exited me. After a couple of days a friend came over and I was telling him what I saw and I took him out and showed him where I saw it and as I was showing him we noticed a bright light in the distance that just shot off into space, and a few minutes later it returned really close to us about half a mile away and it was like a ball of light that threw out multiple different colors and then it flared up really bright and instantly flew off into space in a split second. That was my second encounter. That was a day time encounter.

From there on I would see them all the time, not only would I see them but I would know I would see them beforehand. I would get the feeling that if a would go outside now I would see one, and of cause it would be there...not only that but I could go outside and will them to appear and they would. There was sort of a telepathic messaging going on there. But that was all good and I have to say I don't think I was ever abducted, never had any fear of them or anything threatening happen to me. There was only telepathic contact

Anyway I was going through my astronomy books reading up on the planets when I came across this moon Miranda, and from then on strange things started to happen to me, I would see things on the moon that I never noticed before...and I know it sounds strange but I felt a great opposition from the "UFOs" to what I was seeing and it was trying to scare me away from it. But as the weeks went on I started getting a story from this moon and it sounded familiar to what was written in the bible. The more I delved into the story I was getting from the moon the more satanic attacks I would have, and it got pretty scary, I had lights floating around in my room and I would get, strange as it would seem visions of a giant skull with a roman helmet on its head and with iron teeth coming in to bite my head off. But threw out those few weeks i felt this force of good pushing it through and I would get information about the bible that I shouldn't have known cause I never read it, but in hind sight having read it, it turned out to be true.

Then one night it all came to an end...I got as much of the story I needed from the moon and...and that night lying in my bed thinking about what was given to me I felt aware of this gargoyle type demon sitting on my stomach and I was frozen, I couldn't move and then I became aware of this super evil entity that came in right next to my face and I could feel it breathing down my neck and I was too scared to open my eyes to look at it, then I said the lord's prayer for the first time in 30 years and asked Jesus to get rid of the demons from me, and then instantly within the click of my fingers they were gone. From that day I had never seen another UFO...because they were the demons. And I thank the lord Jesus "Yeshua my Lord and King" for saving me. And 15 years down the track I am free of the influence of these "ALIENS = DEMONS". I have since then found the truth of the bible and am a staunch Christian, I love true Christianity and can see now the falsehood that the main stream media is putting out there to suppress the truth of the bible.

But the strange thing is that after I was freed, I was left there standing with this message I was given. It is something people don't understand because it's been done supernaturally, and it is a warning to the world for the end times. The message was purposefully hidden till the right time and some people see it and some don't, but whether they see it or not don't matter, it is there for the end times.

Thanks Joe

49.   Dear Joe,

I will start with a quick bit of back ground. I was brought up in a Christian home and made a profession of faith about 12 years old and baptized at 16 years olds although I realized a lot later I was not born again at that time. In my early twenties my life style was that of the world. My first encounter with the supernatural was while living with my then fiancée which we shared with a work colleague of mine. Quite often she would wake up paralyzed in the night. She would generally not see anything but on one occasion she saw babies foot prints walk over me and then her while she was in that state. My friend also reported waking up in the morning and heard a baby laughing and felt as if something was jumping on his bed. At that time I hadn't experienced anything. Shortly after, my fiancée went back to university so I was left in the house with just my colleague.

The very first night on my own I woke up paralyzed and felt as if the bed cover was levitating, this was some years ago and the memories vague so whether the floating sheets were an absolute reality of a figment of my imagination I can't tell. I also can't remember if I prayed or call out in Jesus Name (in my head as I was unable to speak). It passed after what seemed like a minute or so and I saw nothing else. I left the house the same night and did not return. My friend stayed there for another year or so and nothing further happened to him.

I moved back in with my parents for a few years and during this time I remember waking up paralyzed at least one more time and seem to remember feeling as if a presence were with me, although it would have been on the other side of the room and I saw (as far as I can remember) nothing concrete. I think I did at that time call out to Jesus and remember the incident concluding shortly after that.

As the years passed I got married and move into our marital home but in providence my marriage lasted only a short time and my wife moved out of the house. This was the event that the Lord used for my actual conversion, up to this point I had not been born again, although I thought I had been. My conversion was fairly dramatic and followed very closely to the conversion narratives given by Jonathan Edwards during the 'Great Awakening'. I had a deep sense of dread and guilty before God and for several days utterly devoid of any hope of salvation but just a fearful dread of my impending judgement and hell. With what seemed like no external helps or internal reasoning in one moment the dread subsided as I was able to happily declare 'If going to Hell brings glory to God I am willing and at peace in going'. I knew I had had a heart change and my life was and still is characterized with a zeal for God's glory and His righteousness, praise His glorious and precious Name.

My life from that point was characterized by intense prayer, most days praying for 3 to 4 hours. Not that there was always a great freedom to do so but my new born zeal was sufficient to drive me to my knees and keep me there. I knew very little of prayer then and wonder how much was of the type that moves mountains. I note this because at that time whether by coincidence or design (I mean human design, all is of God glorious provincial design) I seemed to have attracted the attention of a local coven as recording tape had been put outside my house and where my car is parked. I didn't know what it was at the time but a Christian friend of mine recognized it as recorded curses from a tape cassette. It was about this time (a couple of years ago now) that I had my final encounter with sleep paralysis. I was lying on my bed and woke up paralyzed, I felt as if I was being bodily raised out of bed and if I was going from a flat position to a standing position. I was probably only half a foot off the bed when I frantically called 'Jesus, Jesus, Jesus …….' in my mind, straight away I was back in my bed and able to move freely. I didn't see anything other than the ordinary contents of my room and I do not know if I was being lifted bodily or in my spirit. Since then I have had no further occurrences and sleep at night without fear, which I didn't do for many years.

I guess being brought up in a Christian home and always being aware that there was a spirit world I never acquainted this occurrences with UFO or Aliens but the similarities are marked. Hope this will be of some help in your work. I am happy for you to use this testimony if you wish.

Phil.

50.   Hello!

I came across your site through the work of a brother named Chris White, who participated in the movie Age of Deceit. I rarely watch such videos but they mentioned testimonies and abductions being stopped in the name of Jesus. Let me share my testimony, but let me be anonymous only called "Chris" beyond of what already gets known by me sending this e-mail. Perhaps it is only me being a bit afraid for the sensitivity of this matter. Jesus said for us not to be afraid, but I do not know if I should send this e-mail. On the other hand, the circumstances the last days have led me up to this and perhaps someone can get helped by it. I come from a family, which really cannot be called a family.

I was raised by my mother and my father left us when I was a small child and I was raised by my mother and another man she met later. My mother was since before my birth into astrology and other New Age-teachings, such as the philosophy, cosmology, and theosophy. They are all interconnected anyway. She also had experiences of encounters with interdimensional beings of some sort. Either fallen angelic or angelic of God, or of both. Certainly, there were demons too as it is common. Her testimony in regards of such experiences started when she was a child, she was in her room and a being of light entered the room and moved a chair. She could not get a grip of its physicality and its arms moved strangely. The day after there was a circle outside of the house where the snow had melted, where perhaps its chariot or craft had been but where it likely first had come. The whole family of hers saw this and no one could explain it. This she told me, and more I cannot recall. A few more things my mother told me in regards of other experiences. I can see a pattern in her life, because of her later interest in astrology. My mother whom now passed away as of last year, was a respectable person in society where she was a teacher.

My testimony about abductions and how I came to Christ.

In the fall of 2003 when I was 19 I started to follow a voice, or like an intuition I followed in regards of philosophical thinking where I felt guided to accept that which felt right or true. I was curious about the nature of reality. Do you understand what I am trying to tell you? Early 2004 I came across the theosophical teachings on the world-wide web, and I immersed myself in thinking about these teachings philosophically. Later I too discovered my mother's books in her shelf and at first I started with some theosophical book and later I moved on to cosmology. I never read them that much, I barely opened some of them. I was more into the world-wide web. I was a very picky person, and still am. Also in regards of books. I came across loads of web pages with bad content and design and I sorted amongst page after page to find the right ones. I only had a few web pages I followed back then, for instance official theosophical teachings and some private web pages. Numerology and synchronicity became especially interesting to me over time, and my philosophical thinking was in overall very abstract sorting through a mess looking for knowledge that could answer my questions. I was aiming for order in the chaos I found myself in. I also started to understand that reality was more than mere physical, that it was spiritual at its core. In the summer of 2004 I had an out of body experience where I saw a galaxy and this raised new questions in regards of the nature of reality.

In 2005 and 2006 it all became more intense and I started to get a grasp of what this world is, and later I concluded that the world was of death on good and evil and that life and origin is beyond and is out of reach. That I somehow needed to get there but that the question remained as of how this would happen. After sorting through a mess, I found that the best way per my thinking must be that of Zen Buddhism, and for a while I was interested in becoming a monk. Now I started to think more gnostic in that I could achieve an enlightened state of consciousness to transcend the limits of the lower states of consciousness and thus have my answers for the questions raised about the nature of reality. I thought this could be how to reach that which seemed to be out of reach. But, things did not turn out like this. Things were confusing. For instance, I happened to see the number 33 everywhere, and people around me were surprised at this number really showing up the way it did. It correlated to my birth astrologically speaking in many systems. To this day, I do not know what it meant, but I interpreted it back then as being of a spiritual power of death which occultists such as Crowley called Choronzon. Alternatively, the spirit of Antichrist as the hexagon is his symbol and the numbers can be derived from it. Or a warning from God, that I needed to repent. I do not know to this day and I do not see this number any more.

Somewhere early 2005 when I started to understand how death spiritually permeates the world, I was one night taken out of my body. I was as in the body but outside of my body. I was still in the suburb, but still as if I was not in the suburb. I could see the buildings and the sky with stars and some clouds on which the moon was shining. I have come to understand this as the spiritual realm closest to that of physical earth, or the kingdom of death. I was specifically at a soccer field above my old school a few hundred meters from home when I became conscious, and there were many people there which I saw. Perhaps around 25. They were as if asleep, or dead. A standing mass. Suddenly I looked at the sky and from the east across the sky to the west a light travelled, and when it had gone to the west it made a turn and suddenly it had landed in front of us on the soccer field with its back on the east. It was so intensively light and I could not look at it that easily. Out of this light came a being which was a long and slim figure with big black eyes in a stereotypical "tall grey alien" way. (I have read Communion by Strieber whom I later e-mailed regarding these beings nature.) My arms where forced without being touched to be held out, and in each palm, I had a pentagram without the circle. In my right, it was upward seen from me and in my left, it was downward seen from me. The next thing I know I woke up, and my hands they were itching for a week. These symbols overlapping each other is also the symbol of Choronzon as mentioned in the teachings of Allister Crowley. But, since all of the lies of death I cannot know for certain and I have left this to God to deal with. I am only a sheep in the hoard of my Shepard. Once I was afraid this was the mark of the beast, and there was no return. I do not know but I believe all things are possible for God to restore.

After this experience this reality of spiritual death in the world became more natural to me, I was like: Christians and other religious are of the right-hand path of the tree and they do not know what they are doing and in the left, is the answers which the mystics seek. As if Christians were to be of death too, only fooled. To this day, I stand behind this world-view since all that which is not of Life is still of death and thus of either one side and sphere of it with corresponding spiritual power of the tree of death or knowledge. But, born-again Christians are not any longer of death but of Life and thus this saying cannot be applied to them. They are now hidden in Christ and of another kingdom and the tree of Life. I was back then still longing for something beyond of death even if it had become more natural to me, and I even prayed and received quite instantly things like sex. I had sex and afterwards I left the body. One woman I met I only saw as an unconscious vessel for the spiritual power of lust, and I was confused and paranoid about it and other things. I knew so little. I was interested in joining another order called Dragon Rouge whom explores the spiritual nature of death through the left-side path, which today is a very established order among young people in Europe. This atrophy of my soul continued till I was given a choice as I perceived it, I had to choose and make this philosophical way of thinking of death about the spiritual nature of reality more orderly. It was either to die or to follow it down the rabbit-hole even further.

Somewhere early 2006 I was tired, I did not want death and I still believed life was beyond of it. In May I prayed to Yahveh on a mountain as I barely knew anything about the Bible or about Jesus being the Messiah that came in the flesh. I asked: Let me be re-born in heaven! I guess in other words I asked for God to take me to himself. This literally stirred up a lot of things, and Christians came in my way and I heard about Jesus. I continued to live as before and it just went to become worse and worse. In the end of July I was so sick, I think it was the bird flu. But how sick I was! During this period of more than a week I had out of body experiences where I was taken to heaven, and to the kingdom of death. I was shown some astonishing things which I have a hard time sharing with others. I was also taken to the kingdom of death again, but this time shown the lodge of the Freemasons and the Pentecostal church in my city. The later was like overgrown as if the city was deserted. Two figures told me whom I perceived as human-like: This is the religion you are looking for and this is not the religion you are looking for. When I woke up I continued to chat with the Christians and later prayed a sinner's prayer. I am still skeptical praying such a prayer without the heart, but this was from the heart. I feel asleep again and I dreamt I was in court. I was accused, but was let go. I was freed and taken from one kingdom to another. When I woke up I was healthy and had a sound mind, a lot less confused.

Later I was attacked again and I was taken by two figures outside of my body down through a spiral stair and through a hallway with a valve at its entrance and then I became conscious and levitated from the ground speaking in the Spirit or something. I remember they said: What is happening? I woke up. But these experiences have decreased. But, the few times they have occurred they have been broken in the name of Jesus. But it has been hard to even say it even if it comes through. Like being in a sleep paralysis.

I later fell away from God, and sinned worse than before. In two periods for some years. This last spring I repented, and was as if delivered from such a darkness. I have trust-issues but I am trying to remind myself of reality and trust Jesus even if I have forgotten it sometimes. I sense that death is working hard to make the saints weary, to hinder us from realizing whom we are in Christ. It is of uttermost importance that I stand firm this time and I have lost so much already. It is such a shame, I am sorry. I was almost about to become a member of the Freemasons this fall after someone I know joined but I did not choose to do so since I was reminded of death and its lies. Since then I have had a hard time, but I do not know about any correlation. Please feel free to have me in your prayers since I am struggling with depression and pain.

I hope my testimony can be of some interest and use in preaching the truth to other, because the truth is that there is a lot more things going on around and in us than we are aware of. We are but men but in Christ taken from glory to glory one day to be made fully whole and this is a true promise. I hope I will take part in the resurrection, in the hope of the glory. I have no higher wish either.

Sincerely, Your brother in our beloved Lord and Savior Jesus Christ. Grace be with you, always!

Chris from northern Sweden.

51.   I saw the craft with two strange beings in it that put me in a trance that made me walk to my bedroom and lay on my bed and then I became paralyzed. I could hear my door to my house open and I could hear boot steps making its way towards me which I could turn my head and look out of my bedroom door and on the baseboards of my hall flooring I started to see red pulsating lights reflecting off of it and I could hear farther Vader like breathing. I closed my eyes in terror and when I opened them this being was standing beside me about 4 ft tall in a silver suit with gloves on holding a helmet under his right arm. His eyes were human size and Blue. It had age spots across its small "nose" and across the "cheek" area. We looked at each other for a few seconds and I thought it looked like a hybrid human/"alien". I then thought to myself it was old because of the age spots and it answered me in my brain and said "Yes, I am ancient." I was shocked and

terrified! I then spoke to it in my brain and said, " I am not going with you. ". It said, "Yes, you are going. ". Again I said louder in my head, I am not going with you!" It cocked it's head to the right side and spoke to me in my head again and said, " You Will Go!" I closed my eyes and in my head I started Screaming, JESUS! JESUS! JESUS!   And I waited and didn't hear anything so I opened my eyes and it was gone. I got up immediately and could move again and was freaking out!!! I started speaking out loud to Jesus asking Him what are those things!!!! He told me in my mind and a calm came over me at the same time, " At the name of Jesus, demons shall flee." I said, " Oh!!! Those are Demons!!!!" He said, "Yes!" Then He said to research and tell my loved ones because a strong delusion is coming.

Dee

52.   I give you permission to post this message on your website.

Hello Joe Jordan, in March 2016, I was an intended abductee. All my life I have had insomnia. So I was alone, wide awake in bed trying to go to sleep. It was around 10pm.

Suddenly, I felt a very evil presence around me. My body became temporarily paralyzed. I heard a buzzing noise and felt my whole body vibrating. I saw a blue light glow all around me.

Then I felt a force trying to make my body elevate off of the bed. I did not move because there was another force holding me down. I believe to be the power holding me in place to be either the Holy Spirit or angelic assistance.

From the beginning of this experience, I was trying to speak the Name of Jesus. Yet I could not because I was paralyzed. Finally, I was able to burst out His Name. Once I said Jesus, the whole experience stopped.

Through this whole event, I was not afraid, because I had excerpts of the experience many times before. Each time, I struggled to say the Name of Jesus, then finally did and everything stopped. So I felt assurance that I would be okay.

This experience started in my childhood, and not knowing what was going on, the first early occurrences were very scary. In the past, I felt the evil presence, the paralysis and the vibrating. I heard the buzzing. Yet this was the first and only time I had seen a blue glow in the room or felt the evil force trying to levitate my body.

Please feel free to reply to this e-mail if you have any comments, advice or questions.

Thanks and God bless,

Scott

53.   My experience in 2012

Hello Mr. Jordan, I felt obligated to write to you after watching Unholy Communion: The Fourth Kind Unveiled this evening. I never knew you were from Brevard. That is actually the county I was residing in.

My experience is much different from others. In advance I must tell you that I am a professional. Not a drinker or any type of substance abuser. I will never understand why I went through what I did.

In 2011 I turned off the television and radio. I was going through a rather awakening experience you could say. I wanted to become more spiritual and not influenced by all forms of propaganda. I was becoming more of a truth seeker. I was studying the current world events, government corruption, etc. Of course I've heard stories of grey aliens, but not others!

It was April 2012. I was asleep in my bed. I woke up, but not in my room. There were no lights or physical contact like I have heard from other stories. The room I was in was golden hues. Very warm tones. I was laying on a table. I didn't see anyone in the room. I saw what appeared to be a large bay window. It looked like night. I got up and walked over to it. I saw Earth and became startled! I was terrified! Then I heard two male voices speaking to me. But where were they? They were trying to comfort me and tell me they would bring me back. That they bring everyone back! They could sense my fear. They seemed as if they were trying to comfort me. I remember putting my hands over my face and closing my eyes. I started praying to God! God, god, please bring me back!

I slowly opened my eyes and saw that I was back in my room. I said, "Good, I'm back." Strange thing to say, right? I closed my eyes, reopened them again, and I was back there! I heard the two male voices again! This time they seemed concerned. I was laying on the table. They kept saying don't worry! We will bring you back! Then out of the corner of my eye, I saw a door open. I saw four males. They looked like humans, but even more attractive. They were wearing tight blue suits. As quickly as I saw them, I felt as if someone knocked me out! This time when I opened my eyes and was back in my room, I felt like I couldn't lift myself out of bed!

I went online immediately, looking for similar accounts. When I saw photos and drawings, I was shocked! I saw pictures of the blue suit aliens! I found out they were referred to as the Nordics. Something didn't seem right. I felt like they realized they couldn't get something from me. I made them concerned. Over time I started to feel these are demons! Maybe fallen angels. They were so attractive. When I was praying to God, I think that is when they realized they couldn't control me.

Thank you for your time. If you would like to contact me, you are welcome to. These "aliens" are evil and deceptive.

Sincerely,

Maria

54.   Good afternoon, and may the blessings of Jesus Christ be with you!

This morning I watched "Age of Deceit: Fallen Angel's and the New World Order", and was shocked by a particular section regarding alien abductions. The reason is because I have had 2 occasions in my adult life where I have experienced something that until now, I could not explain.

Both of these experiences came at times when my life was turned upside down, and the foundations of my faith were shaken and weakened, times of great personal turmoil, if you will. On one occasion, I was at my mother's house, visiting during my holiday break from college. At the time, my life was a disaster, drugs, alcohol, and promiscuity were rampant. I was laying in bed one night, I remember the hallway light was on, and there was a small sliver of light passing under the bottom of the door.

One moment, I was just staring at the bottom of the door, hoping to fall asleep and staring at the seams of light emanating from the hallway. The next, I felt this overwhelming and literally paralyzing fear overtake me. I remember trying to call out for my mom, for anybody to help me, but I couldn't so much as open my mouth to speak, it was as if the very breath required to utter even the slightest whimper was stolen from me, as I lay in bed, paralyzed with fear and dread.

It was then, knowing in my soul that I had no chance of help that I began to pray The Lord's Prayer, silently in my head, which gave me just enough breath and strength to call upon The Lord Jesus Christ. At this point, my body jolted, I remember rolling off of the bed, my head was spinning to such an extent that I barely had control of my motor functions. I crawled with what little strength I had to the light switch and turned it on. It was then, at that moment that I knew I had been under some form of spiritual attack. I spoke with some friends of mine, describing what had happened, what I had experienced. They looked at me as though I were crazy, and the only explanation they could give was "oh, those are just night terrors, they're very common."

The second occurrence took place, again, at my mother's house, just 3 years ago. This time, I was living with my mother because my fiancé and I had split up.

Naturally, I felt as though my world had just ended, and thought I would never find comfort or happiness again.

I was laying on the couch watching TV, my dog was laying on the floor, just below and my mother was upstairs in her room, sleeping. I recall laying there, feeling so heartbroken and depressed. I rolled over from lying on my back to lying on my stomach, and then the paralysis hit. Almost immediately I felt a presence standing or hovering over me, combined with an inexplicable fear, overwhelming sense of dread and hopelessness, and sheer panic as I had the sensation that I was floating up through the ceiling, being removed from the house.

I began to fervently recite The Lord's Prayer in my head, after trying to call out for my mom, or my dog, but to no avail. Again, I found the strength to call upon The Lord, and again, my body jolted and I was on the couch again, but this time I was on my back, not on my stomach as I had been seconds prior to this experience. I let my right arm drop off of the side of the couch, hoping that I would feel my dog's fur against my hand, but he was not there. Instead, he was now huddled under the dining room table, shivering and whimpering as though in fear.

It was that night that I realized that this was no simple case of "night terrors", and that whatever tried to get to me in the past, had tried again.

It was also on this night, that I discovered the true meaning of the phrase "There is power in the name of Jesus Christ".

To anyone that has experienced this before, and thought it was "aliens", know this: these beings do not come in peace, they have not come to make mankind "better", and they have come because they seek to destroy men. They seek to destroy faith, and they seek to discredit the existence of Jesus Christ, the Son of God. They are not here to benefit us, and ONLY calling upon The Lord and Savior, Jesus Christ, can save you!

God of Heaven and earth be with you all, and may the blood of Jesus keep you safe!
Michael.

55.   Hello Mr. Joe Jordan,

First I must warn you, what you are about to read is crazy, I mean CRAZY. I am battling with some things right now in my walk with the Lord God. There is more to talk about, besides what you are about to read.....but not by email, it's just too much. If you feel the need to talk further please call anytime.

It is not by chance that I have found you today, it is by Divine appointment.

My name is Anthony, I am a Christian and have been having alien type contacts, as far as I know, since college. At first I thought they were demonic entities, not aliens, just harassing me, every once in a while. Then it progressively got more intense, typically I would wake paralyzed, except I could see in the dark and everything around me, and my tongue would still work partially, but as if I were holding it with my fingers. Naturally being a Christian, my first response was to say, "In Jesus name leave"....in the past whenever this would happen it would be around 3am, almost always the same time. I would never see the actual entity, only feel their presence and complete fearfulness, but at the same time wanting to fight them, as in "beat them down". I am a combat veteran, this is my defensive nature now after serving in the U.S. Infantry pulling tours in Kosovo and in Iraq back in 2002. In the past I would always immediately concentrate on using my tongue to speak as clearly as possible "I command you to leave in Jesus name", and it worked....every time. BUT last night was different.....drastically different. Last night was a first, and new experience. I woke up paralyzed, and actually saw a tall (approx. 7' or so), thin, "invisible" alien reach his hand on my bedroom door and open it, it creeped me out so badly. Now this is hard to explain, the room was black with little light, I saw everything in the room, and don't know how, I saw this alien creature, but he was partially invisible, he also had something shaped like a trumpet or small parabolic disc in his hand, as soon as I saw it opening my door, I said "in Jesus name leave", it didn't work immediately as in the past, so I kept saying it, over and over, it walked over to my bed and got down beside me on my right side and proceeded to place this parabolic disc device up to the right side of my head, I kept commanding it to leave in Jesus name, finally it did, but it didn't. It moved away from me, and I was able to move again, but I felt it still in the house, maybe still in the room, I actually think it was pacing in my room at the foot of my bed.....waiting for me to go back to sleep, This I do not understand. In the past I have always been attacked as I was falling asleep or deep in sleep. I praised God and declared His Glory in all the Earth, I then asked for angels to accompany me to protect me and to minister to me......as in the past, but this time.....it didn't work.   I fell asleep, and it attacked me a 2nd time again, I did the same, saying, in Jesus name leave, then it stopped, again, but would not leave, so I recited The Lord's Prayer........I fell asleep again, and this is where it gets strange......THIS TIME it attacked a 3rd time, paralyzed me as usual BUT I quoted scripture, specifically John 3:16......For God so loved the world that he gave is only begotten Son, that whosoever believeth on Him shall have everlasting life"......it worked, it shut this creature down super-fast, I was able to move again, and began to fight it.....PHYSICALLY, I reached out, grabbed its arm, which was gray and boney, and started slinging it back and forth around the bed, I'm laying down mind you, I am unsure of how I became free from being paralyzed and was able to grab this thing, but I did.......then I think I let go of it and it went away, but not for long, it came back yet again.....If you don't think I'm crazy by now, you're about to brother! Whatever this thing wanted from me, it wanted it badly......I found myself dreaming a dream within a dream, but I knew it was a false reality! so that I would think I was awake, but I wasn't, maybe it was trying to trick me to stop using scripture or Jesus' name, but I was able to become quickly aware of this......this happened twice more, I awoke from the "dream within a dream state" paralyzed using scripture and Jesus' name.......finally it was daylight, I was exhausted, it had all stopped. This was all last night. I'm spending much time today in prayer face down before the Lord God for answers and or help.

I have never had it this bad, all night......a few weeks ago I awoke to a face staring at me, approx. 2 feet from my face....it looked like a "digital grid" face, and it was just staring at me while I slept, I woke to see it in the dark and jumped back in the bed forcefully.....it freaked me out, then it immediately disappeared.

I just wanted to share this with you. Today I've been researching my experience, particularly among Christians, and this is how I found you......I am sure it is by Divine Intervention by the Lord of Hosts.

Anthony

56.   Hello,

My name is Jason, not sure how to categorize this experiences... First, I have no fears in exposure of my experiences I have seen and been through in life... I am not ashamed nor will I hide anything that may help anyone and Glorify CHRIST JESUS... My first experience was when I was 17/18 years old... I grew up as a catholic but had no understanding or real relationship with CHRIST JESUS... I woke up in the middle of the night around 3:00am. I saw a shadow across the room and thought I was seeing things and maybe a reflection from a car passing by casting a shadow from lights hitting the blinds on the 2nd floor in Rochester, NY... This was around 1989/1990..?   The shadow shot across the room and was on top of me, I couldn't move, frozen, I couldn't scream, I couldn't do anything to fight back... I was a black belt in Kyokushin karate and one of the schools top fighter and yet I was hopeless... it was trying to suffocate me and such a paralyzing heaviness on top of me... I noticed our family dog Smokey running in circles next to my bed but he couldn't do anything... The only thing my mom told me in case of something and not sure why she told me? Was "I am covered by the Body and BLOOD of JESUS CHRIST my LORD AND SAVIOR you have no authority or power over me... I said this over and over in my thoughts and drew strength IN HIS NAME... then it flew off me and out the window... As soon as it fled, my dog jumped on the bed next to me to comfort me, and I got on my knees for the first time and prayed over and over throughout the night... the next day was THANKSGIVING and I mentioned this on the dinner table... And my mom who we knew had gifts of psychic? Telekinesis in a way because sometimes things flew when she was angry...   said she never felt anything out of the ordinary in the house?   She did have a strong faith in CHRIST JESUS not necessarily in the

Catholic faith because of a divorce ... Etc... My brother's ex-girlfriend who was from Indonesia turned white as a ghost... As she told me it happened to her on the bedroom downstairs a few nights before... IN THE NAME OF JESUS CHRIST MY LORD AND SAVIOR, I AM COVERED BY HIS BODY AND BLOOD... There are no strongholds or fears the can consume anyone when you call upon HIS NAME... My second event was prior to moving to Las Vegas in 2004... After my mom's death in 1996 I moved to Orlando and hid myself in pain and introduced myself to ecstasy of which as a martial artist was so against drugs and judgmental to those who were... But I'm fast forwarding to 2004 when I was clean and fully engulfed in prayer meetings and serving The LORD... it happened again... Same time around 3:00am. I woke up frozen but this time I felt strong because of faith... but this time it was different? It was calming and peaceful... The whole room illuminated white and everything in it, and a calming peace telling me I was not going to be harmed, its ok... It was of a female figure but white light, calming... Then I started getting flashes... And visions of the future of catastrophes and war... and was told not to be afraid but to prepare..... I have no idea on how to categorize this as abduction? But I know part of my spiritual walk, yes... I'm already categorized as weird and strange... But all the things I've seen and experienced from Las Vegas to now have been right out of a movie... and not even believable if I were to look outside in... I've been shot at from 10 feet half a clip from a 9mm impossible to miss where the person unloaded and couldn't hit me when I was a bouncer... I use to pray Psalms 91 ... And had a bad group of people try to take me out 6 weeks in a row and couldn't touch me... there's more to my story... Lots of things I've broken free from prayers and amulets taught to me from an uncle in the Philippines to slow time to conjuring angels to protect... And gaining power... Etc... Latin prayers from Catholicism supposedly... I broke all chains through baptism and on the CROSS... all this maybe not even believable... Are only a few things I've seen and been through... I share this to help others know that not until you call in the NAME OF JESUS CHRIST Will HE intervene and fight what one cannot see until you call HIS NAME!!! No other NAME... I've been shown purpose and why I've seen what I've seen for the GLORY OF CHRIST JESUS in HIS time... I've been told to write a book based on everything I've seen an been through to share my testimonies... from spiritual things even coming back to life from suicide... because of HIS PERFECT LOVE which goes beyond our understanding... I am not looking for any gain or falsifying anything of which I've stated... it is to share what CHRIST JESUS ALONE has done in my life to share there are no depths HE wouldn't go to fight for us no matter who we are.... close? Lost? Or beyond?   The time to. Prepare IS now!!!

I am not scared nor afraid to share my experiences and have even thrown off pastors in a church and definitely thrown family members off by my boldness... But it's not about me and decisions I've made in the past.. It's All about CHRIST JESUS!!!

GOD BLESS!!!

Jason

57.   Hello,

My name is Mike, and I have a testimony that I believe is sufficient in its attempt to prove the salvation we can have through the acceptance and authority of Jesus Christ.

I had just recently visited New Orleans, a highly occult city, and upon returning home after my visit, I experienced something I never had experienced before. I was lying in bed asleep on my back and I suddenly awoke to the feeling of numerous entities- that looked like grayish-blue aliens. They were surrounding me in a circle and I kept my eyes close, to make it appear I wasn't aware of their presence. I felt extreme fear and knew this wasn't just a dream. Surprisingly in that moment, despite the overwhelming fear, my mind immediately focused on Jesus and remembered a video I had seen online called, Age of Deceit, and I - being a born-again Christian - knew the only chance I had was to call on the name of Jesus because I was in a paralytic state and couldn't move. While I felt those entities reaching down and touching me all over my torso and start towards my private areas I tried with all my might to say something and with every ounce of strength I had, I was barely able to utter out one phrase: Jesus Christ. When I said the name of Jesus, I immediately felt extreme pressure on my chest as it raised up and it felt as if my heart was going to explode. Simultaneously as I called the name of Jesus aloud, I heard a soft, yet high pitched screeching scream as the entities fled in an instance. They fled as if the name of Jesus had seared them like a hot knife. I opened my eyes and sat up in bed and was drenched in sweat and felt an immediate change in energy in the room. I now felt safe. It was one of the most profound moments of my life and reassuring of the power and love Jesus has for those who call on him. I believe, upon doing extensive research, that the alien/visitation and sleep-paralysis occurrences are actually demonic attacks. It is more of a spiritual attack than a mere scientific account in my opinion on most circumstances.

Let's help spread the word of our Lord Jesus and the Salvation we can all have when we accept him as our Savior.

-Mike

58.   Hi there,

let me say that I'm very glad that organization like CE4 exists, I watched your You tube presentation and I decided to contact you, you seem to be decent man with a good will, I hope that God sees what you do and that he will reward you in time. I'm from EU, I had some experience and I already sent an e-mail to one of e mails on your page but I forgot to say that I give permission to you to post it online, use my experience as you will. I decided to send mail directly to you now, the same one, please let me know if you ever heard experience with masks and gloves as I did, yes it's totally strange but I guess that there are many shapes which these creatures/demons can take.

Tonight I will send you the second experience that I had, it includes I would say a classic story with alien gray demon... Also, I never suffered or had diagnosed any kind of schizophrenia etc...Just to make it clear :). Also, sorry for my English, there are probably some mistakes but English is not my native language.

All 3 encounters happened when I was around 4-7 years old. I don't remember exact age but it was before I started attending school, even so, I remember almost everything as it was yesterday. Before my parents totally divorced, I slept with them in a 200x180 bed, after they divorced I slept in the same bed on the right side and mother was on the left side, it lasted till I aged 7 and started attending school. As a child, I occasionally went to bed before my mother did, so once when I was at sleep, I felt like something started to tickle me, I woke up but I couldn't get up from bed because tickling became more intense so I started to swing with my hands in all directions to make whatever it is, leave me alone. But it didn't stop, whole situation soon started to exhaust me, I was about to turn on the light but I couldn't because whenever I was about to do that, tickling increased drastically and then I would again drop on the bed (light switch was very near, one meter from me on the mothers side of the bed), in the end I woke up in the morning, mother was on her side of the bed sleeping and my conclusion was that I had an bad dream, I spoke to mother and she said the same.

Sometime after, it happened again, but this time I instantly decided to turn on the light before tickling become too intense to handle, I did that and I saw white gloves (white hand gloves that had no physical hand inside them or any part of the body visible attached to them), there was 2 or 3 of them, they moved fast all around my body and under the sheets of the bed, I started screaming "Stop, stop please!" and then out of nowhere appeared 2 masks (Venetian type of masks , but without any decor on them, they were completely white) they were flying above the bed and they were also laughing and one of them said "so he finally turned on the light", and the other one still laughed, I was in shock, at that time those gloves disappeared and only two masks and me remained. I asked them who are they and why do they tickle me, one of them asked me back "wasn't it fun", I said it wasn't, and the other said to that "well don't worry we won't harm you", then I asked them what do they want from me and one of them replied "and what do you think we want from you?" , I said I don't know and then I simply entered an rage mode lol, I got up and tried to catch one of them but I couldn't, gloves appeared once more and torture with endless tickling started one more time... I woke up in the morning and then I knew that it wasn't an bad dream, I felt strange because I knew it's something but my mother said it was an bad dream so I didn't say anything about what happened again second time because I felt like she will tell me the same thing as before, "it's an bad dream"....

Again some time passed and this time a final encounter with this masks happened... After the second encounter I said to mother only that I would like to sleep with the light on, so she didn't turn off the light ever again as before , I told her that I want to sleep with the light on until she comes to bed. So she took me to bed, kissed me and she said "sleep well" as always, it was always the same routine, but this time just when she left the room, those two masks appeared out of nowhere , this time there was no tickling and no gloves, masks instantly appeared, just when I saw them I said "I will call my mother now", they replied (one or both) "well so you do, call her" they both laughed, I got up from the bed and then I opened the door, I left the room and I was about to pass the hallway that separated sleeping room from the guest room where mother watched TV, I saw the lights of the TV in the distance but I couldn't pass the hallway, It seemed like there was some sort of invisible barrier between me and the corridor, like some kind of glass in the middle of the hallway that I simply couldn't break or push, I screamed and kicked it but nothing... Few seconds after above my head appeared about 6 to 8 of those masks I described before, they all laughed and said who knows what, there was too many of them, I got scared and I decided to turn back and run inside to the bedroom, I had an idea that I will run inside the bedroom and close the door so that masks will be forced to stay in the hallway lol (I wasn't aware that they can actually pass through the walls etc...), I closed the door and I though my plan succeeded because no mask followed me. I decided to turn to the right and get into the bed, but what I saw then froze me right there. Inside the bedroom, there is a bed, big closet and a chest of drawers with a mirror attached to it. Above that chest of drawers at the very top of the mirror there was an mask, bigger than those other masks I saw few moments before and bigger than any mask from the first two encounters... Now this is a scary part because I know that I spoke to that mask for a few minutes but I don't know exactly what, I remember that I argued with it... First of all, when I just saw it, it said "well, hi Daniel" (Daniel is not my real name but anyway, it said my real name, I will use Daniel as a nickname here), I asked who he/she is, what does it want and how does it know my name... Reply was something like "I know , how couldn't I know you..." after this I don't remember anything, but I remember that after that I argued with it ,but I don't remember the details, whatever I said to the mask, it made it mad, voice of the mask became threatening and more deep, I remember that then I decided to pull one drawer and then I hid under it because I was very scared, I didn't know what to do, but the mask started to laugh when I did that and it said "hahaha, that won't save you!", I don't remember what we talked after that but then, only thing that I remember is my mother entering the room and she was a bit surprised when she saw me laying under the drawer "What are you doing David", I replied "Mama, there were those masks again. They spoke to me and one that was much bigger was here on the top of the mirror...

That's all I remember, I never had any experience with the masks or gloves ever again, but only after I started going to school, In my country we have an class of catholic teachings, it's on the national level, I learned prayers there and I decided to use them, something inside of me pointed to go that way and so I did.

Daniel

59.   Hi there, my name is Deb and I am from South Australia. I just watched Unholy Communion and felt the need to reach out and share some information you may find interesting and or useful.

I want to start off by saying I have believed in God for as long as I can remember. I used to love going to Church as a child with my grandparents, and or mum.

Anyway, one day when I was three years old a priest came over to visit my mum and I took one look at him and said to my mum he's not real, and told her to tell him to leave. But my mum wouldn't and I became very upset and she thought I was possessed and whisked me off to church where they performed an exorcism on me.

Now around that time, my sister said she was seeing this old man in our house and that she would talk to him in the shed. She also thought she saw me once, but chased me around the corner to find I had disappeared. I do not know if this is all relevant but thought I would include it anyway.

After this, we moved into a two story townhouse. I and my little sister shared a room and I slept on the top bunk and she slept on the bottom. Anyway, there were quite a few instances where I would awake to a sensation someone and or something was tickling my back. But no matter how fast I turned around to see who it was no one was there. So one day I plucked up the courage and moved my arm around and tried to grab whatever was doing this. As soon as I did this I felt a hand on my back, and I immediately got a vision it was grey in color and not human. I was so scared that I pulled my arm back and froze on the spot. Then the weirdest thing happened, it hit me really hard on the side of my head and my ear started ringing. I have no memory of going anywhere, or seeing anything else at that time. I do not recall when this stopped, and I never told anyone about it until years later. My mum thought I was nuts (as usual lol) but my sister whom slept on the bottom bunk freaked out because she said she used to feel her feet being tickled.

My next memorable experience was when I was around sixteen. I had never read the bible for myself because we had the old King James Version and the language was difficult to understand. But this night I decided to try and asked God to help me out. That night when I went to sleep, I physically felt my lower body pulled upward off the bed, whilst my head was on the pillow still. I could see what was going on, and saw who I believed was Satan had a hold of my legs. He was grey. I do not recall exactly what I said but it was along the lines of I don't belong to you, and next thing I know he let go of me and I fell back onto the bed and woke up.

I also had one other dream where I was at a small outside amphitheater. It looked ancient, and a few people had gathered to celebrate something. I do not believe they could see me, and I did not know why I was there. Anyway, a short time later I heard the sound of a trumpet, and looked up to see a trumpet in the sky. Then all these small fires popped up everywhere even in the stones of the amphitheater and people ran around in a panic. I tried telling them it was okay but they could not hear me. I again looked up to the sky and saw what I believe was Satan. He was leaning over a huge cloud, and was all grey, while everything else was in color. I again said something along the lines of I don't belong to you and he vanished at which point I woke up.

Now at this stage I never made any connection between demons and aliens mostly because the bible doesn't really discuss aliens, and no one I knew was into them either. However this all changed when I was around 34 years old. I had purchased an old railway station to renovate and was picking up a presence that would come and go. My daughter also picked up on it and started having dreams of a young boy asking her for help. He took her upstairs and pointed to himself hanging from the rafter, and she was convinced this presence was him. I told her I believed it was a trick, and we both prayed for protection as I believed we were under spiritual attack. I think it was that night I went to sleep and I can't recall what I was dreaming about, but I felt a real heaviness in my body and a loud voice saying "Debbie you need to wake up now" and with that I opened my eyes and felt this heaviness rush out of my body. It took a few minutes to realize what happened and I believed this presence tried entering my body and I was so angry I yelled out how dare you, you have no authority, reveal yourself in the name of Christ!

I believe it was the next night or a few nights later, I had a dream about aliens for the first time in my life. At least I think it was the first time. It was very different to what I read in others accounts, and what I see in documentaries. The leader came to me in my dream, along with maybe five others. They stood in the room I was asleep in, and I had a conversation with the leader. I cannot recall what they looked like, but I am sure they had grey skin. I also can't recall much of the conversation anymore but I do specifically remember asking the leader to tell me what they were. He said they were many things to many people, one of which is ghosts. I said why not just reveal your true identity and he said because people would not accept them. He then said it was time to ramp up their presence, and at that moment all these spirits appeared in the room and I watched as they went through my wall and scattered out onto the street. I believe there was thousands and thousands of them, like an eerie zombie apocalypse. I got the distinct impression they would not necessarily all remain spirits but more so shape shift into beings that appealed to people. I do not remember anything else about this dream, or have a memory of being abducted or seeing space craft.

After this dream I never saw them in alien form again, or at least not that I can remember. I assume this is because there is no point hiding their identity, as I would not buy into it. I believe they are demons, they basically said they were demons, and it fits with everything God has revealed to me. Which brings me to my next point. I recently started working on a series of videos that address a variety of dangerous claims made by new agers. One of those topics is aliens, and the claim they are here to help us. Now most people draw this conclusion because aliens say they are concerned for our welfare, but I think it's the other way around. If we wipe ourselves out, and these beings are demons then what happens to them? God said no one comes back to this earth, and demons are not welcome in the new one so to me it makes more sense they are trying to protect themselves, or more so avoid judgement day. Further, if they truly are trying to breed with humans is this because they believe it will gain them entry into heaven, or more an effort to take out as many souls as possible? Either way, it does not appear to be done for our benefit, but more so theirs and I just thought I might share those thoughts while I was here.

I do not know if anyone has written about this, and if they have then I would be interested in learning more from those people (if you have links to videos or books that would be great). Anyway I apologize for the lengthy email, and really have no idea if stories like this are of interest but thought there was no harm in sharing on the off chance it was. If you need anything further, I can be emailed anytime.

Thanks, and keep up the great work!
Deb :)

60.   My New Age deception story

I was raised in a very strict Baptist home as a child and accepted Jesus Christ as my lord and savior at the tender age of 8. I was fortunate in that my start in life was fairly stable, but things changed shortly after and life became hard for me, with my parents divorcing and the addition of a stepfather who was less than fond of me, he seemed to target me with unwarranted punishments daily and was abusive to my mom and sister too, I became withdrawn and sad and by the age of 12 I was busy seeking approval from things and people outside of my family as I felt unloved and unseen at home, this caused more trouble for me and led further into feeling bad about myself and lowering my self-worth, in my own mind.

By the age of 16 I was married and had a child of my own, my husband was 17 and had more difficulties of his own then I had, with similar rebellions and self-esteem issues that caused him to be abusive to us much of the time, By age 26 we had three children and the abuse had escalated to the point where I had to leave with my children for our own safety mentally and physically. It was around this time I began messing with a desk of divination cards with a friend, by my early 30s I was buying New Age books and practicing with out of body experience and psychic expansion techniques, and my home began to get visitors, that these books assured me where lost souls seeking my help, my children began reporting ghosts in their room at night watching them sleep, that soon led to them being attacked and shaken awake at night, entities sitting on their chest at night and waking with sleep paralysis, wicked looking creatures flying over their beds at night.

I was working several jobs to support my family and going to college and had little time to pursue the New Age activities until I was in my mid-40s, at this time I became a certified reiki practitioner, was doing crystal healings and energy clearings, chakra balancing, meditation practices and studying eastern religion, giving card readings and about to start shamanic training. The whole time thinking I was doing good and working for God, I was so sure he had to be very proud of me... I filled my home with all the tools and decoration that correlated with this life style and in 2016 on the 11/11/16 star gate gateway opening that day, I set out to achieve this "love" and "enlightenment" promised by this gateway

I was told about in my reading online. Something gave me the idea to go and sun gaze through a blue tigers eye crystal and I did and soon I felt something cork screw into my left eye, right into the eyeball itself, needless to say this scared the crap out of me and stopped me from this practice any further that day.

Shortly after this I had kundalini go off inside of me and I felt great at first like I was emanating a thousand watts of light from my body, my body pains all vanished, I threw away my depression medication, I felt more intelligent (I even became a bit cocky about my new found intelligence) then it all went really, really bad I became a targeted individual, my house filled with dark entities and I was under psychic attack, they began messing with my grandchildren when they were here daily, and when I would leave my home and drive my car I would have cars riding my bumper pushing me to move or cars in front of me going super slow or cutting me off the whole trip, I even saw a police car that appeared to be from the 1930s turn on its sirens behind and then vanish, the world became very dark, I saw very large dogs being walked all around town, I had 6-7 helicopters flying over my house a day, Emergency Medical Vehicle sirens going past my home repeatedly all day (all sounding exactly the same as the last), squirrels squawking at me for hours at a time on my telephone pole out front, birds sing in the night time outside my bedroom window, electric shock being sent to my heart throughout the night, terrible insomnia that affected everybody that would try to sleep here, I became acutely aware that this place is not what I thought it was all my life and that I was actually surrounded by evil forces working to hurt us constantly, I became exhausted and beat down and in fear of my own husband, that I forced to leave. My home came alive with evil that scared me so badly I spent 3 days and nights trying to shut of all power to my home, block off all mirrors and TV screens they could possibly come through or manifest through the AC/DC, and coaxial cables they all got cut... I proceeded to throw out about half the things in my home as they now felt evil and dangerous I was moving nonstop with very little food or drink and no sleep until I drove myself to the ER and passed out in a hospital bed, "I didn't tell them my true story because I knew it sounded completely crazy", they gave me a few nerve pills and sent me home. I called my husband back home because I just couldn't do it all alone anymore I felt like I was dying and really needed help. I began hearing very large beings walking on my attic floor above me " not possible as it's a crawl space attic" and hearing creatures clawing and scratching inside of my walls, and at my front door, also not physically possible, as time passed the attacks in my home let up gradually and the gang stalking also let up, but still no sleep I looked terrible and felt even worse, I began a two plus year online search trying to figure out what had happened to me, never feeling fully satisfied with my findings until I ran across Doreen Virtue's story a few months ago, I had heard about her transformation but didn't pay much attention to it except for other people attacking her in videos for her choice to leave New Age, and suddenly I knew I was being punished for living in utter sin for many years and seeking after that forbidden knowledge just like Adam and Eve did with the original sin that got them cast out of the garden of Eden and boy did I ever get a spanking for it..

I have since cleaned out my home of these tools and decorations and have turned my whole life over to Jesus Christ and am working hard to get rid of what is left here still causing trouble in my home, my cats "Majorly my male cat" still gets chased and attacked daily in my home, any loud voices or angry attitudes will cause it to start, almost like they feed off of it to attack, and sometimes it just happens out of the blue, the insomnia persists still but has gotten better after a deliverance session, I am still finding stuff I need to throw out all the time and working hard on repentance as I feel so guilty even though it was for lack of knowing better, this too is my own fault for not reading my bible properly and doing this to myself.

I do have a shining Gem though from this story, that makes my heart so happy;

When I was here alone those 3 days running round and round like a crazy lady Jesus came to me and said " If they could hurt you, it would have already been done" I almost fell to floor and hit my knees, his love for me was so powerfully overwhelming, and just that fast he was gone again, I hold this close to my heart and it brings me much joy amidst this horrible story that became my life.

I thank you for reading my story, I pray others can find hope and or understanding from my lessons learned the hard way. God Bless and please seek a closer walk with Jesus and not everything else you will find in the world. Much Love. Christina

Christina

61.   Hello,

I just felt like sharing my testimony with you, since it does pertain to the work you do.

I am going to talk about my experience that I had six years ago in 2013. I had just finished five years of electrical apprenticeship training in 2012 and had quickly been laid off from work after that. I had expected it to happen, so I had been preparing to try some new paths in my time off.

I was looking into health and fitness training and ended up getting a certificate as a health coach. I had to do about a year of training, mostly online to get this. It was good, but I feel that some of it, and maybe the people I was around, had other ideas, other intentions different than me.

I was not making any money still beside my unemployment, so I decided to take a shot at online business work. Some of it seemed legitimate, so I began to learn how to do it. I started making videos and marketing online. It was a new experience. I enjoyed that I was getting to experience new things. I had always been shy, so making videos and expressing myself was helping me to become more confident. I worked at these things for a couple of years, making some money but not enough to sustain myself. I gave up after I realized it was driving me more into the flesh, and causing me to focus more on money-making and things of the world.

Partly because the desire to get my way became so strong that I was willing to read books and listen to people whom I may never have considered to open up to in the past. The first popular book was "Think and grow rich." The second book was "A Course in Miracles."

These play a role in my alien encounter because they fully opened me up to the Occult. Whether it was from the books themselves or possibly people that I had become connected closely to through these, I am not 100%. Either way, it does not matter. These things are leading you into a spiritual world of unseen things and getting you to say yes to their coming.

I realize now I also had been wide open to spiritual attacks because I had been looking at pornography since I was 14. I remember having problems with anxiety and depression all the time after that but never connected the two.

In 2013, I was in a study group with people I did not know reading "A Course in Miracles." I was experiencing lots of pain; most of it caused my being addicted to pornography. Jesus and the bible didn't seem to work for me, so I was turning to other sources. Also, there was a promised financial gain to be had according to others if I followed the ways of some of these books. I was in and committed.

So in 2013, after about six months of being involved with these things, something happened that I could not fully understand. I remember studying one of the books and meditating much of the day. That was a new practice I recently had taken up. The day when things started taken a different turn, I remember becoming a bit hyper. That night suddenly, I began to experience things I had never encountered before.

I started to feel as if something was watching me. What was happening was that I was taking on all the beliefs of these occult thought systems. I went back home and remembered walking outside and experiencing that the heavens had opened up above me, and it was like I was being carried off in my spirit. It felt like my soul was traveling, and I was experiencing what it was experiencing. It all seemed terrific at first. I was being given a revelation and shown amazing things. Later that evening, I went outside again and remembered hearing the sound of a horn, like a trumpet blast. It sounded like possibly the call of some animal, but I had never heard it before. We only have deer where I live.

I was in this hyper state of thinking that I had never had before. It was a bit bizarre to me after hearing that, but I went back into the house, got on my computer, and looked at my email. The number of emails I had was 777. I fell back away from my computer. I then realized something was trying to talk to me. Something was attempting to contact me. Was it God? I remember getting out a piece of paper and writing some things down that seemed to be coming from what I thought was helpful beings.

I remember beginning to experience feelings of being powerful and invincible, but as I got onto my computer, I started looking at some website talking about the devil and demons. For some reason it attracted me and after that things took a turn for the worse. I began to feel afraid, and as the spiritual experience was happening, it seemed as if some evil entity came and tried to possess me. It was making me want to wear a hooded sweater with the hood up all the time which I never did.

At some point I remember hearing a pop in my brain, that startled me, then everything started getting out of control. It seemed like something was taking me over, and I couldn't control myself. It was like I saw visions of things while I was still awake. I had this sense that my spirit was traveling someplace, and I was witnessing all these things. At some point, I remember getting the worst pain in my head. All I could do is scream in pain and pray. After listening to other testimonies of alien abductions, I think these beings were drilling into my head with something. Whatever happens to your spirit body can be felt in your real body.

So I had opened myself up to these entities unknowingly and even after all of these, I stayed in this hyper state of fear. The entities were also attempting to control me to the point that I almost killed myself because the pain was so great. It was attempting to make me commit suicide. I resisted thankfully.

I never experienced bi-polar of schizophrenia, but it was maybe close to what I had experienced. The night when it seemed like I was in the fight for my life and some evil presence was consuming me. I remember having images of seeing a group of beings in space-age style clothing. I had the feeling I was in a UFO. They looked human, they were sitting in chairs, and I was in the middle of the round room. Also, I remember when it felt like my spirit was being carried out, I saw all types of satanic symbols, 5 points stars, and satanic altars.

I have never felt the same since this experience. It has altered me in some ways, and my head felt like it suffered some concussion and trauma, physically and mentally. My stomach has also suffered problems since all of this.

I have given all those occult teaching up and turned back to the Lord Jesus Christ. I was suffering insomnia for a couple of years, and now I am sleeping better again. The ways of the Lord are the best.

These false beliefs convinced me that I could become God and be like Him. But it was through the Tree of the Knowledge of Good and Evil. This way only leads to death. There is only One Creator God. The way I can take my place and be like Him is through Jesus Christ. The Tree of Life. This knowledge brings me to the true God and restores me to the Love that I was created for. Out of selfishness and into the Father. Its amazing God is so good and has loved me even while I was in my sin.

It's only by faith that we come to God, and Jesus has the power to heal us. I am thankful that I still have this opportunity to repent and take responsibility for my life. I see how my own fleshly was, and selfishness has led me to dark places. The Lord is good and forgives all sin when we come to Him in the right way. Amen.

Thanks,

Darren

62.   Hey Joe, I stumbled across your testimony and ministry for the past 3 years or so after doing a bit of research into this myself.

Let me back up to the beginning. In Junior High School, the assistant rector of the Episcopal Church I grew up in introduced me to the Ouija Board while overnighting at the church during a lock-in. From there, I developed quite a fascination for it, and saw just enough to know that it was not just a game.

In time I realized I was entertaining downright demonic thoughts, murderous and otherwise that I knew were not mine. I knew they were from the demons that "took over the board". I did not recognize at the time that the ghosts I was aiming to talk to were demons all along. Then one day, I prayed that God would keep me safe from the demonic. I didn't want to deal with demons on the board, "just dead folk."

That very day, I lost ALL interest in the Ouija Board, and except for one more incident with it that was prompted by a visiting good friend where he and I and a third friend wound up at the police station, I never went back to it.

But fairly shortly after that (1988 or so), I did get into quite a fascination with UFOs and began reading what I could find on them. After some time, I saw and read the book Communion and later Transformation, and was both terrified and infatuated with the experience Whitley Strieber had. While in high school, I also read Betty Andreessen's book as well as a book about the Gulf Breeze sightings (which ends with abduction experiences if I remember right). I read whatever I could find.

I specifically remember reading Betty's testimony and realizing that I was facing a fork in the road between the creation beliefs I was raised with (loosely held and understood at the time), and the concepts of Evolution. If I was going to continue believing what I read there, I would have to abandon my creation views for Evolution. I did.

I also was one of those who would stand out under the stars at night begging for such an experience, even though I found them petrifying to read!

And I had one weird (I believe demonic) incident in high school after school one day where my mom's sewing machine went on the fritz and ran frantically until I unplugged it in a dead panic. I knew it was related to the "poltergeist" activities that Strieber relates in his books.

And I got interested in various New Age concepts later in high school, trying to achieve an out-of-body experience.   What I have wondered in the back of my head through the years is why those things (UFOs, out-of-body experiences) would never happen to me. I sought them earnestly (except for getting involved in drugs). With such a hearty invitation, why did I never experience them? Even though I sought these, something also kept me from drugs and alcohol and premarital sex growing up. Why?

Well, within a couple months of starting college in 1991 (Auburn University), I gave my heart to the Lord to "make me into the person He wants me to be" (through Campus Crusade for Christ) and prayed that He would "keep me safe from the deceptions of the Last Days." I attended some meetings at a nearby Seventh-day Adventist Church that a friend invited me to, and was soon baptized. Based on what I was studying in the Word of God at that time, the prophecies of Daniel and Revelation, I had to dismiss UFOs and the alien abduction scenario I had read so much about, as a demonic delusion to deceive people from the truth. For 17 years, I had to take that on faith, and have been careful not to look back.

Then something 4 or 5 years ago got me curious to know what Strieber was up to these days. I was cautious as I don't want to get sucked back into a fascination of this stuff again and be overcome again. But when I found his website and read his account of letters he received the week before Transformation hit the shelves describing similar experiences he had described in that book (the mysterious knocking noises around the house), something from my Adventist background clicked. If you aren't familiar with Seventh-day Adventists and their beliefs, we are a Bible-based Protestant denomination (the fastest growing and longest lived (in terms of people's lifespans) in the world today) that does believe that God gave the gift of prophecy to a woman named Ellen G. White in the 1800s. She is the most prolific female writer in history, and her counsels on health were 100+ years ahead of her time. At any rate, in one of the compilations of her writings is this statement by the editors, "In 1848 mysterious rapping's were heard in the home of the fox family at Hydesville, a community about thirty-five miles east of the city of Rochester, New York. At a time when there were various conjectures as to the cause of the rapping's, Ellen White announced, on the authority of the vision given to her, that they were a manifestation of spiritualism, that this phenomenon would develop rapidly, and in the name of religion would gain popularity and deceive multitudes, developing into Satan's last-day masterpiece of deception." – Early Writings p.300. That cinched it for me that UFO/alien abductions are indeed just another manifestation of Spiritism -- seducing spirits working miracles. At that point, I had seen enough of Strieber's website and have not been back. I found what I needed. If you haven't already, go check out the history of the Fox Sisters. Fascinating.

Then I came across your testimony and materials 3 years ago while writing a Bible study series on Creation and Evolution, and was blown away by what you have uncovered! Thank you for letting the Lord Jesus Christ use you in this ministry!!!

Since then, as I have preached this in my churches (I am a pastor), I have been amazed at the members who come up to me and thank me for the message, explaining stuff that they had experienced before they became a Christian. And like your collection of testimonies points out so much time and again, there is no line between the demonic/occult and the UFO realm. It is all one and the same.

And, while living as a missionary in the Arctic 2 years ago, I talked with an Inuit lady who was Pentecostal and as this topic came up, she had had abduction experiences and had managed to halt them by calling out to Jesus for help! This truth works even among the Eskimos in the Arctic!! =)

In closing, one of the most moving moments in this for me was to realize the answer 3 years ago to my why questions listed above. Why had I never had any success with New Age and abduction experiences I so craved in high school? God's still small voice brought all the pieces of the puzzle together by pointing out that I had asked Him to keep me safe from the demonic concerning the Ouija Board, and He had been at work to answer that prayer throughout my other spiritualistic pursuits in high school because, He saw what I could not -- they are all of one and the same spirit. Praise God for His mercies and faithfulness!

Joel 2:32, "And it shall come to pass, that whosoever shall call on the name of the LORD shall be delivered.

ACTS 4:12, "Neither is there salvation in any other: for there is none other name under heaven given among men, whereby we must be saved."

Thank you for your ministry! Keep it up!

God bless,

Scott

63.   My story began at an early age, for as long as I can remember I have been experiencing terrifying nightmares. On one occasion I woke up saying "It's happened again". I would literally be too scared to go to sleep for fear of what could happen. Every nightmare involved in an attack from an unseen entity in which I would be scratched, bitten and have pressure applied to me. I would always try to defend myself but it was never enough to overpower whatever it was. It's hard to remember exactly but I think there could have been a connection to numerous sessions on the Ouija board with various people (including my mother and younger sister). I didn't really think about this possibility at the time even though some very strange and creepy things happened. I have always had an attraction to the occult, I've dabbled in so many things including tarot cards, psychics and spiritualism. Again I never even considered that I could be playing with fire and opening doors to the dark side. Also I was fascinated with UFO's and strongly believed that other planets were inhabited. The nightmares continued, the only way I could stop them was to force myself to wake up. I was so scared and angry and upset but whenever I tried to talk to anyone about them, they would laugh or tell me they were just dreams and nothing to worry about. So for 35 years or so I have on the whole lived with this fear always in the back of my mind, sometimes I wouldn't have a nightmare for 5 months or so and I would be lulled

into a false sense of security and then it would happen again. Last year I was in bed reading and I fell asleep and was raped by the entity, I was horrified and traumatized. As I've mentioned I never see what attacks me although I have had dreams about repulsive many limbed creatures or aliens with grasshopper heads. A while ago I was out with a friend and I drove back to her house, when she got out of the car she left the door open. Suddenly the door swung almost shut with a real force then opened again on its own. Later on that night when I was driving home I was looking in the rearview mirror and I saw a demonic creature that looked like a little thin grey on the backseat. What it was doing there I have no idea!! I guess the real essence of this testimony is to convey how relieved and hopeful I am to have discovered that through Jesus Christ these invasions can be stopped. During the last two I called out to Jesus and it did have an effect which after suffering for so long is a miracle. The main thing is that I'm not scared anymore, I feel protected, I pray each night too before I go to sleep. Joanne. Please feel free to post this on your site if you wish. God Bless.

Joanne

64.   I came across your interview from several years ago on Future Shock. Here is my testimony:

About three months ago I was visiting a friend (not Christian and truly a disbeliever of God) at this mountain house in Cumberland, Maryland. It was around 10 pm, and we had been having a discussion in his living room about God, family crisis and other subjects. We decided to come out to see the sky, it was pitch dark. All of a sudden the light of what seemed like two flood lights like the ones you see in WWII movies looking for enemy planes, in the shape of cones, began rising from a mountain right in front of us, about a quarter of a mile away. There are no houses there nor way of climbing it, since it is a steep mountain covered with thick vegetation. The moment I saw how these lights slowly emanated from the mountain and lit the clouds above it, I became terrified. I was immobilized with terror, as this is what it inspired. Immediately I realized there was something ominous about them. Since I couldn't talk, I was paralyzed with fear, I prayed in my mind and asked for Jesus' protection, to cover us with His holy blood. The minute I started praying in my mind, the lights slowly began to go down and to disappear into the mountain.

Needless to say that my friend was dismissive about the whole thing, deriding me and my spiritual Christian beliefs. I am not crazy, nor am I easily impressed. I am not a coward either. But I can tell you that the terror I felt was not human induced, but induced by something I cannot explain. My friend is a lost cause, he is a drunkard and promiscuous, but has a good heart. We have known each other for over 40 years, and I have tried to make him see the errors of his ways. I have been in the Christian walk for over 28 years, falling at times, but lifted up by the grace of God on many occasions! My Lord has been truthful and loyal, it is me who has been beyond contempt. But I feel that He protected me that night. The same way He has done so in who knows how many times.

I thought I'd share this with you. Needless to say that I have not returned to that house, nor intend to either. By the way, I had spent last year three weeks alone there, and was never afraid, though it is dark and removed from civilization.

O.

65.   Hi, I am a Christian and have had this same kind of experience very early on in my Christian life. I personally believe that dreams can be effected by either God Himself, angels or demonic influence. My experience has been shunned by my many fellow Christians, even my wife doesn't like to talk about.

To tell you of my first experience with manifestations we would have to go back to the mid-1980's, when I was around 10 years old. I had cycled to a spot near where I and my brother were permitted to climb some tall Poplar trees. I saw these trees and my brother trying to climb the trees. With him was some other children who were causing trouble. I could hear their voices as if they were standing right alongside me (strange now, but not then). In addition to the voices I sensed was something else trying to pull me away and telling me to not allow them to speak to me. This same voice continued to speak to on my way home trying to convince me that what I saw and heard was not real. It was like if I had a guardian angel trying to protect me. I did not listen to this voice. When I got back home my dad was outside. He was having trouble with his car, which was over-heating. On hearing what I told him that my brother was in trouble he got in his car a drove down to the place where these trees are. It was only then I realized that there was nothing there. I couldn't understand why. My dad's car was steaming, and so was he! When we got home my brother was there. He told us that he didn't go anywhere near the place where the tall poplar trees where. I felt angry with myself that I didn't listen to the voice telling me leave and not listen to the other voices. I knew from that point what those voices were. At that point the devil had crossed the line, and this meant war! It was like Satan want to drive a rift between me and my dad (as he was a Christian). After this I did not have any further occurrence until about 2000.

To give some background, in 1990 I committed myself to Christ. After this point my life instead of becoming better it became worse. I was confronted at school being surrounded by people mocking me for being a Christian. They asked "why?", "How can you prove God exists?" The usual stuff. I felt that this moment was like the disciples denying Christ. I felt that I couldn't deny Jesus! "Take up your cross and follow me!" came to mind. I answered their questions from the bottom of my heart and I believe lead by Christ. One of my teachers overheard my answers and testimony. He was a staunch Atheist. One my final externally marked coursework, he marked my work down from an "A" to and "F", with no explanation. My parents were furious. Up to this point I had been getting mainly all "A" grades for my work. I got an "A" for my exam (a paper that he could not mark)! Both grades together gave me an overall grade "D", not enough to do my A levels as I needed a "C". This wasn't the only time I downgraded. On an item of course work I refused to write about evolution and wrote about the geologic record from Adam, and that there couldn't have been millions of years. I confronted my teacher and told them they would get the "F" one day, and they would find I would receive the "A". Yet another moment to stand my ground!

Well now for the year 2000 event.

My brother had a girlfriend who was not a Christian, and was even involved in the occult. My brother, even though he professed to be saved, had brought her in to the house of my parents to sleep with her. On one such night I had just gone to my room, turned the light out and was lying on my back when something came in to my bedroom through the top of part of the window. I was frozen in fear! I felt, should I grab it? I couldn't believe what I was seeing. There was no way I was asleep as I had just got in to bed and turned the light out! It was like a dark colored monkey crawling on all its fours, on my bedroom ceiling!! It stopped for a moment, look down at me, then decided to carry on crawling on my ceiling finally going through the wall in to my brother's bedroom where he was sleeping with his girlfriend. (To note my dad was too scared to make my brother stop what he was doing). I jumped out of my bed and turning the light on. I looked behind my wardrobe to see if was still in the room. It wasn't it really freaked me out and got my heart racing.

Over this period of time I was having re-occurring nightmares where a dark shadowy figure haunted my dreams. Everything used to turn from day to night. Then the shadow character would approach me to lay hold of me. I never saw its face by felt its presence. I would feel the evil and try to flee upwards, but people would come and grab me by my feet and hold me back down.

After seeing this monkey thing in my room I kept my Bible next to me in bed.

It wasn't enough to stop the dreams. They only stopped when I began to realize in my own dreams what I was seeing was a dream. It gave me a very weird sense when being asleep and knowing in every thought that you are asleep and dreaming. It's made me more aware when I do sleep and dream. I knew I had to confront this spirit, and I though one way of confronting it was to believe I was indestructible. The Terminator character fitted that role perfectly. I went to sleep and dreamed my dad stumbling down the loft ladders. (We lived in a bungalow). His cloths were torn and he was bleeding. He wanted to go back up, but I held him back. I told my dad "You can't stop this. Only I can". I then proceeded up the ladders to meet my Nemesis. On meeting this shadow character again in my dreams I rose up about a foot off the ground and went up to it and told it by its arms and said; "I know who you are, and what you are!" It tried to install fear in me by running its fingers down my arms to draw blood. I looked up at his face again and said "Do you think I am going to fear you? You cannot hurt me as I know that I am dreaming and you are not meant to be here. I know what you are! Here in my dreams I am indestructible!" I then grabbed it and ripped it apart, saying "You are... TERMINATED!" It fell apart like leaves. I was still troubled one final time. This time it wasn't coming for me, but it was possessing everyone where I live, even my own family. The sky became dark, as it usually did when I felt evil coming near. Everyone was cursing God as well as speaking a language I could not understand. I knew the only thing that would make it stop was to start singing Christian hymns like "Onward Christian soldiers". My brother who was possessed grabbed me and told me to "Shut up". I knew my singing was bad, but I continued even louder. Then the clouds began to separate and the sun began to shine in, like I had never seen in a dream before and ever seen again! It was so bright! I saw a vortex being opened up by a voice coming from heaven. All of the dark spirits began to be drawn in to the vortex, still cursing God, until they were all gone and the vortex was closed. I then heard the voice say to me "Thank you for believing in me my faithful servant". Now if there was any dream one could have that symbolized the day of judgement I had that dream. It gave me a happy feeling that by trusting in God we are on the winning side and "All will be well".

When seeing and reading your website I know I am not alone in having similar experiences. My dad now knows that demons can be seen and effect your dreams. It's worrying to some, but I know these things exist and there is war going on until God calls "enough is enough".

It has been prophesized that people in the last days leading up to Christ's return people will have dreams and visions.

To and a note. When in my dream I confronted the evil spirit I saw its face in full close-up detail. It was exactly like the pictures you see as aliens! It was exactly like a man. Standing the same height. It was a shadow, as you could see through it. It eyes though where the blackest black you could imagine. You could feel the evil and fear emanating from it, but I drove through the fear. They say the eyes are the window to the soul, when this thing had no soul to speak of as it was pure evil and lacking light. My fear was trying to wake me, but I tried my hardest to stay asleep just to make sure I gave it a good whipping! Payback time! Each time I've seen aliens mentioned on TV and seen the images people have drawn I tell my wife "that is what the demon I confronted looks like". It's not an alien but an evil spirit, and now they fear me! As I say I am at war with them! It's like I am Neo from the Matrix films or the Terminator in 'Rise of the Machines'. "It is time!" I've been made fully aware and I'm not afraid to confront them, but now they seem to say clear. I just know they will change tactics, so I should be always aware of their possible attacks.

Regards,

Neil

66.   Hello CE4. How are you? I guess I'll start by telling you about myself. I have 3 kids. Single mom. I work 3rd shift right now... it seems like my whole life the enemy has been after me. I am not baptized yet but i believe in The Almighty and Messiah. I have tried to reach out to someone before to talk about the things that have happened to me but no response so I'm actually shocked you responded. Thank you. I have been to Heaven before. I met The Watchers. I have been face to face with Satan himself in another dimension...I think maybe it was like a small part of hell. But in Heaven ...wow... I heard angels singing. They sang Hallelujah. Was so beautiful. I was asleep when anything like this happened. It was like I was taken.... but with the greys.... they are demonic like you said...they never abducted me because of my strong faith...I believe...but they have tried to get me to follow and go with them willingly.... the one time a couple years ago they showed up as I was sleeping... they were in my room on 2nd story... it was a taller one... I saw a

short one also before. He had a craft outside and was telling me to go with him. He had his hand out to me. I rebuked him and woke up.... the most recent encounter with these greys.... was over a year ago I think... I was asleep but found myself walking through this forest and there was a path and it was rather dark. And I came upon pieces of a fallen craft scattered... there was a dead alien in it and I tried leaving and a short grey showed up... next thing i know I'm lying next to it on a large round stump in the same area.... I was actually talking to it like it was a friend... he was right next to me... it was telling me it wanted to impregnate me and I was going to have a son and I'll never have to worry about anything again ... it only needed my permission.... these entities mess with your mind...at this point I almost completely forgotten about Yahweh God about the Messiah. Like my mind was blank...so I stood up and as I was thinking about it and I come to remember these things are evil and the name of God came back to me and so I started rebuking it.... I woke up after that.... sounds almost unreal...but what happened the following year is crazier. Now I'm very spiritual. I teach my kids about God and everything... I pray and have even rebuked demons from my homes before... I have dealt with spiritual warfare with demons throughout my life.....so anyways ... I am separated... I left my husband in April 2018 because he became abusive and went on various drugs and it wasn't getting better. I became homeless when I got away from him... I just didn't want my kids growing up seeing their mom fighting all the time and thinking its ok...they can't put up with that...I didn't want the cycle to continue... so at one point being homeless an ex of mine from years prior reached out and offered us a room. Well this was like 2 months after leaving my husband so I was really upset and depressed as ever.... that night I got drunk with my ex. Smoking pot...drinking... I just didn't care at that point... it was like my life was so messed up and it was just awful.... now this ex didn't believe in God. He probably wasn't very good... so we fornicated that night.... I left the next day.... so I ended up moving in with relative. Going to work... I ended up getting my own place... for over a month I got so sick.... I couldn't eat. Barely could drink. My blood pressure would spike in the middle of the night... I would be in a ball on the floor crying. My insides hurt so badly and I never had this pain before. I had what felt like electrical shocks going up my spine... if I even ate a little. I felt like i was going to explode... I describe it to my family as ...I feel like there is something dead inside me.... one night I woke up sweating.... in pain...heart beating rapidly. My sister heather went with me to the emergency room at like 4 am. So they did a urine and came back and told me i was pregnant... I couldn't even believe it. I have 3 kids already and I was bleeding also and it wasn't my period ... so they did a sonogram but would not let me see the screen. When the doctor went out my sister told me she caught the picture and it wasn't a normal looking fetus. She said it had what resembled a cone looking shape on its head... she said ...lea it didn't look normal. And she has kids. My whole family has kids and has seen sonograms a lot... the doctor came in but didn't say much. They told me they don't know why I'm bleeding or nothing. I was still getting shocks up my spine as I sat on the hospital bed. Basically I was 6 weeks when I found out. I couldn't work because of this ...I lost a lot weight in 2 weeks like 20 pounds. I was so messed up and sick and knew I had to work to care for my kids. I ended up making a trip to Pittsburgh and getting a medical abortion at round 8 or 9 weeks. Went home after taking a pill and starting having contractions the next day... look I do not think abortions are right. I am actually against them and I have prayed and prayed to God to forgive my actions in this.... but when that small fetus came out.... I felt my whole body being relieved... I was immediately able to eat again. I felt 110 percent better. I know this all sounds made up or crazy but I think because of my sins that night with my ex... The greys did something to me.... I have been pregnant 4 times before. I had a miscarriage at 18. Then had 3 kids after the following years that came... and never...never was I so messed up and sick and my body just was not healthy. I believe that fetus was evil or something... idk... I feel bad about the abortion but I feel like it had to be done... so that was like last year I had that happen. I want to say august....

My dad has had encounters with the greys. He believes in God but says they been after him and put a chip in his leg and it moved when he tried cut it out. He is a very smart man, he was in the navy before. He was with my mom recently in the Alleghany forest in pa and he goes there often at night. They both told me a spacecraft stopped in front of his vehicle in middle of road and shown the light down and he stopped so he didn't drive under it. He got out and started talking to it. Saying... I know you guys are following me and I'm not falling for your trick again. Last time you shown your light down I got this chip in me...and been sick since... my mom yelled at him to get back in and they drove other way. He doesn't believe they are evil. I tried multiple times to tell him they were. So I mean yea he has seen a lot stuff too. My sister Becky has saw a grey show up in her sleep and she said it had rows of razor sharp teeth. She rebukes them also and they go away.

Alysha

67.   The experience as I remember clearly occurred during the winter of 1993. I was back home from college during Christmas break and was lying in bed, completely awake and completely sober. Although it was late at night, I had a serious case of insomnia and was counting the minutes go by on my alarm clock, with every minute feeling like an eternity. I wished I could go to sleep, but could not.

Eventually, out of extreme boredom, I began to 'speak' to God. In my mind, I was asking God for a sign of His presence and existence. I would ask for Him to give me proof of His existence and then wait for long minutes for any sign. I continued this for some time until eventually I began to speak audibly and ask God "If you are here, show me a sign". Over and over I continued, at first whispering it, and then with a more loud voice, almost demanding it.

After a long time doing this, without a hint of any 'sign', I tried going back to sleep again and still found I couldn't. By now it was around 3 am, and in my frustration and exasperation at not being able to fall asleep, I decided to lie down on the floor, hoping that perhaps laying on the hard ground, I would finally find sleep.

I got out of bed and lay on my back on the floor and the insomnia continued. Next to me was an exercise bike, and in my boredom I began to gently spin the pedal. At first it would spin a few times, according to how forcefully I spun it, and then eventually slow down and stop. After doing this for a short while, I began to notice that at the end of the spinning, as it slowed to a stop, it would suddenly make a full steady turn in the opposite direction. I found this peculiar, not understanding how this could happen, especially since it was just previously slowing down and stopping. I figured there was a mechanical reason why and then thought nothing more of it, even as I continued to play with it.

It was at that time, that I decided that maybe if I laid on my stomach, I would finally get some sleep. I turned to lay on my stomach and almost immediately I saw bright lights (although my eyes were closed) and heard a loud repeating buzzing noise. The best I could describe the noise is what you hear after leaving a phone off the hook for too long- a rhythmic alarm sound. The noise was extremely loud and filled my head and the bright light blinded me. I tried to move and found that I could not. As hard as I tried to get up or squirm, I was completely frozen and felt as if something behind (above) me, was holding me. I felt constrained, held, and a fearsome presence above me. I then felt that whatever was holding me was raising me off the ground. I was rising into the air, although because of the blinding light, I could not see how far I was off the ground.

I was in sheer terror at this point, trying to scream out, and I couldn't move a muscle or make any sound whatsoever.

I then called in my mind desperately "Lord Jesus Christ, help me! Lord Jesus Christ, help me!"

With that, the next thing I knew I was already jumping in the air, springing free from whatever was confining me, with my vision and hearing completely restored.

I ran to my parent's bedroom to tell them what happened.

Although the experience itself was horrifying during the event, while explaining what happened to my parents, I began to feel quite elated, almost thrilled by the experience. My initial conclusions were that God had answered by prayers and had shown me a sign. I figured this was a divine vision.

For the next two weeks while at home during Christmas break, every night at 3 am I would inexplicably wake up for no rhyme or reason. And after waking up, the thought of the phone ringing would enter into my head, and no sooner had the thought formed in my mind, the phone on my night stand would ring. I would answer the phone and there would be no sound from the other end. No dial tone or anything, just silence.

It wasn't until some years later after maturing and doing more research into the teachings and experience of the Saints of the Christian Church that I realized that what I experienced was not at all a divine vision, but rather, a demonic attack.

Since that time, I have had a few (much less dramatic) episodes of spiritual attacks, and every time, I have found that I can repel these attacks by uttering the Jesus Prayer, namely, "Lord Jesus Christ, Son of God, have mercy on me a sinner".

Tony

68.   by Joseph G. Jordan

To close out this section of testimonials, I wanted to share one of my personal encounters with the name and authority of Jesus Christ being used. I hope you too, will be as blessed and filled with Hope as I was.

In 2012, a few months after arriving in South Korea, I had an opportunity to see the power in the name and authority of Jesus Christ in action. No, it had nothing to do with the UFO phenomenon at all.

I had been hearing and recording these testimonies for years. But I was forever changed by this experience that I had an opportunity to see unfold.

I had been attending a little church here in Korea call New Testament Fellowship, Pastored by David Stevens, and supported by his wife Lillian. I really enjoyed the fellowship of the small congregation of U.S. soldiers, Government employees, civilian contractors, and foreign nationals.

On Friday or Saturday nights we would do safe fellowship outings, as an alternative to staying home, or the bar scene, which is prevalent here. The outings ranged from local Korean restaurants to the downtown Daegu center city scene (shopping area), to amusement parks.

It was on one of these outings, to downtown, the Deagu center city area, that I had a chance opportunity to see the name and authority of Jesus Christ in action.

I will be sharing the experience through the blog posting below by the Pastors wife, Lillian Stevens, done many years later in retrospect. I will be interjecting my perspective into her blog posting as JGJ).

HOW TO GUARD YOUR HEART AGAINST ANXIETY

By Lillian Stevens

It took great courage for me to share and write this blog post Up until now, 7 years after the day when my husband collapsed and was diagnosed with three brain aneurysms, (one of which hemorrhaged) I haven't fully shared my story. I cannot thank those enough who prayed for us, who sent us offerings and were there for us during the most difficult time in our life. If this story and Scriptures resonate with you, could you please share this blog post so others can read? I would be so grateful!

JGJ) After having dinner at an awesome hamburger restaurant, and following up with cold slab ice cream, we all headed to an outdoor gaming area that had many games like, batting cages, and basketball shooting, just to name a few. The Pastor loved this place. Anytime we went to Deagu, we would finish up the night there before going home. He would try and park the van we all went in close by.

He was shooting baskets in a game against one of the female soldiers we had with us. Most of the rest of us were standing behind and to the side of him watching. It was the last game of the evening, then we would be heading home.

After taking a shot at the basket, he paused, stepped back to a ledge where his wife was sitting watching, and sat down.

I thought he was kidding.

I was about to razz my husband and make a snarky joke about him not being able to hang with the "big boys" as he shot some baskets at an arcade game.

He looked tired.

As he moved back about 10 steps to sit down on a ledge next to me, that's when I noticed his eyes.

JGJ) He had a blank stare on his face, no expression at all. His eyes were fixed forward, not blinking at all. He said nothing.

He was looking at me but there was no connection. It was the expression-something was missing. He sat down next to me and the next thing I knew he went unconscious and collapsed into my chest.

That's when the frenzy began.

"He's having a stroke".

"It's a heart attack".

"Somebody get help".

JGJ) Everybody panicked at that moment, but Lillian. She started repeating, out loud, over and over, "Thank you Jesus for healing my husband, thank you Jesus for healing my husband..."

I grabbed their dog Poley because we needed to move fast, and he wasn't on a leash. Two big soldier guys grabbed Pastor Steven and got him to the ground. He started vomiting. But still with fixed stare and no sounds. They tried to keep him from choking on his vomit.

We knew trying to get an ambulance to us would be difficult due to the language barrier. Lillian had remembered that there was a police station within a couple of blocks of us. She said she was going to run to the police station, the soldiers said they would be behind carrying the Pastor to the main street where the ambulance could see us. As Lillian ran off, I could still hear her saying out loud, "Thank you Jesus for healing my husband, thank you Jesus for healing my husband…"

I ran to the nearby fire department as I left my dear husband with my beloved friends.

I ran quickly at first, but my pace decreased as I got tired. I was out of shape and my breathing was labored. I was angry at myself because my body wasn't going as fast as I wanted it to.

This was when the first fiery dart of anxiety from Satan himself was aimed at my heart and hit target.

"Your delay in getting an ambulance will cause your husband to die."

After telling the fire station staff where to go, I ran back down the street. My husband was laying lifeless on the sidewalk with our friends surrounding him. I'll never know how they combat carried him through the parking lot to the street for easy access to the ambulance, but I'm grateful they did.

JGJ) We made it to the main street to be seen by the ambulance, we were performing the best First Aid we all new to do, not knowing what was really wrong with him.

Even when Lillian returned to us on the main street sidewalk, she was still saying, "Thank you Jesus for healing my husband, thank you Jesus for healing my husband…"

Those beautiful people are forever my heroes.

On the sidewalk, they were doing first aid on him and passersby walked by without a second glance.

I threw myself on the sidewalk next to my beloved husband of 22 years and pulled his long arms towards me to scoop up his head in my lap.

And then I prayed. Loud.

JGJ) Lillian kept praying, really loud, "Thank you Jesus for healing my husband, thank you Jesus for healing my husband…" Lillian will tell the rest of the story. Enjoy.

I needed divine intervention.

When Paul was writing to the church at Philippi, they were going through some serious tribulation. Back in that time they didn't have a handy dandy concordance of New Testament Bible verses of anxiety for the New Testament saint. But we do.

In the middle of the battle, Paul's desire for them was to walk in joy- even in the midst of hardship and trouble.

Is it even possible? Can a person really live a life of fear over faith and cast aside anxiety?

THE FEAR FOLLOWED ME ACROSS CONTINENTS

Time went on and we moved from Korea to Chicagoland.

Hubby fully recovered with only one side effect- he has a constant ringing in his ears that sounds like white noise.

The days seemed torturous for me as I went through self-diagnosed PTSD.

When you've watched the most beloved person in your world nearly die before your eyes, it does something to you.

Enter another fiery dart of the devil.

"You will bury your husband in Chicago Heights."

And Creative Sister, let me tell you- the grip employed by satan hit me in the midst of my heart and reverberated in my soul for 5 years.

Five LONG years.

I had God's promises. I knew His working.

I knew the miracle that God had done when he survived three brain aneurysms, one of which hemorrhaged, with no memory loss or brain damage.

But Satan kept sewing his seeds of anxiety.

Every single day I cried for (seemingly) no reason.

I cried while getting ready in the morning.

I cried while at the stove cooking.

I cried in the car.

Who am I kidding? I cried everywhere.

The fiery pit of hell sent my heart a message on a daily basis- that I was going to bury my husband in Chicagoland. Every time we passed a funeral home (and there are PLENTY) I'd be reminded.

Have you ever prayed and asked God how to get over a fear?

Have you ever wondered how to get help with anxiety according to the Bible?

Can the Bible really show you how to overcome of anxiety, stress and worry?

There are many true stories about fear in Bible and verses of anxiety that we can apply to our lives.

The word anxiety might not be mentioned in the Bible but there are plenty of instances where anxiety in Bible terms can be seen.

LORD, YOUR WILL BE DONE

One of my most memorable prayers during my husband's 2 week hospitalization was a breaking of my will- where I finally gave it all to the Lord.

"If you want to take Dave home, Lord, your will be done."

I was literally powerless over life. I resigned my will and put everything at the feet of my Master.

And that's when I was flooded with God's peace. I knew that whatever happened, in the life or death of my husband, the Lord would take care of me.

It was during this time that two songs became my anthems in life, Matt Redman's 10.000 Reasons and Vince Gill's Threaten me with Heaven/

These songs were mainstays that reminded me that no matter what I go through, I have so many things to be thankful for. The end goal for the saints of God is an eternity with Him.

SPIRITUAL WARFARE USING GOD'S WORD

Satan's Lies are Strong but God is Stronger Do you think that you can battle Satan in your own strength?

I can't say this enough.

You can't.

You need the divine power of God and His word to back you up and give you authority.

Satan's lies are strong but the truth of God is stronger.

The truth of God's word stands strong and is meant for us to use against the spiritual warfare that the devil throws at us. The word of God is our spiritual armor.

Does fear ever take hold? You bet it does.

Do the same fears crop up again? They do.

But the key to guarding the heart against anxiety lays in applying God's timeless truth by way of Scripture.

It wasn't until the end of 5 years that we finally stepped on a plane to relocate to Germany that I sat down and verbally told Satan where he could go-and where he could put his wicked lies- back to the pit of hell for all eternity. All of the filth and lies he had told me were not true.

And then I praised God.

VERSES OF ANXIETY IN BIBLE SCRIPTURES

How to get over a Fear as a Christian with Bible Scriptures on Overcoming Anxiety. The epistle of Paul to the Philippians focuses on joy and the word joy is mentioned multiple times in the book.

Paul's desire was for the Philippian church to walk in joy to further their joyful faith. (Philippians chapter 2 is full of admonition and encouragement for the Philippian saints to be full of joy.

What is JOY? The Greek word for joy is chara χαρά, khar-ah'; from G5463; which means cheerfulness, calm delight and gladness.

It was Satan's desire to squash out that joy by sowin seeds of worry into the hearts of the Philippian believers. God has given us His word to combat worry and anxiety.

So lovely sister, it's with my life experience that I offer you these Bible verses on how to help with anxiety are a balm to your soul in times of trial.

Let's dig in, shall we?

Be Anxious in Nothing Verse Don't be anxious- Pray

Paul told the believers at Philippi to be careful in nothing.

Be careful for nothing; but in everything by prayer and supplication with thanksgiving let your requests be made known unto God. -Philippians 4:6

How and why would Paul be telling them to be careful? It doesn't make sense, does it? It does when we do a bit of Greek word study.

The word for careful in the Greek is merimnaō (me-rēm-nä'-ō) which means to be anxious and troubled with cares.

Paul was telling them to not be full of anxiety over anything.

And then he gives the first solution to that anxiety.

But in everything by prayer and supplication with thanksgiving let your requests be made known unto God. -Philippians 4:6

Are you anxious?

Are you drowning in the cares of this world?

Take it to HIM in prayer this very moment.

He is waiting for you to go to Him in prayer!

SCRIPTURE ABOUT THE PEACE OF GOD

The Peace of God Scripture to Fight Anxiety

Allow the peace of God to keep your heart and mind through Christ Jesus

And the peace of God, which passes all understanding, shall keep your hearts and minds through Christ Jesus. – Philippian 4:7

When everything is out of control, pray and ask the Lord to help you with His Scripture about the peace of God.

Peace- a state of national tranquility, exempted to the rage and havoc of war, security, safety, harmony and concord

Heart- kardia- the center of all physical and spiritual life

Mind- mental perception

THINK ON THESE THINGS SCRIPTURE

This is where our mind and thought process is brought into the subjection of Christ as we reign in our thoughts and focus on what is good. This think on these things Scripture is beneficial for your spiritual warfare battle

Finally, brethren, whatsoever things are true, whatsoever things are honest, whatsoever things are just, whatsoever things are pure, whatsoever things are lovely, whatsoever things are of good report; if there be any virtue, and if there be any praise, think on these things. -Philippians 4:8

Do you allow the father of lies to run havoc in your mind?

Do you entertain those lies in your heart and mind?

Creative Sister, God is commanding us to think on things that are:

True, honest, just, pure, lovely, of a good report, things that are virtuous and things that are worthy of praise.

Surely, in my case, focusing on the seed of satan only caused turmoil and sewed seeds of doubt and unbelief.

If you have a bit of time, look up the words in Philippians 4:8 in your Greek Lexicon or over at the Blue Letter Bible.

It is really eye opening.

True- not focusing on lies

Just- upright, righteous, virtuous, innocent, faultless, guiltless

Pure- reverent, venerable, sacred, pure from carnality, chaste, clean

Lovely- acceptable and pleasing

Good report- things that sound well

Virtue- moral goodness and excellence

Praise- commendation or praise

In thinking and focusing on good things, we won't have time to think about:

The lies of Satan

Negativity that hinders our growth in God

STAY FOCUSED ON GOD SCRIPT

Thou wilt keep him in perfect peace, whose mind is stayed on thee: because he trusteth in thee. Isaiah 26:3

Perfect peace is completeness. It is soundness.

When you fasten your heart upon God's truth, you are resting in, laying in, being supported, being held and sustained by the lover of your soul.

Is perfect peace the desire of your heart?

This stay focused on God Scripture will eliminate the noise and anxiety and allow you to have the perfect peace of God.

SPIRITUAL WARFARE SCRIPTURES

The next few Bible verses are Spiritual Warfare Scriptures.

Our war is not against flesh and blood, but is a spiritual warfare waged in the heavenlies. You might think that a person is attacking you but it is so much more than that. It's spiritual warfare when a person is motivated by satan to attack you.

USE SPIRITUAL WEAPONS TO CAST DOWN THOUGHTS OF WORRY AND ANXIOUSNESS

For the weapons of our warfare are not carnal, but mighty through God to the pulling down of strong holds; Casting down imaginations, and every high thing that exalteth itself against the knowledge of God, and bringing into captivity every thought to the obedience of Christ; 2 Corinthians 10:3-6

The weapons of our warfare are mighty through God– The word mighty in the Greek is dunatos which means to be able, powerful, mighty and strong.

What is our part in this spiritual warfare? We must CAST DOWN the fiery darts of the devil.

For me, it was those lies that I was going to bury my husband and that he would die while we were still living in Chicago Heights.

Those imaginations are fleshly reasoning, judgements and decisions that exalt themselves against God's truth and promises.

When we cast those thoughts down we are bringing them into obedience.

OUR MISSION IN FIGHTING ANXIETY AS FOUND IN THE SCRIPTURE

Finally, my brethren, be strong in the Lord, and in the power of his might. Put on the whole armour of God that ye may be able to stand against the wiles of the devil. For we wrestle not against flesh and blood, but against principalities, against powers, against the rulers of the darkness of this world, against spiritual wickedness in high places. Wherefore take unto you the whole armour of God that ye may be able to withstand in the evil day, and having done all, to stand. Stand therefore, having your loins girt about with truth, and having on the breastplate of righteousness; And your feet shod with the preparation of the gospel of peace; Above all, taking the shield of faith, wherewith ye shall be able to quench all the fiery darts of the wicked. And take the helmet of salvation, and the sword of the Spirit, which is the word of God: Praying always with all prayer and supplication in the Spirit, and watching thereunto with all perseverance and supplication for all saints; -Ephesians 6:10-18

Your mission, if you wish to accept it, (and I hope you do) is to:

Be strong in the Lord (not in yourself)

Be strong in the power of His might

Put on the entire armor of God. Your job is a full time soldier. Wear your armor.

Stand in God's confidence against the wiles of the devil. The confidence comes from God and not you.

Realize you are not warring against flesh and blood but against spiritual wickedness in high places. Your attack might come from a person, but realize that the motivation is of Satan.

Girt your loins with God's truth- quote God's word to yourself daily.

Stand in battle.

Wear God's breastplate of righteousness for protection against the fiery darts of satan

Part of your spiritual armor are your spiritual shoes which are the gospel of peace.

Share the gospel even during difficult times because others need to hear your testimony as you go through the fire.

Quench all the fiery darts of the wicked one with the shield of faith.

Guard your mind with the helmet of salvation and the sword of the Spirit, which is the word of God

With God's spiritual armor you can quench all of the fiery darts of the wicked one.

SCRIPTURES OF CONFIDENCE

As a child of God, we can have confidence in our God and what he has done for us. It's important to mention that we cannot muster up this confidence in our own strength because our righteousness is as filthy rags.

Christ has made us righteous and that should give us Godly confidence.

God doesn't want you to walk in doubt always questioning who you belong to.

When someone asks you who your earthly father is, you respond with His name. The same is true with your Heavenly Father.

Who is your Daddy? GOD is!

Read, learn and study these Scriptures of confidence until you are able to apply God's divine confidence in your life.

Take heed, brethren, lest there be in any of you an evil heart of unbelief, in departing from the living God. -Hebrews 3:12

Having therefore, brethren, boldness to enter into the holiest by the blood of Jesus, -Hebrews 10:19

Surround Yourself with Products that Proclaim God's Peace

As a result of applying these Scriptures of confidence you will be able to fully dwell in victorious confidence over your anxiety.

Ultimately, worry can grow a heart of distrust and unbelief in God.

HE CARES FOR YOU SCRIPTURE

The world can be fickle. Relationships fade and feelings ebb and flow.

But God's love is everlasting and does not change. That steadfast love of the Lord towards us can reassure our hearts on a daily basis and help us to overcome anxiety in life.

Casting all your care upon him; for he careth for you. -1 Peter 5:7

I love the visuals of this verse after doing a word study in the Greek.

The word casting means to place upon or throw upon. My burdens are wearisome. They are heavy. I try to carry them for as long as possible but God is telling me to throw them to him. I'm heaving them HIS way because He can handle them so much better than myself.

How to- Help with Anxiety

The Greek word for care is anxiety. ANXIETY!

365 FEAR NOT SCRIPTURES

Did you know that there are 365 fear not Scriptures? That's ONE for every day of the year.

BIBLICAL HOW TO-HELP WITH ANXIETY

Are you ready to cast all of your CARES and ANXIETY upon the Lord today?

The world will disappoint. But God has given us His word for a Biblical how to. Help with Anxiety is just a prayer away.

Knowing what the Lord has promised us in Scripture will pave the way for us to claim victory in the name of Jesus.

The Bible is full of real life stories of those who have overcome their fear and anxiety by reading scripture and trusting God for the outcome.

Does anxiety and fear ever creep in again? I'd be a liar if I said it didn't.

The upkeep of our souls is still part of the spiritual warfare that continues to take place and I have to constantly renew my mind in the Scripture as long as Satan buffets me.

THE GREAT CHANGE

The day my husband collapsed into my arms was a pivotal moment in my life and in my walk with God.

There has been a great metamorphosis that would have never taken place had I not experienced such a great time of anxiety and sorrow.

I have learned to not take every day for granted.

I am more thankful for even the smallest things.

I appreciate my husband whereas before I would take him for granted.

My husband's and I relationship has grown in ways that would have never happened pre brain aneurysms.

The trials have drawn me closer to the Lord in ways I could never have imagined.

My faith walk with God is deeper than ever.

I can see clearly that God REALLY DOES work all things together for His good- even our anxiety and the most difficult hardships.

BITTER OR BETTER- WE DO HAVE A CHOICE

Satan wants to destroy your soul and he does that by way of anxiety and trials. Don't allow the anxiety of life to make you become bitter with God. Allow it to help you rely on Him, pray to him and draw you closer to Him.

It is my hope and prayer that these Bible verses on How to Help with Anxiety will resonate in your heart and mind and that you will be victorious in the Lord!

JGJ) What an absolutely awesome testimony. I was blessed to see this myself. I needed to see it myself. All doubt of the name and authority of Jesus Christ being real and all powerful is gone. I pray, I too, will have that Faith, and Strength, through Jesus, when it is needed in my own life.

Pastor Stevens and his wife Lillian are at this time continuing to do God's work at a Church in Germany. His medical checkups have been giving him a report of a fit and healthy man. God bless you both. And thank you so much, Lillian for allowing me to share your testimony.

69. Jason Dezember

I could share my personal testimony of a life changed through a personal relationship with Jesus Christ, but, I'll let you read it from my daughter's words, as she can testify to that change. The following is an interview paper that my daughter had to do for a class in school. She decided to interview me.

Charlene Dezember
English 101
2 March 2017

Battle with the Demon

Overcoming addiction is no easy task; it takes a person who is strong enough to beat the odds. That person is my eccentric, down to earth, beatnik-esque father. When I asked my father what he thought the most major turning point in his life had been, I assumed it was going to be his final divorce, or his first band. Nothing could have prepared me for his answer. My father, Jason, sat at the dining room table in his apartment, and was excited that I was going to write about him. He had no idea what the interview might be about, just that it was a way to get to understand him as a human being on a deeper level. Throughout his interview my father became very emotional. When asked if he wanted to take a break he said, "No let's keep on going, let's knock it out." Giving up is not something my father does easily. It had been a long time since I had seen this big, burly, bearded, and heavily tattooed man in such a vulnerable state. I discovered that despite my father's painful past, and battling with an alien encounter hand in hand with addiction, he was strong enough to defy the odds and crawl out of the grave that had been dug.

Growing up, my father had no idea where he was going to live. The numerous times he moved made childhood messy and unbearable at times. His mom, Anita, always bad mouthed his dad, Lonnie, and demonized him. She instilled a terror within my father in regards to Lonnie. While my father would be forced to visit Lonnie, he instilled hatred towards Anita. Lonnie would tell my father that Anita was a nut job bible thumper. Without a sane parental figure my father was left with no one to look up to. When I asked him what childhood was like he explained, "Scary, I was always scared. I didn't know where I was going to live. I must've gone to twenty different middle schools." Based on that description and the stories of his childhood, I was left envisioning a dark and depressing childhood that seemed impossible to cope with. He shared how much he envied the stability of his friends' homes. How their home lives were so peaceful, consisting of eating meals around the table together, and compassionate support. Social normality appeared to be a luxury to my father. So much turmoil filled the memories of my father's upbringing; it made me curious to if he could recall anything pleasant. When I asked him to tell me an anecdote of something pleasant from childhood he had to mull it over for a while. He finally shared, "Probably when I and my friends started playing together in middle school." Playing guitar had been my father's tool to escape. The best thing in his life at this point had been starting a band with a group of his friends. Once he picked up the guitar he never stopped playing.

It all began at Calvary Chapel in Costa Mesa, during Wednesday night rock in his Christian youth group. My father attended when he was twelve where he gazed upon a punk band. The guitarist had a pink Mohawk and was covered head to toe in tattoos. Amazed that you could be a Christian and look that way and rock that way, my father was inspired to pick up the guitar for himself. His uncle Jeff, and Anita got him his first guitar when he turned thirteen, and that instrument became his escape. He played for two to four hours every single day for three years to learn the guitar, and by the time he was fourteen he writing songs and starting bands. My father would play anywhere someone would let him. I asked him what show he remembered playing that stood out the most and he described, "Centennial Park, Santa Ana, headlining for New Years, There were hundreds of people, at least five hundred people, and the stage was huge! I felt so small up there looking across at the other dudes on stage, we were shredding and everyone loved it." Hearing that made my heart light up. After that performance my father's band had an interview over the radio station at UCI. They were getting pretty well known. However, through all the glitter and success, there was a darkness lurking. My father admitted that is when his addiction first began, mainly with alcohol.

Playing shows was my father's life for about fifteen to twenty years, I remember him performing ever since I was a kid. The other aspects of his life were always chaotic. My father and mother got a divorce when I was four and he re-married. He started a new family with his new wife and in the beginning things seemed perfect. Having a man with a good job, money, and a nice house were the only things on his wife's agenda. When my father lost his job and the economy crashed she left. She took everything. Once my father finally got back on his feet she came back while things were successful, then they weren't so successful, and again she left and took everything. He was married to her three times. After each divorce the addiction just spiraled out of control, and that last divorce appeared to be the nail on the coffin. My father was gone, and the person he knew himself to be had vanished.

Years had passed and he met someone new, someone genuine and kind, with a beautiful heart. My father was still heavily drinking and there was a time where he was consuming any drug he could get his hands on, waiting for his life to end. He had reached rock bottom. It appeared nothing could drag him out of the pit he fell into until the day he was driving to work, and saw a huge light hovering above the hospital, which he found quite peculiar but ignored. Then he saw it again on his way home, and again ignored it. That night he went out with his friend, Dulce. My father explained to me, "Dulce was driving my car up Newport Boulevard, and I look over to see a huge mall sized square object in the sky. I scream at her to pull over, she sees it too. I get out of the car and it looks like this thing was floating in water, it was made of metal. It made no sound. It was moving away when I screamed what the fuck are you!? That's when it paused and started coming back again. We hopped back in my car and that's when we were fleeing. I saw more crafts then coming from behind it, at least twelve, all different kinds." That experience haunted him for years, but the drug use continued. He finally settled down with the beautiful woman he met, Katie, and they moved in together. He told me one night Katie was out of town and he was sitting on the couch. He always closed the blinds because he didn't want to see the sky. When he looked over at the window, through the cracks in his blinds he started seeing a bunch of eyes. Then he screamed as loud as he could for his neighbor, but his neighbor did not come. My father thought he was dead or dying and that was the reason for seeing this living nightmare. Finally he screamed out for Jesus Christ, and when he did, he looked up to see an apparition of him. When he looked away everything disappeared, including all the eyes and the figures that had begun to form around them. That is when he realized that Jesus is real, and found his faith. My father turned to the church and they enlightened him that all these alien encounters were actually demons. Demons that my father had been battling with. Were these encounters real, or a manifestation from addiction? Maybe a combination of both? Perhaps something did happen. Either way my father received the biggest wakeup call of his life.

Life for my father now is much more peaceful. He managed to let all of his guilt and turmoil go, that he held onto so tightly because of all the mistakes he has made. Recognizing how painful it was to learn the hard way, he finally managed to get sober. Believing in a bigger picture, and being in tune with his spirituality really humbled my father. Nowadays he has less drive to write or pick up his guitar. My father shared that, "The less you need to escape, the less you use that tool to escape." Going through the phases of this interviewing process has really given me a sense of catharsis after hearing a happy ending to such a dark story, the story of my father's life. Crawling out of a traumatic childhood, and an even more traumatic adulthood is something most people will never accomplish. The people dealt these cards in life often turn to substances, and that is what claims their lives. That is not the case for my father. When I asked him what he would like the reader to know, what piece of advice he wanted to share to end the interview he said, "If you are young enough to not have gotten married, have kids, done drugs, lied, cheated, etc. Pay attention to my story. What you reap is what you sow. Think twice before you make decisions. Save yourself from years and years of turmoil." These are wise words from a man who has gone through hell and back.

(Works Cited: Dezember, Jason. Personal Interview. 20 Feb. 2017.)

Conclusion

Wrapping it Up

By Jason Dezember

Most of the damage from this unusual, "so-called" alien abduction experience, comes when someone who believes they have had an experience goes looking for answers away from God's Word. When they do this, it takes them down a long road of lies and deception, only making the situation worse. It causes them to take their eyes off of the one true God, the true source of help. That, I believe is the purpose of the evil force that manipulates humanity with this delusion. It can eventually become the experiencer's new religion, and at least their new perspective in which they view life.

But the best finding of all to come from CE4 Research, is that no matter what the experience is that has happened to you, those that have had their lives destroyed by the belief of having an experience (actual or not), can stop the experiences, and get their lives back, through a personal relationship with Jesus Christ. Joe Jordan said it back in 1997 and it still fits CE4 Research today:

"The one thing we can offer people in this field, that nobody else anywhere is offering, is hope. Hope that they can stop this experience."

The Unwanted Piece of the UFO Puzzle

The testimonies that you have read in this book are the most powerful evidence in the world today, showing the true nature of the deceptive entities behind the UFO phenomenon.

The testimonies that you have read in this book, show us beyond a shadow of a doubt, that the name and authority of Jesus Christ will terminate the so-called alien abduction experience and the UFO sighting experience.

The testimonies that you have read in this book show us that if you ask for this help in terminating the experience in this way, it too can work for you. That, my friends, is a repeatable event. There is no other repeatable event in all of Ufology.

The testimonies that you have read in this book show us that the power in the name and authority of Jesus Christ is real.

The testimonies that you read in this book show us that Jesus Christ is real.

The testimonies that you have read in this book show us that God is real.

And, the testimonies that you have read in this book show us that the so-called aliens are actually demonic spiritual entities, masquerading as highly technological other worldly beings, here to cheat humanity out of their blessed hope of salvation by perpetrating a delusion.

Now, what about this ability to stop and/or terminate this experience?

The findings of CE4 Research show that these so-called beings from other worlds or realms can be stopped. Not just stopped, but they will be made harmless to you, regarding this phenomenon.

These entities give the appearance of having very highly advanced futuristic technology, well beyond our wildest dreams or abilities. The so-called technology that they display, no matter how seemingly advanced, can be stopped. The abduction experience and the sighting experience can be stopped. The affect it has on human thinking can be stopped. Humanity has the choice within their grasp, to wield the most powerful weapon in the entire universe—one that actually puts these deceptive entities in their place. And the over 60 testimonies in this book will attest to that fact.

That weapon is the power in the Name and authority of Jesus Christ. Yup, you read it right. Not a high tech ray gun, or even a thermonuclear device, but rather Jesus Christ, and your relationship with Him.

And access to that weapon is available and free, to any believer and follower of Jesus Christ, the Creator of the Universe itself.

How does one obtain access to that weapon to put these entities in their place?

It's a very simple process, actually. But I have to tell you, looking back, it was the hardest thing I ever did. And after you do it, you realize it is the easiest thing you could ever do.

Joe Jordan told me that a good friend and Christian Brother, John Algermissen, put it this way for him, "for non-believers (in Jesus Christ), they have to see it, to believe it... but for believers (in Jesus Christ), when they believe it, they see it." I know I must sound confusing, but I will try to explain.

Those that follow Jesus Christ are Christians, and Christians have access to the power in the name and authority of Jesus Christ, which is the name above all names. The testimonies you will read in this book give proof to just that.

What gives Christians that access? The answer is found in a mystery, a mystery that was once secret, but later revealed.

The mystery goes like this. The demonic realm has been running this world for quite some time. Then, Jesus was born into the world. They knew who He was (God manifest in the flesh on earth), and they knew there was going to be trouble. They knew the ancient written prophesies, and they were seeing them being fulfilled. During His time on Earth, Jesus did give the demonic realm a hard time, putting them in their place.

> Matthew 28:18 Then Jesus came to them and said, "All authority in heaven and on earth has been given to me." New International Version

So the demonic realm planned to turn the people against Him, to have Him eliminated. They thought that once He was gone, things would return to normal. So they influenced the minds of the people and they had Him crucified. But He rose from the grave on the third day, He defeated death, but He didn't stay. He rose to the right hand of the Father (God) in Heaven. The demonic realm thought they had won since He was gone.

But wait, Jesus had told His disciples something before He rose up to Heaven, found in Acts 1:4 New International Version (NIV):

On one occasion, while he was eating with them, he gave them this command: "Do not leave Jerusalem, but wait for the gift my Father promised, which you have heard me speak about."

On the day of Pentecost, in the Upper Room where they were gathered together, they received the promised gift from the Father, the indwelling of the Holy Spirit.

From that day forward, believers in the Lord Jesus Christ would all receive the indwelling of the Holy Spirit. Christ in you.

This was the mystery revealed. Because every believer in the Lord Jesus Christ would have access to the power in the name and authority of Jesus Christ through the indwelling of the Holy Spirit. The power to defeat the demonic entities that come against them. And the testimonies that you read in this book, show just that.

This can be best seen, in the sixth chapter of Ephesians, the spiritual warfare chapter.

Verse 12 identifies who we war against:

> Ephesians 6:12 "For our struggle is not against flesh and blood, but against the rulers, against the authorities, against the powers of this dark world and against the spiritual forces of evil in the heavenly realms." New International Version

Verses 13 through 17 are about protecting yourself from these demonic forces by putting on the whole armor of God in your daily life:

> Ephesians 6:13-17 "Therefore put on the full armor of God, so that when the day of evil comes, you may be able to stand your ground, and after

you have done everything, to stand. Stand firm then, with the belt of truth buckled around your waist, with the breastplate of righteousness in place, and with your feet fitted with the readiness that comes from the gospel of peace. In addition to all this, take up the shield of faith, with which you can extinguish all the flaming arrows of the evil one. Take the helmet of salvation and the sword of the Spirit, which is the word of God."

But you as human beings will tire, you will let down your defenses. Because of that, you have an offensive weapon that will put the demonic realm in its place. The most powerful weapon in the Universe. Those are verses 18 through 20:

Ephesians 6:18-20 "And pray in the Spirit on all occasions with all kinds of prayers and requests. With this in mind, be alert and always keep on praying for all the Lord's people. Pray also for me, that whenever I speak, words may be given me so that I will fearlessly make known the mystery of the gospel, for which I am an ambassador in chains. Pray that I may declare it fearlessly, as I should."

In simple terms, prayer is a powerful weapon, especially silent prayer, (in the spirit), to God the Father. Why silent prayer? Because the demonic realm cannot read your thoughts, but they will make you think they can. I do believe they can influence your thoughts though. This is warfare, don't give anything away to them.

Now look at verse 19, it says, "that whenever I speak," but speak to who? Remember, this is the spiritual warfare chapter dealing with the demonic realm. You are speaking, out loud, to the demonic realm. Why? Because they can't read your thoughts. But, they can hear your voice.

"Words may be given me," by who? The Holy Spirit, that indwells in the believer of Jesus Christ.

"So that I will fearlessly make known the mystery of the gospel." What mystery? The mystery I shared with you earlier. That we have Christ in us, through the indwelling of the Holy Spirit, and access to call on the power in the name and authority of Jesus Christ, the name above all names, the power over all the Universe and the earth.

"For which I am an ambassador in chains," I am a child of God, blood bought by Son of God, Jesus Christ, whom I follow, and are committed to sharing with others. And they have no power over you.

That, my friends, is the most powerful force in the Universe, able to break down any stronghold.

And it's freely available to anyone who earnestly asks for it.

And that is what these many testimonies show you.

Remember that original hypothesis, or question that we put forward as CE4 Research over twenty years ago? "Are Christians being abducted by aliens?" I believe we have the evidence to finally answer the question honestly and proudly, with a resounding no.

In the words of the late Dr. David Allen Lewis:

"In dealing with the mystery of UFO's, we are not on the lunatic fringe of theology. Instead, we stand in your behalf in front line of battle. We are in defensive warfare at a major point of assault on humanity."

Dr. David Allen Lewis in, <u>UFO, End Time Delusion</u>, July 1, 1991 by David Allen Lewis and Robert Shreckhise

In July of 1947, in Roswell, New Mexico, a UFO myth was born.

But in the end, the Creator of this Universe will expose this myth.

"And the four and twenty elders and the four beasts fell down and worshipped God that sat on the throne, saying, Amen; Alleluia.

And a voice came out of the throne, saying, Praise our God, all ye his servants, and ye that fear him, both small and great.

And I heard as it were the voice of a great multitude, and as the voice of many waters, and as the voice of mighty thunderings, saying, Alleluia: for the Lord God omnipotent reigneth.

Let us be glad and rejoice, and give honour to him: for the marriage of the Lamb is come, and his wife hath made herself ready."

Revelations 19:4-7

"He that dwelleth in the secret place of the most High shall abide under the shadow of the Almighty. I will say of the LORD, He is my refuge and my fortress: my God; in him will I trust.

Surely he shall deliver thee from the snare of the fowler, and from the noisome pestilence. He shall cover thee with his feathers, and under his wings shalt thou trust: his truth shall be thy shield and buckler.

Thou shalt not be afraid for the terror by night; nor for the arrow that flieth by day; Nor for the pestilence that walketh in darkness; nor for the destruction that wasteth at noonday.

A thousand shall fall at thy side, and ten thousand at thy right hand; but it shall not come nigh thee. Only with thine eyes shalt thou behold and see the reward of the wicked.

Because thou hast made the LORD, which is my refuge, even the most High, thy habitation; There shall no evil befall thee, neither shall any plague come nigh thy dwelling.

For he shall give his angels charge over thee, to keep thee in all thy ways.

They shall bear thee up in their hands, lest thou dash thy foot against a stone.

Thou shalt tread upon the lion and adder: the young lion and the dragon shalt thou trample under feet.

Because he hath set his love upon me, therefore will I deliver him: I will set him on high, because he hath known my name.

He shall call upon me, and I will answer him: I will be with him in trouble; I will deliver him, and honour him.

With long life will I satisfy him, and shew him my salvation."

Psalms 91:1-16 KJV

"The one thing we can offer people in this field, that nobody else elsewhere is offering, is hope. Hope that they can stop this experience," - Joe Jordan

"We shall nobly save, or meanly lose, the last best hope of earth. Other means may succeed; this could not fail. The way is plain, peaceful, generous, just — a way which, if followed, the world will forever applaud, and God must forever bless."
– Abraham Lincoln

GOD BLESS HUMANITY

About the Authors

<u>Joseph G. Jordan</u>

Joseph Jordan is the President and co-founder of the CE4 Research Group, an alien abduction investigation and research team (originally) based out of Cocoa, Florida. Following his work for NASA's Kennedy Space Center as a Safety Specialist, he took a position in South Korea as a Safety Professional contractor supporting the US Military presence there.

Joe has been a Mutual UFO Network Field Investigator since 1992, and currently is the MUFON International Director for South Korea He is a member of MUFON's STAR Team "Rapid Response Special Unit" and recently MUFON's Inner Circle.

Joe has shared his research findings from his alien abduction investigations through many radio shows, newspaper and magazine articles, DVDs, and lectures. His research findings on alien abductions have been written about in over 30 different authored books over the past two decades. He has spoken during six Roswell UFO Festivals in Roswell, New Mexico, including the 60th Anniversary Conference in 2007 and the 70th Anniversary Festival Conference in 2017, as well as other domestic and international venues. He was also honored to host the Roswell UFO Festival Conference for the city of Roswell in 2008.

The findings of the CE4 Research Group are without a doubt the most powerful and controversial evidence of the true nature of the alien abduction phenomenon to ever be presented in the field of Ufology.

Jason Dezember

Jason Dezember, born and raised in Huntington Beach, CA, is father to three beautiful children and husband to his wife, Katerina. He serves at First Love Church in Costa Mesa, CA, on the worship team and occasionally in the children's ministry. He's gone from nomadic surfer in rock bands, to a successful career in the financial sector, and warrior for Christ (and everything in between).

His most recent endeavor is joining forces with Joseph G. Jordan in a ministry for Christ, to help people being deceived by the world view of alien abduction and UFO encounters; in an effort to prevent them from going down rabbit holes, and instead find the Truth, Jesus Christ.

About the Cover Artist

Robert "Bobby" Marsee is an award winning painter and artist proficient in multiple mediums. While he enjoys painting and drawing various subjects in a variety of mediums, he specializes in painting oil portraits. In 1993 he received his B.A. in Fine Art from the University of Science and Arts of Oklahoma in Chickasha, OK. There he studied under Western Oklahoma artists Hollis Howard and Angus "Kent" Lamar. Bobby's studio, named Marsee's Fine Art & Framing, is located in Weatherford, OK, where he does most of his commissioned paintings, provides custom picture framing, and teaches several weekly oil painting classes. He enjoys living in Western Oklahoma with his wife, Angela, and their two rescue dogs, Rembrandt and Kona.

Marsee has been a featured artist at multiple shows and festivals, including "Arts Festival Oklahoma (OCCC)," the "Global Oklahoma" (Rose State College) cultural festival, and "Septemberfest" held at the Oklahoma Governor's mansion, where he created crowd pleasing sidewalk chalk murals of legendary Oklahomans, including astronaut Thomas P. Stafford, Olympic champion Jim Thorpe and Yankee great Mickey Mantle. His colorful acrylic portrait of Dr. Ben Carson currently hangs Mr. Carson's office at HUD in Washington D.C. Some of his more recent high profile commissions include a portrait of singer Jon Bon Jovi. Commissioned by the Chesapeake Energy Center (home of the NBA's Oklahoma City Thunder), Bobby painted a group portrait of Jon Bon Jovi and his band while they played at "The Peake." It was presented to the band after the concert. His latest commissioned oil painting "The Cottonwood Band" can be viewed at the Oklahoma state capitol in Oklahoma City, where it was presented on the floor of the house in May, 2020, and will be included in the permanent capitol collection.

A Word from the Cover Artist

Let me begin by saying I've never witnessed a UFO, been abducted by aliens, or even met someone who has. My story is how I met Joe Jordan, and how his research and ministry has impacted my faith. In 2009, while traveling with friends and family to watch my beloved Oklahoma Sooners face off against Stanford in the Sun Bowl in El Paso, TX, we spent the night in Roswell, NM. It was the day before the game and we had some time to explore the town. I was excited to visit the UFO museum. I have always been entertained by science fiction and was familiar with the lore surrounding the famed 1947 UFO crash in Roswell. The next day we travelled to El Paso, watched our Sooners defeat Stanford, and then made our way back to Roswell before heading back to Oklahoma the next day. It was New Year's Eve. My friend James, a fellow Sooner fan and running buddy, joined me and my family along for the trip. While eating dinner that night, we spotted a poster on the door of the restaurant advertising the Roswell UFO festival. It took place that next July. James and I were currently training for the upcoming New Orleans marathon in February of 2010, and noticed one of the events during the UFO festival; it was a 10k fun run called the "Alien Chase". We thought that sounded fun and something to encourage us to maintain our training regimen for the months following our upcoming marathon. That next July we arrived in Roswell expecting nothing more than a relaxing, if not amusing, diversion from everyday life. Little did I know how meaningful it would become. The festival had much to offer. A parade, car show, BBQ contest, visitors expo, flag football tournament, free movies, and the Alien Chase of course. But the most intriguing of the festival events, was the lineup of Ufologists speaking at the visitors center. It was a who's who of famed Ufologists. After the 10k that morning, I showered and headed down to take in a few of the speakers presentations. I arrived at the conference room towards the end of Guy Malone's presentation about the 47 Roswell crash. It was very provocative. After the conclusion of his presentation, he invited everyone to attend an additional presentation at the Roswell Library the following day called "The Ancient of Days." Presenters would include himself and "fellow Christian Ufologist," Joe Jordan. The term "Christian Ufologist" really intrigued me. Although I had grown up in the church, it had only been in more recent years that I had truly accepted Jesus as my Lord and Savior. Surprisingly, studying the bible and scripture with fellow Christians became exciting and edifying. And I was curious to learn more. Knowing that UFOs and the possibility of extraterrestrials was not something discussed in church or Sunday school. I was curious to hear how these guys were going to approach the issue through a biblical lens. Honestly, I was quite excited about it, hoping they could provide some good answers to a subject that had become such a pervasive subject. As entertaining as I find Science Fiction and the UFO culture, I never did want to sincerely contemplate the possibility of something that could potentially shake my faith, for the opposite reason. Just as Mr. Jordan's colleagues within MUFON have told him when confronted with evidence of abduction experiences being spiritual in nature, "I didn't want to go there." God definitely wanted me to go there! Roswell, that is. Had I not been there, and not heard Guy Malone's invitation to hear his and Joe Jordan's lectures on alien abductions, I doubt I would have ever known the truth about this phenomenon. Mr. Jordan's presentation, steeped full of deliverance testimonies and decades of research, all juxtaposed with scripture, convinced me these things are real and are demonic spirits on a "psyop" for Satan. Like I stated earlier, thanks be to God I have never experienced such attacks, but am aware of the truth on what is really happening. It has opened my eyes to how creative and insidious demons are when waging spiritual warfare, and how easily they can be unwittingly invited into your life through open doorways. Mr. Jordan has had a most positive and profound effect on my faith. I'm blessed to have crossed paths with him and his ministry.

Resources

CE4 Research

Website: www.ce4research.com

Email: ce4president@yahoo.com

Jasondezember237@gmail.com

Facebook: https://www.facebook.com/CE4Research/

YouTube: https://www.youtube.com/channel/UC06K8J1Een7cPNi1s6zCiAQ/

Mutual UFO Network

Website: www.mufon.com

Roswell Mission

Guy Malone

Website: http://www.roswellmission.org/

Creation Ministries International

Website: https://creation.com/

You Tube: https://www.youtube.com/user/creationclips

Alien Intrusion

Website: https://alienintrusion.com/

Book: https://www.amazon.com/Alien-Intrusion-Updated-Expanded-Bates/dp/0890514356/ref=sr_1_2?dchild=1&keywords=alien+intrusion&qid=1591943483&sr=8-2

Ian Juby of Genesis Week

Website: https://ianjuby.org/

Michael Heiser

Website: https://drmsh.com/

Derek Gilbert

Website: https://www.derekpgilbert.com/

A More Excellent Way, Be in Health

Website: https://resources.beinhealth.com/products/amew

Tear/cut out the following to post as a reminder.

_ _

8R's to Freedom in Relation to Alien Abductions

1. <u>Recognize</u> - You must recognize what it is.

The UFO/Alien Abduction experience is a powerful delusion from the enemy. The purpose is to take your eyes off the one true God. It is a war for your soul and the enemy will use whatever it takes for you to believe his lies.

2. <u>Responsibility</u> - You must take responsibility for what you recognize.

You must take action to stop this experience of the enemy now that you see it for what it is.

3. <u>Repent</u> - Repent to God for participating with what you recognize.

Repent for falling for the enemy's lies. Usually the experiences are from open doors in our lives that allow the enemy in. Even repent for not knowing what you had become part of. A lot of times we don't even know that we have opened doors.

4. <u>Renounce</u> - You must make what you recognize your enemy and renounce it.

Renounce any part of your life that is not of God. Anything not of God is of the enemy and it is our enemy.

5. <u>Remove it</u> - Get rid of it once and for all.

Remove all participation, involvement, research for information or answers, associations, books, charms, crystals, and anything related to the enemy's tactics of perpetrating the delusion or opening doors in your life to allow him back in.

6. <u>Resist</u> - When it tries to come back, resist it.

When it tries to come back? Oh yeah, he will, he used to own you, he knows your weaknesses. But keep in mind you now can see his methods and purpose, to destroy. But through Jesus Christ, the authority is given to make him flee.

7. <u>Rejoice</u> - Give God thanks for setting you free. Free from the bondage of the enemy's delusion and having to live in fear.

8. <u>Restore</u> - Help someone else to get free.

We are told we reach the lost through the Word of God, and our testimony. Our testimony is the most powerful evidence, (proof), that God is real. The testimony of a changed life through the name and authority of Jesus Christ is the real evidence that exposes the lies of the enemy. When you share your testimony you give someone else the hope that they too can also be free.

www.ingramcontent.com/pod-product-compliance
Lightning Source LLC
Chambersburg PA
CBHW031230090426
42742CB00007B/142